Comed

Comedy

MEANING AND FORM

SECOND EDITION

Robert W. Corrigan

THE UNIVERSITY OF WISCONSIN—MILWAUKEE

1817

HARPER & ROW, PUBLISHERS, New York

Cambridge, Hagerstown, Philadelphia, San Francisco,
London, Mexico City, São Paulo, Sydney

Sponsoring Editor: Phillip Leininger
Project Editor: Jo-Ann Goldfarb
Production Manager: Marion A. Palen
Compositor: TriStar Graphics

Cover: Irving Bogen

Comedy: Meaning and Form, Second Edition

Library of Congress Cataloging in Publication Data

Corrigan, Robert Willoughby, 1927–   ed.
  Comedy, meaning and form.

  Bibliography: p.
  1. Comedy—Collected works. 2. Comic, The—
Collected works. I. Title.
PN1922.C63 1981 809.2 80-23864
ISBN 0-06-041370-0

For Eric Bentley—artist, critic, scholar, and friend.

Contents

V
THE PSYCHOLOGY OF COMEDY

VI
FARCE, SATIRE, AND TRAGICOMEDY

VII
THE CRITICISM OF COMEDY

VIII
FROM THE CLASSICS OF COMIC THEORY

Preface

The first edition of this book was published over fifteen years ago (1965). During the subsequent years it had a satisfying, if albeit modest, success. It became a standard reference work in libraries, a volume frequently used by teachers, scholars, and (much to my pleasure) theatre practitioners; and it was almost always mentioned in bibliographies and footnotes as the most ample and wide-ranging collection of essays on comedy. But, more important, for more than a decade it was a regularly used textbook in countless college courses. As I went about the country, I would invariably meet people who had used the "comedy anthology" (or its counterpart on tragedy) when they were in school.

Thus I was overjoyed when Harper & Row asked me to do a second edition. This would give me an opportunity to reassess the book's contents, to incorporate changes that had been suggested to me over the years, to add some of the important new essays on comedy that had been written since the first edition appeared, and to revise and expand my introduction to the earlier edition. The problem: what to leave out? The first cuts were easy—no author would be represented by more than one essay. Next, I realized that it was no longer as necessary to fight the battle for the legitimacy of farce as a dramatic form, so that section could be reduced. Finally, there were a number of essays that had either become so readily available or for any number of reasons could not be used in a new edition that they eliminated themselves. However, before commenting on their replacements, let me say a word about the book's organization.

I am still satisfied with the organizational plan of the first edition and have repeated it. The eight sections into which I have divided the book probably do not need much explaining. Section I deals with the spirit of comedy, which I discuss in my introduction. In Sections II through IV I have included essays which are primarily concerned with the nature and form of comedy. While I do not believe that comedy has a fixed form, the essays in these sections do discuss several basic formal patterns which generally apply to most comedy written before the twentieth century, and they can also be helpful to us in our attempts to understand the comedies of today insofar as they describe what the modern writer of comedy is rebelling against. Section V is still, regrettably, too short. A whole book of essays could be devoted to the question "Why do we laugh?" My only consolation is that even if such a book existed, we probably would not be much closer to a definitive answer to this sticky question. Section VI had to be entirely rethought. As I said earlier, the need to establish the legitimacy of farce was no longer pressing. Increasingly, people have come to see that farce is the basic ore from which much theatre derives. As for the essays on satire, I never thought they really worked, although I have retained Al Capp's little piece because I still think this "buried" classic reveals so much about the nature of comic satire and its relationship to political freedom. Finally, I believed it was essential to include something on tragicomedy, that hybrid form that has come to dominate the theatre of the twentieth century. The rationale of Section VII is fairly obvious. I have tried to select relatively recent essays which discuss the comedy of some of the great masters of the comic. In Section VIII I have included excerpts from four of the classics of comic theory. Most of this material is readily available elsewhere; however, I have included it for those teachers who may, quite legitimately, want to relate the modern essays to the earlier thinking on comedy.

Now, a word about the new material. Walter Kerr and Robert Bechtold Heilman have written the most important books on comedy since the first edition was published, and it was essential that they be represented. The eloquent Mr. Kerr is the current dean of American drama critics, and his ideas on the subject have been shaped and tested within the context of current and ongoing theatre practice. Professor Heilman's book, which was recently awarded the 1979 Christian Gauss prize of Phi Beta Kappa, is a landmark of scholarship. Clara Claiborne Park's essay (published in the summer of 1979) is a brief but penetrating analysis of the state of the comic muse as we enter the decade of the 1980s. The inclusion of the section on comedy from Duerrenmatt's *Problems of the Theatre* needs no explanation. This remarkable little monograph is one of the major documents of the twentieth-century theatre. Another one is the collection of Jean-Paul Sartre's theatre essays, which was published in this country in 1976. I can think of no one who brings deeper philosophic and psychological insights to the subject of comedy than this great existentialist thinker. Professor Hurrell's short piece is a valuable response to Eric Bentley's groundbreaking work on farce, and I included my own discussion of tragicomedy. Section VII presented the biggest problem. Obviously, I could have replaced all of the essays used in the first edition with ones written more recently. But newness could not be the only criterion. So I replaced two and added a third. As the country's leading scholar on classical Greek drama during the past few decades, Professor Whitman had to be included. The section from Leonard C. Pronko's book on Feydeau is a concrete analysis of some of the dynamics of farce. And who wouldn't want to include something by Lionel Trilling, who fortunately wrote on Shaw in the last years of his life?

Finally, I must thank the authors and permission editors of the various publishers with whom I have corresponded. Each of them was most cooperative. Thanks also to Phillip Leininger, the senior editor at Harper & Row who shepherded every step of this new edition, and to my always dependable and cheerful secretary, Margaret Rotter. In the first edition, I acknowledged my debt to and admiration for Eric Bentley by dedicating the book to him. That dedication still stands.

Robert W. Corrigan

Comedy

Introduction

Comedy and the Comic Spirit

I. Mystery and the Forms of Drama

The theatre's long history confirms the fact that the stage is a realm of spirits, demons, and primordial gods; of wild fantasy and transcendental aspiration. It is a place of foreboding darkness and brightest light. It is a world of fear and loss, and also one of triumph and joyous fulfillment. To enter this world is to enter the realm of mystery.

It is precisely because the theatre does make manifest the other world of mystery that it has always had such a powerful hold upon our imagination. Ultimately, the central concern of all human beings has been to deal with the mysteries of life, with those aspects of the numinous which haunt our experience. While it is true that the nature and definition of the numinous may differ from culture to culture and may change from age to age, because our experience proves to us that what was thought to be mysterious need not be so, nonetheless there are certain abiding mysteries in human life which we can never totally understand or explain in rational terms no matter how hard we might try to do so. Life continually mocks the efforts of our intelligence to fathom it fully, and hence its mysteries never cease to haunt our imagination. And it is just because they do haunt us that we inevitably use our imagination in an effort to find some way of dealing with them. We create imaginative constructs which will explain the mysterious in the hopes that by doing so, we will be endowed with the power to control it.

One of the most remarkable characteristics of the human imagination is the fact that whenever we confront an unfamiliar situation or enter into an unfamiliar setting or milieu we invariably perceive it as having a theatrical quality, and we tend to react to it in theatrical terms. When we travel in foreign countries and observe what we perceive as alien behavior, it is almost like watching a play. Even in societies with customs more attuned to our own, we experience the same thing. Whenever we feel that we are outsiders, all unfamiliar customs and behavior will appear to us as theatrical. We are spectators at a play.

But what happens when circumstances make it impossible for us to remain outside the action? Whether we like it or not, we have to give up our spectator role and become a participant. Again, we perceive both ourselves and our behavior in theatrical terms. We become actors; we imitate what we believe is expected behavior as a way of making it our own. Acting is a means of mastering an alien reality. Moreover, we are aware of the many roles—roles which have no sense of innate or necessary consistency—which we play as an actor plays roles.

1

The point is that the more we think about it, the more aware we become of how much of life is perceived, experienced, and judged in theatrical terms. We are always conscious of the fact that there is a theatricality in all human action.

This explains why one of the oldest metaphors to express the fundamental nature of human experience is voiced by the melancholy Jacques in the well known lines from Shakespeare's *As You Like It:*

> All the world's a stage,
> And all the men and women merely players.

From the beginnings of history and in every known culture, the idea that we play our lives out as if on stage cast in a divinely authored script before an audience of our fellow human beings has been a dominant image of man's view of himself. Even in markedly secular ages, such as our own, the theatrical metaphor has had a persisting power.

The reasons for this are numerous. To begin with, no matter how boldly each of us may assert that "I am the master of my fate; I am the captain of my soul," we are nonetheless haunted by a nagging sense that there are unseen, undefined, or unknowable forces which shape our lives; that there is a script of someone else's making which directs what happens to us. We feel this because no matter how deeply involved we may be in our ordinary, everyday lives, we are always aware that somehow our experience is unreal, or at least it could be closer to reality. We are conscious of the fact that no matter how close to other people we may be, we really do not know them; in fact, we feel we can never really know ourselves. This leads us to wonder if there may not be another world that is as valid (or even more valid) than the world we commonly accept as real. Primitive man believed that there was another world—a world of the Gods—which was more real than his. Plato insisted that what we experienced as real was, in fact, only a shadow of a reality which could never be fully known. In the Middle Ages, life was viewed as part of God's grand design which man could never comprehend and would only be revealed to him at Judgment Day. According to Hindu thought, man and the world are but images in God's dream; and consequently, man's sense of reality is nothing but an illusion (*Maya*). The fairy tales of our childhood invariably begin by referring to an earlier time ("Once upon a time") when the Gods walked the earth, which was more real than all subsequent history. Even in our rationalistic scientific age, much of our daily experience strikes us as illusory, and we are increasingly conscious of the existence of other realities.

However, thinking this way makes us feel very uncomfortable, and while we can acknowledge the theatrical nature of much of our everyday lives, it provokes negative responses within us as well. For example, it is a commonplace observation that people tend to describe, and often judge, everyday experience in terms of the arts. We refer to landscapes as "poetic," or an individual's struggle with adversity as "epic," a beautiful body as "statuesque," graceful moments as "balletic," a woman's beauty as "lyric," a powerful image as "graphic," any kind of happy blending together of diverse elements as "symphonic," and so on. Invariably, epithets from the arts tend to have positive and praiseworthy connotations. But just think of those that come from the theatre-related arts! When life experience is described as "theatrical," "operatic," "melodramatic," or "stagey," the connotation is invariably hostile and reveals our feelings that somehow that experience is insincere or inauthentic and therefore not to be trusted. Certainly, when we use such terms or phrases as "acting," "putting on an act," "playing up to," "making a scene," "making a spectacle of oneself," or "playing to the gallery," we are usually indicating some form of disapproval. The pejorative tone of these expressions reveals a deep-seated prejudice against the theatre. Why is this?

On the conscious level, it is probably due to the fact that while we can see a certain validity to the idea that life is experienced in theatrical terms, we nonetheless reject it. Ultimately we abhor the thought that we are helpless puppets performing in a play over which we have no control. We really believe that we can and do make choices which alter the direction of our lives. We know that we do have an effect on the lives of other people that cannot be predetermined. While we acknowledge the fact that we play many different roles in life, we believe there is a unifying consciousness which binds all of those roles together in a meaningful way—that role playing in life is not the same thing as what actors do in the theatre. In short, no matter how apt the idea that "all the world's a stage" may seem, we reject it as an adequate expression of how our life really is. In a sense this is true, but it isn't the whole story. If it were, the theatrical metaphor would have lost its power long ago, and certainly there would be no reason for theatrical terms to have such negative connotations or be indications of such a negative response.

There is probably a deeper and largely unconscious reason for our strongly held prejudice against the theatre, and it has the same roots as those impulses which make the theatre not only attractive but even necessary to our lives. Most of us, most of the time, have of necessity to go about with the business of living without giving too much thought to life's mysteries. There's the house to clean, the job to do, the children to get to school, the car and house to pay for. We haven't time for mysteries. Like the women of Canterbury in T. S. Eliot's play, *Murder in the Cathedral,* we go on "living and partly living" with "our private terrors, our particular shadows, our secret fears." But there is something about those private terrors, particular shadows, and private fears: they have a way of creeping into our consciousness no matter how busy we are carrying out our mundane daily tasks. They keep coming back to haunt us. We are all aware of the many ways in which we attempt to escape or to be distracted from their disturbing presence—work, drugs, alcohol, shopping, indiscriminate sex, etc.—and we sometimes try to deal with them in more creative and constructive ways, such as entering into some form of psychiatric therapy or sincerely embracing a religious belief.

However, because it is just these terrors, shadows, and fears that are the unique subject matter of the theatre, human beings throughout history have found themselves turning to the theatre as one of the most satisfactory ways of confronting them. But this confrontation is as fearful as it is necessary. It is precisely because the theatre's chief function is to make present mystery, make manifest the unknown or the inexplicable, that it evokes such ambivalent responses within us. And the complexity of these responses is compounded by the very nature of the theatrical medium itself. Unlike the other arts which communicate through inanimate or abstract means (or some combination of the two), the theatre does so primarily through living human beings. Human beings as actors who confront and present mystery at the same time; human beings who are more and less than human; human beings whose feelings and responses are real and not real. Just as we go to the theatre as a way of confronting and dealing with those mysteries that haunt us, so the theatre deals with them in ways that are haunting. There is something strange and almost ghostly about the whole experience, and this accounts for the contradictoriness of our responses to everything related to the theatre. It is this quality of ghostliness which prompts our fears, even as it fulfills our needs. This ambivalence—this combination of attraction and apprehension—is at the heart of our response to the theatrical event.

Thus, whenever we go to the theatre, we enter into a situation where those anxieties provoked by our never resolved confrontations with separation, loss and strangeness come back to haunt us. It is for this reason that the theatre is often referred to as a realm of mystery. It is a place where those ghosts which we carry with us all of our lives are made present in such a way that we experience them as if directly without having to fear the consequences of that confrontation. The "as if" is important. Our experience of most events taking place on the stage— even in the frothiest comedy—would at best be anxious-making, and in most instances would be too difficult to bear if we were dealing with them directly. But we do not. We are always conscious that what's going on only appears to be real. It is all an illusion; it is representation of reality, not reality itself; it is make believe. In fact, one of the most interesting characteristics of theatre is the way it continually draws our attention to its essential theatricality. (The play within the play is a good example.) We tend to forget that the word "illusion" is derived from the Latin word "to mock." One of the reasons we experience theatre without directly experiencing fear, pain, or anxiety is that it is always mocking the unreality of its own nature. The theatre can speak the unspeakable and show that which should not be shown because we are never allowed to forget that we are watching a play with players playing.

Mention of the "as if" leads us to a discussion of one of the most interesting yet most frequently misunderstood concepts of theatre: imitation. In his very important book, *Play, Dreams and Imitation in Childhood*, which has shaped so much of our thinking about developmental psychology in the twentieth century, the French psychologist Jean Piaget presents overwhelming evidence that we tend to imitate those things which cause the most ambivalent emotions within us. His central thesis is that the source of all imitation (and subsequently of all play and playing) resides in those deeply rooted fears which are derived from the "ghost reaction" of our infancy, when we first became conscious of otherness and which creates that condition of uncertainty of the self that haunts us for the rest of our lives. Anthropologists and historians of religion (particularly Claude Lévi-Strauss and Mircea Eliade) confirm that this pattern of behavior has always and everywhere been operative and applies as much to the tribes of primitive cultures—both past and present—as it does to the civilizations of modern man. Like the infant or the members of a primitive tribe, we imitate the unknown and the strange as a way of handling the fears which, because of their very strangeness, they evoke. The rhythm of imitation is fear and aggressive response and the working out of the rhythm is directly related to others, to spirits, to ghosts. We imitate the unknown as a way of mastering and gaining dominance over it. We give form to and identify with our secret terrors in the belief that by accommodating ourselves to them we will gain control over them by assimilating them to ourselves. (One of the basic premises of Bruno Bettelheim's fascinating book, *The Uses of Enchantment*, is that the frightening figures in the fairy tales of our childhood serve a very similar function in our development to maturity.)

Imitation, then, is the process by which we confront and transform our fear of the strange and unknown by becoming at one with it. And it is no accident that imitation is the essential process of the theatre. Every play is an imitation of an action which makes manifest a mystery, and the presentation of the play transforms the ghost by making it present and thus confrontable. The special power of the theatrical metaphor is that it is capable of dealing with those mysteries which are the central concern of all human beings and which never cease to haunt our imaginations. And it does so in human—not abstract—terms through the living presence of the actor, who is both a real person and at the same time a fictional character. This explains why we are so attracted to the theatre, and why we are so fearful of it too. It also explains why each of the forms of drama is in some essential way ultimately concerned with dealing mediately with some aspect of the numinous or mysterious in human experience. This is as true of comedy as it is of tragedy, of farce as it is of melodrama, or of tragicomedy as it is of any of the various mutations of dramatic form enumerated by Polonius in the "Players' Scene" of *Hamlet*.

But having made this generalization, we must at once acknowledge that our experience of theatre—no matter how limited it may be—tells us that not only do plays take different forms, but the mysteries they manifest can be significantly different as well. Both *Oedipus the King* and *The Importance of Being Earnest* are foundling stories and hence are concerned with identity; but no one would ever confuse the two plays or what they are about. The governing spirit of each of them is so different that we can easily distinguish that not only is one a tragedy and the other a comedy, but they are centrally concerned with quite different aspects of experience. Similarly, while both *Antigone* and Webster's *The Duchess of Malfi* deal with great suffering, we perceive that they do so in ways that make them different in kind and not degree. The mysteries of life can be viewed from a number of perspectives, and throughout history certain dominant forms or types of drama have established themselves as ways that the theatre has given expression to them. One of the oldest, most persistent, and most satisfying of these forms is comedy.

II. The Comic View of Life

Everything in nature is . . . . comic in its existence.
GEORGE SANTAYANA

Several years ago an article appeared in a New Orleans newspaper which in no way dealt with the subject of comedy, and yet in a strange and grotesque fashion, it points to some of the significant elements of this most complex of all dramatic forms. The article reads as follows:

MAN'S CORK LEG CHEATS DEATH
Keeps Him Afloat After Leap Into River

A carpenter's cork leg kept him afloat and prevented him from taking his life by jumping into the Mississippi River from a Canal St. Ferry, Fourth District police reported Monday.

Taken to Charity hospital after his rescue was Jacob Lewis, Negro, 52, 2417 Annette. Suffering from possible skull fracture and internal injuries, he was placed in a psychiatric ward for examination.

Police said that after his release from the hospital he would be booked for disturbing the peace by attempting to commit suicide.

The incident occurred about 11:25 P.M. Sunday while the Ferry M.P. Crescent was tied up on the Algiers side of the river.

Police quoted a ferry passenger as saying he saw the man leap from a rest-room window into the water. When the call was sounded, Johnson, 54, 21113 Whitney, Algiers, both Negroes, lowered a boat and rescued Lewis.

He was brought into the boat about 100 yards from the ferry after he refused to grab life preservers the men threw him.

Ferry employees said he told them he had no desire to live. His attempt on his life might have succeeded if his cork leg had not kept him afloat, police said.

(New Orleans Times Picayune)

We cannot help laughing at this report of a thwarted suicide. The situation is ludicrous, if not downright absurd; death and utter despair are cheated in such a preposterous fashion that they are not taken seriously. Even the physical injury is all but ignored, and we are more conscious of the insult—being booked for disturbing the peace—than we are of the pain. And, finally, in its own grim way the story underscores that comedy and laughter are serious business.

However, as we enter the realm of comedy, we must proceed with caution. There are countless pitfalls to be avoided, the most important of them being the tendency to get so caught up in related but peripheral issues—the psychology or physiology of laughter, the politics of humor, conventions of comic acting, etc.— that we forget the main subject altogether. Nor should we forget the lesson to be learned from the first recorded attempt to take comedy seriously. Recall the prophecy of Plato's *Symposium:* It is early morning and Socrates is still rambling on. He finally begins talking about comedy and proposes his theory that tragedy and comedy spring from the same roots. "To this they were constrained to assent, being drowsy, and not quite following the argument. And first of all Aristophanes dropped off to sleep." "Such was the charm," as Henry Myers has pointed out, "of the first theory of comedy! We leave the *Symposium* with an unforgettable picture of an eminent philosopher putting an eminent comic poet to sleep with a lecture on the comic spirit."

A second warning: Going all the way back to the time of Aristotle there has been a tendency to discuss comedy in terms of form. That is, we tend to describe, define, and judge comedy in terms of certain formal or structural characteristics which we assert must pertain to all comedies, as if a comedy were a sonnet or a sonata, a symphony or a Chinese landscape scroll. Such an approach to comedy—or any of the other forms of drama—could not be more misleading. It cannot begin to be a fruitful approach when dealing with the broad diversity of the modern theatre. Nor is it helpful as a way of studying Elizabethan comedy (consider how different the comedies of Shakespeare and Jonson are—not to mention those of lesser known playwrights). It won't work for the Greek theatre when we compare Menander to Aristophanes. The issue of defining comedy in terms of form and/or structure gets even more confusing if we start comparing and contrasting its manifestations in different periods of history or in different countries and cultures. There is no way we can relate *The Miser* to *The Clouds* or *Arms and the Man* to *A Midsummer Night's Dream* in terms of form. If they share something in common—and they do—it is something other than form.

Therefore, if we want to deal with all of those plays we tend to think of as comedies in a meaningful way, we must resist falling victim to what I have called the "formalistic fallacy in the study of dramatic genres." That is, we must avoid the kind of thinking about drama which assumes that comedy (or tragedy) of all ages has certain formal or structural characteristics in common. The essential qualities of comedy are not structural, nor can its nature be defined in terms of form. The structure of each play is unique, and even within the work of an individual playwright there is an evolution of form which makes it impossible to consider his or her plays in terms of consistent structural patterns.

Finally, we should not be misled by one other false but widely held assumption about comedy. Namely, that there are certain themes, situations, or character types which are the special province of comedy, or are more compatible to the comic muse. The history of drama reveals more exceptions than there are rules. *Oedipus The King,* for example, is the story of "the lost one found." As such, it is, like *The Importance of Being Earnest,* a "success" story, a story type which traditionally has been particularly well-suited to comedy. There is no doubt that *Oedipus The King* is a success story, but no one would ever call it a comedy. The reverse is equally true: J. M. Synge's *The Playboy of the Western World* is a story of Oedipal murder, but no one has ever thought of it as a tragedy. Or to take the most striking example of all: There is no question that we invariably associate fools with comedy; yet one of the most deeply tragic scenes in the history of the theatre is the storm scene between King Lear and the Fool on the heath.

All of the materials available to the dramatist, whether they be from his own experience, from history, or from the accrued traditions of the drama itself are, in fact, neutral. It is only by the playwright's shaping of them that they take on meaning—a meaning which may be tragic, comic, melodramatic, farcical, or what have you. Not to understand this fact is to blur the crucial distinctions which exist between art and life. In life, the meaning we assign to any situation will be the product of personal determinants. But our response to an event which occurs in a play will be the product of the causes built into that play by the playwright. In both cases it is the view and the value assigned to it which will determine whether we consider a situation serious or comic, or remain completely indifferent to it. For example, the "battle of the sexes" is usually mentioned as a typical comic plot. While it is true that the struggle for power in the home has provided a comic impetus for many plays, from Aristophanes' *Lysistrata* to Neil Simon's latest hit, this same struggle is also at the heart of such eminently serious works as *Macbeth* and Strindberg's *The Father.* Or again, a girl surrounded by a host of suitors has been used as the basic predicament of countless comic plots, but this is also the situation of Ibsen's *Hedda Gabler* and O'Neill's *Strange Interlude* as well. Even plays universally accepted as tragic or comic can be transformed. Tom Stoppard turned *Hamlet* into an absurdist comedy with *Rosencrantz and Guildenstern Are Dead,* and many productions of *The Cherry Orchard* have been played as a tragedy rather than as the comedy Chekhov intended.

In short, for every comic use made of a given situation, one can find examples of a serious use of the same situation. And the reverse of this is equally true. In each case, the deciding factor is the way the artist has used his materials so they will assume a comic or a serious shape. In so doing, the playwright will also shape the audience's response to his or her creation. The common denominator from comedy to comedy is not a certain kind of plot or character or structure but the playwright's comic view of life.

What is the comic view of life? All comedy celebrates humankind's capacity to endure; it dramatizes the fact that no matter how many times we may get knocked down or fall short, we somehow manage to pull ourselves up and keep on going. There is something almost biological about the comic—and this is the source of its energy as well as its appeal to audiences. It reveals the unquenchable vitality of our impulse to survive. The central intuition of comedy is an innate and deeply felt trust in life. In spite of the many failures we may and do experience—our tragic fate—the comic spirit expresses elation over our condition because it is so supremely conscious of the way life pushes on, of the many ways it continually asserts itself. The spirit of comedy is the spirit of resurrection, and the joy that attends our experience of the comic is the joy that comes from the realization that despite all our individual defeats, life does nonetheless continue on its merry way. This is the spirit Susanne Langer was describing when she wrote about "the comic rhythm" as follows: (see page 70.)

> Comedy is an art form that arises naturally wherever people are gathered to celebrate life, in spring festivals, triumphs, birthdays, weddings, or initiations. For it expresses the elementary strains and resolutions of animate nature, the animal drives that persist even in human nature, the delight man takes in his special mental gifts that make him the lord of creation; it is an image of human vitality holding its own in the world amid the surprises of unplanned coincidence. The most obvious occasions for the performance of comedies are thanks or challenges to fortune. What justifies the term "Comedy" is not that the ancient ritual procession, the Comus, honoring the god of that name, was the source of this great art form—for comedy has arisen in many parts of the world, where the Greek god with his particular worship was unknown—but that the Comus was a fertility rite, and the God it celebrated a fertility god, a symbol of perpetual rebirth, eternal life.

(Feeling and Form)

That all comedy celebrates life's capacity to renew itself is underscored by the central presence of lovers in every comic action. There are invariably obstacles or misunderstandings for them to overcome—parents who separate them, mistaken identities, petty jealousies or temporary rivals, enforced absences, money problems—but by the end of the play, they are happily united, and the closing note is always bright with hope for the future. The lovers embody the energy and elation of that life, which is always pushing on.

However, when we think about any of the comedies we may have seen or read, we realize that for all of our talk about elation and energy, at the heart of comedy we will find a condition of misery, discord, confusion, or threat. Comedies may end happily, but along the way there is nothing but trouble. Parents thwart the wishes of their children; children rebel against their parents; people lie, cheat, steal, insult, and behave in countless petty ways; the social system is often corrupt or breaking down. One could extend the list, but pick any comedy ever written, and one will discover that the essential fact of the comic world is disturbance. It is a world of lost fortunes, separated lovers, mistaken and/or threatened identities, tyrannical and/or threatening imposters, knavishness, blind and willful authority figures, exile, and melancholy. Yet we laugh at and enjoy these unpleasant characters and unhappy goings-on! Why do we have such a joyous response to events and situations which are so clearly painful, unhappy, or uncomfortable? To answer this question, we must discover the special world in which comedy takes place and the boundaries that define it.

For a comedy to ring true, the characters in the play must experience the same kinds of social pressures and restraints that we in the audience experience in our daily lives. They may fail or do with less than they hoped for; they may be embarrassed, humiliated, or threatened. Yet, somehow, we always feel that they exist in a protected realm—one which is characterized by an absence of pain because we know that eventually the threats to their condition will be cut off or removed. The repressive forces of authority (usually in the form of a parental figure or an imposter) are there, but they are always overcome by some form of antic daring. Life has its shortcomings, but this situation is not viewed as irremediable, for everything about comedy confirms the possibility for change. The inauthentic is seen for what it is, and a new and more honest reality seems possible because in comedy good sense always triumphs. And because it does, the discord is assimilated, and social order is restored. At the end of every comedy, we have a condition of momentary stability—there is a balance and equilibrium.

The mysterious freedom which characterizes comedy's protected world is probably most fully embodied by the figure of the fool or trickster who appears in some form in most comic plays. From Greek and Roman comedy, through Shakespeare and Moliere, to Charlie Chaplin and the Marx Brothers, the fool has had a primitive and magical license to strip us naked as he reflects the folly of all human endeavor. He can act free of law and order, seemingly independent of the constraints of space and time, and always untouched by the terrors of reality. Like the heroes of the fairy tales of our childhood, he moves through the play as if protected by a shining halo of bright and joyous light. His presence assures us that the discord at the heart of the comic situation will eventually be made right.

The wisdom of fools and tricksters is the wisdom of the comic world. They possess what Susanne Langer described as a quality of "brainy opportunism in the face of an essentially dreadful universe." Through a kind of logical luck, which does not seem like luck while we experience the play in performance, the fool assures us that somehow our freakishly individual fortune is capable of triumphing over our tragic fate. This explains why we take such pleasure in the predicaments of the comic. We know that at all times the world of the play is protected by an indefatigable and undefeatable spirit of life.

What are the boundaries of this protected world of comedy? Although Aristotle said very little about comedy, he did provide us with some clues that will be helpful in dealing with this question. At the beginning of the fifth chapter of the *Poetics*, he defines comedy as follows:

> Comedy is, as we have said, an imitation of characters of a lower type—not, however, in the full sense of the word bad, the ludicrous being merely a subdivision of the ugly. It consists in some defect or ugliness which is not painful or destructive. To take an obvious example, the comic mask is ugly and distorted, but does not imply pain.

The two key ideas in this definition are the *ludicrous* and *the absence of pain;* and although it is clear from what follows that Aristotle is more concerned with their contrasts—*the serious* and *the painful*—he does establish two fundamental boundaries of the comic. Let us examine them briefly.

In making this distinction between the ludicrous and the serious, Aristotle was not denying the potential seriousness of comedy; rather, much like Plato, he was postulating the idea that comedy—as well as tragedy—derives from positive attitudes toward value. For something to be serious, we must assign it serious value, and this can occur only when there exists a larger system of values which we accept as valid and of which the specific value is a part. Thus, while Aristotle describes the ludicrous as a species of the ugly which has no painful effects, it is impossible to set the limits of the ludicrous until the serious has first been defined and accepted. A thing cannot be ugly or immoral until we have first agreed on what is beautiful and moral. This explains why we can discuss tragedy (which deals directly with the serious) without reference to comedy, but, when talking about comedy, must always refer to the standards of seriousness which give it its essential definition.

Thus, for all of its positive characteristics, comedy is negative in its definition. (Which explains why Samuel Johnson was so correct when he observed that comedy "has been particularly unpropitious to definers.") An audience will refuse to react positively—in this case, laugh—to any presentation in a ludicrous manner of what it believes to be the true, the good, or the beautiful. We laugh, for example, at the absent-minded professor not because of his learning, but because his absent-mindedness is not consistent with his erudition. When Trofimov falls down the stairs in the Third Act of *The Cherry Orchard,* it is a comic event. Not because falling down stairs is funny—it obviously is not—but because it undercuts the pompous posturings which preceded his fall. Similarly, we can never be induced to laugh at the beautiful *as* beautiful. A beautiful woman is not funny; a beautiful woman who speaks in a high, squeaking voice is very funny because she fails to measure up to the standard which her appearance has established. Such a standard may not always be a logically defensible one—more often than not it is not—but it holds in the theatre so long as the audience takes it to be so. Such is also the case with the beautiful but dumb blonde. The dumbness is an analog to the squeaking voice, though there is no logical, necessary relationship between beauty and intelligence. It is merely that we somehow expect it.

However, our laughter in these instances cannot be explained in the simple terms of incongruity. For incongruity, no matter how it is conceived—expectation and consequence, tension and elasticity, reality and illusion—does not, as many theorists have maintained, necessarily evoke a comic response, nor is it unique to the comic form. Incongruity has been effectively used in all dramatic forms—serious and comic. It can produce dire emotions as well as side-splitting laughter. The coming of Birnam Wood to Dunsinane in *Macbeth* is unquestionably incongruous, but no one in the play or the audience thinks it is funny. The same is true of Richard III's seduction of Lady Anne. Indeed, as Aristotle pointed out in Chapter XIV of the *Poetics,* to show a terrible act committed by a character from whom we expect love (hence, an incongruous act) is the most effective way of producing a tragic effect. In fact, a good case could be made for the idea that incongruity is the cause of horror in the theatre as well as laughter. What is operative in the ludicrous is not a question of mere incongruity, but a perceptible falling short of an already agreed-upon standard of seriousness which we have set for the object, or which is set by the object itself.

One boundary of the comic's realm, then, is that line where the ludicrous and the serious meet. We turn now to its other boundary, the absence of pain. Pain is never funny in itself. Painful circumstances that turn out to have no serious consequences do provoke laughter. In comedy, action has definite consequences, but these consequences have had all of the elements of pain and permanent defeat removed. The pratfall is a fitting symbol of the comic. Even death is never taken seriously or considered as a serious threat in comedy. Aristotle perceived, correctly, that while the ludicrous (whether it takes the form of the grotesque, of exaggeration, or of physical deformity) was the proper subject matter for comedy, manifestations of the ludicrous must be made painless before they can become comic. The writhings of the cartoon character who has just received a blow on the head, the violent events in some of Molière's plays, or the mayhem committed by slapstick clowns remains funny only as long as it is quite clear that no real pain is involved. One reason why the violence of slapstick is so effective in films (one thinks of the pies and boppings of the Three Stooges or the Ritz Brothers) is that it is virtually impossible to fear for the characters, since the actors have no physical reality. If a fight on the stage—even one intended to be funny—appears to be an actual fight, the audience may well begin to fear for the actors, that is, take seriously the possibility of pain.

Whenever a serious deed or event is allowed to enter the field of comedy (as frequently happens), the serious effect must, in some way, be cut off. Such is the case in Jonson's *Volpone* in which the possibility of the rape is never seriously considered because of the circumstances in which the scene occurs. Similarly, in *The Playboy of the Western World*, we never take Christy Mahon's threat to murder his father seriously because all of the prior fantasizing about Oedipal murder assures us that the dreadful threat will never be carried out. Conversely, one of the reasons *The Cherry Orchard* is so difficult to interpret is that the line between the characters' self-dramatizing about suffering and actual pain is such a tenuous one. If we miss all of the subtle clues Chekhov gives us to indicate that Madame Ranevsky does not really care about the orchard and is actually enjoying being at the center of a teapot drama, then it is impossible for us to think of it as the comedy ("at times even a farce") which Chekhov intended. The same kind of ambiguity exists in *Twelfth Night* with Malvolio. Shakespeare pushes the cruelty almost too far, and, if we begin to feel sorry for Malvolio, the comic effect of the rest of the play is jeopardized.

Comedy, then, operates in that middle zone between the serious and the absurd which Aristotle called the ludicrous. It is an area which excludes nobility of character, painful consequences, and the consummation of any events which are likely to offend our moral sensibilities.

So life pushes on! The spirit of comedy celebrates our capacity not only to endure our tragic fate, but to overcome it with a kind of energy and exuberance which insists that our good fortune is every bit as much an active force in our lives as our limitations. Our fate may be tragic, but comedy, in all its forms, is an assertion of that life force which enables us to be joyous survivors in an acceptable and accepting world.

Finally, there is one other broad area of misunderstanding which I should like to clarify at least a little before the reader enters comedy's labyrinthine world. One of the most striking characteristics of the modern drama is the obliteration of the age-old distinctions between the tragic and the comic (the serious and the ludicrous, the painful and the painless). This has not been a process of commingling as so many critics have, I believe, erroneously asserted. The combining of the tragic and the comic in a single play is nearly as old as the drama itself—I can trace it back at least to Sophocles. But what is happening today is something quite different. So much so, that it is questionable whether we should even use the terms comedy and tragedy any longer.

As I said earlier in this introduction, both tragedy and comedy depend upon generally accepted standards of values. Such norms make it possible to establish those hierarchies of seriousness upon which the drama has been traditionally based. However, in these muddled and menacing times, there seem to be no generally accepted values, no universally valid systems, no publicly meaningful hierarchies. Without them, all experience becomes equally serious or equally ludicrous. Or, as Ionesco said, "It all comes to the same thing anyway; comic and tragic are merely two aspects of the same situation, and I have now reached the stage when I find it hard to distinguish one from the other."

The first playwright to reflect this changed perception in the theatre was Chekhov. Critics are continually telling us that Chekhov is funny, and furthermore we know that both *The Sea Gull* and *The Cherry Orchard* were called comedies by their author, and that he did not conceive of any of his plays as tragedies. But Chekhov's plays are so unlike most of the comedies of the past that we are not sure we should trust even the author's calling them comedies. Perhaps a better way of understanding what is meant when we describe Chekhov as a comic writer is to recall that he was writing a drama that was to show "life as it is." Another way of putting Chekhov's phrase, "life as it is" is expressed in Santayana's statement, "Everything in Nature is lyrical in its ideal essence, tragic in its fate, and comic in its existence." This provides a very important insight not only into the nature of Chekhovian comedy but also into much of the drama of the twentieth century. The most significant characters in the contemporary theatre respond to all three of Santayana's levels with unique intensity. They are comedians by necessity, smitten with a tragic sense of life, and lyrically in love with the ideal in a world poorly equipped to satisfy such aspirations.

The essential quality of the "is-ness" of life is its absurdity, its futility. Some would argue that this is tragic, perhaps the most tragic condition of all, but as Dorothy Sayers has wisely pointed out: "The whole tragedy of futility is that it never succeeds in achieving tragedy. In its blackest moments it is inevitably doomed to the comic gesture." But make no mistake, this is a special kind of comedy, a grotesque kind of comedy, which makes us laugh with a lump in our throats. This is so because for all of its awareness of the absurdity of experience, it is also extremely conscious of the suffering struggle, and failure of experience. Both the complexity of this condition and the difficulty that the playwright has in giving it dramatic form is beautifully described by Christopher Fry in the essay which opens this volume.

> I know that when I set about writing a comedy the idea presents itself to me first of all as tragedy. The characters press on to the theme with all their divisions and perplexities heavy about them; they are already entered for the race to doom, and good and evil are an infernal tangle skinning the fingers that try to unravel them. If the characters were not qualified for tragedy there would be no comedy, and to some extent I have to cross the one before I can light on the other. In a century less flayed and quivering we might reach it more directly, but not now unless every word we write is going to mock us.

In the past fifty years, the Chekhovian form has come to dominate much of the theatre. We see it in the plays of such different writers as Beckett, Ionesco, Pinter, and Albee, all of whom use what were once considered comic techniques to serve serious aims. Their belief that life is a grand guignol, but with less sense—that to live is only to make the comic gesture, or what Pirandello called the comic grimace—employs the ludicrousness of comedy to show that life is itself absurd. It is a view of life and drama which employs the comic to make its point, a point that is comic only in the sense that Baudelaire found life comic. In the work of all these playwrights, the lines of the comic mask have become those of the tragic; in them we find that the relationship of means to ends is a paradox. Whereas in the comedy of earlier times, comic means were used to comic ends, in the modern theatre, comic means are employed to serious ends. The comic has become a transparency through which we see to the serious. Comedy is unquestionably the proper mirror of our times; but it is also true that it reveals our life to us as "through a glass darkly."

I
THE SPIRIT
OF COMEDY

Comedy[*]

Christopher Fry

A friend once told me that when he was under the influence of ether he dreamed he was turning over the pages of a great book, in which he knew he would find, on the last page, the meaning of life. The pages of the book were alternately tragic and comic, and he turned page after page, his excitement growing, not only because he was approaching the answer but because he couldn't know, until he arrived, on which side of the book the final page would be. At last it came: the universe opened up to him in a hundred words: and they were uproariously funny. He came back to consciousness crying with laughter, remembering everything. He opened his lips to speak. It was then, that the great and comic answer plunged back out of his reach.

If I had to draw a picture of the person of Comedy, it is so I should like to draw it: the tears of laughter running down the face, one hand still lying on the tragic page which so nearly contained the answer, the lips about to frame the great revelation, only to find it had gone as disconcertingly as a chair twitched away when we went to sit down. Comedy is an escape, not from truth but from despair: a narrow escape into faith. It believes in a universal cause for delight, even though knowledge of the cause is always twitched away from under us, which leaves us to rest on our own buoyancy. In tragedy every moment is eternity; in comedy eternity is a moment. In tragedy we suffer pain; in comedy pain is a fool, suffered gladly.

Charles Williams once said to me—indeed it was the last thing he said to me: he died not long after: and it was shouted from the tailboard of a moving bus, over the heads of pedestrians and bicyclists outside the Midland Station, Oxford—"When we're dead we shall have the sensation of having enjoyed life altogether, whatever has happened to us." The distance between us widened, and he leaned out into the space so that his voice should reach me: "Even if we've been murdered, what a pleasure to have been capable of it!"; and, having spoken the words for comedy, away he went like the revelation which almost came out of the ether.

He was not at all saying that everything is for the best in the best of all possible worlds. He was saying—or so it seems to me—that there is an angle of experience where the dark is distilled into light: either here or hereafter, in or out of time: where our tragic fate finds itself with perfect pitch, and goes straight to

* Christopher Fry, "Comedy," *Vogue* (January), 1951; © 1951 by Christopher Fry. Reprinted by permission of Actac, Ltd, 16 Cadoqan Lane, London SWI.

the key which creation was composed in. And comedy senses and reaches out to this experience. It says, in effect, that, groaning as we may be, we move in the figure of a dance, and, so moving, we trace the outline of the mystery.

Laughter did not come by chance, but how or why it came is beyond comprehension, unless we think of it as a kind of perception. The human animal, beginning to feel his spiritual inches, broke in on to an unfamiliar tension of life, where laughter became inevitable. But how? Could he, in his first unlaughing condition, have contrived a comic view of life and then developed the strange rib-shaking response? Or is it not more likely that when he was able to grasp the tragic nature of time he was of a stature to sense its comic nature also; and, by the experience of tragedy and the intuition of comedy, to make his difficult way. The difference between tragedy and comedy is the difference between experience and intuition. In the experience we strive against every condition of our animal life: against death, against the frustration of ambition, against the instability of human love. In the intuition we trust the arduous eccentricities we're born to, and see the oddness of a creature who has never got acclimatized to being created. Laughter inclines me to know that man is essential spirit; his body, with its functions and accidents and frustrations, is endlessly quaint and remarkable to him; and though comedy accepts our position in time, it barely accepts our posture in space.

The bridge by which we cross from tragedy to comedy and back again is precarious and narrow. We find ourselves in one or the other by the turn of a thought; a turn such as we make when we turn from speaking to listening. I know that when I set about writing a comedy the idea presents itself to me first of all as tragedy. The characters press on to the theme with all their divisions and perplexities heavy about them; they are already entered for the race to doom, and good and evil are an infernal tangle skinning the fingers that try to unravel them. If the characters were not qualified for tragedy there would be no comedy, and to some extent I have to cross the one before I can light on the other. In a century less flayed and quivering we might reach it more directly; but not now, unless every word we write is going to mock us. A bridge has to be crossed, a thought has to be turned. Somehow the characters have to unmortify themselves: to affirm life and assimilate death and persevere in joy. Their hearts must be as determined as the phoenix; what burns must also light and renew: not by a vulnerable optimism but by a hard-won maturity of delight, by the intuition of comedy, an active patience declaring the solvency of good. The Book of Job is the great reservoir of comedy. "But there is a spirit in man . . . Fair weather cometh out of the north . . . The blessing of him that was ready to perish came upon me: And I caused the widow's heart to sing for joy."

I have come, you may think, to the verge of saying that comedy is greater than tragedy. On the verge I stand and go no further. Tragedy's experience hammers against the mystery to make a breach which would admit the whole triumphant answer. Intuition has no such potential. But there are times in the state of man when comedy has a special worth, and the present is one of them: a time when the loudest faith has been faith in a trampling materialism, when literature has been thought unrealistic which did not mark and remark our poverty and doom. Joy (of a kind) has been all on the devil's side, and one of the necessities of our time is to redeem it. If not, we are in poor sort to meet the circumstances, the circumstances being the contention of death with life, which is to say evil with good, which is to say desolation with delight. Laughter may seem to be only like an exhalation of air, but out of that air we came; in the beginning we inhaled it; it is a truth, not a fantasy, a truth voluble of good which comedy stoutly maintains.

The Meanings of Comedy*

Wylie Sypher

I. Our New Sense of the Comic

Doubtless Meredith and Bergson were alike wearied by the "heavy moralizings" of the nineteenth century, with its "terrific tonnage," and thus sought relief in comedy of manners. For both really confine their idea of comedy within the range of comedy of manners; and they have given us our finest, most sensitive theory of that form. Comedy, says Bergson, is a game—a game that imitates life. And in writing the introduction to *The Egoist*, Meredith thinks of this game as dealing with human nature in the drawing room "where we have no dust of the struggling outer world, no mire, no violent crashes." The aftertaste of laughter may be bitter, Bergson grants, but comedy is itself only "a slight revolt on the surface of social life." Its gaiety happens like froth along a beach, for comedy looks at man from the outside: "It will go no farther."

For us, today, comedy goes a great deal farther—as it did for the ancients with their cruel sense of the comic. Indeed, to appreciate Bergson and Meredith we must see them both in a new perspective, now that we have lived amid the "dust and crashes" of the twentieth century and have learned how the direst calamities that befall man seem to prove that human life at its depths is inherently absurd. The comic and the tragic views of life no longer exclude each other. Perhaps the most important discovery in modern criticism is the perception that comedy and tragedy are somehow akin, or that comedy can tell us many things about our situation even tragedy cannot. At the heart of the nineteenth century Dostoevsky discovered this, and Søren Kierkegaard spoke as a modern man when he wrote that the comic and the tragic touch one another at the absolute point of infinity—at the extremes of human experience, that is. Certainly they touch one another in the naïve art of Paul Klee, whose "little scrawls" tell the ridiculous suffering of modern man. Klee adopts the child's drawing because there is a painful wisdom in the hobgoblin laughter of children: "The more helpless they are, the more instructive are the examples they offer us." The features of modern man, whose soul is torn with alarm, are to be seen in Klee's daemonic etchings. Perseus, The Triumph of Wit Over Suffering, of which the artist himself said: "A laugh is mingled with the deep lines of pain and finally gains the upper hand. It reduces to absurdity the unmixed suffering of the Gorgon's head, added at the side. The face is without nobility—the skull shorn of its serpentine

* Wylie Sypher. "The Meanings of Comedy," in *Comedy*, Wylie Sypher, ed. (Doubleday & Company, 1956), pp. 193–258.

adornment except for one ludicrous remnant." In our sculpture, too, the image of modern man is reduced to absurdity—in, for example, Giacometti's figures, worn thin and naked nerve patterns and racked by loneliness.

Our comedy of manners is a sign of desperation. Kafka's novels are a ghastly comedy of manners showing how the awkward and hopelessly maladroit hero, K, is inexorably an "outsider" struggling vainly somehow to "belong" to an order that is impregnably closed by some inscrutable authority. Kafka transforms comedy of manners to pathos by looking, or feeling, from the angle of the alien soul. He treats comedy of manners from the point of view of Dostoevsky's "underground man," and his heroes are absurd because their efforts are all seen from below, and from within. In his notebooks Kafka described the anxiety with which his characters try to bear up under a perpetual judgment life passes upon them: "Watching, fearing, hoping, the answer steals round the question, peers despairingly in her enigmatic face, follows her through the maddest paths, that is, the paths leading farthest away from the answer." Kafka is a modern Jeremiah laughing in feverish merriment, prophetically writing the incredible—the depraved—comedy of our concentration camps, which are courts where the soul of contemporary man undergoes an absurd Trial by Ordeal. His comedy reaches the stage of the inarticulate, as tragedy does when Lear frets about the button.

Our new appreciation of the comic grows from the confusion in modern consciousness, which has been sadly wounded by the politics of power, bringing with it the ravage of explosion, the atrocious pain of inquisitions, the squalor of labor camps, and the efficiency of big lies. Wherever man has been able to think about his present plight he has felt "the suction of the absurd." He has been forced to see himself in unheroic positions. In his sanest moments the modern hero is aware that he is J. Alfred Prufrock, or Osric, an attendant lord—"Almost, at times, the Fool." Or else Sweeney, the apeneck, seeking low pleasures while death and the raven drift above.

We have, in short, been forced to admit that the absurd is more than ever inherent in human existence: that is, the irrational, the inexplicable, the surprising, the nonsensical—in other words, the comic. One of the evidences of the absurd is our "dissociation of sensibility," with the ironic lack of relation between one feeling and another; and the artist now must, as Eliot once said, accept the chaos which serves for our life, span the unstable consciousness of the ordinary man: "The latter falls in love or reads Spinoza, and these two experiences have nothing to do with each other, or with the noise of the typewriter or the smell of cooking." The fragmentary lives we live are an existential comedy, like the intense schizoid lives of Dostoevsky's characters. In *The Brothers Karamazov*, Ivan says, "Let me tell you that the absurd is only too necessary on earth. The world stands on absurdities, and perhaps nothing would have come to pass without them." In our modern experiences the ethical "golden mean" seems to have broken down, and man is left face to face with the preposterous, the trivial, the monstrous, the inconceivable. The modern hero lives amid irreconcilables which, as Dostoevsky suggests, can be encompassed only by religious faith—or comedy.

The sense of the absurd is at the root of our characteristic philosophy—existentialism. The existential religious hero is Kierkegaard, who wrote "In truth, no age has so fallen victim to the comic as this." Kierkegaard, like Kafka, finds that "the comical is present in every stage of life, for wherever there is life there is contradiction, and wherever there is contradiction the comical is present." Kierkegaard's highest comedy is the comedy of faith; since the religious man is the one who knows by his very existence that there is an endless, yawning difference between God and man, and yet he has the infinite, obsessive passion to devote himself to God, who is all, whereas man is nothing. Without God man does not exist; thus "the more thoroughly and substantially a human being exists, the more he will discover the comical." Finite man must take the full risk of encountering an infinite God: "Existence itself, the act of existing, is a striving, and is both pathetic and comic in the same degree." Faith begins with a sense of "the discrepancy, the contradiction, between the infinite and the finite, the eternal and that which becomes." So the highest form of comedy is that "the infinite may move within a man, and no one, no one be able to discover it through anything appearing outwardly." The earnestness of one's faith is tested by one's "sensitiveness to the comical," for God is all and man is nothing, and man must come to terms with God. If one exists *as* a human being, he must be hypersensitive to the absurd; and the most absurd contradiction of all is that man must risk everything without insurance against losing everything. This is precisely what ordinary "Christians" refuse to do, Kierkegaard finds; they wish to find a "safe" way to salvation, to find God without being tormented, and to base their faith on what is probable, reasonable, assured. This is itself ludicrous—the despicable comedy of "Christendom," which requires religion to be comforting and "tranquilizing." Even in his religious life man is always being confronted with the extreme hazard in the guise of the absurd.

This sense of having to live amid the irrational, the ludicrous, the disgusting, or the perilous has been dramatized by the existentialists; and it has also been boldly exploited by propagandists and those who seize power by using "the big lie," the most cynical form of modern political comedy. For all our science, we have been living through an age of Un-reason, and have learned to submit to the Improbable, if not to the Absurd. And comedy is, in Gautier's words, a logic of the absurd.

In his notebooks Kafka explained that he wanted to exaggerate situations until everything becomes clear. Dostoevsky has this sort of comic clarity—a frightening clarity of the grotesque, reducing life, as totally a tragedy, by means of a perspective that foreshortens everything, to absurdity. From this perspective, which is often Goya's or Picasso's, man looks puppetlike, and his struggles diminish to pathos. For example, in the closing pages of *The Brothers Karamazov* when Ilusha is buried, Snegiryov runs distracted about the corpse of his boy, strewing flowers on the coffin, scattering morsels of bread for sparrows on the little grave. These scenes cause a laughter so raw that it brings grimaces hardly to be distinguished from tragic response. The force of this comic "shock" is like the "qualm" stirred by tragedy; it can disorient us, "disturb" us as confusingly as tragic calamity. Melville's tormented Captain Ahab sets his course headlong "outward," driven on by the modern "delight in foundering." Like Conrad's character Kurtz, he is a madman in the grip of "merciless logic for a futile purpose." We are now more sensitive to these absurd calamities than to tragic recognitions. We appreciate Rouault, who sees man as a Clown. In its style Picasso's giant Guernica, that premonition of total war, is a shocking comic strip in black and white, showing how the ridiculous journalese of painting can be an idiom for modern art.

Guernica is like a bad dream and Kafka's novels are nightmares. The dream is nonsensical and free, having none of the logic and sobriety of our waking selves; the very incongruity of the dream world is comic. Freud interprets the dream and the jest as a discharge of powerful psychic energies, a glimpse into the abyss of the self. We have learned to read our dreams to tell us what we really are, for we now find that the patterns of our conscious life have meanings that can be explained only by looking below them into the chaos of the unconscious life always there, old, irrational, and inarticulate except in the language of the sleeping self when, as Banquo warned Macbeth, the instruments of darkness tell us truths. By exploiting the dream, surrealism plays the comedy of modern art, and psychoanalysis plays the comedy of modern medical practice.

Freud is not the only one to suggest that the joke, like the dream, is an upsurge from the unconscious, a mechanism for releasing powerful archaic impulses always there below the level of reason.[1] The caricaturist and the masters of grotesque art have long employed a kind of dreamwork, charged with the spell of mania, like medieval gargoyles or paintings by Bosch and Gruenewald, where there is fiendish zest in wracking man's body. Expressionist art has always been one of the most potent forms of caricature, whether it be paintings by Van Gogh and Kokoschka or Michelangelo's unfinished sculptures. The caricaturist and expressionist use comic distortions that often are the overstatements of a soul shaken by neurosis. Long before Di Chirico and Yves Tanguy painted their dream-fantasies, Bergson guessed that comic automatism resembles the automatism of the dream: *"L'absurdité comique est de même nature que celle des rêves."* Bergson adds: "Whenever the comic personage mechanically holds his idea, he ends by thinking, speaking, acting as if he dreamed." Surrealism is "dream play" (*les jeux du rêve*) since the surrealist painter represents the involuntary "free" associations of the hidden life, which have their own "absurdity" and "improbability." As Bergson remarked, psychological automatism is as comic as the physical automatism of gesture. Dickens is the great artist of physical automatism with his Uriah Heeps and his Mrs. Gamps. Molière is not the only great artist of psychological automatism, for Dostoevsky's "split" characters have the mechanism of surrealist art. His people move, as we do in dreams, by involuntary impulses; they make "psychological gestures." Surrealism surprises us with the *imprévu*, the unexpected psychic gesture controlled by the Id.

Thus the comic gesture reaches down toward the Unconscious, that dim world usually assigned to tragedy, the midnight terrain where Macbeth met the witches. The joke and the dream incongruously distort the logic of our rational life. The joke and the dream are "interruptions" in the pattern of our consciousness. So also, possibly, is any truly creative work of art a form of "interruption" of our normal patterns or designs of seeing and speaking, which are mere formulas written on the surface layer of the mind. Underneath this surface layer is the pattern-free (non-Gestalt) activity of the unconscious, undisciplined self, which cannot be expressed by the forms consciousness imposes on our vision and thought. The deepest "meanings" of art therefore arise wherever there is an interplay between the patterns of surface-perception and the pressures of depth-

---

[1] Most of what I say about Freud's interpretation of comedy derives from *Wit and Its Relation to the Unconscious*. But I have also drawn upon Ernst Kris: *Psychoanalytic Explorations in Art* (1952) to describe what the unconscious contributes to comic art, especially the grotesque; and also on A. P. Rossiter: *English Drama from Early Times to the Elizabethans* (1950), which has some useful passages on caricature. The remarks upon art as an "interruption" in normal consciousness are based on Anton Ehrenzweig: *Psycho-Analysis of Artistic Vision and Hearing*, 1953.

perception. Then the stated meanings will fringe off into unstated and unstatable meanings of great power, felt dimly but compellingly. Behind the trim scaffolding of artistic "form" and logic there whispers, for a moment, the wild voice of the unconscious self—using the disturbed language of the dream and the jest, as well as the language of tragedy. This uncivilized but knowing self Nietzsche once called Dionysian, the self that feels archaic pleasure and archaic pain. The substratum of the world of art, Nietzsche says, is "the terrible wisdom of Silenus," and Silenus is the satyr-god of comedy leading the ecstatic "chorus of natural beings who as it were live ineradicably behind every civilization." The confused statements of the dream and the joke are intolerable to the daylight, sane, Apollonian self.

No doubt the tragic experience reaches deeply down into the "interruptions" of conscious life, conjuring up our grimy disinherited selves and expressing the "formless" intimations of archaic fear and archaic struggle. But in an artist like Dostoevsky the comic experience can reach as deeply down, perhaps because the comic artist begins by accepting the absurd, "the improbable," in human existence. Therefore he has less resistance than the tragic artist to representing what seems incoherent and inexplicable, and thus lowers the threshold of artistic perception. After all, comedy, not tragedy, admits the disorderly into the realm of art; the grotesque depends upon an irrational focus. Ours is a century of disorder and irrationalism.

Is it any wonder that along with our wars, our machines, and our neuroses we should find new meanings in comedy, or that comedy should represent our plight better than tragedy? For tragedy needs the "noble," and nowadays we seldom can assign any usable meaning to "nobility." The comic now is more relevant, or at least more accessible, than the tragic. As Mephisto explains to God, one cannot understand man unless one is able to laugh: "For man must strive, and striving he must err."

Man has been defined as a social animal, a tool-making animal, a speaking animal, a thinking animal, a religious animal. He is also a laughing animal (Malraux takes the "archaic smile" in sculpture as a sign man has become aware of his soul). Yet this definition of man is the obscurest of all, for we do not really know what laughter is, or what causes it. Though he calls his essay "Laughter," Bergson never plumbs this problem. We have never agreed about the motives, mechanism, or even the temper of laughter. Usually the Greeks laughed to express a disdain roused by seeing someone's mischance, deformity, or ugliness. One of the least agreeable scenes in classical literature is the cruel, casual slaying of wretched Dolon, a Trojan spy caught skulking one night by Diomedes and Ulysses near the Greek camp; after tormenting Dolon with a hint he can save his life, the gleeful Ulysses, smiling no doubt an archaic smile, watches Diomedes strike off the head of their captive, "green with fear." There is also scandalous Homeric mirth among the Olympians themselves when lame Hephaistos calls the gods together to ridicule his wife Aphrodite, lying trapped with brazen Ares, god of war. To be laughed at by the ancients was to be defiled.

Malice, however, is only one of the many obscure motives for laughing, which has been explained as a release from restraint, a response to what is incongruous or improper, or a sign of ambivalence—our hysteric effort to adjust our repulsion from, and our attraction to, a situation. Certainly laughter is a symptom of bewilderment or surprise. Sometimes it is said that a laugh detonates whenever there is a sudden rupture between thinking and feeling.[2] The rupture occurs the instant a situation is seen in another light. The shock of taking another point of view causes, in Bergson's words, a momentary "anesthesia of the heart."

During the Middle Ages people seem to have laughed at the grotesque as when, for instance, Chrétien de Troyes brings among the dainty knights and ladies of his romance *Yvian* a rustic lout whose "ears were big and mossy, just like an elephant's," or when Dante's gargoylelike demons caper through the lower circles of hell making obscene noises. In pious legends like "The Tumbler of Our Lady" medieval laughter is charitable, becoming almost tender in anecdotes about Friar Juniper, that tattered soul who in meekness and humility played seesaw with children.

Renaissance laughter was complex. Sometimes it was like Cellini's, swaggering with contempt—*sprezzatura*. When Machiavelli laughs he almost sneers, notably in his play *Mandragola*, showing how a stupid old husband is cuckolded. We can fancy that his Prince would laugh somewhat like a Borgia. Then there is Erasmus' satire, quiet and blighting; less boisterous than Rabelais' monstrous glee. Ben Jonson's plays ridicule the classic-bourgeois "types" (as Bergson would call them) who, like Rabelais' mammoths, are laughable because they have an excess of one "humor" in their disposition or "complexion." Shakespeare's theatre is filled with medically "humorous" persons like Falstaff, who raise a laugh at once brutal, loving, and wise. The laughter in Cervantes' *Quixote* is gentler and more thoughtful, and not so corrosive as Hamlet's wit, which is tinged with Robert Burton's melancholy.

Hamlet's "disturbed" laughter was very "modern," as was also the strained, joyless grimace of Thomas Hobbes, who explained laughter as a sense of "sudden glory" arising from our feeling of superiority whenever we see ourselves triumphantly secure while others stumble. Hobbes brings in the note of "biological" laughter, for he takes life to be a struggle for power waged naturally in a brutish combat "where every man is enemy to every man." Some three hundred years later Anthony M. Ludovici rephrased Hobbes's theory in Darwinian form by supposing that a laugh is man's way of showing his fangs.[3] And man needs, like any animal, to show his fangs only when he is threatened; we laugh in self-defense and bare our teeth to recruit our sinking spirits or to ease our aching sense of inferiority or danger. Laughter is a tactic for survival, a mark of "superior adaptation" among gregarious animals. The weak and the savage both laugh. Ludovici agrees with Nietzsche that man laughs only because he can suffer excruciatingly; and his direst, most inward sickness is the thwarting of his will.

On this latter theme we can play every variation of modern comedy with all its satanic ironies and romantic dreamwork. The "genial" romantics of the early nineteenth century assumed, with Charles Lamb, that laughter is an overflow of sympathy, an amiable feeling of identity with what is disreputably human, a relish for the whimsical, the odd, the private blunder. Carlyle (of all people!) cheerfully supposed that the man who smiles is affectionate. But there were the diabolic romantics, too, driven by the Will to Power or consumed by their own poisons, and they laughed menacingly, frantically. Baudelaire's laugh,

---

[2] This theory of laughter as being due to a "bisociation" of sensibility is discussed at length in Arthur Koestler: *Insight and Outlook*, 1949.

[3] Anthony M. Ludovici: *The Secret of Laughter*, 1932.

heard in the dark bohemian world of Paris—the Paris which drove men desperate and betrayed their ideals—is "a nervous convulsion, and involuntary spasm," a proof of man's fallen state.[4] The feverish laugh of Baudelaire's hero sears his lips and twists his vitals; it is a sign of infinite nobility and infinite pain. Man laughed only after the Exile, when he knew sin and suffering; the comical is a mark of man's revolt, boredom, and aspiration. "The laugh is satanic; it is likewise deeply human." It is the bitter voice of nineteenth-century disillusion. Schopenhauer was the first to define the romantic irony in this desolate laugh of the "underground man": laughter "is simply the sudden perception of incongruity" between our ideals and the actualities before us. Byron jested "And if I laugh at my mortal thing/'Tis that I may not weep."

The mirth of the disenchanted and frustrated idealist, frenzied by his sense of the impassable distance between what might be and what is, reaches its shrillest pitch in Nietzsche, the scorpion-philosopher, exempt from every middle-class code, whose revolt is, unlike Bergson's comedy of "slight revolt on the surface of social life," savage. Nietzsche is able to transvalue all social values by pain, disgust, fury. This sickly laughter of the last romantics is the most confused and destructive mirth Western man has ever allowed himself. It has all the pessimism which Bergson chose not to consider. Rimbaud's laugh is a symptom of anguish, and a glimpse into the abyss of the self. It is a terrifying scorn, a shameless expense of lust, an eruption of the pleasure-principle in a world where pleasure is denied. Nietzsche's laughter is a discharge far more "possessed" than the Freudian sexual release.

So Bergson's analysis of laughter is incomplete, which may explain why he thinks comedy works only from "the outside." Comedy may, in fact, not bring laughter at all; and certain tragedies may make us laugh hysterically. It was Shelley who found the comedy in *King Lear* to be "universal, ideal, and sublime." Ben Jonson himself noted "Nor is the moving of laughter always the end of comedy." When Coleridge lectured on *Hamlet* and *Lear* he pointed out that terror is closely joined with what is ludicrous, since "The laugh is rendered by nature itself the language of extremes, even as tears are." Thus *Hamlet* "will be found to touch on the verge of the ludicrous," because "laughter is equally the expression of extreme anguish and horror as of joy." The grimace of mirth resembles the grimace of suffering; comic and tragic masks have the same distortion. Today we know that a comic action sometimes yields tragic values.[5] In Balzac's *human* comedy (*Comédie humaine*) we meet Old Goriot and Cousin Pons, those heroes of misery.

If we have no satisfactory definition of laughter, neither do we have any satisfactory definition of comedy. Indeed, most of the theories of laughter and comedy fail precisely because they oversimplify a situation and an art more complicated than the tragic situation and art. Comedy seems to be a more pervasive human condition than tragedy. Often we are, or have been, or could be, Quixotes or Micawbers or Malvolios, Benedicks or Tartuffes. Seldom are we Macbeths or Othellos. Tragedy, not comedy, limits its field of operation and is a

---

[4] Probably the most important discussion of "satanic," laughter is Baudelaire's brief essay "On the Essence of Laughter, and In General, On the Comic in the Plastic Arts," which appeared as early as 1855 and was reprinted in *Aesthetic Curiosities*. [See in this volume p. 313.]

[5] According to L. C. Knights "comedy is essentially a serious activity" ("Notes on Comedy" in *Determinations*, ed. F. R. Leavis, 1934).

more closely regulated form of response to the ambiguities and dilemmas of humanity. The comic action touches experience at more points than tragic action. We can hardly hope that our various definitions of comedy will be more compatible than our definitions of laughter; yet each of the many definitions has its use in revealing the meanings of comedy. Bergson's alone will not suffice, or Meredith's either; and they both will mean more when seen against the full spectrum of comic values.

Ordinarily we refer to "high" and "low" comedy; but we cannot speak of "low" tragedy. All tragedy ought to be "high." There are, of course, various orders of tragic action, such as *drame* and "heroic tragedy"; however, as tragedy falls away from its "high" plane it tends to become something else than tragedy. Tragedy is indeed "an achievement peculiarly Greek"—and needs a special view of man's relation to the world.[6] But comedy thrives everywhere and fearlessly runs the gamut of effects from "high" to "low" without diminishing its force or surrendering its values or even jeopardizing them. Once Mme. de Staël said: "Tragedies (if we set aside some of the masterpieces) require less knowledge of the human heart than comedies." What a strange opinion! Yet which of Shakespeare's plays really shows a more profound knowledge of the hearts of fathers and children: *Lear*, or *Henry IV*, 1 and 2, and *Henry V*? Is not the crisis luridly overstated in *Lear* and met with greater insight in the figures of Henry IV, Hal, Hotspur, and Falstaff? Can we honestly claim that Shakespeare reveals more about life in the tragedy of Lear than in the conflicts between Henry and his wild son? Are not many of the problems raised in the great tragedies solved in the great comedies?

Mme. de Staël continues: "The imagination without much difficulty can represent what often appears—the features of sorrow. Tragic characters take on a certain similarity that blurs the finer distinctions between them, and the design of a heroic action determines in advance the course they must take." (Whereas Bergson claims it is comedy that deals with types.) Surely the comic action is more unpredictable, and delight is an emotion quite as individual as grief, remorse, or guilt.

Further, and illogically, "low" comedy is as legitimate as "high." In fact, the lower the range, the more authentic the comedy may be, as we know when we behold the Wife of Bath, that slack daughter of Eve, or Falstaff, that ruffian always on the point of untrussing. At the bottom of the comic scale—where the human becomes nearly indistinguishable from the animal and where the vibration of laughter is longest and loudest—is the "dirty" joke or the "dirty" gesture. At this depth comedy unerringly finds the lowest common denominator of human response, the reducing-agent that sends us reeling back from our proprieties to the realm of old Pan. The unquenchable vitality of man gushes up from the lower strata of Rabelais' comedy, inhabited by potbellied monsters who tumultuously do as they wish in a world built entirely with the apparatus of a gargantuan pedagogy. There we drop the mask which we have composed into the features of our decent, cautious selves. Rabelais strips man of his breeches; he is the moral *sans-culotte*. Psychologists tell us that any group of men and women, no matter how "refined," will, sooner or later, laugh at a "dirty" joke, the question being not whether they will laugh but when, or at precisely what "dirty" joke;

[6] As Edith Hamilton says in *The Greek Way*.

that is, under exactly what the human co-efficient of stress a code of "decency" breaks apart and allows the human being to fall steeply down to the recognition of his inalienable flesh.

Yet laughter at the obscenest jest forever divides man from animal, because the animal is never self-conscious about any fleshly act whatever; whereas man is not man without being somehow uneasy about the "nastiness" of his body. One of the deepest paradoxes in comedy thus reveals itself in obscenity, which is a threshold over which man enters into the human condition; it is a comic equivalent to the religious state of original sin or of tragic "error," and man may as justly be thought human because of his sense of what is "dirty" as because of his sense of what is "evil," "sinful," or fearful. This elemental self-awareness—this consciousness of shame at one's flesh—sets one of the lowest margins for civilization; and, conversely, a hypersensitivity to what is "obscene" is a mark of a decadent society. The paradox in comic filth was madly intensified in the satire of Jonathan Swift, that puritan pornographer, who wrote in his notebook that "A nice man is a man of nasty ideas." Swift forces comic obscenity to its extremes in Gulliver's disgust at the Yahoos; his fastidiousness is insane when Gulliver is frightened by the red-haired female Yahoo who stands gazing and howling on the bank, inflamed with desire to embrace his naked body.

As we move "up" the scale of comic action, the mechanisms become more complex but no more "comic."[7] Physical mishaps, pratfalls, and loud collisions are the crudest products of Bergson's comic "automatism." It is hard to distinguish these pleasures from our glee at physical deformity; and here we detect the cruelty inherent in comedy, which may perhaps be another form of the cruelty inherent in tragic disaster. Essentially our enjoyment of physical mishap or deformity springs from our surprise and delight that man's motions are often absurd, his energies often misdirected. This is the coarsest, most naïve, comedy of manners. Another sort of mechanical comedy is the farce—mistaken identities, coincidences, mistimings—which can be a very complicated engine of plot devices. In this range of comedy the characters need only be puppets moved from the outside, as events require. There is the right key to the wrong door, or the wrong key to the right door; and it does not matter very much who is inside, provided it is the unexpected figure. In these comic vehicles fate takes the guise of happy or unhappy chance, which is, of course, only a tidy arrangement of improbable possibilities. On this sort of artificial framework comedy displays some of its most glittering designs.

Or comedy can be a mechanism of language, the repartee that sharply levels drama and life to a sheen of verbal wit. Congreve's cool, negligent persons like Fainall are beings who have a *verbal* existence, of extremely delicate taste, and able to refine all their pleasures to raillery: "I'd no more play with a man that slighted his ill fortune than I'd make love to a woman who undervalued the loss of her reputation." The transparent Mrs. Fainall lives and moves in the same dry atmosphere and speaks with the same brittle tongue: "While I only hated my husband, I could bear to see him; but since I have despised him, he's too offensive." Such comedy of manners does not hesitate to sacrifice humanity to dialogue. Or rather, the dialogue itself may be a fragile mechanism of wit to elevate the comedy to "intellectual" heights. Shakespeare's intricate wit in *Love's La-*

---

[7] The "scale" of comic effects is arranged in Alan Reynolds Thompson: *The Anatomy of Drama*, 1942, Chapter VI. I have modified Thompson's scale in certain ways.

bour's Lost, with its "flowers of fancy, the jerks of invention," demands of us an agility that makes the brain spin. The play is a thin fabric of banter dazzling us with preciosity, its quick venue of phrase—"snip, snap, and home." At its gilded moments this comedy feeds upon dainties, delights to drink ink, to eat paper, to replenish the spirit with joy, to come to honorable terms with a code of manners, and to leave trudging far behind those who are sensible only in the duller parts.

But it is more than a parterre of devices: it is a drama played by those odd, lovable Shakespearean creatures for whom Bergson seems to have so little feeling—they are "characters" in the British sense of the word. Berowne and Don Armado are among them, and they inhabit the higher domain of comedy where we meet Fielding's Squire Western, Chaucer's Monk, Cervantes' Quixote, Sterne's Uncle Toby, and Dickens' Sam Weller. Such persons cannot exist in the dry seclusion of farce. They require the mellow neighborhood of a comedy of humors which gathers into its action spirits of strong and perverse disposition and convincing weight. These characters thrive at more genial latitudes than Ben Jonson allowed them in his comedy of humors, which was too harshly satiric. English literature is, as Taine said, the native province of these unruly creatures whose life blood pulses richly, whose features are odd, and whose opinions, gestures, vices, and habits control the mechanism of the plot in which they happen to be cast. Indeed, such dispositions may temper the whole climate in which events happen and constantly threaten to wreck the tight logic of a fiction. Mercuito and Benedick are incorrigible fellows of this sort. We never take them seriously. They live for us as Falstaff lives; for Falstaff is more than a sack of guts. He moves the whole play from within; he is a temperamental as well as an anatomical grotesque.

These "characters" realized in depth stand at the threshold of "high" comedy, which is really a transformation of comedy of manners. Whenever a society becomes self-conscious about its opinions, codes, or etiquette, comedy of manners may serve as a sort of philosophic engine called "comedy of ideas." Frail as they are, and known best in their moments of raillery, Millamant and Mirabell raise Congreve's *Way of the World* to a bolder order of comedy of manners: "Let us," says Millamant to Mirabell, "be as strange as if we had been married a great while, and as well bred as if we were not married at all." The edge of this comedy is sharpened by sanity as well as verbal wit, and, as Meredith clearly saw, Molière magnified comedy of manners to the dimensions of a criticism of life. Our most provoking social critic is Shaw, although Pirandello soars farther into a crystalline sphere of ideas. The world of Aristophanes could have been shaped only in the sophisticated theatre of an Athens that had begun to examine its own conventions. Aristophanes is like Erasmus or Gide, who serve as the intellectual conscience of a nervous and self-scrutinizing society where all is not now so well as it might be or has been or seems to be.

At the radiant peak of "high" comedy—a peak we can easily sight from Meredith's essay—laughter is qualified by tolerance, and criticism is modulated by a sympathy that comes only from wisdom. Just a few writers of comedy have gained this unflinching but generous perspective on life, which is a victory over our absurdities but a victory won at a cost of humility, and won in a spirit of charity and enlightenment. Besides Shakespeare in, perhaps, *The Tempest*, one might name Cervantes and Henry James and Jane Austen, or Thomas Mann in his *The Magic Mountain*, when pliable, diseased Clavdia yields carelessly to the stricken Hans Castorp in a scene where the grimness of human life, its folly and its error, are seen clearly and with a perverse tenderness: "*Petit bourgeois!*" she says to him—"*Joli bourgeois à la petite tache humide.*" For they both know that the body, love, and death are all three the same thing, and that the flesh is sickness and desire, and life only a fever in matter. This is how "high" comedy chastens men without despair, without rancor, as if human blunders were seen from a godlike distance, and also from within the blundering self. The deep humiliation and reassurance in Don Quixote's madness and recovery, with his resignation, detachment, and self-awareness, are all confirmed by the experience of Shakespeare's Benedick—to whom Meredith appealed. After proving himself as foolish as the rest of the world, Benedick comes to a vision of the human condition: "For man is a giddy thing, and this is my conclusion." Benedick speaks without bitterness, bias, or pride; and has learned, like Hans Castorp, to accept the insufficiency of man without being damaged.

So the range of comedy is more embracing than the range of tragedy; and if tragedy occurs at some middle point in ethical life where failure is weighed against man's nobility of spirit, comedy ventures out into the farther extremes of experience in both directions, toward the bestial or "obscene," and at the other end of the spectrum toward the insane heroics of Nietzsche or the vision of Prospero, who sees sin as the last mistake of all our many mistakes, dispelled before our clearer reason whenever hate seems more absurd than charity.

We may prefer one theory of comedy to another; but we shall find it hard to get along without the other. In *Winter's Tale*, Autolycus meditates on his lot: "I am courted now with a *double occasion.*" The phrase is useful, for comedy is built upon double occasions, double premises, double values. "Nothing human is alien to me," says the character in Terence. Nothing human is alien to comedy. It is an equivocal art. If we now have trouble isolating comedy from tragedy, this is not because comedy and tragedy are identical, but rather because comedy often intersects the orbit of tragic action without losing its autonomy. Instead, comedy in its own right, boldly and illogically, lays claim to some of the values that traditionally are assigned to tragedy alone. Think, for example, of Henry James's "Beast In the Jungle," which really is comedy of manners suddenly consumed in the flame of Marcher's grief that he has lost May forever through his own selfishness. Here is comedy seen ruthlessly "from within" as Bergson did not allow. Marcher is a fool—but a sinister fool, an egoist far more barbaric than Meredith's sleek Sir Willoughby Patterne. And James's London, a society of genteel manners and frail nerves, is a scene where savage eyes glare behind the social simper.

II. The Ancient Rites of Comedy

In fact, to interpret the complications and contradictions in comedy, we must look far backward toward Aristotle and the Greeks; for the meanings in comedy are tribally old, and Bergson and Meredith refine almost beyond recognition the primitive violence of comedy, which, curiously, reappears again in James, Kafka, and "us moderns."

The notion of an affinity between tragedy and comedy would not be strange to the Greeks: not to Socrates, we know, because of what happens in *The Symposium*, a very dramatic dialogue where Plato brings together in debate the comedian Aristophanes, the tragedian Agathon, and along with them the goat-faced Socrates, the philosophic clown, a figure who stands near the center of all the larger problems of comedy. In the course of this night-long dialogue Socrates is described by Alcibiades as looking "exactly like the masks of Silenus." He turns to Socrates and asks: "You will not deny that your face is like that of a satyr? And there is a resemblance in other points too. For example, you are a bully." Yet Socrates makes the notorious Alcibiades ashamed of his misdeeds. Alcibiades complains, "Mankind are nothing to him; all his life is spent in mocking and flouting at them." This Socrates, resembling a caricature of a man, is the person who alone is able to make the dissolute Athenians care for their souls; his words "amaze and possess the soul of every man." Plato reports that by daybreak only Aristophanes and Agathon are still awake to hear Socrates insisting that anyone who can write tragedy can also write comedy because the craft (*techne*) of writing comedy is the same as the craft of writing tragedy.

Surely Socrates, comedian and martyr, mocker and moralist, was the proper one to hold this notion, which has gained new implication now that the social anthropologists have discovered what Aristotle already knew—namely, that comedy is a primal rite; a rite transformed to art. As F. M. Cornford puts it, comedy is "a scene of sacrifice and a feast."[8] Aristotle intimated as much in the *Poetics* by stating that at first both tragedy and comedy were improvisations, the one rising from the Dithyramb, the other from phallic songs "still used as ritual in many of our cities." These improvisations having evolved in different ways, each found its "natural form," the comic writer presenting men as "worse than they are," the tragic writer as "better," and the comic being a version of the Ludicrous—which in turn is a variety of the Ugly without being painful or destructive. Comedy, he adds, has no history—that is, it passed unnoticed for a long time, although it had definite "forms" (*schemata*) even in the early poets. Aristotle thinks that tragedy gained its "magnitude" after it passed its "satyric" phase and took on a "stately manner" at a "late phase" of its history. Thereafter tragedy imitated "noble actions" of "noble personages," whereas comedy dealt with the "meaner sorts of actions among the ignoble." He also says that comedy turned from an early use of "invective" to a "dramatizing of the ridiculous." In early satyric dramas, poetry was adapted to dancing.

However cryptic Aristotle's comment may be, it is clear that he traces the origins of drama to some sort of fertility rite—Dionysiac or phallic—the primitive "sacrifice and feast" mentioned by Cornford. It is now accepted that art is born of rites and that the comic and tragic masks are themselves archetypal symbols for characters in a tribal "semantics of ritual." Behind tragedy and comedy is a prehistoric death-and-resurrection ceremonial, the rite of killing the old year (the aged king) and bringing in the new season (the resurrection or initiation of the adolescent king). Associated with killing the old king and devouring his sacrificial body was the ancient rite of purging the tribe by expelling a scapegoat on whose head were heaped the sins of the past year. Frazer describes what happened during this "public expulsion of evils" at a season when there was an "oblation of first fruit:"

---

[8] Behind my whole discussion of this rite and my whole account of the inconsistent theories necessary to explain comedy is Francis M. Cornford: *The Origin of Attic Comedy*, 1914. Cornford's interpretation seems to me to offer our only means of understanding the incompatibles in comedy without laying ourselves open to a charge of willful illogicality. These incompatibles in comedy are also dealt with effectively in Johan Huizinga: *Homo Ludens* and in Élie Aubouin: *Technique et psychologie du comique*. See also Northrop Frye: "The Argument of Comedy" in *English Institute Essays, 1948*.

> . . . the time of year when the ceremony takes place usually coincides with some well-marked change of season. . . . this public and periodic expulsion of devils is commonly preceded or followed by a period of general license, during which the ordinary restraints of society are thrown aside, and all offences, short of the gravest, are allowed to pass unpunished. (*The Golden Bough*)

At this public purging or catharsis the scapegoat was often the divine man or animal, in the guise of victim, to whom were transferred the sins and misfortunes of the worshipers. Eventually the divine character of the scapegoat was forgotten; as Frazer notes, he became an ordinary victim, a wretch who was a condemned criminal perhaps, actually as well as ritually guilty. This ancient death-and-resurrection rite, then, seems to have had a double meaning: the killing of the god or king to save him and the tribe from the sterility of age, and the expulsion of evils (or devils) amid rejoicing of a people who were redeemed by the sacrifice of a hero-victim.

From this rudimentary sacrifice-and-feast evolved comic and tragic poetry, using a "canonical" plot formula older than either art, an elemental folk drama from which derived in obscure ways the "action" (myth) of the Athenian theatre. In its typical form the archaic fertility ceremony—involving the death or sacrifice of a hero-god (the old year), the rebirth of a hero-god (the new year), and a purging of evil by driving out a scapegoat (who may be either god or devil, hero or villain)—requires a contest or *agon* between the old and new kings, a slaying of a god or king, a feast and a marriage to commemorate the initiation, reincarnation, or resurrection of the slain god, and a final triumphal procession or *komos*, with songs of joy. Behind the marriage ceremonial probably lies the myth of the primal union between the earth-mother and the heaven-father. Following this revelation of the mysteries of life, the new hero-king is proclaimed and elevated; there is an "apotheosis," epiphany, or manifestation of the young hero-god (a theophany).

The rites may take the guise of an initiation or testing of the strength of the hero or his fertility, perhaps in the form of a "questioning" or catechism, after which there comes to him a "discovery" or "recognition"—an *anagnorisis* or new knowledge. Or else the sacrifice may be interrupted by an unwelcome intruder (an *alazon*) who views the secret rites; he is a profaner of the mysteries, an alien. This character must be put to flight or else confounded in a "struggle" that may also occur in the form of a catechism, to which he does not know the proper answers. In either case there is a debate, a dialectic contest, which is preserved in Aristophanes' *Clouds*, for instance, as an argument between "Right Logic" and "Wrong Logic." Thus again the comic action is double, since it is both a rational debate and a phallic orgy. Logic and passion appear together in the primal comic formula.

In Cornford's opinion the dramatic form known as tragedy eventually suppressed the sexual magic in this canonical plot, leaving only the portrayal of the suffering and death of the hero, king, or god. Comedy, however, kept in the foreground the erotic action, together with the disorderly rejoicing at the rebirth or resurrection of the god-hero who survives his *agon*. In this sense comedy preserves the archaic "double occasion" of the plot formula, the dual and wholly incompatible meanings of sacrifice and feast, cruelty and festival, logic and license. So much we may read into Aristotle's remark that comedy was, like tragedy, originally an improvisation, its "action" being a procession of the devotees of Phales carrying the emblem of the god, that profane and sacred symbol, the ithyphallus, the *penis erectus*. After pausing at the place of sacrifice to pray to Dionysus they continued their procession to the burden of phallic songs.

If this indeed be the origin of comedy we can guess why Aristotle said that "tragedy advanced by slow degrees, and having passed through many changes, found its natural form and then stopped evolving." Unlike comedy, tragedy is a "closed" form of art, with a single, fixed, and contained meaning (by contrast to the disorderly relaxed meanings in comedy). Tragedy demands a law of necessity or destiny, and a finality that can be gained only by stressing a logic of "plot" or "unified action" with a beginning, middle, and end. Within the confines of this action the hero is given to sacrifice or death. That is, tragedy performs the sacrificial rite without the festival—which means that it is a less complex, less ambiguous form of drama than comedy. Retaining its double action of penance and revel, comedy remains an "improvisation" with a loose structure and a precarious logic that can tolerate every kind of "improbability."

The coherent plot is vital to tragic theatre (Aristotle says that plot is the very soul of tragedy); and a tragic action needs to convey a sense of destiny, inevitability, and foreordination. The tragic poet often implies there are unchanging moral laws behind the falling thunderbolt. The fate of a tragic hero needs to be made "intelligible" as the comic hero's fate does not; or at least tragic fate has the force of "necessity" even if it is not "intelligible." Somehow tragedy shows what "must" happen, even while there comes a shock of unsurmised disaster. As Aristotle said, in tragedy, coincidence must have an air of probability. Then too, tragedy subordinates "character" to the design of the plot; for the purpose of tragedy, says Aristotle, is not to depict "character," but, rather, to show "men in action," so that the "character" of a tragic hero reveals itself in a deed which expresses his moral disposition. Comedy, on the contrary, can freely yield its action to surprise, chance, and all the changes in fortune that fall outside the necessities of tragic myth, and can present "character" for its own sake.

Following what Aristotle implied, Cornford is able to say that if tragedy requires plot first of all, comedy is rooted so firmly in "character" its plot seems derivative, auxiliary, perhaps incidental. Unlike tragedy, comedy does not have to guard itself by any logic of inevitability, or by academic rules. Comedy makes artistic all the unlikely possibilities that tragic probability must reject. It keeps more of the primitive aspect of *play* than does tragedy.

From the anthropologist's view the tragic action, however inspiring and however perfect in artistic form, runs through only one arc of the full cycle of drama; for the entire ceremonial cycle is birth: struggle: death: resurrection. The tragic arc is only birth: struggle: death. Consequently the range of comedy is wider than the tragic range—perhaps more fearless—and comic action can risk a different sort of purgation and triumph.[9] If we believe that drama retains any of the mythical values of the old fertility rite, then the comic cycle is the only fulfilled and redemptive action, and, strange to think, the death and rebirth of the god belong more fittingly to the comic than to the tragic theatre. Is this the reason why it is difficult for tragic art to deal with Christian themes like the Crucifixion and the Resurrection? Should we say that the drama of the struggle,

[9] Gertrude Rachel Levy in *The Gate of Horn* (1948), p. 319 ff., stresses this interpretation; but, again, my primary debt is to Cornford.

death, and rising—Gethsemane, Calvary, and Easter—actually belongs in the comic rather than the tragic domain? The figure of Christ as god-man is surely the archetypal hero-victim. He is mocked, reviled, crowned with thorns—a scapegoat King.

If the authentic comic action is a sacrifice and a feast, debate and passion, it is by the same token a Saturnalia, an orgy, an assertion of the unruliness of the flesh and its vitality. Comedy is essentially a Carrying Away of Death, a triumph over mortality by some absurd faith in rebirth, restoration, and salvation. Originally, of course, these carnival rites were red with the blood of victims. The archaic seasonal revel brought together the incompatibles of death and life. No logic can explain this magic victory over Winter, Sin, and the Devil. But the comedian can perform the rites of Dionysus, and his frenzied gestures initiate us into the secrets of the savage and mystic power of life. Comedy is sacred and secular.

Thus it happens that from the earliest time the comic ritual has been presided over by a Lord of Misrule, and the improvisations of comedy have the aspect of a Feast of Unreason, a Revel of Fools—a *Sottie*. Comedy is a release, a taking off the masks we have put on to deal with others who have put on decent masks to deal with us. The Church herself knew how salutary is this comic rite of unmasking, for near the season of Lent the monks used to appoint one of their number to be Lord of Unreason and chant the liturgy of Folly, during which an Ass was worshiped and the mass parodied in a ceremony no less religious, in its profane way, than the Dionysian and Saturnalian revels of Greece and Rome.[10] During these *ludi inhonesti* the monks at vespers gave the staff of office to a Lord of Misrule while they chanted "*deposuit potentes de sede, et exultavit humiles.*" In performing the mock mass the celebrants brayed the responses. The first Herod of the mystery plays may have been *Rex Stultorum*, and we know that medieval drama never excluded the comic from its religious ritual. Those in the thrall of carnival come out, for a moment, from behind the façade of their "serious" selves, the façade required by their vocation. When they emerge from this façade, they gain a new perspective upon their official selves and thus, when they again retire behind their usual *personae*, they are more conscious of the duplicity of their existence. That is why Freud thought of the comic as an "unmasking," a mechanism that allows, whether we watch or play it, a "free discharge" of impulses we daily have to repress. The carnival is an hour when we are permitted to recover our "lost infantile laughter" and to rejoice again with the pleasure of a child. It redeems us from our "professional" life.

Aristotle said that tragedy works a purgation or "catharsis" and carries off harmful passions by means of an allowed public cleansing of the self, enabling us to face with poise the calamities of life. Tragedy has been called "mithridatic" because the tragic action, inoculating us with large doses of pity and fear, inures the self to the perils we all face. Comedy is no less mithridatic in its effects on the self, and has its own catharsis. Freud said that nonsense is a toxic agent acting like some "poison" now and again required by the economy of the soul. Under the spell of this intoxication we reclaim for an instant our "old liberties," and after discharging our inhibited impulses in folly we regain the sanity that is worn away by the everyday gestures. We have a compulsion to be moral and decent,

---

[10] This parody is described in A. P. Rossiter: *English Drama from Early Times to the Elizabethans*, 1950.

but we also resent the obligations we have accepted. The irreverence of the carnival disburdens us of our resentment and purges our ambivalence so that we can return to our duties as honest men. Like tragedy, comedy is homeopathic. It cures folly by folly.

The tragic law works a transformation: from sin and suffering come calm of mind and resistance to disaster, to fears that weaken us. The transformations in comedy are equally miraculous: from license and parody and unmasking—or putting on another mask—come renewed sanity and responsibility, a confidence that we have looked at things from a lower angle and therefore know what is incorruptible. In Shakespeare's play the madness of midsummer night is necessary to purge doting and inconstant lovers. After the fierce vexation of their dreams comes the bright Athenian dawn, with secure judgement. As Hippolyta says:

> And all their minds transfigured so together,
> More witnesseth than fancy's images,
> And grows to something of great constancy;
> But howsoever, strange and admirable.

The comic perspective can be reached only by making a game of "serious" life. The comic rites are necessarily impious, for comedy is sacrilege as well as release. That is one reason why comedy is intolerable to the sober moralist Rousseau, who gravely protests that the women of Geneva will be corrupted by going to the theatre to see how Molière satirizes virtuous men like Alceste. Plato has the same puritan timidity, despising the art that stirs up "the rebellious principle" in men, "especially at a public festival when a promiscuous crowd is assembled in a theatre" where passions are roused and fed. Plato's high-minded snobbism, like Rousseau's petty-bourgeois "seriousness," is brought to bear chiefly against tragedy; yet both have an abiding fear of the carnival, which has the power "of harming even the good" by its contagious impieties. Plato warns his Guardians of the ideal State not to be given to laughter, for "violent laughter tends to provoke an equally violent reaction." He especially fears buffooneries or any "impulse to play the clown"—"and by encouraging its impudence at the theatre you may be unconsciously carried away into playing the comedian in your private life." But Freud saw what this impudence means, for the comic action is a mode of "representation through the opposite," and man must periodically befoul the holy and reduce himself to folly. We find ourselves reflected in the comedian, who satisfies our need for impieties.

Nietzsche believed that we discover truth in the excesses of a Dionysiac orgy, which is ecstasy as well as pain. This orgy takes place in the theatre he calls "epidemic" because it sweeps the individual into the tide of a mass emotion. In *The Birth of Tragedy* Nietzsche says that Greek drama was played at a point of conflict between our Apollonian and our Dionysian selves. The Apollonian self is reason (*logos*), while the unruly Dionysiac self finds its voice in song (*melos*)— the song of the chorus. Who are the chorus, singing before the actors (who stand apart to speak of their dialogue)? They are the satyr-selves, the natural beings madly giving out cries of joy and sorrow that arise from the vast cosmic night of primordial existence. "Is it possible," Nietzsche asks, "that madness is not necessarily a symptom of degeneration, of decline, of a decadent culture? Perhaps this is a question for alienists—there are neuroses of *health*?" Nietzsche finds the substratum of both comedy and tragedy in the old satyr-self: "Our deepest insights must—and should—appear as follies, and under certain circumstances as

crimes." So Zarathustra rejoices in the Ass-Festival: "A little valiant nonsense,
some divine service and ass-festival, some old joyful Zarathustra-fool, some blus-
terer to blow your souls bright." When he sings the wild songs of Bacchus, man
loses his personal identity, his "differentiation," and ceases to be a thinker. He
becomes the Dionysiac hero, the archetypal Reveller. In the epidemic theatre
there is a metamorphosis, for civilized man finds again his archaic being among
the throng.

The Dionysiac theatre consecrates truth by outbursts of laughter. Comedy
desecrates what it seeks to sanctify. The orgiastic cleansing of the self and the
tribe is ritually performed in Shakespeare's *Henry IV*, 1 and 2, which is a Feast
of Unreason ceremonially held in the taverns of Eastcheap, with Falstaff presiding as Lord of Misrule. The Lancastrian king Henry IV, Bolingbroke, has under
the guise of just causes usurped the throne and slain the anointed king, Richard
II. After this stroke of power politics Henry has ventured to put on the mask of
repute and piety; but behind this decent royal *persona* is the "shadow" self of
the old unscrupulous Bolingbroke, and he confesses to Hal:

> ... God knows, my son,
> By what by-paths and indirect crookt ways
> I met this crown; and I myself know well
> How troublesome it sat upon my head ...

Henry cannot wear the royal garments easily because he has come to his throne
by the unholy cunning of the opportunist. Richard's blood will not out, and like
a tragic guilt it stains the grace of Henry's rule. Yet Bolinbroke cannot drop the
mask. So Hal's heritage is tainted, and the Lancastrian line must be purged. This
false righteousness can be washed away only by rites acted hilariously on Gadshill, where Hal connives at another, baser thievery that is detected—a parody of
his father's practice. In the depths of bohemia, amid whores, parasites, and cow-
ards, a realm where Falstaff is king and priest, young Hal is initiated into the
company of Fools and Rogues. Falstaff asks the ruthless question: "What is hon-
or?" The Lancastrians must answer before they are legitimate kings. With all the
lewdness of the comedian Falstaff reduces to absurdity the lineage of Bolingbroke when he jests at the parentage of young Harry and knows him to be his father's son only by a villainous hanging lip, which proclaims him honestly begot.
In this pit of degradation Hal cleanses himself and his line from the policy of his
ancestors, and by coming out from behind the façade of Lancastrian pompous-
ness he proves that he is, indeed legitimately, the heir apparent. By stooping to
Doll Tearsheet, Harry makes himself eligible to woo Kate of France. Falstaff is
at once devil and priest, coward and hero, tempter and scapegoat, and essentially the satyr who lives ineradicably behind the façade of every culture. Without
his ribaldry, his drunken wisdom, Britain cannot be redeemed.

III. The Guises of the Comic Hero

Hence the range of comic action is far wider than Bergson supposed when he remarked that the comic is something mechanical encrusted on what is living and
that the comic hero is dehumanized because he makes only gestures, automatic
motions, which look ridiculous when they are "interrupted." Bergson, perhaps

following Stendhal's notion that we remain untouched by the plight of the comic figure, saw him from only one angle, treating him as if he were a toy manikin which, wound up, is geared to execute the same motion wherever he is put. Bergson's comic hero is only a caricature of a man. Yet Don Quixote, even while making mechanical gestures, enters the realm of *human* action as a figure like Tartuffe cannot. In Dickens and Dostoevsky, too, the characters are geared to make a few stormy gestures, but are not merely comic machines like Tartuffe and Harpagon, who by contrast merely gesticulate. Chaucer's Wife of Bath is another creature capable of only a few responses who is, nevertheless, more than an automaton.

Above all other comic heroes, perhaps, Falstaff is a grotesque who has by no means disqualified himself from being a man; in fact, he has a kind of massive "probability" and authentic selfhood-in-depth. Behind his great belly there is an ample personality, and his gesticulations, mechanical as they seem, are comparable to the moral "action" of a tragic hero. Nor is Falstaff isolated from us like Tartuffe, even when his cowardly motions are "interrupted" as he is caught red-handed at Gadshill or on the field at Shrewsbury. Exactly when Falstaff is driven into the tightest corner—when like Tartuffe he is "caught" firmly in the mechanical trap of comedy—he asks his most troublesome questions: What is honor? What is so much like a counterfeit man as a dead hero? Tartuffe does not have this ingenuity, this power to come to grips with us at close quarters. Falstaff is never so dangerous as when he is at bay—which proves that he has an existence of his own apart from the intrigue in which he has a role. Some of Dostoevsky's grotesque people who have obsessive notions also have this power to challenge us as we stand outside the comic arena and watch them from a position of presumed safety. The sickly hero of *Notes from the Underworld* faces us with some very awkward problems which a character so absurd and artificial has no right to raise. Furthermore, at the basest level of his "low" comedy Falstaff ventures to address himself directly to us, making us doubt Bergson's opinion that only "high" comedy is close to life. Indeed, Falstaff shows how narrow the margin sometimes is between high and low comedy, for he was doubtless born a comic machine of a very low order—the *miles gloriosus*—yet as if by a leap he traverses the whole distance between "low" and "high" and is able to dwell disturbingly among us in his own libertine way.

The truth is that the comic hero has a complexity of character Bergson and Meredith did not suspect. Falstaff and Hal are both comedians who take part in the ancient ritual of feast and sacrifice, orgy and debate. In the oldest comedy there was a struggle, or *agon*, with the Imposter (or *alazon*) who looked with defiling eye upon the sacred rites that must not be seen. The alazon was put to flight after a contest with either the young king or with a character known as the *eiron*, "the ironical man." The alazon is a boaster who claims, traditionally, more than a share of the agonist's victory. It was the duty of the eiron, who often professed ignorance, to reduce the alazon, to bring him to confusion. Sometimes the king himself assumed the character of the eiron—"the ironical buffoon"—to deflate the boaster or "unwelcome intruder" who appeared to know more than he actually did. Thus somewhere at the heart of old comedy—ritual comedy—was a combat of the king-eiron against the imposter-intruder-alazon.

This ancient struggle was still being waged in Aristotle's *Ethics* (II, 7; IV, 7, 8) in the contrast between the boaster (alazon) and the self-depreciator (eiron);

and midway between these two characters is the "straightforward" man who neither exaggerates nor understates. Here, as in old comedy, the alazon is the alter ego of the eiron. The two extremes appear together.

Aristotle mentions Socrates as the "mock-modest" character who understates things; and, in fact, Socrates is a kind of alter ego to Falstaff, the boaster-buffoon. The double nature of the comic hero is symbolized in these two: Falstaff and Socrates. They are of opposite disposition, yet not so unlike as we might think. The essential charcacter of the eiron is incarnate in Socrates, who was "ignorant" and who also had the disposition of the "buffoon" or "fool," the features of the comic spirit itself, the coarse, ugly mask of the satyr or clown. The Socratic method is a tactic of winning victory by professing ignorance, by merely asking questions of the "impostors," the so-called "wise" men of Athens. Irony "defeats the enemy on his own ground," for in the course of the comic debate the supposed wisdom of the alazon is reduced to absurdity, and the alazon himself becomes a clown. Thus Socrates, without risking any dogmatic answers, corrects the folly of those sophists who claimed to know the truth, or who were ignorant enough to presume there is no truth. So the ironical man by his shrewd humility ("lying low beneath the gods and saying nothing") proves to be wiser than the wisdom of the world. Irony has been called one of the faces of shame. Yet we must remember that Falstaff the buffoon and impostor used the same sort of interrogation Socrates the ironist used. He asks the same sort of questions: What is honor? Socrates asked: What is justice?

Socrates, like Falstaff, is both ironist and buffoon; he is the questioner using a philosophic buffoonery to seek the truth. In *The Republic* Thrasymachus speaks of Socrates' "shamming ignorance" in his "imbecile way." Socrates is a sort of supersophist who inquires or doubts, and thus again resembles Falstaff. He has a double or triple character, for he is, as Falstaff was, both victor and victim—a victim, eventually, of the thinking Athenians who refused to have their creed unsettled. He was finally condemned to drink the hemlock because he asked too many impious questions. And Falstaff is rejected by King Hal. The eiron himself, with the rude face of the satyr, is at last, like the king in the fertility rite, sacrificed by the tribe. Socrates is a kind of alazon too, since he did claim to have his "wisdom," given him by his daemon, a still small voice he held sacred. When he is comdemned to death by the court he stubbornly insists that if they kill him they will injure themselves far more than they injure him, for they will not find another like him, a gadfly given to the city by God. This is a considerable claim. He adds, "I know but little, and I do not suppose that I know. But I do know that injustice and disobedience to a better, whether God or man, is evil and dishonorable." Here we need to recall that Aristotle classified comic characters as being of three kinds: buffoon, ironist, and impostor. Socrates is all three—and so is Falstaff.

Thus is revealed the deep ambiguity in the comic hero: the Impostor, the enemy of God, is not only the alter ego of the ironist; he is, in Cornford's phrase, the double of the very god himself. The god must be slain and devoured; therefore the guilt feeling of the tribe arising from sacrificing their god-king is transferred to the figure of the alazon, the antagonist and profaner who serves as scapegoat for the injury done the god during the fertility ceremony. The impostor profanes the rites; then he is beaten and driven out. So the tribe rationalizes its sin by persecuting the One Who Dares To Look. Cornford says: "The reviling and expulsion of the Antagonist-Impostor is the darker counterpart of the Kô-

mos, which brings in the new God, victorious over him in the *Agon*." The god who is savior must be hated and slain. He has a double nature: he who is venerated, he who is reviled. Before the resurrection there is the crowning with thorns. The alazon is one of the disguises worn by the god-hero before he is sacrificed; he is also, by the same token, the "antagonistic" self that must be disowned before the worshiper is "possessed" by the god. Hence the ambivalence toward the comic hero.

Or the alazon-eiron may be simply the agent of God, like Goethe's Mephisto, who explains how he is "the spirit that endlessly denies" but is also "part of a power that would alone work evil, but engenders good." The Impostor, Profaner, or Devil is a "darkness that is part of light." Evil is inherent in Good, and to reach salvation man must pass through a "negation of negation." Therefore Faust finds himself bound to the impudent spirit who is only his darker self. Faust exclaims: "Why must I be fettered to this infamous companion who battens upon mischief and delights in ruin?" He does not yet know that the one who goads him—the Tempter—is a deputy of God. And the eiron, who can put on the features of the buffoon and scapegoat, is, in his other self, a mocker, blasphemer, and Offender. He embodies, again, the side of the god that must be rebelled against before the god can be worshiped. God must be hated before he can be loved, denied before he is believed. The comedian plays the role of Doubting Thomas. He is at once a stone rejected by the builder, and the cornerstone of the temple. Comedy is destructive and creative. So Falstaff, like Socrates, has a double nature and a double fate: eiron and alazon, tempter and clown, hero and knave, the great god Pan and also Pharmakos—he who is expelled with communal sins heaped on his head.

Falstaff is a central image in comedy. Symbolically he is the Fool; and the province of the Fool is the whole wide circuit of life and death, laughter and tears, wisdom and ignorance.[11] The fool is comic man. He is no mechanical figure. His gestures have daemonic power, and he carries his scepter by right of ancient rule. We fear him as god; we laugh at him as clown. All the ambiguities and ambivalences of comic action pivot on this archetypal hero of many guises. The fool wears motley—the particolor of human nature—and quickly changes one mask for another, putting on indifferently and recklessly the shifting features of man, playing with gusto more roles than are suitable to the tragic hero. The fool at last proves to be the clown; and the clown is He Who Gets Slapped—and "is none the worse for his slapping." He is resilient with a vitality lacking to the tragic hero, who must accept his misfortune and his responsibility with a stoic face, with a steadier logic than the absurd logic of comedy.

In general one may distinguish two orders of fool, natural and artificial. The natural fool is the archaic victim who diverts the wrath of the gods from the anointed figure of the king. He is the alter ego of the Successful Man, who needs to exempt himself from the jealousy and ill will of the Olympians and who therefore provides himself with someone insolent or ignorant, whom the gods smite. The fool is vicarious Sufferer. He is reviled, beaten, and stricken; but he has the privilege of vilifying the Prosperous Man; he is free to humble the Exalted by mockery. The fool saves the hero from the awful sin of pride (*hubris*). He

[11] In discussing the nature of the Fool and his many roles, I have relied heavily on Enid Welsford: *The Fool*, 1935, as well as on Kris: *Psychoanalytic Explorations in Art*, 1952, and J. A. K. Thomson: *Irony*, 1927.

is the Ugly One who by slandering, guards the king, or even the priest, from the evil eye. He may be dwarfed and deformed; he may be an idiot. But the idiot has the widsom of innocence and the naïveté of the child.

To this order of natural fools belongs Friar Juniper, the holy clown of the Franciscan order, whose antics were a token of grace, who had great power against the Devil and went about in ragged cowl, greatly comforted when the people called him blockhead. In his mind the fool bears the stigmata of holiness. Dostoevsky's saintly prostitutes like Sonia, or his "idiots" like Muishkin and Alyosha, have a close kinship with the natural fool. Kafka's heroes—those anonymous abused innocents known only as K—are natural fools who behold their own affliction with wide, credulous eyes. Everything strikes K with wonder and surprise, since he is the amateur in living who cannot be sophisticated by custom, who never learns his way around. For him life is always astonishment, effort, and uncertainty.

At his most contemptible the artificial fool may be the parasite of the old Greco-Roman comedies, a servile instrument in the hands of wealth and power. These fools use the oily manners of Rosencrantz and Guildenstern, or Osric, that yeasty, superserviceable knave spacious only in the possession of dirt.

But the fool can also be the seer, the prophet, the "possessed," since the madness of the fool is oracular, sibylline, delphic. He may be the voice crying in the wilderness, an Evangelist or Baptist, or an Imbecile-Prince like Muishkin, whose friends tell him he will always be a child, and who has revelations: "The recognition of God as our Father, and of God's joy in men as His own children, which is the chief idea of Christ." The fool may be the godly Dolt like the medieval Tumbler of Our Lady, or the poetic Seer like Rimbaud. He may, like Touchstone, look askance at life with a cool reluctance to commit himself. Sometimes his intuition is tragic, like the naïve cynicism of Lear's Fool, who sees the folly of playing Machiavellian games in a world rent by tempest. In the Sermon on the Mount, Jesus tells us with the voice of Innocence that we must accept the ridiculous as the basis of morality: "Blessed are the meek, for they shall inherit the earth."

The comedian is indeed a "revolutionary simpleton." No modern has claimed this more emphatically than Kierkegaard, who saw how the religious man must first of all be a comedian: "The religious individual has as such made the discovery of the comical in largest measure." Kierkegaard's religious man is not necessarily the comic poet or actor, but he is the one who has seen that our deepest experiences come to us in the form of contradictions. Therefore he is afflicted with the "higher madness" that is the comedy of faith, a passionate belief in the absurd. The knight of faith knows that the pathetic is inherent in the comic, that suffering is a mark of blessedness: "And hence it comes about that one is tempted both to weep and to laugh when the humorist speaks." Kierkegaard restates in another key the theme of Nietzsche's existential comedy: that one who suffers "by virtue of his suffering *knows more* than the shrewdest and wisest can ever know." Like a modern saint Nietzsche writes: "Suffering makes noble: it separates."

Thus in almost all his roles the fool is set apart, dedicated, alienated, if not outcast, beaten, slain. Being isolated, he serves as a "center of indifference," from which position the rest of us may, if we will, look through his eyes and appraise the meaning of our daily life. Archimedes is said to have promised "Give me a place to stand, and I will move the earth." In art, in ethics, in religion the fool finds a place to stand, for he is the detached spectator who has been placed, or has placed himself, outside accepted codes. From this point "outside"—this extrapolated fulcrum—he takes his leverage on the rest of us, and from his point of vantage can exclaim with Puck, the comic avenger, "Lord, what fools these mortals be."

There is something malign in Puck's spirit; he is scornful and delights in confusion. When this scorn is fierce enough we have the comic spirit of Swift, who frightens us out of laughter into dismay, if not despair. Just as Kierkegaard discovers the extreme absurdities of faith by extrapolating the attitude of the humorist, so Jonathan Swift leads us to the verge of a gulf of hopelessness by extrapolating the mischievous attitude of Puck. His Majesty of Brobdingnag tells Gulliver, after deliberation, "I can not but conclude the bulk of your natives to be the most pernicious race of little odious vermin that nature ever suffered to crawl upon the surface of the earth." The most galling of all comic figures are Swift's loathsome Yahoomen who reduce us all to intolerable shame.

There is something Puckish, also, in Hamlet's spirit, taunting and curious as it is. Amid the rottenness of Denmark the Prince serves as a philosophic and temperamental fool, a center of "indifference." He stands apart from gross revelry under his own melancholy cloud; and from his distance he is able to perceive more things than philosophy can dream; for the dust of great Alexander may stop a bunghole, and however thick my lady paints, she comes to a foul grave, the noisome state of Yorick, who is eaten by the same worms that feed upon Polonius, that duller fool. Hamlet is humorist and sufferer existing alone with his disdainful soul. He allows himself every incaution, and with midsummer lunacy puts an antic disposition on. Some of Hamlet's motives are devilish— Mephistophelian; his vocation is picaresque, to ask impudent questions and lead us along the narrow ledge where the immoralist walks, making us quarter our thoughts with an obsessive guile. Hamlet, Mephisto, Byron, Stendhal, Nietzsche, and Gide are heroes who belong in a comic theatre where man is goaded and teased, led down the dimmest passes of sin, to see what is learned by evil.

When he appears as tempter, the fool—the comic hero who stands "outside"—must put on the mask. He disguises himself as clown or devil, wearing as need arises the garb of buffoon, ironist, madman. He must lead us, finally, to the witches' kitchen and the Walpurgis Night; or to the wilderness where we meet our "shadow" selves face to face, although we have disowned these selves in our public life. There in the wilderness or on the Brocken the god in us is confronted by the Adversary, our "other" self, who lays before us illusions of pomp, knowledge, and pleasure. In tempting us the Adversary must have the features of innocence, must charm us with mannerly good will, gaiety, finesse, and high spirits. He may seem as honest as Iago, whose motiveless malignity wears the bland mask of friendship. Iago is the Socratic interrogator who destroys us with our own ideals; yet he is an illusion: "I am not what I am," he says. This Adversary may speak folly or profanity; or jest insanely, as did Nietzsche, who tempted the whole respectable middle class with his madness. His Satyr-Heroes have recognized Dionysus as god and they "*revert* to the innocence of the beast-of-prey conscience, like jubilant monsters, who perhaps come from a ghostly bout of murder, arson, rape, and torture with bravado and moral equanimity, as though merely some wild student's prank had been played."

The rebel, the immoralist, the free and licensed self in this terrible comedy of the future has passed "beyond" and looks back from a new and daring perspective upon the morality of the herd, which is hollow. Nietzsche's comic hero is the Despiser, the Blond Beast; or else he is the Great Sick Man overcome by his disgust, his nausea as he examines, from his point "outside," the premises of a morality we have never examined. To feel the spell of this Tempter we must take the awful risk of entering into a "boundary-situation" where nothing is taken for granted and where all our values must be found anew without help from "the others." Here we walk alone upon the margin of Reason. The Adversary goes with us to this highest precipice of comedy, the edge of the abyss where we glance with Nietzsche into Chaos. There we must stand on the brink of Nonsense and Absurdity and not be dizzy. If we do not fall, or plunge, we may be saved. Only by taking this risk can we put Satan behind us. Only thus can the Rebel learn what is Good. The comic Feast of Unreason is a test and a discovery, and our season spent mumming with the Lord of Misrule can show what will redeem us. The Adversary must be expelled. The Tempter must perish. That is, we must sacrifice him to save ourselves.

Young Hamlet, late from Wittenberg, stands alone on the brink of this abyss, sees himself as a ridiculous fellow crawling between heaven and earth with more sins at his beck than he has time to act. So he puts on the antic disposition of the fool. And if a sense of contradiction and absurdity is a cause of comedy, then Hamlet is a profoundly comic character. He encounters what Kierkegaard calls either/or choices, the extremes that cannot be mediated but only transcended. That is, the comic hero and the saint accept the irreconcilables in man's existence. Both find themselves face to face with the Inexplicable and the Absurd. When, for example, as Kierkegaard points out, Abraham holds the knife above Isaac and at the command of God is about to slay his son, he places himself outside and beyond all moral norms and is either, quite simply, a murderer or a believer. He stands alone in a situation that allows no middle term whatever. He meets an extreme peril that cannot be related to "virtue" or any human ethic. His dilemma can only be transcended by a "perspective from infinity"—looking at it from the infinite distance of faith, a perspective so far extrapolated beyond ethics that it extends from "eternity." Then Abraham is rescued from the irreconcilables in his crisis.

The comic hero finds himself in situations like Abraham's because comedy begins from the absurd and the inexplicable and, like faith, tolerates the miraculous. Dostoevsky, as usual, begins with the Unaccountable when old man Karamazov lies with Stinking Lizaveta and begets Smerdyakov, who is as truly his son as the saintly Alyosha. In the same way Miranda in *The Tempest* knows that good wombs have borne bad sons: Antonio is proof. Prospero accepts these incompatibles in reality, then transcends them by his "perspective from infinity," for at the farthest reaches of his magical vision life is like some dream that seems to come and fade. Precisely because he is face to face with the Inexplicable the comic hero is eligible for "rescue," like Don Quixote, who is mad to the degree of pouring curds over his poor head but who dies, like a saint, in a state of grace.

Often the comic hero is rescued because Improvisation and Uncertainty are the premises of comic action, and the goddess Fortuna presides over great tracts of the comic scene. But the law of Inevitability or Necessity bears heavily on the tragic hero, who is not eligible for rescue because in tragedy man must somehow take responsibility for the flaws in the nature of things or at least pay a penalty for them. To be sure, the tragic hero meets the Inexplicable—by what logic does Oedipus happen to confront his father on the road to Thebes and kill him in a narrow pass? Behind tragedy, too, is a riddle of the Sphinx, the warning of oracles only hoarsely spoken. In any case the tragic poet feels some compulsion to look backwards across the gulf of disaster and help us understand why the hero met his doom. Or he must fortify us against the Inexplicable and reassure us that Justice is not wrecked by it; whereas the comic artist can accept absurdities as the open premises of his account of life and not be troubled by them. The comedian practices an art of exaggeration, or overstatement.

The tragic hero, however, must heed some "golden mean" between extremes; he does not dare *play* with life as the comic hero does. The tragic hero meets either/or dilemmas but must pay some penalty for not being able to conciliate incompatibles. His only refuge from despair is a stoic endurance between those incompatibles; he must somehow prove himself adequate to the disasters he suffers. The tragic poet cannot, like the comic artist or the religious hero, look at man's struggle from infinite distances and revise its human weight or its penalties. Tragedy is a form of ethical heroism, suggesting that "man is the measure," even between desperate choices.

The tragic hero, noble and magnified, can be of awesome stature. The comic hero refuses to wear the trappings of moral or civil grandeur, usually preferring motley, or the agility of the clown. He is none the less man, and Hamlet more than once rouses our suspicion that the tragic hero is eligible for comic roles: or is it the other way round, that Hamlet is a comic hero who generates tragic values? The Prince touches his deepest meanings when he has on his antic humor. Then he needs no grandeur to hide his weakness, which is laughably naked.

Under the auspices of Fortuna comedy allows a play of character impossible in tragedy, which requires a hero "greater and better than most men" but capable of "error." As Aristotle says, the tragic hero cannot be either "depraved" or simply a victim of "bad luck." Comedy, however, delights to deal with those who are victims of bad luck, along with those who are "depraved" or "vicious"—by means of the grotesque. By disfiguring the hated person in caricature, comedy is able to elevate hatred to art. Swift evidently saw man as depraved and vicious, and projected his hatred into the grotesques called Yahoos. At the severest phase of grotesque we can behold the unnatural figures of King Lear and his daughters, who seem to have reduced life to horrors from which tragedy turns away. The crazy Lear wails:

> When we are born, we cry that we are come
> To this great stage of fools.

In this savage play men seem to be puppets (but not automatons).

Cornford tells us why comedy can utilize the grotesque. In Greece and Rome comedy was gradually transmuted from religious Mystery to theatrical Mime. So when comedy lost its appearance of being what originally and essentially it was, a fertility celebration, the characters tended to become grotesques, and the comedian continued using many of the stock masks tragedy had discarded. The original chorus of celebrant animal-figures gave a name to some of Aristophanes' comedies like *The Birds* and *The Wasps*. The old goat-chorus and satyr-masks invaded the final comic unit of tetralogy. The Impostor, particularly, became a stylized, sterotyped figure, like the Vice in medieval plays with his lath dagger and his sortie from Hell-Mouth. In this way the comic personality did indeed become dehumanized when it was a vehicle for making certain ges-

tures—the automatic gestures of Punch and Pierrot. Are not these lively creatures the ancestors of Tartuffe and other caricatures? They are born of Mime
and live the repetitive existence of Bergson's manikins, oscillating between life
and art. Yet we must once more remind ourselves that Falstaff born of a "mask,"
generates a personality and temperament more human than his gestures entitle
him to.

IV. The Social Meanings of Comedy

The tradition of Mime, Mask, and Caricature, then, explains why Bergson
thought, with Stendhal, that comedy requires a certain rigidity in the comic personage, an *insociabilité* in the hero and a degree of *insensibilité* in the spectator.
But Falstaff breaks down this insensibility and offers us a sort of release and purgation Pierrot cannot. Falstaff proves what Freud suspected: that comedy is a
process of safeguarding pleasure against the denials of reason, which is wary of
pleasure. Man cannot live by reason alone or forever under the rod of moral obligation, the admonition of the superego. In the person of Falstaff the superego
"takes a holiday." The comedian is the self behaving as prodigal and bohemian.
From its earliest days comedy is an essential pleasure mechanism valuable to the
spectator and the society in which he lives. Comedy is a momentary and publicly useful resistance to authority and an escape from its pressures; and its mechanism is a free discharge of repressed psychic energy or resentment through
laughter. Its purpose is comparable to the release of the dream, except that the
dream is private and asocial, whereas the comic uproar is "infectious." Freud
goes so far as to say "The comical appears primarily as an unintentional discovery in the social relations of human beings." Meredith, of course, emphasized
more strongly than Bergson that comedy is "the ultimate civilizer."

The ambivalence of comedy reappears in its social meanings, for comedy is
both hatred and revel, rebellion and defense, attack and escape. It is revolutionary and conservative. Socially, it is both sympathy and persecution.

One of the strongest impulses comedy can discharge from the depths of the
social self is our hatred of the "alien," especially when the stranger who is "different" stirs any unconscious doubt about our own beliefs. Then the comedian
unerringly finds his audience, the solid majority, itself a silent prey to unrecog-
nized fears. He can point out our victim, isolate him from sympathy, and cruelly
expose him to the penalty of our ridicule. In this role the comic artist is a "conservative" or even a "reactionary" who protects our self-esteem. Wherever comedy serves as a public defense mechanism, it makes all of us hypocrites: we try to
laugh our doubts out of existence. Whenever comedy is a symptom of fear, our
mirth indicates the zeal with which we are maltreating our scapegoat. Certainly
the laugh of the satirist is often a sneer; and there is an undercurrent of satire in
most comedy.

To this extent the comic response is tribal and, if it is malicious, uncivilized.
Any majority secretes venom against those who trouble it, then works off this
venom in mocking some figure like Shylock the Jew, and Usurer, hated by right-
thinking Christians precisely because he lives in the free and open market on a
premise of ruthless competition. Shylock is the naked image of renaissance "initiative," whose thrift is called greed only because he is Hebrew. "And thrift,"
Shylock protests, "is blessing if men steal it not." Could any gentile entrepreneur

put it better? The inconsistency is implied by the shadow of pathos falling across Shylock's ugly figure. Let us avoid the old dispute whether Shylock is tragic: it is clear enough that according to the confused premises of the play a Christian without money is tragic and a Jew without money is funny. And Jews should be without money. Unless the Jew is Jessica, who becomes Christian by gilding herself with ducats.

Granted that Shakespeare sees his victim in double perspective (for Shylock the monster becomes Shylock the man when he asks "If you prick us, do we not bleed?"), the Elizabethan audience probably did not see the Jew in this double way but took his grotesque figure to be a hateful and hated image of greed. The higher the social charge in comedy, the less the audience is likely to care about distinguishing truth from prejudice. The classical instance would be *The Clouds*, a play in which Aristophanes evidently leads a pack of right-minded Athenians in hounding down sophists who have insulted the gods and shaken the ordinary pieties. Never mind what questions the sophists really asked; never mind whether we can answer their questions—we must quell these troublemakers;:

> Strike, smite them, spare them not, for many reasons: BUT MOST BECAUSE THEY HAVE BLASPHEMED THE GODS.

The attack in Molière's *Highbrow Ladies* is not so blunt, but it is none the less based on the premise that women are not entitled to be foppish; they must be conveniently stupid.

Usually the comedian will address us with most assurance when he is conservative, when he affirms the security of any group already unsure of itself. In middle-class societies, particularly, the comic artist often reassures the majority that its standards are impregnable or that other standards are not "normal" or "sane." Then the comedian banishes doubt by ridicule and is the "diplomatic artist."[12]

Yet this defense of the *status quo* occurs in a society where there is a hidden conflict in social standards; and the comedian may appear on the other side of the barricades, with the revolutionaries. Falstaff gleefully invites us to join him in making bohemian sallies among the ranks of the Philistines, bringing confusion to their hosts. The very appearance of Shylock as a sympathetic villain indicates the malaise in Elizabethan society about "rugged individualism." Similarly the figure of Tartuffe is a focus for the conflict between an ideal of personal integrity and the unscrupulous piety of an acquisitive class. In despising Tartuffe we despise our own hypocrisy, whether it be a false puritan asceticism or the slippery indulgence of the Jesuits. Tartuffe could be born only in a society anxious about its honesty. He is a sign of what we reject.

Or else the comedian can evade the conflict, relieving the stress between competing ideals by laughter. He may enable us to "adjust" incompatible standards without resolving the clash between them. Thus we laugh when Tartuffe

---

[12] In *The Dark Voyage and the Golden Mean* Albert Cook advances the ingenious but somewhat narrow-gauge theory that tragedy ventures to make the Dark Voyage toward Risk and Wonder, whereas comedy stays safely within the limits of a Golden Mean. This is a tenable argument, certainly; however, the distinction can hardly be made this simply, and the comedian is often a "revolutionary" as well as a "diplomatic" artist.

brings our conflict into the open, because we may not wish to recognize that we, too, seek power, women, and money, and that all these may be more desirable than piety. We laugh at Tartuffe because we do not intend to see clearly what he means. We may also laugh at Falstaff because we do not—must not—grant that good sherris sack is, after all, the real value of life, and honor only a word. Falstaff raises questions we wish to blink, and we laugh at him to prevent his damaging our convictions which are taboo.

In its boisterous moods comedy annihilates the power of evil in the person of the scapegoat. Yet we have already seen that this triumphant laughter is a mode of defense, because the enemy who has power over us must be neutralized by transforming him into a harmless victim.[13] Falstaff, we have said, has the sacred power of a god of fertility; therefore he must be disguised before he can be laughed out of existence, lest he threaten us too closely. Comedy is at once a defense against the Enemy and a victorious assault upon Him. He vanishes in an explosion of choral mirth.

At its most triumphant moments comic art frees us from peril without destroying our ideals and without mustering the heavy artillery of the puritan. Comedy can be a means of mastering our disillusions when we are caught in a dishonest or stupid society. After we recognize the misdoings, the blunders, we can liberate ourselves by a confident, wise laughter that brings a catharsis of our discontent. We see the flaws in things, but we do not always need to concede the victory, even if we live in a human world. If we can laugh wisely enough at ourselves and others, the sense of guilt, dismay, anxiety, or fear can be lifted. Unflinching and undaunted we see *where we are*. This strengthens us as well as society.

When comic art is generous enough, it is a triumphant affirmation of truth—which, we see, cannot be damaged by our failures. "Great comic artists assume that truth may bear all lights."[14] In this belief lies the heroic courage of the comedian. The unvanquishable Falstaff is an ageless witness that truth can bear all lights: this comic giant proves that honor cannot be sullied in Eastcheap or on Gadshill. He breaks down our unreliable attitudes—unreliable because they are overguarded. His obscene questions strip us of our linen decencies and free us from the iron yoke of conformity. This high priest of comedy is doing us the service John Milton gravely did in *Areopagitica* when he protested against fugitive and cloistered virtues. "That which purifies us is trial," Milton writes, "and trial is by what is contrary." Milton requires trial by "dust and heat." Falstaff challenges us from alleys and bawdy houses. He asks us to walk out of the whited sepulchre we have made into our world; and when we walk abroad with Falstaff we discover what John Milton discovered: that truth is strong next to the Almighty and will not be put to the worse when she grapples with falsehood in open encounter.

To be able to laugh at evil and error means that we have surmounted them. Comedy may be a philosophic, as well as a psychological, compensation. When-

---

[13] The best discussion of the complicated psychology behind this sort of comedy seems to me Hugh Dalziel Duncan: *Language and Literature in Society*, 1953, which I have utilized in the following comments.

[14] So argues Duncan, p. 53 ff. Ernst Cassirer has also written a major comment on the "sympathetic vision" of the great comic artists who, he says, bring us close to the realities of our human world and dissolve our scorn in a laughter that liberates us (*Essay on Man*).

ever we become aware that this is not the best of possible worlds, we need the help of the comedian to meet the "insuperable defects of actuality."[15] We escape with him into a logical order by laughing at the imperfections of the world about us; the comic artist releases us from the limitations in things as they are. Chafed by the deficiencies in reality the comedian may be more intransigent than the tragedian. Tragedy accepts the flaw in the world as it is, then ventures to find nobility in "the inexorable march of actual situations." If the tragic illusion is potent enough we are reconciled to the tears at the heart of things. But unless he is in his "diplomatic" mood, the comedian refuses to make these concessions to actuality and serves, instead, as chief tactician in a permanent resistance movement, or rebellion, within the frontiers of human experience. By temperament the comedian is often a fifth columnist in social life.

An outrageous rebel is that same picaresque knave Falstaff, who dares us to stride with him across the boundaries of caution into the Walpurgis Night of a new philosophic order where one lives completely at ease. Even the rococo comedy in *Tristram Shandy* is daring, for Sterne trespasses smirkingly against every decency for the sake of liberating his exquisite feelings. One of the annoying intransigents in our own society was André Gide, who temperamentally was unable to write tragedy but insisted on publishing, in the teeth of his "serious" friends, his diabolical *Corydon*. Gide kept saying, "My function is to disturb." He is the classic type of comic artist who is *agent provocateur*. In Gide and Goya and Swift the tenor of comedy is uncompromising, irreverent.

In her own quiet way Jane Austen devastates our compromises and complacencies—especially male complacency. It is said one can read her novels and never guess that France was red with terror or that British troops were dying at Waterloo. She leaves all that turmoil to the "romantics." Meanwhile Miss Austen placidly undermines the bastions of middle-class propriety. Her irreverence is calm, but she knows better than the "romantics" that one must not compromise one's honesty. She is not the less dangerous because she operates inconspicuously. There she resembles Henry James, who lays bare in his overbred prose the shameless vulgarity of the *haute bourgeoisie*. We must not be deceived, either, about Miss Austen's cool disposition, which seems defensive, wary of being taken in. She is using the caution native to those comic artists who contrive to protect themselves against scorn while they are making us scorn others. Her contempt is polite.

This is comedy near its "highest," which, Bergson and Meredith agree, is a game played in social life. In *Two Sources of Morality and Religion* Bergson described two orders of society, the one unchanging, mechanical, stratified, conservative, and "closed"; the other mobile, organic, fluid, and "open." A colony of insects is a "closed" order, alert for danger, attack, defense. It is a society with Spartan efficiency and ability to survive. The members of a closed society care nothing for humanity but live untroubled by dreams or doubts. The open society has a different morality because it is sensitive to the fringe of intuition, "vague and evanescent," that envelops every clear idea. Those living in an open society are self-aware, responsive to the nuance, the not-wholly-formulated. The open society gives play to individuality, true selfhood. Stendhal's hero Julien Sorel be-

---

[15] James Feibleman: *In Praise of Comedy*, p. 178 ff., develops this view and shows how comedy is a form of "rebellion" against "things as they are."

longs in an open society but is trapped within the confines of a closed caste system. So his adventures become a picaresque comedy played at the expense of the insensitive people about him and of his own malaise.

To expand Bergson's idea a little, we may say that the "lower" the comedy, the more it needs a "closed" social order, and the "higher" the comedy, the more the situation is "open" socially and morally. The mechanics of Shakespeare's *Comedy of Errors* are possible in a situation firmly "closed," where events exactly balance each other in a series of neatly arranged coincidences. The moral rigidity in this world is suggested by the Duke's mechanical, paralyzing ethic which causes him to say to Aegeon: "For we may pity, though not pardon, thee."

The situation in *Twelfth Night* seems to be more "open" but really is not. Behind the delicate manners in Illyria is a tightly closed social order, as the aspiring Malvolio finds, to his distress and our delight. The fellow is a bounder; his eye is fixed hard on Olivia; he is the butler who woos his mistress. The man is a yellow-stockinged fool; and he is a fool first of all because he wishes to leap the barriers, which are far too high. At all costs Malvolio must not climb. Obviously Malvolio is an ass—obviously. Yet no more so than Sir Andrew Aguecheek, at whom we laugh, but not malignly as we do at Malvolio. Sir Andrew has a prerogative of asininity in virtue of his birth. He is a natural, not a bounder. Hardmindedly we identify our scapegoat, Malvolio parading cross-gartered, even if we do not choose to see him for what, socially, he is: the Impostor who must be expelled with a vengeance. Sir Andrew cannot be devalued by the sneer alone, because he is guarded by his rank. But Malvolio the popinjay rouses our archaic wrath at the Pretender—who is, in this event, our own social alter ego to be publicly tormented, disclaimed, icily denied. Comedy of manners often releases the cruelty in a closed society; and the stiff ranks in this society put us in unnatural positions.

At the height of comedy the whole situation "opens" in many directions. *Love's Labour's Lost* begins as if it were to be a "closed" comedy like *Twelfth Night*, for the scene is the fastidious Academe in Navarre where some precious fools are pledging themselves to an ascetic life for three years, depriving themselves of sleep, food, and love. Berowne alone protests, in the name of "grace." Then one by one the lordly fantasticoes fall in love with very frail women and break their vows, yielding to the flesh. These wits bring themselves face to face with human realities. But before they can readjust, the King of France dies, and they all find themselves standing at the mouth of the grave, where they must pause. The entire company disperses with a curiously somber and hesitant benediction: "You that way, we this way." The play shows how the movement of high comedy is expanding, scattering itself from situation to situation always farther abroad, opening toward other possibilities, holding all in suspense.[16] Berowne is one of those who, with Benedick and Mercutio and Hamlet, cannot be at home in a closed plot, a closed society, a closed ethic.

Shakespeare's most "open" comedy—nearly mystic in Bergson's sense—is *The Tempest*, where all the machinery of plot is suspended in evanescent meanings that are almost musical. This play disperses into unknown modes of being, where even Caliban can seek for grace. The act of forgiveness is the moral pole of this comedy, and under the spell of Prospero's sea-change we are able to look

---

[16] The point is made by Paul Goodman: *The Structure of Literature*, 1954, p. 89 ff.

as if from afar, backward upon the wrongs done in the dark abysm of the past. Evil is there, in Antonio and Sebastian, in Stephano and Trinculo and Caliban; but at these moral latitudes we can see even the vicious Antonio as if he were only a troubling recollection. Amid devouring shows and strange noises human nature is transfigured. Prospero's magic is the godlike charity of understanding, thus enduring, all. Using the tolerance of high comedy, and its confidence, Prospero speaks gently to those who tried to kill him. In this larger perspective sin seems to be the last delusion of man's mind, an error that is absurd. Prospero's vision of life is not tragic because sin is seen from distances that exempt man from disastrous penalties. All miracles are performed at this height of comedy, which brings us into a shifting, open world that continuingly transforms itself without being emptied of the cruelest actualities. Antonio is eager to murder with his three inches of obedient steel; yet these failings in men cannot damage the illusion that is truth. The vile Antonio cannot destroy what is good. Tragic danger is here cancelled by a feat of moral insight. The drama of Prospero's isle, the farthest reach of comedy, is an insubstantial pageant. It is also a triumphant revision of life, a politics of illusion.

Bergson must have seen life as Prospero did, since he described this politics of illusion in *Two Sources of Morality and Religion*:

> The open society is the society which is deemed in principle to embrace all humanity. A dream dreamt, now and again, by chosen souls, it embodies on every occasion something of itself in creations, each of which, through a more or less far-reaching transformation of man, conquers difficulties hitherto unconquerable.

Prospero's charity is the imaginative fulfillment of an ethic such as Bergson mentions. There is nothing in actuality to justify his mercy, his confidence, or his vision; yet these master the failings of nature and work a change in man. Comedy is, indeed, like a dream, as even Bergson perhaps did not suspect. In saying that life is rounded with a sleep, Prospero is but repeating the words spoken by Theseus, king of a realm where there were midsummer-night dreams; for when Theseus saw the silly interlude rudely played by the mechanicals in honor of him and Hippolyta he explained: "The best in this kind are but shadows, and the worst are no worse if imagination amend them." Theseus saw that the drama was there, even if it was badly played; and he was grateful to the wretched players, who gained their triumph not on their poor stage but in Theseus' fancy.

The high comic vision of life is humane, an achievement of man as a social being. Meredith addressed himself to "our united social intelligence, which is the Comic Spirit." He suspected that comedy is "the ultimate civilizer." If Prospero's comedy is transcendentally "open," Meredith's social comedy remains a worldly discipline with, nevertheless, full moral overtones. In all civilized societies, Meredith insists, the comic spirit must hover overhead, its lips drawn in a slim, hungry smile, wary and tense, thoughtfully eager to see the absurdities of polite men and women. Kierkegaard might have been describing Meredith's faun when he said the "comic spirit is not wild or vehement, its laughter is not shrill." For Kierkegaard, too, the highest comedy, like the highest pathos, rarely attracts attention by making great shows. Only the "lower forms of the comical do show themselves by something extrinsic. The highest in life does not make a showing, because it belongs to the last sphere of inwardness." No society is in good health without laughing at itself quietly and privately; no character is sound without self-scrutiny, without turning inward to see where it may have overreached itself. The perception of the self as comic touches the quick; and honest self-inspection must bring a sense of the comical. This kind of awareness is an initiation into the civilized condition; it lightens the burden of selfishness, cools the heat of the ego, makes us impressionable by others.

So the comic spirit keeps us pure in mind by requiring that we regard ourselves skeptically. Indeed this spirit is an agent of that civilizing activity Matthew Arnold called "criticism," which is essential to "culture." It is an activity necessary to middle-class society, where we gravitate easily toward that dead center of self-satisfaction, the Philistine. Arnold tells us why criticism brings salvation, and why culture *is* criticism:

> And thus culture begets a dissatisfaction, which is of the highest possible value in stemming the common tide of men's thoughts in a wealthy and industrial community, and which saves the future, as one may hope, from being vulgarized, even if it cannot save the present.
>
> (*Culture and Anarchy*)

Shakespeare's plays, says Meredith, are saturated with the golden light of comedy—the comedy that is redemptive as tragedy cannot be. Consider what happens in *Much Ado About Nothing* when Benedick makes the startling comic discovery that he himself, together with the other mistaken people in the play, is a fool. Here is a moral perception that competes with tragic "recognition." The irony of Benedick's "recognition" is searching, for he has boasted, all along, that he cannot find it in his heart to love any of Eve's daughters, least of all Beatrice. And Beatrice, for her part, has avowed she will never be fitted with a husband until God makes men of some other metal than earth. Both these characters are too deep of draught to sail in the shoal waters of sentimentality, and both have bravely laid a course of their own far outside the matchmaking that goes easily on in Messina. Each is a mocker, or eiron; but in being so, each becomes the boaster (alazon) betrayed into the valiant pose that they are exempt from love. Then they both walk, wide-eyed, like "proud" Oedipus, into the trap they have laid for themselves. There they see themselves as they are. When Benedick hears himself called hard-hearted he suffers the bewilderment of comic discovery and knows that his pose as mocker is no longer tenable. So he turns his scornful eye inward upon his own vanity: if Beatrice is sick for love of his ribald self he must give up his misogyny and get him a wife. He yields himself, absurdly, to Beatrice, saying "Happy are they that hear their detractions and can put them to mending." At the extreme of his own shame Benedick is compelled to see himself as he sees others, together along a low horizon. Thus occur the comic purgation, the comic resignation to the human lot, the comic humbling of the proud, the comic ennobling after an act of blindness. Those who play a comic role, like Benedick or Berowne or Meredith's Sir Willoughby Patterne, wrongheadedly are liable to achieve their own defeat and afterwards must hide their scars. The comic and the tragic heroes alike "learn through suffering," albeit suffering in comedy takes the form of humiliation, disappointment, or chagrin, instead of death.

There is a comic road to wisdom, as well as a tragic road. There is a comic as well as a tragic control of life. And the comic control may be more usable, more relevant to the human condition in all its normalcy and confusion, its many unreconciled directions. Comedy as well as tragedy can tell us that the vanity of the world is foolishness before the gods. Comedy dares seek truth in the slums of Eastcheap or the crazy landscape Don Quixote wanders across or on the enchanted Prospero isle. By mild inward laughter it tries to keep us sane in the drawing room, among decent men and women. It tells us that man is a giddy thing, yet does not despair of men. Comedy gives us recognitions healing as the recognitions of tragic art. They are sometimes revelations and come in the moonlit forest of a summer night; then Bottom, with his ass head, is transformed to a Seer, a Visionary, and Bottom's Dream is apocalyptic. For Bottom, the poor weaver, reports: "I have had a dream; past the wit of man to say what dream it was. Man is but an ass if he go about to expound this dream." After this midnight dream everything is seen from a new distance; as Hermia says:

> Methinks I see these things with parted eye
> When every thing seems double.

Tragedy needs a more single vision than comedy, for the comic perception comes only when we take a double view—that is, a human view—of ourselves, a perspective by incongruity. Then we take part in the ancient rite that is a Debate and a Carnival, a Sacrifice and a Feast.

The Comic Mask
and Carnival*

George Santayana

The Comic Mask

The clown is the primitive comedian. Sometimes in the exuberance of animal life a spirit of riot and frolic comes over a man; he leaps, he dances, he tumbles head over heels, he grins, shouts, or leers, possibly he pretends to go to pieces suddenly, and blubbers like a child. A moment later he may look up wreathed in smiles, and hugely pleased about nothing. All this he does hysterically, without any reason, by a sort of mad inspiration and irresistible impulse. He may easily, however, turn his absolute histrionic impulse, his pure fooling into mimicry of anything or anybody that at the moment happens to impress his senses; he will crow like a cock, simper like a young lady, or reel like a drunkard. Such mimicry is virtual mockery, because the actor is able to revert from those assumed attitudes to his natural self; whilst his models, as he thinks, have no natural self save that imitable attitude, and can never disown it; so that the clown feels himself immensely superior, in his rôle of universal satirist, to all actual men, and belabours and rails at them unmercifully. He sees everything in caricature, because he sees the surface only, with the lucid innocence of a child; and all these grotesque personages stimulate him, not to moral sympathy, nor to any consideration of their fate, but rather to boisterous sallies, as the rush of a crowd, or the hue and cry of a hunt, or the contortions of a jumping-jack might stimulate him. He is not at all amused intellectually; he is not rendered wiser or tenderer by knowing the predicaments into which people inevitably fall; he is merely excited, flushed, and challenged by an absurd spectacle. Of course this rush and suasion of mere existence must never fail on the stage, nor in any art; it is to the drama what the hypnotizing stone block is to the statue, or shouts and rhythmic breathing to the bard; but such primary magical influences may be qualified by reflection, and then rational and semi-tragic unities will supervene. When this happens the histrionic impulse creates the idyl or the tragic chorus; henceforth the muse of reflection follows in the train of Dionysus, and the revel or the rude farce passes into humane comedy.

Paganism was full of scruples and superstitions in matters of behaviour or of *cultus*, since the *cultus* too was regarded as a business or a magic craft; but in expression, in reflection, paganism was frank and even shameless; it felt itself inspired, and revered this inspiration. It saw nothing impious in inventing or recasting a myth about no matter how sacred a subject. Its inspiration, however,

* George Santayana, "The Comic Mask" and "Carnival," in *Soliloquies in England and Later Soliloquies* (Charles Scribner's Sons, 1922), pp. 135–144. Copyright 1922. Used by permission of Charles Scribner's Sons.

soon fell into classic moulds, because the primary impulses of nature, though intermittent, are monotonous and clearly defined, as are the gestures of love and of anger. A man who is unaffectedly himself turns out to be uncommonly like other people. Simple sincerity will continually rediscover the old right ways of thinking and speaking, and will be perfectly conventional without suspecting it. This classic iteration comes of nature, it is not the consequence of any revision or censorship imposed by reason. Reason, not being responsible for any of the facts or passions that enter into human life, has no interest in maintaining them as they are; any novelty, even the most revolutionary, would merely afford reason a fresh occasion for demanding a fresh harmony. But the Old Adam is conservative; he repeats himself mechanically in every child who cries and loves sweets and is imitative and jealous. Reason, with its tragic discoveries and restraints, is a far more precarious and personal possession than the trite animal experience and the ancestral grimaces on which it supervenes; and automatically even the philosopher continues to cut his old comic capers, as if no such thing as reason existed. The wiseacres too are comic, and their mask is one of the most harmlessly amusing in the human museum; for reason, taken psychologically, is an old inherited passion like any other, the passion for consistency and order; and it is just as prone as the other passions to overstep the modesty of nature and to regard its own aims as alone important. But this is ridiculous; because importance springs from the stress of nature, from the cry of life, not from reason and its pale prescriptions. Reason cannot stand alone; brute habit and blind play are at the bottom of art and morals, and unless irrational impulses and fancies are kept alive, the life of reason collapses for sheer emptiness. What tragedy could there be, or what sublime harmonies rising out of tragedy, if there were not spontaneous passions to create the issue, no wild voices to be reduced to harmony? Moralists have habitually aimed at suppression, wisely perhaps at first, when they were preaching to men of spirit; but why continue to harp on propriety and unselfishness and labour, when we are little but labour-machines already, and have hardly any self or any passions left to indulge? Perhaps the time has come to suspend those exhortations, and to encourage us to be sometimes a little lively, and see if we can invent something worth saying or doing. We should then be living in the spirit of comedy, and the world would grow young. Every occasion would don its comic mask, and make its bold grimace at the world for a moment. We should be constantly original without effort and without shame, somewhat as we are in dreams, and consistent only in sincerity; and we should gloriously emphasize all the poses we fell into, without seeking to prolong them.

Objections to the comic mask—to the irresponsible, complete, extreme expression of each moment—cut at the roots of all expression. Pursue this path, and at once you do away with gesture: we must not point, we must not pout, we must not cry, we must not laugh aloud; we must not only avoid attracting attention, but our attention must not be obviously attracted; it is silly to gaze, says the nursery-governess, and rude to stare. Presently words, too, will be reduced to a telegraphic code. A man in his own country will talk like a laconic tourist abroad; his whole vocabulary will be *Où? Combien? All right! Dear me!* Conversation in the quiet home will dispense even with these phrases; nothing will be required but a few pragmatic grunts and signals for action. Where the spirit of comedy has departed, company becomes constraint, reserve eats up the spirit, and people fall into a penurious melancholy in their scruple to be always exact, sane, and reasonable, never to mourn, never to glow, never to betray a passion or

a weakness, nor venture to utter a thought they might not wish to harbour for
ever.

Yet irony pursues these enemies of comedy, and for fear of wearing a mask
for a moment they are hypocrites all their lives. Their very reserve becomes a
pose, a convention imposed externally, and their mincing speech turns to cant.
Sometimes this evasion of impulse sentiment fosters a poignant sentimentality
beneath. The comedy goes on silently behind the scenes, until perhaps it gets the
upper hand and becomes positive madness; or else it breaks out in some shy, indirect fashion, as among Americans with their perpetual joking. Where there is
no habitual art and no moral liberty, the instinct for direct expression is atro-
phied for want of exercise; and then slang and a humorous perversity of phrase
or manner act as safety-valves to sanity; and you manage to express yourself in
spite of the censor by saying something grotesquely different from what you
mean. That is a long way round to sincerity, and an ugly one. What, on the contrary, could be more splendidly sincere than the impulse to play in real life, to
rise on the rising wave of every feeling and let it burst, if it will, into the foam of
exaggeration? Life is not a means, the mind is not a slave nor a photograph: it
has a right to enact a pose, to assume a *panache*, and to create what prodigious
allegories it will for the mere sport and glory of it. Nor is this art of innocent
make-believe forbidden in the Decalogue, although Bible-reading Anglo-Saxon-
dom might seem to think so. On the contrary, the Bible and the Decalogue are
themselves instances of it. To embroider upon experience is not to bear false witness against one's neighbour, but to bear true witness to oneself. Fancy is playful
and may be misleading to those who try to take it for literal fact; but literalness
is impossible in any utterance of spirit, and if it were possible it would be deadly.
Why should we quarrel with human nature, with metaphor, with myth, with
impersonation? The foolishness of the simple is delightful; only the foolishness of
the wise is exasperating.

Carnival

In this world we must either institute conventional forms of expression or else
pretend that we have nothing to express; the choice lies between a mask and a
fig-leaf. Art and discipline render seemly what would be unseemly without
them, but hypocrisy hides it ostentatiously under something irrelevant, and the
fig-leaf is only a more ignominious mask. For the moment it is certainly easier to
suppress the wild impulses of our nature than to manifest them fitly, at the right
times and with the proper fugitive emphasis; yet in the long run suppression
does not solve the problem, and meantime those maimed expressions which are
allowed are infected with a secret misery and falseness. It is the charm and safety of virtue that it is more natural than vice, but many moralists do their best to
deprive it of this advantage. They seem to think it would lose its value if they
lost their office. Their precepts, as distinguished from the spontaneous apprecia-
tions of men, are framed in the interests of utility, and are curiously out of sympathy with the soul. Precept divides the moral world materially into right and
wrong things; but nothing concrete is right or wrong intrinsically, and every object or event has both good and bad effects in the context of nature. Every passion, like life as a whole, has its feet in one moral climate and its head in another.
Existence itself is not a good, but only an opportunity. Christians thank God for
their creation, preservation, and all the blessings of this life, but life is the condi-

tion and source of all evil, and the Indians thank Brahma or Buddha for lifting them out of it. What metaphysical psychologists call Will is the great original sin, the unaccountable and irrational interest which the spirit takes, when it is incarnate, in one thing happening rather than another; yet this mad interest is the condition of generosity and of every virtue. Love is a red devil at one end of its spectrum and an ultraviolet angel at the other end.

Nor is this amphibious moral quality limited to the passions; all facts and objects in nature can take on opposite moral tints. When abstracted from our own presence and interests, everything that can be found or imagined is reduced to a mere essence, an ideal theme picked out of the infinite, something harmless, marvellous, and pure, like a musical rhythm or geometrical design. The whole world then becomes a labyrinth of forms and motions, a castle in the clouds built without labour and dissolved without tears. The moment the animal will reawakes, however, these same things acquire a new dimension; they become substantial, not to be created without effort nor rent without resistance; at the same time they become objects of desire and fear; we are so engrossed in existence that every phenomenon becomes questionable and ominous, and not so much a free gift and manifestation of its own nature as a piece of good or bad news. We are no longer surprised, as a free spirit would be, at the extraordinary interest we take in things turning out one way rather than another. We are caught in the meshes of time and place and care; and as the things we have set our heart on, whatever they may be, must pass away in the end, either suddenly or by a gentle transformation, we cannot take a long view without finding life sad, and all things tragic. This aspect of vanity and self-annihilation, which existence wears when we consider its destiny, is not to be denied or explained away, as is sometimes attempted in cowardly and mincing philosophies. It is a true aspect of existence in one relation and on a certain view; but to take this long view of existence, and look down the avenues of time from the station and with the emotions of some particular moment, is by no means inevitable, nor is it a fair and sympathetic way of viewing existence. Things when they are actual do not lie in that sort of sentimental perspective, but each is centred in itself; and in this intrinsic aspect existence is nothing tragic or sad, but rather something joyful, hearty, and merry. A buoyant and full-blooded soul has quick senses and miscellaneous sympathies: it changes with the changing world; and when not too much starved or thwarted by circumstances, it finds all things vivid and comic. Life is free play fundamentally and would like to be free play altogether. In youth anything is pleasant to see or to do, so long as it is spontaneous, and if the conjunction of these things is ridiculous, so much the better: to be ridiculous is part of the fun.

Existence involves changes and happenings and is comic inherently, like a pun that begins with one meaning and ends with another. Incongruity is a consequence of change; and this incongruity becomes especially conspicuous when, as in the flux of nature, change is going on at different rates in different strands of being, so that not only does each thing surprise itself by what it becomes, but it is continually astonished and disconcerted by what other things have turned into without its leave. The mishaps, the expedients, the merry solutions of comedy, in which everybody acknowledges himself beaten and deceived, yet is the happier for the unexpected posture of affairs, belong to the very texture of temporal being; and if people repine at these mishaps, or rebel against these solutions, it is only because their souls are less plastic and volatile than the general flux of nature. The individual grows old and lags behind; he remembers his old pain and resents it when the world is already on a new tack. In the jumble of existence there must be many a knock and many a grief; people living at cross purposes cannot be free from malice, and they must needs be fooled by their pretentious passions. But there is no need of taking these evils tragically. At bottom they are gratuitous, and might have been avoided if people had not pledged their hearts to things beyond their control and had not entrenched themselves in their illusions. At a sufficient remove every drama seems pathological and makes much ado about what to other people is nothing. We are interested in those vicissitudes, which we might have undergone if placed under the given circumstances; but we are happy to have escaped them. Thus the universe changes its hues like the chameleon, not at random but in a fashion which moral optics can determine, as it appears in one perspective or another; for everything in nature is lyrical in its ideal essence, tragic in its fate, and comic in its existence.

Existence is indeed distinguishable from the platonic essences that are embodied in it precisely by being a conjunction of things mutually irrelevant, a chapter of accidents, a medley improvised here and now for no reason, to the exclusion of the myriad other farces which, so far as their ideal structure is concerned, might have been performed just as well. This world is contingency and absurdity incarnate, the oddest of possibilities masquerading momentarily as a fact. Custom blinds persons who are not naturally speculative to the egregious character of the actual, because custom assimilates their expectations to the march of existing things and deadens their power to imagine anything different. But wherever the routine of a barbaric life is broken by the least acquaintance with larger ways, the arbitrariness of the actual begins to be discovered. The traveller will first learn that his native language is not the only one, nor the best possible, nor itself constant; then, perhaps, he will understand that the same is true of his home, religion, and government. The naturalist will begin by marvelling at the forms and habits of the lower animals, while continuing to attribute his own to their obvious propriety; later the heavens and the earth, and all physical laws, will strike him as paradoxically arranged and unintelligible; and ultimately the very elements of existence—time, change, matter, habit, life cooped in bodies—will reveal themselves to him in their extreme oddity, so that, unless he has unusual humility and respect for fact, he will probably declare all these actual things to be impossible and therefore unreal. The most profound philosophers accordingly deny that any of those things exist which we find existing, and maintain that the only reality is changeless, infinite, and indistingishable into parts; and I call them the most profound philosophers in spite of this obvious folly of theirs, because they are led into it by the force of intense reflection, which discloses to them that what exists is unintelligible and has no reason for existing; and since their moral and religious prejudices do not allow them to say that to be irrational and unintelligible is the character proper to existence, they are driven to the alternative of saying that existence is illusion and that the only reality is something beneath or above existence. That real existence should be radically comic never occurs to these solemn sages; they are without one ray of humour and are persuaded that the universe too must be without one. Yet there is a capital joke in their own systems, which prove that nothing exists so strenuously, that existence laughs aloud in their vociferations and drowns the argument. Their conviction is the very ghost which it rises to exorcise; yet the conviction and the exorcism remain impressive, because they bear witness to the

essential strangeness of existence to the spirit. Like the Ghost in *Hamlet* this apparition, this unthinkable fact, is terribly disturbing and emphatic; it cries to us
in a hollow voice, "Swear!" and when in an agony of concern and affection we
endeavour to follow it, " 'Tis here! 'Tis here! 'Tis gone!" Certainly existence can
bewitch us; it can compel us to cry as well as to laugh; it can hurt, and that is its
chief claim to respect. Its cruelty, however, is as casual as its enchantments; it is
not cruel on purpose but only rough, like thoughtless boys. Coarseness—and existence is hopelessly coarse—is not an evil unless we demand refinement. A gig-
gling lass that peeps at us through her fingers is well enough in her sphere, but
we should not have begun by calling her Dulcinea. Dulcinea is a pure essence,
and dwells only in that realm. Existence should be met on its own terms; we may
dance a round with it, and perhaps steal a kiss; but it tempts only to flout us, not
being dedicated to any constant love. As if to acknowledge how groundless existence is, everything that arises instantly backs away, bowing its excuses, and saying, "My mistake!" It suffers from a sort of original sin or congenital tendency to
cease from being. This is what Heraclitus called *Dikê*, or just punishmeent; because, as Mephistopheles long afterwards added, *alles was entsteht ist wert dass
es zugrunde geht*—whatsoever arises deserves to perish; not of course because
what arises is not often a charming creation, but because it has no prerogative to
exist not shared by every Cinderella-like essence that lies eternally neglected in
that limbo to which all things intrinsically belong—the limbo of unheard melo-
dies and uncreated worlds. For anything to emerge from that twilight region is
inexplicable and comic, like the popping up of Jack-in-the-box; and the shock
will amuse us, if our wits are as nimble as nature and as quick as time. We too
exist; and existence is a joy to the sportive side of our nature, itself akin to a
shower of sparks and a patter of irrevocable adventures. What indeed could be
more exhilarating than such a rout, if only we are not too exacting, and do not
demand of it irrelevant perfections? The art of life is to keep step with the celes-
tial orchestra that beats the measure of our career, and gives the cue for our exits
and our entrances. Why should we willingly miss anything, or precipitate anything, or be angry with folly, or in despair at any misadventure? In this world
there should be none but gentle tears, and fluttering tip-toe loves. It is a great
Carnival, and amongst these lights and shadows of comedy, these roses and vices
of the playhouse, there is no abiding.

No Time for Comedy*

Clara Claiborne Park

A LONG TIME AGO, back at the beginning of literature, Achilles got angry. Out of that came destruction, for enemy and friend. Odysseus, on the other hand, kept his cool; he got to eat his cake and have it too. The Iliad and the Odyssey are the fundamental narratives of Western consciousness, even for those who have not read them: two masks, two modes, two stances; minor chord and major; two primary ways of meeting experience. The Iliad sets the type of tragedy, as Aristotle tells us, where greatness shines amid violence, error, defeat, and mortality. The Odyssey celebrates survival among the world's dangers and surprises, and then homecoming, and order restored. It is the very archetype of a prosperous outcome, of Comedy.

Comedy? Laughs are not the point. It is that primary sense of comedy that Dante explained to his patron:

> It differs, then, from tragedy in its content, in that tragedy begins admirably and tranquilly, whereas its end or exit is foul and terrible . . . whereas comedy introduces some harsh complication, but brings its matter to a prosperous end. . . . And hence it is evident that the title of the present work is "the Comedy."

Evident from the Inferno's first lines, in which Dante tells what he means to do: to give account of the *good* he found in that dark and harsh and savage wood where he had lost the straight way.

Tragedy and Comedy: the masks are two. Iliad and Odyssey go together, and not only as they trip off the tongue. One requires the other. A reading of Homer which stops with the lament for Hector must be in every sense partial. As surely as we experience the Iliad in the knowledge that Achilles will die and Troy will fall, we must experience it in the awareness that there is another kind of story to be told, that Odysseus will survive the war and the journey and make it home.

Tragedy and Comedy: though the words are paired, their order is not reversible. We do not speak of Comedy and Tragedy, or Odyssey and Iliad. "To make a sombre action end happily is easy enough," writes Northrop Frye, "to reverse the procedure almost impossible." The direction of this statement runs directly counter to what our gloomy age expects. Yet it tests true. We can imagine Iliad and Odyssey in only one sequence. To turn back from the long voyage home to the fall of the city, from Odysseus in Penelope's arms to Hector dead and Achilles' death to come, would be to turn experience upside down. It is not merely chronology that forbids it, or arguments from archaeology or technique, but the requirements of the imagination itself, as it balances What Is and What Should Be to make the kind of sense we call art—sense which is enough more than the first to take on shape, and enough less than the second to be felt as real. Historically indeed, but above all emotionally, the Odyssey comes last.

Last—as Sophocles at 90, his proud city collapsing around him, in defeat returned to the bitter legend and brought old Oedipus to the healing grove of Colonus, insisting that though suffering is disproportionate, it is not meaningless but mysteriously confers blessing; last, as Matisse with crippled fingers cut singing color into immense shapes of praise. Not everyone survives, of course. But those who do have a bequest to make. Shakespeare's sequence makes the same statement; what comes last is not the sovereign "Nothing" of *King Lear*, but the benign vision of *The Winter's Tale* and *The Tempest*.

Perdita, Miranda; Nausicaa, Telemachus—in comedy the young grow up, the lost are found, the separate joined, as the rhythms of renewal are recognized, and luck, and wonder.

> How many goodly creatures are there here!
> How beauteous mankind is! O brave new world
> That has such people in it!

The comic spirit knows well enough that the goodly creatures Miranda sees are only ourselves, the clowns and criminals and honest men that Prospero has assembled for what Eric Henry, speaking of the characteristic comic ending, calls "that burst of good will in which, at the close, the aberrant society is forgiven and invited to rejoin the mainstream." " 'Tis new to thee," says Prospero to his only daughter, whom he has just betrothed to his enemy's son. Prospero's revels are near ended, and he knows that. Yet here on stage stand Miranda and Ferdinand, undertaking once more to live happily ever after—the young, our own, that simple investment in the future we're all capable of, our built-in second chance. For them the tragic past is only a story that grownups remember. Untendentiously, insouciantly, they will go about their business, the business of comedy, making new beginnings of our bad endings, showing us that they were not endings at all, that there are no endings. Even Odysseus has one more journey to make. But though there are no endings, we are not trapped in stasis either, since boy gets girl, the prince and the princess marry and renew the world. Whatever competing structures of enmity and loss we have taught ourselves to call deep, this is one we cannot do without. What Prospero wished for he has accomplished. Ferdinand and Miranda will make their fathers' errors good. Odysseus will come home and when he does, Telemachus will fight at his side and succeed him, making his father glad. The story of Oedipus is not the only story we know. Our Odysseys and *Tempests* stand, permanent challenges to Ivan Karamazov's terrible question, "Who doesn't desire his father's death?", reminding us to read it, not as the late-revealed archetype of all human development, but as Dostoevsky took the trouble to write it, the cry of a mind diseased.

What is at issue today is whether we have grown too conscious and too clever for comedy's burst of good will. In every age but this the creators of our great fictions have regularly accorded us happy endings to stand beside those others that evoke our terror and our pity. Happy endings still exist, of course. But they have lost their ancient legitimacy. Diminished into trash and Tolkien (not, of course, at all the same thing), they awaken an automatic distrust. Though we'll greet any cheap irony with adolescent acceptance, for a contemporary work to end happily seems in itself enough to make us refuse it full intellectual respectability. At least let it be ambiguous—as some critics convert even the ultimate "Yes" of Joyce's great modern Odyssey into fashionable dubiety. Art accommodates itself to our educated expectations; for all the romantic cult of the outsider, writers are as anxious to be thought respectable as readers, nearly as anxious as critics. And so for the first time since the beginning of our literature there is no major artistic mode to affirm the experience of comedy: healing, restoration, winning through.

In the wilderness, a few voices are newly audible. John Fowles makes his Daniel Martin reflect "how all through his writing life, he had avoided the happy ending, as if it were somehow in bad taste. . . . It had become offensive, in an intellectually privileged caste, to suggest publicly that anything might turn out well." Is the writer's creative freedom, he asks, "compatible with such deference to a received idea of the age: that only a tragic, absurdist, black-comic view . . . of human destiny could be counted as truly representative and 'serious' "? In *Daniel Martin* the hero is denied disaster, or even the copout of the "open ending," in a refreshing authorial decision that there is no sufficient reason why intelligent and privileged people, even those who have not "fulfilled their promise," even those whose somber fate is to have become highly paid screenwriters, need permeate our fictions with narcissistic bellyaching. Saul Bellow attacks the same orthodoxies in his Nobel Prize address (the general neglect of which eloquently illustrates its thesis):

> Essay after essay, book after book . . . maintain . . .the usual things about mass society, dehumanization, and the rest. How weary we are of them. How poorly they represent us. The pictures they offer no more resemble us than we resemble the reconstructed reptiles and other monsters in a museum of paleontology. We are much more limber, versatile, better articulated; there is much more to us; we all feel it.

Our claims to *angst* override realism, common sense; they override our own experience.

Consider the ending of Heller's *Something Happened*. The unpleasant, trapped, pathetic musings of its unpleasant, trapped, pathetic narrator cannily suppress until the last few pages what is offered as the climactic fact: what's happened is that this suburban father has somehow managed to kill the little boy who is the one creature he loves in the world. Our interest in whether it was a true accident or consciously or unconsciously willed shrivels before the event's blank incredibility, even in its own fictional circumstances. The ending is absurd indeed, but in no cosmic sense; it is merely implausible. We have come full circle. In a hundred years, the unhappy ending has become as gratuitous as the conventional happy conclusion the nineteenth century novelists came to find so confining.

"Fairy-tale endings" we have come to call them—the phrase itself is a repudiation. In *The Uses of Enchantment* Bruno Bettelheim has made another old man's bequest; he has tried to give us back fairy-tales. He has dressed his insights in the Oedipal garments of twentieth-century respectability, but they shine brighter naked. "The fairy tale leaves no doubt in the child's mind that the pain must be endured and the risky chances taken"; it can do this because "despite all anxieties, there is no question about the happy ending." "The message that fairy tales get across to the child in manifold form [is] that struggle . . . is an intrinsic part of human experience—but that if one does not shy away, but steadfastly meets unexpected and often unjust hardships, one masters all the obstacles and at the end emerges victorious." Yet children are not the only ones among us who have deep uses for archetypes of success. Bettelheim quotes Schiller: "Deeper meaning resides in the fairy tales told to me in my childhood than in the truth that is taught by life"; he reminds us that "only if a fairy tale met the conscious and unconscious requirements of many people was it repeatedly retold." It was not children who invented these stories. The message of fairy tale is the message of the Odyssey—the indispensable message of comedy.

Yet even Schiller's tribute reinforces the conventional opposition between the meanings of fairy tales and "the truth that is taught by life." To speak of a fairy-tale ending is another way of saying "untrue," an assertion that the story ends, not according to our experience but our wishes. Dying gods may rise again and winter give place to spring—a secular society knows, if only from anthropology, that people might think that. But even those who recognize the ancient emotional uses of such mythic happy endings will concede, all too readily, that the mythic is also mythical in the common sense: false. The most they dare claim is that the truth of comedy is somehow deeper than the real world's. The hard-nosed simply reiterate "untrue."

Yet mythic need not mean mythical. Stories can be archetypal, and still show us how people and events can interrelate for good in a world we recognize, how character attracts luck and makes the prosperous outcome not only wished-for but likely. It is important to distinguish a kind of happy ending different from those of fairy-tale or myth, where miraculous escapes and supernatural assistants invite the hard-nosed to dismiss them (or ghetto them into innocent, old-fashioned art-forms like the Tolkien romances). From Homer on, there have always been fiction-makers who have interested themselves in what may be called *earned* happy endings. Putting their resources of language and invention to dramatising the qualities of personality that conduce to happy outcomes, they have been fascinated by the human capacity for adaptation, moderation, for perseverance without obsessiveness; by the quality that bends but does not break.

Comedy can contain pain. The name "Odysseus" comes from the same "pain" root which gives us "anodyne," and every Greek knew that to be Odysseus meant to have more than one man's share of trouble. In the Odyssey, we are made to wait through five books to meet the hero; when we do, he is sitting on the shore, his eyes "never dry, weeping for a way home," weary of adventures and Calypso. Almost all those familiar adventures—Cyclops, Sirens, Circe, Hades and the rest—took place in the first eighteen months of his ten-years' voyage. They are crammed into a small fraction of the Odyssey's twenty-four books; more than half the action takes place in Ithaca. The Odyssey is a poem of wandering, but primarily of homecoming, its prosperous outcome seconded by luck, but earned by intelligence. It is mythic and realistic at once. It offers all the accoutrements of fairy tale—giants and witches, magic beasts and herbs, supernatural helpers. Yet it displays in its array of survivor characters—not Odysseus only but wise Penelope and prudent Telemachus, sleek old Nestor, Menelaus and the lady Helen—the personal resilience that is a necessary aspect of the power to endure.

That resilience may include a certain deviousness; more kindly we might call it tact. We need continually to be reminded that too strong an integrity, however it may command admiration, can work devastation, like Cordelia's and Lear's. Odysseus himself, joined later by the versatile slave of New Comedy (recently resurrected in *A Funny Thing Happened on the Way to the Forum*), shows the alternative type. Like the slave, Odysseus in the Cyclops' cave is not in a position to fail grandly. The tragic poets were fascinated by the Antigones and Creons, who will die—or kill—rather than disguise what they are or compromise what they are sure they know. The comic vision contemplates and celebrates the reverse. These are the characters who have all the luck, who are happy-accident-prone. Comedy shows us how they make their luck. If Shakespeare, in his late comedies, affirms the mythic vision of restoration, his earlier comedies, as Hugh Richmond has shown,[1] interest themselves in the flexibility, adaptability, the willingness to climb down from preestablished positions that is necessary to earn happy endings. It is the quality that Richard Wilbur has noted in Molière's comedies, of those who respond to life and do not coerce it.

These are the happy endings in which we can believe. We think of Trollope, who applied himself seriously and successfully to the task of investigating what behavior in human beings tended to bring about the kind of endings his public demanded and he himself would wish for his characters. His modest gifts did not include myth-making. But he accepted, as Dickens never did, the responsibility for imagining the prerequisites for happy endings which should be organic and not imposed.

It is a grand claim we make when we reject happy endings: that we are very special, that whatever songs previous ages could sing, in our terrible century all success is shallow or illusory, all prosperity a fairy tale; that the only responses to our world which can command adult assent are compulsive ironies and cries of pain; that the world which seems to lie before us like a world of dreams, so various, so beautiful, so new, hath, in short, really neither joy nor love nor light, nor certitude, nor peace, nor help for pain, and we are here as on a darkling plain waiting for Godot. But what is true enough when recognized as half the story rings counterfeit when it aggrandizes the whole. Since misery loves company, it will find it. But second-hand misery is as inauthentic as second-hand cheerfulness, and far less attractive. It used to be possible to laugh at melancholy Jacques.

In the world of unparalleled safety and comfort which most contemporary readers and writers inhabit, it takes real chutzpah to deny that there can be true tales of victory, unscrambling, fortunate coming together, that literature can weightily concern itself with imagining a world in which luck is frequently on our side, and dramatizing the social wisdom which knows how prosperous outcomes are commonly brought about. Was Homer's vision—Chaucer's—Shakespeare's—Molière's—so much less searching than our own? There is an ugly arrogance in the insistence that our age, alone among all, is too terrible for comedy. In the city of York, in the years when Shakespeare was writing, only ten percent of the population lived to the age of forty. Aristocrats indeed did better; they had nearly an even chance. We cannot imagine what the words "the shadow of death" meant to our forefathers. The Thirty Years War left two of every three in Germany dead. Chaucer's pilgrims rode to Canterbury through a countryside which a generation before had been devastated by the Black Death. In 1348 Oxford lost two-thirds of her academic population. It was not out of his

[1] *Shakespeare's Sexual Comedy: A Mirror for Lovers* (Indianapolis: Bobbs, Merrill, 1971).

prosperity that Dante wrote of the good he found. Any realistic consideration of the life of the past, both in its day-to-day precariousness and its vulnerability to repeated holocaust, will show up our claims to unique misery as uniquely self-centered.

> It is incorrect [wrote Auden] to say . . . that all men have a right to the pursuit of happiness. . . . Happiness is not a right; it is a duty. To the degree that we are unhappy we are in sin (and vice versa).

The idea is old enough to be ready for rediscovery. In Kierkegaard's formulation, Despair is Sin, related like all other sins to Pride, first of the deadly company. Happiness is our business. Hope is not the lucky gift of circumstance or even disposition, but a virtue like faith and love, to be practiced whether or not we find it easy, or even natural, because it is necessary to our survival as human beings.

Christian thinkers of course go farther. Survival suggests safety, and the other way to say that is salvation. "My duty to God," continues Auden, "is to be happy." It is what Dostoevsky's Father Zossima says to silly Mme Holakhov, when on the day before his death she tells him how well and happy he's looking. He understands his illness, and does not deceive himself or her. "But if I seem happy to you, you could never say anything that would please me more. For men were made for happiness and anyone who is completely happy has a right to say to himself, 'I am doing God's will on earth.' All the righteous, all the saints, all the holy martyrs were happy."

Poignant enough, since Dostoevsky himself so evidently was not. But to cite the Christian version of the comic imperative is unnecessarily to limit the application of what Homer knew as well as Chaucer and Dante and Shakespeare. Plato and Aristotle knew it too: Aristotle saw happiness as virtue's serene by-product, and Father Zossima's cheerfulness before death pays its debt to the Socrates of the *Phaedo*. The art that affirms survival reaches through rite to reality; that babies are born, that pain passes, that spring comes again, is as sure as that the sun will rise tomorrow. It is, says Frye, speaking of Shakespearean comedy, an archetypal function of literature to visualize "the world of desire, not as an escape from 'reality,' but as the genuine form of the world that human life tries to imitate."

Nor need one be religious to speak up for happy endings. Georg Lukàcs, that gallant and sensitive Marxist, demonstrates how our time's great secular locus of Faith imposes the same demands. For Marxism, like Christianity and Judaism, establishes for history a direction which gives life meaning beyond mere process. Speaking of the fruitfulness of "justified historical optimism," Lukàcs carefully distinguishes it from that "schematic optimism" which gives rise to unearned happy endings. He writes impatiently of the gift for misery of the modern existential hero, "basically solitary . . . , constitutionally unable to establish relationships with things or persons outside himself," trapped in a world in which it is considered "impossible to determine theoretically the origin and goal of human existence." In *The Meaning of Contemporary Realism* Lukàcs, discussing the literature of *angst*, refuses to accept it as a justified response to a decadent and oppressive capitalism. Rather it is "a rejection of reality, . . . an escape into nothingness." He castigates the glorification of the pathological which is now everywhere around us, as "distortion becomes the normal condition of human existence . . . the formative principle of art and literature." He sees in

Kafka and Beckett, for all their marvelous inventiveness, an apotheosis of impotence and paralysis, which makes "the denial of history, of development the mark of true insight into the nature of reality." And when "the static nature of reality and the senselessness of its surface phenomena" are accepted as "absolute truths requiring no proof, . . . *angst* becomes supreme."

For the artist, whether bourgeois or socialist, has an obligation to the whole truth. "The question," for Lukàcs, "is not: is *x* present in reality? But rather: does *x* represent the whole of reality?"

> What counts is the personal decision. . . . : acceptance or rejection of *angst*. Ought *angst* to be taken as an absolute or ought it to be overcome? Should it be considered one reaction among others, or should it become the determinant of the *condition humaine*? These are not primarily, of course, literary questions—they relate to a man's behavior and experience of life. The crucial question is whether a man escapes from the life of his time into a realm of abstraction—it is there that *angst* is engendered in human consciousness—or confronts modern life determined to fight its evils and support what is good in it.

Bellow is more Platonic, but he comes out in the same place:

> The value of literature lies in these "true impressions." A novel moves back and forth between the world of objects, of actions, of appearances, and that other world from which these "true impressions" come and which moves us to believe that the good we hang on to so tenaciously—in the face of evil, so obstinately—is no illusion.

Tragedy and Comedy: the masks are two. Iliad and Odyssey require each other—or rather, it is we who require them both. It is imperative to hail winners as well as heroic losers; to refuse credence or admiration to those who manage to get what they want and want what they get announces a perverse and envious romanticism. It is that sulky refusal of good that Dante knew, according it no grand extremes of fire or ice, but the unlovely muck of Styx. "Tristi fummo"— "Sullen were we in the sweet air the sun made glad, bearing within us a sluggish smoke."

Since there are no endings, tragedy can be no more *final* than comedy. In every fiction, the pause we call an ending has been imposed by a mind, and reflects a choice. Our solemn rejection of happy endings would be lethal, personally and socially, if it were not by nature partial and temporary. Yet it may most sanely, perhaps, be seen as comic, comic in the familiar sense: ludicrous. We may recall the cry of the Frenchman at the beach resort, in that story grammarians used to tell to illustrate the difference between "shall" and "will," in the days when people still cared about such things: "I will be drowned, and nobody shall save me!"

II
THE FORM
OF COMEDY

The Comic Rhythm*

Susanne Langer

Of all the arts, the most exposed to non-artistic interpretation and criticism are prose fiction and the drama. As the novel has suffered from being treated as a psycho-biographical document, drama has suffered from moralism. In the theater, most people—and especially the most competent spectators—feel that the vision of destiny is the essence of the work, the thing that unfolds before their eyes. In critical retrospect they forget that this visibly growing future, this destiny to which the persons in the play are committed, is the artistic form the poet set out to make, and that the value of the play lies in this creation. As critics, they treat the form as a device for conveying a social and moral content; almost all drama analysis and comment is concerned with the moral struggle involved in the action, the justice of the outcome, the "case" of society against the tragic hero or the comic villain, and the moral significance of the various characters.

It is true that tragedy usually—perhaps even always—presents a moral struggle, and that comedy very commonly castigates foibles and vices. But neither a great moral issue, nor folly inviting embarrassment and laughter, in itself furnishes an artistic principle; neither ethics nor common sense produces any image of organic form. Drama, however, always exhibits such form; it does so by creating the semblance of a history, and composing its elements into a rhythmic single structure. The moral content is thematic material, which, like everything that enters into a work of art, has to serve to make the primary illusion and articulate the pattern of "felt life" the artist intends.

"The tragic theme" and "the comic theme"—guilt and expiation, vanity and exposure—are not the essence of drama, not even the determinants of its major forms, tragedy and comedy; they are means of dramatic construction, and as such they are, of course, not indispensable, however widespread their use. But they are to European drama what the representation of objects is to painting: sources of the Great Tradition. Morality, the concept of deed and desert, or "what is coming to the doer," is as obvious a subject for the art of creating a virtual future as the depiction of objects is for the art of creating virtual space. The reason for the existence of these two major themes, and for their particular respective contents, will be apparent as soon as we consider the nature of the two great forms, comic drama and tragic.

It is commonly assumed that comedy and tragedy have the same fundamental form, but differ in point of view—in the attitude the poet and his inter-

*Susanne Langer, "The Comic Rhythm," in *Feeling and Form* (Charles Scribner's Sons, 1953), pp. 326-350. [Footnotes have been renumbered.]

preters take, and the spectators are invited to take, toward the action.[1] But the difference really goes deeper than surface treatment (i.e., relative levity or pathos). It is structural and radical. Drama abstracts from reality the fundamental forms of consciousness: the first reflection of natural activity in sensation, awareness, and expectation, which belongs to all higher creatures and might be called, therefore, the pure sense of life; and beyond that, the reflection of an activity which is at once more elaborate, and more integrated, having a beginning, efflorescence, and end—the personal sense of life, or self-realization. The latter probably belongs only to human beings, and to them in varying measure.

The pure sense of life is the underlying feeling of comedy, developed in countless different ways. To give a general phenomenon one name is not to make all its manifestations one thing, but only to bring them conceptually under one head. Art does not generalize and classify; art sets forth the individuality of forms which discourse, being essentially general, has to suppress. The sense of life is always new, infinitely complex, therefore infinitely variable in its possible expressions. This sense, or "enjoyment" as Alexander would call it,[2] is the realization in direct feeling of what sets organic nature apart from inorganic: self-preservation, self-restoration, functional tendency, purpose. Life is teleological, the rest of nature is, apparently, mechanical; to maintain the pattern of vitality in a non-living universe is the most elementary instinctual purpose. An organism tends to keep its equilibrium amid the bombardment of aimless forces that beset it, to regain equilibrium when it has been disturbed, and to pursue a sequence of actions dictated by the need of keeping all its interdependent parts constantly renewed, their structure intact. Only organisms have needs; lifeless objects whirl or slide or tumble about, are shattered and scattered, struck together, piled up, without showing any impulse to return to some pre-eminent condition and function. But living things strive to persist in a particular chemical balance, to maintain a particular temperature, to repeat particular functions, and to develop along particular lines, achieving a growth that seems to be performed in their earliest, rudimentary, protoplasmic structure.

That is the basic biological pattern which all living things share: the round of conditioned and conditioning organic processes that produces the life rhythm. When this rhythm is disturbed, all activities in the total complex are modified by the break; the organism as a whole is out of balance. But, within a wide range of conditions, it struggles to retrieve its original dynamic form by overcoming and removing the obstacle, or if this proves impossible, it develops a slight variation of its typical form and activity and carries on life with a new balance of functions—in other words, it adapts itself to the situation. A tree, for instance, that is bereft of the sunshine it needs by the encroachment of other trees, tends to grow tall and thin until it can spread its own branches in the light. A fish that has most of its tail bitten off partly overcomes the disturbance of its locomotion patterns by growing new tissue, replacing some of the tail, and partly adapts to its new

---

[1] Cf., for instance, the letters of Athene Seyler and Stephen Haggard, published under the title: *The Craft of Comedy*. Miss Seyler writes: "... comedy is simply a point of view. It is a comment on life from outside, an observation on human nature. . . . Comedy seems to be the standing outside a character or situation and pointing out one's delight in certain aspects of it. For this reason it demands the cooperation of . . . the audience and is in essence the same as recounting a good story over the dining-table." (p. 9.)

[2] S. Alexander, *Space, Time and Deity*. See Vol. I, p. 12.

condition by modifying the normal uses of its fins, swimming effectively without trying to correct the list of its whole body in the water, as it did at first.

But the impulse to survive is not spent only in defense and accommodation; it appears also in the varying power of organisms to seize on opportunities. Consider how chimney swifts, which used to nest in crevasses among rocks, have exploited the products of human architecture, and how unfailingly mice find the warmth and other delights of our kitchens. All creatures live by opportunities, in a world fraught with disasters. That is the biological pattern in most general terms.

This pattern, moreover, does not develop sporadically in midst of mechanical systems; when or where it began on the earth we do not know, but in the present phase of this planet's constitution there appears to be no "spontaneous generation." It takes life to produce further life. Every organism, therefore, is historically linked with other organisms. A single cell may die, or it may divide and lose its identity in the reorganization of what was formerly its protoplasm round two nuclei instead of one. Its existence as one maturing cell is a phase in a continuum of biological process that varies its rhythm at definite points of growth, starting over with multiplied instances of the immature form. Every individual in this progression that dies (i.e. meets with disaster) instead of dividing is an offshoot from the continuous process, an end, but not a break in the communal biography.

There are species of such elementary life that are diffused in air and water, and some that cohere in visible colonies; above all, there are genetically related organic structures that tend to interact, modify each other, vary in special ways, and together—often by hundreds, thousands, millions together—produce a single higher organism. In such higher organisms, propagation no longer occurs by binary fission, and consequently the individual is not a passing phase in an endless metabolic process; death, which is an accident in amoeboid existence, becomes the lot of every individual—no accident, but a phase of the life pattern itself. The only "immortal" portion of such a complex organism is a class of cells which, during its lifetime, forms new individuals.

In relatively low forms of individualized life, for instance the cryptograms, new specimens may spring entirely from one parent, so that the entire ancestry of an organism forms a single line. But the main evolutionary trend has been toward a more complex form of heredity: two cells of complementary structure, and from different individuals, fuse and grow into a common offspring. This elaborate process entails the division of the race into two sexes, and radically affects the needs and instincts of its members. For the jellyfish, the desire for continuity is enough; it seeks food and avoids destructive influence. Its rhythm is the endless metabolic cycle of cellular growth, punctuated by fissions and rearrangements, but ageless except for the stages of each passing individuation, and in principle deathless. The higher organisms, however, that do not give themselves up by division into new units of life, are all doomed to die; death is inherent in a form of life that achieves complete individuation. The only vestige in them of the endless protoplasmic life passing through organism after organism is their production of the "immortal" cells, ova or spermatozoa; this small fraction of them still enjoys the longer life of the stock.

The sex impulse, which presumably belongs only to bisexual creatures (whatever equivalents it may have in other procreative processes), is closely intertwined with the life impulse; in a mature organism it is part and parcel of the whole vital impetus. But it is a specialized part, because the activities that maintain the individual's life are varied and adaptable to many circumstances, but procreation requires specific actions. This specialization is reflected in the emotional life of all the higher animals; sexual excitement is the most intense and at the same time the most elaborately patterned experience, having its own rhythm that engages the whole creature, its rise and crisis and cadence, in a much higher degree than any other emotive response. Consequently the whole development of feeling, sensibility, and temperament is wont to radiate from that source of vital consciousness, sexual action and passion.

Mankind has its rhythm of animal existence, too—the strain of maintaining a vital balance amid the alien and impartial chances of the world, complicated and heightened by passional desires. The pure sense of life springs from that basic rhythm, and varies from the composed well-being of sleep to the intensity of spasm, rage, or ecstasy. But the process of living is incomparably more complex for human beings than for even the highest animals; man's world is, above all, intricate and puzzling. The powers of language and imagination have set it utterly apart from that of other creatures. In human society an individual is not, like a member of a herd or a hive, exposed only to others that visibly or tangibly surround him, but is consciously bound to people who are absent, perhaps far away, at the moment. Even the dead may still play into his life. His awareness of events is far greater than the scope of his physical perceptions. Symbolic construction has made this vastly involved and extended world: and mental adroitness is his chief asset for exploiting it. The pattern of his vital feeling, therefore, reflects his deep emotional relation to those symbolic structures that are his realities, and his instinctual life modified in almost every way by thought—a brainy opportunism in face of an essentially dreadful universe.

This human life-feeling is the essence of comedy. It is at once religious and ribald, knowing and defiant, social and freakishly individual. The illusion of life which the comic poet creates is the oncoming future fraught with dangers and opportunities, that is, with physical or social events occurring by chance and building up the coincidences with which individuals cope according to their lights. This ineluctable future—ineluctable because its countless factors are beyond human knowledge and control—is Fortune. Destiny in the guise of Fortune is the fabric of comedy; it is developed by comic action, which is the upset and recovery of the protagonist's equilibrium, his contest with the world and his triumph by wit, luck, personal power, or even humorous, or ironical, or philosophical acceptance of mischance. Whatever the theme—serious and lyrical as in *The Tempest*, coarse slapstick as in the *Schwänke* of Hans Sachs, or clever and polite social satire—the immediate sense of life is the underlying feeling of comedy, and dictates its rhythmically structured unity, that is to say its organic form.

Comedy is an art form that arises naturally wherever people are gathered to celebrate life, in spring festivals, triumphs, birthdays, weddings, or initiations. For it expresses the elementary strains and resolutions of animate nature, the animal drives that persist even in human nature, the delight man takes in his special mental gifts that make him the lord of creation; it is an image of human vitality holding its own in the world amid the surprises of unplanned coincidence. The most obvious occasions for the performance of comedies are thanks or challenges to fortune. What justifies the term "Comedy" is not that the ancient ritual procession, the Comus, honoring the god of that name, was the source of this great art form—for comedy has arisen in many parts of the world, where the Greek god with his particular worship was unknown—but that the Comus was a fertility rite, and the god it celebrated a fertility god, a symbol of perpetual rebirth, eternal life.

Tragedy has a different basic feeling, and therefore a different form; that is why it has also quite different thematic material, and why character development, great moral conflicts, and sacrifice are its usual actions. *It is also what makes tragedy sad,* as the rhythm of sheer vitality makes comedy happy. To understand this fundamental difference, we must turn once more to the biological reflections above, and carry them a little further.

In the higher forms of life, an organism is not split up into other organisms so as to let its career as an individual properly end without death and decay; each separate body, on the higher levels, having completed its growth, and normally having reproduced, becomes decadent and finally dies. Its life has a definite beginning, ascent, turning point, descent, and close (barring accidental destruction of life, such as simple cells may also suffer); and the close is inevitably death. Animals—even highly developed ones—instinctively seek to avoid death when they are suddenly confronted with it, and presumably do not realize its coming if and when they die naturally. But human beings, because of their semantically enlarged horizon, are aware of individual history as a passage from birth to death. Human life, therefore, has a different subjective pattern from animal existence; as "felt life" (to borrow Henry James' phrase once more) it has a different dimension. Youth, maturity, and age are not merely states in which a creature may happen to be, but are stages through which persons must pass. Life is a voyage, and at the end of it is death.

The power to conceive of life as a single span enables one also to think of its conduct as a single undertaking, and of a person as a unified and developed being, a personality. Youth, then, is all potentiality, not only for physical growth and procreation, but also for mental and moral growth. Bodily development is largely unconscious and involuntary, and the instincts that aid it are bent simply upon maintaining the vital rhythms from moment to moment, evading destruction, letting the organism grow in its highly specialized fashion. Its maturation, procreative drive, then a fairly long period of "holding its own" without further increase, and finally the gradual loss of impetus and elasticity—these processes form one organic evolution and dissolution. The extraordinary activity of man's brain, however, does not automatically parallel his biological career. It outruns the order of animal interests, sometimes confusing his instincts, sometimes exaggerating them (as simple sexual passion, for instance, is heightened by imagination into romantic passion and eternal devotion), and gives his life a new pattern dominated by his foreknowledge of death. Instead of simply passing through the natural succession of his individualized existence, he ponders its uniqueness, its brevity and limitations, the life impulses that make it, and the fact that in the end the organic unity will be broken, the self will disintegrate and be no more.

There are many ways of accepting death; the commonest one is to deny its finality, to imagine a continued existence "beyond" it—by resurrection, reincarnation, or departure of the soul from the body, and usually from the familiar world, to a deathless existence in hades, nirvana, heaven or hell. But no matter how people contrive to become reconciled to their mortality, it puts its stamp on their conception of life: since the instinctive struggle to go on living is bound to meet defeat in the end, they look for *as much life as possible* between birth and death—for adventure, variety and intensity of experience, and the sense of growth that increase of personality and social status can give long after physical growth has stopped. The known limitation of life gives form to it and makes it appear not merely as a process, but as a career. This career of the individual is variously conceived as a "calling," the attainment of an ideal, the soul's pilgrimage, "life's ordeal," or self-realization. The last of these designations is, perhaps, the most illuminating in the present context, because it contains the notion of a limited potential personality given at birth and "realized," or systematically developed, in the course of the subject's total activity. His career, then, appears to be performed in him; his successive adventures in the world are so many challenges to fulfill his individual destiny.

Destiny viewed in this way, as a future shaped essentially in advance and only incidentally by chance happenings, is Fate; and Fate is the "virtual future" created in tragedy. The "tragic rhythm of action," as Professor Fergusson calls it, is the rhythm of man's life at its highest powers in the limits of his unique, death-bound career. Tragedy is the image of Fate, as comedy is of Fortune. Their basic structures are different; comedy is essentially contingent, episodic, and ethnic; it expresses the continuous balance of sheer vitality that belongs to society and is exemplified briefly in each individual; tragedy is a fulfillment, and its form therefore is closed, final and passional. Tragedy is a mature art form, that has not arisen in all parts of the world, not even in all great civilizations. Its conception requires a sense of individuality which some religions and some cultures—even high cultures—do not generate.

But that is a matter for later discussion, in connection with the tragic theater as such. At present I wish only to point out the radical nature of the difference between the two types of drama, comedy and tragedy; a difference which is, however, not one of opposites—the two forms are perfectly capable of various combinations, incorporating elements of one in the other. The matrix of the work is always either tragic or comic; but within its frame the two often interplay.

Where tragedy is generally known and accepted, comedy usually does not reach its highest development. The serious mood is reserved for the tragic stage. Yet comedy may be serious; there is heroic drama, romantic drama, political drama, all in the comic pattern, yet entirely serious; the "history" is usually comedy. It presents an incident in the undying life of a society that meets good and evil fortunes on countless occasions but never concludes its quest. After the story comes more life, more destiny prepared by the world and the race. So far as the story goes, the protagonists "live happily ever after"—on earth or in heaven. That fairy-tale formula is tacitly understood at the close of a comedy. It is implicit in the episodic structure.

Dante called his great poem a comedy, though it is entirely serious—visionary, religious, and sometimes terrible. The name *Divina Commedia*, which later generations attached to it, fits it, even if not too literally since it is not actually a drama as the title suggests.[3] Something analogous to the comedy pattern, togeth-

---

[3] Professor Fergusson and Mr. T. S. Eliot both treat *The Divine Comedy* as an example of genuine drama. The former even speaks of "the drama of Sophocles and Shakespeare, the *Divine Commedia* of Dante—in which the idea of a theater has been briefly realized." (*The Idea of a Theater*, p. 227.) But between drama and dramatic narrative there is a world of difference. If everything these two eminent critics say of great drama holds also for Dante's poem, this does not mean that the poem is a drama, but that the critics have reached a generalization applying to more than drama.

er with the tones of high seriousness that European poets have generally struck only in tragedy, yields a work that invites the paradoxical name.

Paradoxical, however, only to our ears, because our religious feeling is essentially tragic, inspired by the contemplation of death. In Asia the designation "Divine Comedy" would fit numberless plays; especially in India triumphant gods, divine lovers united after various trials (as in the perennially popular romance of Rama and Sita), are the favorite themes of a theater that knows no "tragic rhythm." The classical Sanskrit drama was heroic comedy—high poetry, noble action, themes almost always taken from the myths—a serious, religiously conceived drama, yet in the "comic" pattern, which is not a complete organic development reaching a foregone, inevitable conclusion, but is episodic, restoring a lost balance, and implying a new future.[4] The reason for this consistently "comic" image of life in India is obvious enough: both Hindu and Buddhist regard life as an episode in the much longer career of the soul which has to accomplish many incarnations before it reaches its goal, nirvana. Its struggles in the world do not exhaust it; in fact they are scarcely worth recording except in entertainment theater, "comedy" in our sense—satire, farce, and dialogue. The characters whose fortunes are seriously interesting are the eternal gods; and for them there is no death, no limit of potentialities, hence no fate to be fulfilled. There is only the balanced rhythm of sentience and emotion, upholding itself amid the changes of material nature.

The personages in the nataka (the Sanskrit heroic drama) do not undergo any character development; they are good or evil, as the case may be, in the last act as they were in the first. This is essentially a comedy trait. Because the comic rhythm is that of vital continuity, the protagonists do not change in the course of the play, as they normally do in tragedy. In the latter there is development, in the former developments. The comic hero plays against obstacles presented either by nature (which includes mythical monsters such as dragons, and also "forces," personified like the "Night Queen," or impersonal like floods, fires, and pests), or by society; that is, his fight is with obstacles and enemies, which his strength, wisdom, virtue, or other assets let him overcome.[5] It is a fight with the uncongenial world, which he shapes to his own fortunes. Where the basic feeling of dramatic art always has the comic rhythm, comedy enjoys a much fuller development than it does where tragedy usurps its highest honors. In the great cultures of Asia it has run through all moods, from the lightest to the most solemn, and through all forms—the one-act skit, the farce, the comedy of manners, even to dramas of Wagnerian proportions.

In the European tradition the heroic comedy has had a sporadic existence; the Spanish *Comedia* was perhaps its only popular and extended development.[6] Where it reaches something like the exalted character of the nataka, our comedy has generally been taken for tragedy, simply because of its dignity, or "sublimity," which we associate only with tragedy. Corneille and Racine considered their dramas tragedies, yet the rhythm of tragedy—the growth and full realiza-

[4] Cf. Sylvain Lévi, *Le théâtre indien*, p. 32: "The heroic comedy (nataka) is the consummate type of Indian drama; all dramatic elements can find their place in it."

[5] In Chinese drama, even exalted heroes often conquer their enemies by ruse rather than by valor; see Zucker, *The Chinese Theater*, especially p. 82.

[6] Brander Matthews describes the *Comedia* as "often not a comedy at all in our English understanding of the term, but rather a play of intrigue, peopled with hot-blooded heroes. . . ." (Introduction to Lope De Vega Carpio's *The New Art of Writing Plays*.)

tion of a personality—is not in them; the Fate their personages meet is really misfortune, and they meet it heroically. This sad yet non-tragic character of the French classical drama has been noted by several critics. C. V. Deane, for instance, in his book, *Dramatic Theory and the Rhymed Heroic Play,* says of Corneille: "In his tragedies the incidents are so disposed as to bring out to the full the conflict between an overmastering will and the forces of Fate, but the interest centres in the dauntless endurance of the individual, and there is little attempt to envisage or suggest the universal moral problem inherent in the nature of Tragedy, nor do his chief characters submit to ordinary morality; each is a law unto himself by virtue of his particular kind of heroism."[7] Earlier in the book he had already remarked on the fact that the creation of human personalities was not the aim of these playwrights;[8] and in a comment on Otway's translation of Racine's *Bérénice* he really exposed—perhaps without realizing it himself—the true nature of their tragedies, for he said that Otway was able "to reproduce the spirit of the original," though he was not scrupulously true to the French text. "Even Otway, however, adapts rather than translates," he observed, "and the tilt toward the happy ending in his version betrays an acquiescence in the stereotyped poetic justice which the English playwrights (appreciably influence by Corneille's practice) deemed inseparable from the interplay of heroism and honor." (p. 19.)

How could a translator-editor bring a tragic play to a happy ending and still "reproduce the spirit of the original"? Only by virtue of the non-tragic structure, the fundamentally comic movement of the piece. These stately Gallic classics are really heroic comedies. They are classed as tragedies because of their sublime tone, which is associated, in our European tradition, with tragic action,[9] but (as Sylvain Lévi pointed out)[10] they are really similar in spirit and form to the nataka. Corneille's and Racine's heroic characters are godlike in their rationality; like the divine beings of Kalidasa and Bhavabhuti, they undergo no real *agon,* no great moral struggle or conflict of passions. Their morality (however extraordinary) is perfect, their principles clear and coherent, and the action derives from the changes of fortune that they meet. Fortune can bring sad or happy occasions, and a different course of events need not violate "the spirit of the original." But there is no question of how the heroes will meet circumstances; they will meet them rationally; reason, the highest virtue of the human soul, will be victorious. This reason does not grow, through inner struggles against passional

---

[7] *Dramatic Theory and the Rhymed Heroic Play,* p. 33.

[8] *Ibid.,* p. 14: "It is true that during the course of its history the heroic play seldom succeeded in creating characters which were credible as human beings; this, however, was really foreign to its purpose."

[9] The strength of this association is so great that some critics actually treat "sublimity" as the necessary and sufficient condition for tragedy. Racine himself said: "It is enough that its action be great, its actors heroic, that the passions be excited in it; and that the whole give the experience of majestic sadness in which the whole pleasure of tragedy resides." (Quoted by Fergusson, *op. cit.,* p. 43.)

The same criteria are evidently applied by Professor Zucker when he writes: "Tragedy is not found in the Chinese drama. The plays abound in sad situations, but there is none that by its nobility or sublimity would deserve to be called tragic." (*Op. cit.,* p. 37.) Jack Chen, on the other hand, in his book *The Chinese Theater,* says that during the Ching dynasty "Historical tragedy was greatly in vogue. *The Bloodstained Fan* dealing with the last days of the Mings and *The Palace of Eternal Life . . .* are perennially popular even today." (p. 20.) The last-named play, which deals with the death of Lady Yang, is certainly a genuine tragedy.

[10] See *Le théâtre indien,* p. 425.

obstacles, from an original spark to full enlightenment, as "the tragic rhythm of action" would demand, but is perfect from the outset.[11]

Romantic drama such as Schiller's *Wilhelm Tell* illustrates the same principle. It is another species of serious heroic comedy. Tell appears as an exemplary personage in the beginning of the play, as citizen, husband, father, friend and patriot; when an extreme political and social crisis develops, he rises to the occasion, overcomes the enemy, frees his country, and returns to the peace, dignity and harmonious joy of his home. The balance of life is restored. As a personage he is impressive; as a personality he is very simple. He has the standard emotions—righteous indignation, paternal love, patriotic fervor, pride, anxiety, etc.—under their obvious conditions. Nothing in the action requires him to be more than a man of high courage, independent spirit, and such other virtues as the mountaineers of Switzerland boasted, to oppose the arrogance and vanity of foreign oppressors. But this ideal male he was from the start, and the Gessler episode merely gives him opportunity to show his indomitable skill and daring.

Such are the serious products of comic art; they are also its rarer examples. The natural vein of comedy is humorous—so much so that "comic" has become synonymous with "funny." Because the word "comic" is here used in a somewhat technical sense (contrasting "the comic rhythm" with "the tragic rhythm"), it may be well to say "comical" where the popular sense is intended. There are all degrees of humor in comedy, from the quick repartee that elicits a smile by its cleverness without being intrinsically funny at all, to the absurdity that sets young and old, simple or sophisticate, shouting with merriment. Humor has its place in all the arts, but in comic drama it has its home. Comedy may be frivolous, farcical, ribald, ludicrous to any degree, and still be true art. Laughter springs from its very structure.

There is a close relation between humor and the "sense of life," and several people have tried to analyze it in order to find the basis of that characteristically human function, laughter; the chief weakness in their attempts has been, I think, that they have all started with the question: What sort of thing makes us laugh? Certainly laughter is often evoked by ideas, cognitions, fancies; it accompanies specific emotions such as disdain, and sometimes the feeling of pleasure; but we also laugh when we are tickled (which may not be pleasurable at all), and in hysterics. Those predominantly physiological causes bear no direct relation to humor; neither, for that matter, do some kinds of pleasure. Humor is one of the causes of laughter.

Marcel Pagnol, who published this theory of laughter in a little book entitled *Notes sur le rire*, remarks that his predecessors—he names particularly Bergson, Fabre, and Mélinand—all sought the source of laughter in funny things or situations, i.e. in nature, whereas it really lies in the subject who laughs. Laughter always—without exception—betokens a sudden sense of superiority. "Laughter is a song of triumph," he says. "It expresses the laugher's sudden discovery of his own momentary superiority over the person he laughs at." This, he

---

[11] Cf. Fergusson's analysis of *Bérénice:* "The scenes of dialogue correspond to the agons; but the polite exchange between Arsace and Antiochus, in the first act, is far from the terrible conflict between Oedipus and Tiresias, wherein the moral beings of the antagonists are at stake. . . . [In *Bérénice*] the moral being is unmistakable and impossible to lose while the stage life continues at all . . . the very possibility of the interchange depends upon the authority of reason, which secures the moral being in any contingency. . . . But if the moral being is *ex hypothesi* secure, . . . there cannot be a pathos in the Sophoclean sense at all." (*Op. cit.*, p. 52.)

maintains, "explains all bursts of laughter in all times and all countries," and lets us dispense with all classifications of laughter by different kinds or causes: "One cannot classify or arrange in categories the radii of a circle."[12]

Yet he proceeds directly to divide laughter into "positive" and "negative" kinds, according to its social or antisocial inspiration. This indicates that we are still dealing with *ludicrous situations*, though these situations always involve the person to whom they are ludicrous, so it may be said that "the source of the comical is in the laughter."[13] The situation, moreover, is something the subject must discover, that is, laughter requires a conceptual element; on that M. Pagnol agrees with Bergson, Mélinand, and Fabre. Whether, according to Bergson's much-debated view, we see living beings following the law of mechanism, or see absurdity in midst of plausibility as Mélinand says, or, as Fabre has it, create a confusion only to dispel it suddenly, we feel our own superiority in detecting the irrational element; more particularly, we feel superior to those who perform mechanical actions, introduce absurdities, or make confusions. Therefore M. Pagnol claims that his definition of the laughable applies to all these supposedly typical situations.

It probably does; but it is still too narrow. *What is laughable* does not explain the nature of the laughter, any more than what is rational explains the nature of reason. The ultimate source of laughter is physiological, and the various situations in which it arises are simply its normal or abnormal stimuli.

Laughter, or the tendency to laugh (the reaction may stop short of the actual respiratory spasm, and affect only the facial muscles, or even meet with complete inhibition) seems to arise from a surge of vital feeling. This surge may be quite small, just so it be sudden enough to be felt distinctly; but it may also be great, and not particularly swift, and reach a marked climax, at which point we laugh or smile with joy. Laughter is not a simple overt act, as the single word suggests; it is the spectacular end of a complex process. As speech is the culmination of a mental activity, laughter is a culmination of feeling—the crest of a wave of felt vitality.

A sudden sense of superiority entails such a "lift" of vital feeling. But the "lift" may occur without self-flattery, too; we need not be making fun of anyone. A baby will laugh uproariously at a toy that is made to appear suddenly, again and again, over the edge of the crib or the back of a chair. It would take artful interpretation to demonstrate that this fulfillment of his tense expectation makes him feel superior. Superior to whom? The doll? A baby of eight or nine months is not socialized enough yet to think: "There, I knew you were coming!" and believe that the doll couldn't fool him. Such self-applause requires language, and enough experience to estimate probabilites. The baby laughs because his wish is gratified; not because he believes the doll obeyed his wishing, but simply because the suspense is broken, and his energies are released. The sudden pleasure raises his general feeling tone, so he laughs.

In so-called "gallows humor"—the harsh laugh in distress—the "lift" of vital feeling is simply a flash of self-assertion. Something similar probably causes the mirthless laughter of hysterics: in the disorganized response of a hysterical person, the sense of vitality breaks through fear and depression spasmodically, so that it causes explosive laughter, sometimes alternating with sobs and tears.

[12]*Notes sur le rire*, p. 41. His argumentation is, unfortunately, not as good as his ideas, and finally leads him to include the song of the nightingale and the rooster's crow as forms of laughter.
[13]*Ibid.*, p. 17.

Laughter is, indeed, a more elementary thing than humor. We often laugh without finding any person, object, or situation funny. People laugh for joy in active sport, in dancing, in greeting friends; in returning a smile, one acknowledges another person's worth instead of flaunting one's own superiority and finding him funny.

But all these causes of laughter or its reduced form, smiling, which operate directly on us, belong to actual life. In comedy the spectator's laugh has only one legitimate source: his appreciation of humor in the piece. He does not laugh with the characters, not even at them, but at their acts—at their situations, their doings, their expressions, often at their dismay. M. Pagnol holds that we laugh at the characters directly, and regards that as a corroboration of this theory: our pleasure in the comic theater lies in watching people to whom we feel superior.[14]

There is, however, one serious defect in that view, namely that it supposes the spectator to be aware of himself as a being in the same "world" as the characters. To compare them, even subconsciously, to himself he must give up his psychical Distance and feel himself copresent with them, as one reads an anecdotal news item as something apart from one's own life but still in the actual world, and is moved to say: "How could she do such a thing! Imagine being so foolish!" If he experiences such a reaction in the theater, it is something quite aside from his perception of the play as a poetic fabrication; he has lost, for the moment, his Distance, and feels himself inside the picture.

Humor, then, would be a by-product of comedy, not a structural element in it. And if laughter were elicited thus by the way, it should not make any difference to the value of the work where it occurred: a stage accident, a bad actor who made every amateur actor in the audience feel superior, should serve as well as any clever line or funny situation in the play to amuse the audience. We do, in fact, laugh at such failures; but we do not praise the comedy for that entertainment. In a good play the "laughs" are poetic elements. Its humor as well as its pathos belongs to the virtual life, and the delight we take in it is delight in something created for our perception, not a direct stimulus to our own feelings. It is true that the comical figures are often buffoons, simpletons, clowns; but such characters are almost always sympathetic, and although they are knocked around and abused, they are indestructible, and eternally self-confident and good-humored.

The buffoon is, in fact, an important comic personage, especially in folk theater. He is essentially a folk character that has persisted through the more sophisticated and literary stages of comedy as Harlequin, Pierrot, the Persian Karaguez, the Elizabethan jester or fool, the *Vidusaka* of Sanscrit drama; but in the humbler theatrical forms that entertained the poor and especially the peasantry everywhere before the movies came, the buffoon had a more vigorous existence as Hans Wurst, as Punch of the puppet show, the clown of pantomine, the Turkish Karagöz (borrowed from Persian tradition) who belongs only to the shadow play.[15] These anciently popular personages show what the buffoon really is: the indomitable living creature fending for itself, tumbling and stumbling (as the clown physically illustrates) from one situation into another, getting into scrape after scrape and getting out again, with or without a thrashing. He is the personified *élan vital*; his chance adventures and misadventures, without much

---

[14] *Ibid.*, p. 92. There is further discussion of the problem at the end of the present chapter [selection].
[15] See N. N. Martinovitch. *The Turkish Theater, passism.*

plot, though often with bizarre complications, his absurd expectations and disappointments, in fact his whole improvised existence has the rhythm of primitive, savage, if not animalian life, coping with a world that is forever taking new uncalculated turns, frustrating, but exciting. He is neither a good man nor a bad one, but is genuinely amoral,—now triumphant, now worsted and rueful, but in his ruefulness and dismay he is funny, because his energy is really unimpaired and each failure prepares the situation for a new fantastic move.[16] The most forthright of these infantilists is the English Punch, who carries out every impulse by force and speed of action—chastises his wife, throws his child out of the window, beats the policeman, and finally spears the devil and carries him out triumphantly on a pitchfork. Punch is not a real buffoon, he is too successful; his appeal is probably a subjective one, to people's repressed desires for general vengeance, revolt, and destruction. He is psychologically interesting, but really a degenerated and stereotyped figure, and as such he has little artistic value because he has no further poetic progeny. What has caused his persistence in a single, mainly vulgar, and not particularly witty role, I do not know, nor is this the place to investigate it; but when he first appeared in England as Punchinello, borrowed from the Italian marionettes, he was still the pure comic protagonist. According to a statement of R. M. Wheeler in the *Encyclopaedia Britannica*, which we may, presumably, take as authority, "The older Punchinello was far less restricted in his actions and circumstances than his modern successor. He fought with allegorical figures representing want and weariness as well as with his wife and the police, was on intimate terms with the patriarchs and the seven champions of Christendom, sat on the lap of the Queen of Sheba, had kings and dukes for his companions, and cheated the Inquisition as well as the common hangman."

The high company this original Punch keeps is quite in accordance with the dignified settings in which he makes his appearance. From the same article we learn that the earliest recorded appearances of Punch in England were in a puppet play of the Creation of the World, and in another representing the Deluge. To the modern, solemn religious mind, scriptural stories may seem a strange context for such a secular character, and perhaps this apparent incongruity has led to the widespread belief that the clown in modern comedy derives from the devil of mediaeval miracle plays.[17] The devil is, of course, quite at home in sacred realms. It is not impossible that this relation between devil and fool (in his various forms as clown, jester, freak) really holds; yet if it does, that identifies the devil with the flesh, and sin with lust. Such a conception brings the spirit of life and the father of all evil, which are usually poles apart, very close together. For there is no denying that the fool is a red-blooded fellow; he is, in fact, close to the animal world. In French tradition he wears a cockscomb on his cap, and Punchinello's nose is probably the residue of a beak. He is all motion, whim, and impulse—the "libido" itself.

But he is probably older than the Christian devil, and does not need any connection with that worthy to let him into religious precincts. He has always been close to the gods. If we view him as the representative of mankind in its struggle with the world, it is clear at once why his antics and impertinences are

---

[16] Falstaff is a perfect example of the buffoon raised to a human "character" in comedy.

[17] See the article "Clown" (unsigned) in the *Encyclopaedia Britannica*.

often an integral part of religious rites—why, for instance, the clowning orders in Pueblo society were held in high honor:[18] the clown is Life, he is the Will, he is the Brain, and by the same token he is nature's fool. From the primitive exuberant religions that celebrate fertility and growth he tends ever to come into the ascetic cults, and tumble and juggle in all innocence before the Virgin.

In comedy the stock figure of the buffoon is an obvious device for building up the comic rhythm, i.e. the image of Fortune. But in the development of the art he does not remain the central figure that he was in the folk theater; the lilt and balance of life which he introduced, once it has been grasped, is rendered in more subtle poetic inventions involving plausible characters, and an *intrigue* (as the French call it) that makes for a coherent, over-all, dramatic action. Sometimes he remains as a jester, servant, or other subsidiary character whose comments, silly or witty or shrewd, serve to point the essentially comic pattern of the action, where the verisimilitude and complexity of the stage-life threaten to obscure its basic form. Those points are normally "laughs"; and that brings us to the aesthetic problem of the joke in comedy.

Because comedy abstracts, and reincarnates for our perception, the motion and rhythm of living, it enhances our vital feeling, much as the presentation of space in painting enhances our awareness of visual space. The virtual life on the stage is not diffuse and only half felt, as actual life usually is: virtual life, always moving visibly into the future, is intensified, speeded up, exaggerated; the exhibition of vitality rises to a breaking point, to mirth and laughter. We laugh in the theater at small incidents and drolleries which would hardly rate a chuckle offstage. It is not for such psychological reasons that we go there to be amused, nor are we bound by rules of politeness to hide our hilarity, but these trifles at which we laugh are really funnier *where they occur* than they would be elsewhere; they are employed in the play, not merely brought in casually. They occur where the tension of dialogue or other action reaches a high point. As thought breaks into speech—as the wave breaks into form—vitality breaks into humor.

Humor is the brilliance of drama, a sudden heightening of the vital rhythm. A good comedy, therefore, builds up to every laugh; a performance that has been filled up with jokes at the indiscretion of the comedian or of his writer may draw a long series of laughs, yet leave the spectator without any clear impression of a very funny play. The laughs, moreover, are likely to be of a peculiar sameness, almost perfunctory, the formal recognition of a timely "gag."

The amoral character of the comic protagonist goes through the whole range of what may be called the comedy of laughter. Even the most civilized products of this art—plays that George Meredith would honor with the name of "comedy," because they provoke "thoughtful laughter"—do not present moral distinctions and issues, but only the ways of wisdom and of folly. Aristophanes, Menander, Molière—practically the only authors this most exacting of critics admitted as truly comic poets—are not moralists, yet they do not flaunt or deprecate morality; they have, literally, "no use" for moral principles—that is, they do not use them. Meredith, like practically all his contempories, labored under the belief that poetry must teach society lessons, and that comedy was valuable for

---

[18] On the secret societies of clowns, see F. H. Cushing, *Zuni Creation Myths* (Report of the Bureau of American Ethnology, 1892), concerning the order of "Koyemshi" ("Mudheads").

what it revealed concerning the social order.[19] He tried hard to hold its exposé of foibles and vindication of common sense to an ethical standard, yet in his every efforts to justify its amoral personages he only admitted their amoral nature, and their simple relish for life, as when he said: "The heroines of comedy are like women of the world, not necessarily heartless from being clear-sighted. . . . Comedy is an exhibition of their battle with men, and that of men with them. . . ."

There it is, in a nutshell: the contest of men and women—the most universal contest, humanized, in fact civilized, yet still the primitive joyful challenge, the self-preservation and self-assertion whose progress is the comic rhythm.

This rhythm is capable of the most diverse presentations. That is why the art of comedy grows, in every culture, from casual beginnings—miming, clowning, sometimes erotic dancing—to some special and distinctive dramatic art, and sometimes to many forms of it within one culture, yet never seems to repeat its works. It may produce a tradition of dignified drama, springing from solemn ritual, even funereal, its emotional movement too slow to culminate in humor at any point; then other means have to be found to lend it glamor and intensity. The purest heroic comedy is likely to have no humorous passages at all, but to employ the jester only in an ornamental way reminiscent of tragedy, and in fact to use many techniques of tragedy. It may even seem to transcend the amoral comic pattern by presenting virtuous heroes and heroines. But their virtue is a formal affair, a social asset; as Deane remarked of the French classic heroes,[20] they do not submit to ordinary morality; their morality is "heroism," which is essentially strength, will, and endurance in face of the world. Neither have the divinities of oriental drama any "ordinary morality"; they are perfect in virtue when they slay and when they spare, their goodness is glory, and their will is law. They are Superman, the Hero, and the basic pattern of their conquest over enemies whose only wickedness is resistance, is the amoral life pattern of fencing with the devil—man against death.

Humor, then, is not the essence of comedy, but only one of its most useful and natural elements. It is also its most problematical element, because it elicits from the spectators what appears to be a direct emotional response to persons on the stage, in no wise different from their response to actual people: amusement, laughter.

The phenomenon of laughter in the theater brings into sharp focus the whole question of the distinction between emotion symbolically presented, and emotion directly stimulated; it is, indeed, a *pons asinorum* of the theory that this distinction is radical, because it presents us with what is probably the most difficult example. The audience's laugh at a good play is, of course, self-expressive, and betokens a "lift" of vital feeling in each laughing person. Yet it has a differ-

---

[19] His well-known little work is called *An Essay on Comedy, and the Uses of the Comic Spirit*. These uses are entirely non-artistic. Praising the virtues of "good sense" (which is whatever has survival value in the eyes of society), he says: "The French have a school of stately comedy to which they can fly for renovation whenever they have fallen away from it; and their having such a school is the main reason why, as John Stuart Mill pointed out, they know men and women more accurately than we do." (pp. 13–14.) And a few pages later: "The *Femmes Savantes* is a capital instance of the uses of comedy in teaching the world to understand what ails it. The French had felt the burden of his new nonsense [the fad of academic learning, new after the fad of excessive nicety and precision in speech, that had marked the *Precieuses*]; but they had to see the comedy several times before they were consoled in their suffering by seeing the cause of it exposed." (pp. 19–20.)

[20] Cf. *supra*, p. 336.

ent character from laughter in conversation, or in the street when the wind carries off a hat with the "hair-do" attached, or in the "laugh house" at an amusement park where the willing victims meet distorting mirrors and things that say "boo." All these laughs of daily life are direct responses to separate stimuli; they may be as sporadic as the jokes bandied in a lively company, or may be strung along purposely like the expected and yet unforeseen events in the "laugh house," yet they remain so many personal encounters that seem funny only if one is in the mood for them. Sometimes we reject witticisms and are bored with tricks and clowning.

It is different in the theater: the play possesses us and breaks our mood. It does not change it, but simply abrogates it. Even if we come in a jovial mood, this does not notably increase our appreciation of humor in the play; for the humor in a good comedy does not strike us directly. What strikes us directly is the dramatic illusion, the stage action as it evolves; and the joke, instead of being as funny as our personal response would make it, seems as funny as its occurrence in the total action makes it. A very mild joke in just the right place may score a big laugh. The action culminates in a witticism, an absurdity, a surprise; the spectators laugh. But after their outburst there is not the letdown that follows an ordinary laugh, because the play moves on without the breathing spell we usually give our own thought and feeling after a joke. The action carries over from one laugh to another, sometimes fairly far spaced; people are laughing *at the play*, not at a string of jokes.

Humor in comedy (as, indeed, in all humorous art) belongs to the work, not to our actual surroundings; and if it is borrowed from the actual work, its appearance in the work is what really makes it funny. Political or topical allusions in a play amuse us because they are *used*, not because they refer to something intrinsically very comical. This device of playing with things from actual life is so sure to bring laughs that the average comic writer and improvising comedian overdoes it to the point of artistic ruin; hence the constant flood of "shows" that have immense popularity but no dramatic core, so they do not outlive the hour of their passing allusions.

Real comedy sets up in the audience a sense of general exhilaration, because it presents the very image of "livingness" and the perception of it is exciting. Whatever the story may be, it takes the form of a temporary triumph over the surrounding world; complicated, and thus stretched out, by an involved succession of coincidences. This illusion of life, the stage-life, has a rhythm of feeling which is not transmitted to us by separate successive stimulations, but rather by our perception of its entire *Gestalt*—a whole world moving into its own future. The "livingness" of the human world is abstracted, composed, and presented to us; with it the high points of the composition that are illuminated by humor. They belong to the life we see, and our laugh belongs to the theatrical exhilaration, which is universally human and impersonal. It is not what the joke happens to mean to us that measures our laughter, but what the joke does in the play.

For this reason we tend to laugh at things in the theater that we might not find funny in actuality. The technique of comedy often has to clear the way for its humor by forestalling any backsliding into "the world of anxious interest and selfish solicitude." It does this by various devices—absurd coincidences, stereotyped expressions of feeling (like the clown's wails of dismay), a quickened pace of action, and other unrealistic effects which serve to emphasize the comic structure. As Professor Fergusson said, "when we understand a comic convention we see the play with godlike omniscience. . . . When Scaramouche gets a beating, we do not feel the blows, but the idea of a beating, at that moment, strikes us as funny. If the beating is too realistic, if it breaks the light rhythm of thought, the fun is gone, and the comedy destroyed."[21]

That "light rhythm of thought" is the rhythm of life; and the reason it is "light" is that all creatures love life, and the symbolization of its impetus and flow makes us really aware of it. The conflict with the world whereby a living being maintains its own complex organic unity is a delightful encounter; the world is as promising and alluring as it is dangerous and opposed. The feeling of comedy is a feeling of heightened vitality, challenged wit and will, engaged in the great game with Chance. The real antagonist is the World. Since the personal antagonist in the play is really that great challenger, he is rarely a complete villain; he is interesting, entertaining, his defeat is a hilarious success but not his destruction. There is no permanent defeat and permanent human triumph except in tragedy; for nature must go on if life goes on, and the world that presents all obstacles also supplies the zest of life. In comedy, therefore, there is a general trivialization of the human battle. Its dangers are not real disasters, but embarrassment and loss of face. That is why comedy is "light" compared to tragedy, which exhibits an exactly opposite tendency to general exaggeration of issues and personalities.

The same impulse that drove people, even in prehistoric times, to enact fertility rites and celebrate all phases of their biological existence, sustains their eternal interest in comedy. It is in the nature of comedy to be erotic, risqué, and sensuous if not sensual, impious, and even wicked. This assures it a spontaneous emotional interest, yet a dangerous one: for it is easy and tempting to command an audience by direct stimulation of feeling and fantasy, not by artistic power. But where the formulation of feeling is really achieved, it probably reflects the whole development of mankind and man's world, for feeling is the intaglio image of reality. The sense of precariousness that is the typical tension of light comedy was undoubtedly developed in the eternal struggle with chance that every farmer knows only too well—with weather, blights, beasts, birds and beetles. The embarrassments, perplexities and mounting panic which characterize that favorite genre, comedy of manners, may still reflect the toils of ritual and taboo that complicated the caveman's existence. Even the element of aggressiveness in comic action serves to develop a fundamental trait of the comic rhythm—the deep cruelty of it, as all life feeds on life. There is no biological truth that feeling does not reflect, and that good comedy, therefore, will not be prone to reveal.

But the fact that the rhythm of comedy is the basic rhythm of life does not mean that biological existence is the "deeper meaning" of all its themes, and that to understand the play is to interpret all the characters as symbols and the story as a parable, a disguised rite of spring or fertility magic, performed four hundred and fifty times on Broadway. The stock characters are probably symbolic both in origin and in appeal. There are such independently symbolic factors, or residues of them, in all the arts,[22] but their value for art lies in the degree to which their significance can be "swallowed" by the single symbol, the art

---

[21] *Op. cit.*, pp. 178–179.

[22] E.g., the symbolization of the zodiac in some sacred architecture, of our bodily orientation in the picture plane, or of walking measure, a primitive measure of actual time, in music. But a study of such non-artistic symbolic functions would require a monograph.

work. Not the derivation of personages and situations, but of the rhythm of "felt life" that the poet puts upon them, seems to me to be of artistic importance: the essential comic feeling, which is the sentient aspect of organic unity, growth, and self-preservation.

The Mythos of Spring: Comedy*

Northrop Frye

Dramatic comedy, from which fictional comedy is mainly descended, has been remarkably tenacious of its structural principles and character types. Bernard Shaw remarked that a comic dramatist could get a reputation for daring originality by stealing his method from Molière and his characters from Dickens: if we were to read Menander and Aristophanes for Molière and Dickens the statement would be hardly less true, at least as a general principle. The earliest extant European comedy, Aristophanes' *The Acharnians*, contains the *miles gloriosus* or military braggart who is still going strong in Chaplin's *Great Dictator*; the Joxer Daly of O'Casey's *Juno and the Paycock* has the same character and dramatic function as the parasites of twenty-five hundred years ago, and the audiences of vaudeville, comic strips, and television programs still laugh at the jokes that were declared to be outworn at the opening of *The Frogs*.

The plot structure of Greek New Comedy, as transmitted by Plautus and Terence, in itself less a form than a formula, has become the basis for most comedy, especially in its more highly conventionalized dramatic form, down to our own day. It will be most convenient to work out the theory of comic construction from drama, using illustrations from fiction only incidentally. What normally happens is that a young man wants a young woman, that his desire is resisted by some opposition, usually paternal, and that near the end of the play some twist in the plot enables the hero to have his will. In this simple pattern there are several complex elements. In the first place, the movement of comedy is usually a movement from one kind of society to another. At the beginning of the play the obstructing characters are in charge of the play's society, and the audience recognizes that they are usurpers. At the end of the play the device in the plot that brings hero and heroine together causes a new society to crystallize around the hero, and the moment when this crystallization occurs is the point of resolution in the action, the comic discovery, *anagnorisis* or *cognitio*.

The appearance of this new society is frequently signalized by some kind of party or festive ritual, which either appears at the end of the play or is assumed to take place immediately afterward. Weddings are most common, and sometimes so many of them occur, as in the quadruple wedding at the end of *As You Like It*, that they suggest also the wholesale pairing off that takes place in a dance, which is another common conclusion, and the normal one for the masque. The banquet at the end of *The Taming of the Shrew* has an ancestry

* Northrop Frye, "The Mythos of Spring: Comedy," in *The Anatomy of Criticism* (Princeton University Press, 1957), pp. 163–186.

that goes back to Greek Middle Comedy; in Plautus the audience is sometimes jocosely invited to an imaginary banquet afterwards; Old Comedy, like the modern Christmas pantomine, was more generous, and occasionally threw bits of food to the audience. As the final society reached by comedy is the one that the audience has recognized all along to be the proper and desirable state of affairs, an act of communion with the audience is in order. Tragic actors expect to be applauded as well as comic ones, but nevertheless the word "plaudite" at the end of a Roman comedy, the invitation to the audience to form part of the comic society, would seem rather out of place at the end of a tragedy. The resolution of comedy comes, so to speak, from the audience's side of the stage; in a tragedy it comes from some mysterious world on the opposite side. In the movie, where darkness permits a more erotically oriented audience, the plot usually moves toward an act which, like death in Greek tragedy, takes place offstage, and is symbolized by a closing embrace.

The obstacles to the hero's desire, then, form the action of the comedy, and the overcoming of them the comic resolution. The obstacles are usually parental, hence comedy often turns on a clash between a son's and a father's will. Thus the comic dramatist as a rule writes for the younger men in his audience, and the older members of almost any society are apt to feel that comedy has something subversive about it. This is certainly one element in the social persecution of drama, which is not peculiar to Puritans or even Christians, as Terence in pagan Rome met much the same kind of social opposition that Ben Jonson did. There is one scene in Plautus where a son and father are making love to the same courtesan, and the son asks his father pointedly if he really does love mother. One has to see this scene against the background of Roman family life to understand its importance as psychological release. Even in Shakespeare there are startling outbreaks of baiting older men, and in contemporary movies the triumph of youth is so relentless that the moviemakers find some difficulty in getting anyone over the age of seventeen into their audiences.

The opponent to the hero's wishes, when not the father, is generally someone who partakes of the father's closer relation to established society: that is, a rival with less youth and more money. In Plautus and Terence he is usually either the pimp who owns the girl, or a wandering soldier with a supply of ready cash. The fury with which these characters are baited and exploded from the stage shows that they are father-surrogates, and even if they were not, they would still be usurpers, and their claim to possess the girl must be shown up as somehow fraudulent. They are, in short, impostors, and the extent to which they have real power implies some criticism of the society that allows them their power. In Plautus and Terence this criticism seldom goes beyond the immorality of brothels and professional harlots, but in Renaissance dramatists, including Jonson, there is some sharp observation of the rising power of money and the sort of ruling class it is building up.

The tendency of comedy is to include as many people as possible in its final society: the blocking characters are more often reconciled or converted than simply repudiated. Comedy often includes a scapegoat ritual of expulsion which gets rid of some irreconcilable character, but exposure and disgrace make for pathos, or even tragedy. *The Merchant of Venice* seems almost an experiment in coming as close as possible to upsetting the comic balance. If the dramatic role of Shylock is ever so slightly exaggerated, as it generally is when the leading actor of the company takes the part, it is upset, and the play becomes the tragedy of

the Jew of Venice with a comic epilogue. *Volpone* ends with a great bustle of
sentences to penal servitude and the galleys, and one feels that the deliverance of
society hardly needs so much hard labor; but then *Volpone* is exceptional in being a kind of comic imitation of a tragedy, with the point of Volpone's hybris
carefully marked.

The principle of conversion becomes clearer with characters whose chief
function is the amusing of the audience. The original *miles gloriosus* in Plautus
is a son of Jove and Venus who has killed an elephant with his fist and seven
thousand men in one day's fighting. In other words, he is trying to put on a good
show: the exuberance of his boasting helps to put the play over. The convention
says that the braggart must be exposed, ridiculed, swindled, and beaten. But
why should a professional dramatist, of all people, want so to harry a character
who is putting on a good show—*his* show at that? When we find Falstaff invited
to the final feast in *The Merry Wives*, Caliban reprieved, attempts made to mol-
lify Malvolio, and Angelo and Parolles allowed to live down their disgrace, we
are seeing a fundamental principle of comedy at work. The tendency of the
comic society to include rather than exclude is the reason for the traditional importance of the parasite, who has no business to be at the final festival but is nevertheless there. The word "grace," with all its Renaissance overtones from the
graceful courtier of Castiglione to the gracious God of Christianity, is a most important thematic word in Shakespearean comedy.

The action of comedy in moving from one social center to another is not unlike the action of a lawsuit, in which plaintiff and defendant construct different
versions of the same situation, one finally being judged as real and the other as illusory. This resemblance of the rhetoric of comedy to the rhetoric of jurispru-
dence has been recognized from earliest times. A little pamphlet called *Tractatus Coislinianus*, closely related to Aristotle's *Poetics*, which sets down all the
essential facts about comedy in about a page and a half, divides the *dianoia* of
comedy into two parts, opinion (*pistis*) and proof (*gnosis*). These correspond
roughly to the usurping and the desirable societies respectively. Proofs (i.e., the
means of bringing about the happier society) are subdivided into oaths, compacts, witnesses, ordeals (or tortures), and laws—in other words the five forms of
material proof in law cases listed in the *Rhetoric*. We notice how often the action
of a Shakespearean comedy begins with some absurd, cruel, or irrational law: the
law of killing Syracusans in the *Comedy of Errors*, the law of compulsory marriage in *A Midsummer Night's Dream*, the law that confirms Shylock's bond,
the attempts of Angelo to legislate people into righteousness, and the like, which
the action of the comedy then evades or breaks. Compacts are as a rule the con-
spiracies formed by the hero's society; witnesses, such as overhearers of conversations or people with special knowledge (like the hero's old nurse with her reten-
tive memory for birthmarks), are the commonest devices for bringing about the
comic discovery. Ordeals (*basanoi*) are usually tests or touchstones of the hero's
character: the Greek word also means touchstones, and seems to be echoed in
Shakespeare's Bassanio whose ordeal it is to make a judgment on the worth of
metals.

There are two ways of developing the form of comedy: one is to throw the
main emphasis on the blocking characters; the other is to throw it forward on the
scenes of discovery and reconciliation. One is the general tendency of comic irony, satire, realism, and studies of manners; the other is the tendency of Shakespearean and other types of romantic comedy. In the comedy of manners the

main ethical interest falls as a rule on the blocking characters. The technical hero and heroine are not often very interesting people: the *adulescentes* of Plautus and Terence are all alike, as hard to tell apart in the dark as Demetrius and Lysander, who may be parodies of them. Generally the hero's character has the neutrality that enables him to represent a wish-fulfilment. It is very different with the miserly or ferocious parent, the boastful or foppish rival, or the other characters who stand in the way of the action. In Molière we have a simple but fully tested formula in which the ethical interest is focussed on a single blocking character, a heavy father, a miser, a misanthrope, a hypocrite, or a hypochondriac. These are the figures that we remember, and the plays are usually named after them, but we can seldom remember all the Valentins and Angeliques who wriggle out of their clutches. In *The Merry Wives* the technical hero, a man named Fenton, has only a bit part, and this play has picked up a hint or two from Plautus's *Casina*, where the hero and heroine are not even brought on the stage at all. Fictional comedy, especially Dickens, often follows the same practice of grouping its interesting characters around a somewhat dullish pair of technical leads. Even Tom Jones, though far more fully realized, is still deliberately associated, as his commonplace name indicates, with the conventional and typical.

Comedy usually moves toward a happy ending, and the normal response of the audience to a happy ending is "this should be," which sounds like a moral judgement. So it is, except that it is not moral in the restricted sense, but social. Its opposite is not the villainous but the absurd, and comedy finds the virtues of Malvolio as absurd as the vices of Angelo. Molière's misanthrope, being committed to sincerity, which is a virtue, is morally in a strong position, but the audience soon realizes that his friend Philinte, who is ready to lie quite cheerfully in order to enable other people to preserve their self-respect, is the more genuinely sincere of the two. It is of course quite possible to have a moral comedy, but the result is often the kind of melodrama that we have described as comedy without humor, and which achieves its happy ending with a self-righteous tone that most comedy avoids. It is hardly possible to imagine a drama without conflict, and it is hardly possible to imagine a conflict without some kind of enmity. But just as love, including sexual love, is a very different thing from lust, so enmity is a very different thing from hatred. In tragedy, of course, enmity almost always includes hatred; comedy is different, and one feels that the social judgement against the absurd is closer to the comic norm than the moral judgement against the wicked.

The question then arises of what makes the blocking character absurd. Ben Jonson explained this by his theory of the "humor," the character dominated by what Pope calls a ruling passion. The humor's dramatic function is to express a state of what might be called ritual bondage. He is obsessed by his humor, and his function in the play is primarily to repeat his obsession. A sick man is not a humor, but a hypochondriac is, because, *qua* hypochondriac, he can never admit to good health, and can never do anything inconsistent with the role that he has prescribed for himself. A miser can do and say nothing that is not connected with the hiding of gold or saving of money. In *The Silent Woman*, Jonson's nearest approach to Molière's type of construction, the whole action recedes from the humor of Morose, whose determination to eliminate noise from his life produces so loquacious a comic action.

The principle of the humor is the principle that unincremental repetition, the literary imitation of ritual bondage, is funny. In a tragedy—*Oedipus Tyrannus* is the stock example—repetition leads logically to catastrophe. Repetition overdone or not going anywhere belongs to comedy, for laughter is partly a reflex, and like other reflexes it can be conditioned by a simple repeated pattern. In Synge's *Riders to the Sea* a mother, after losing her husband and five sons at sea, finally loses her last son, and the result is a very beautiful and moving play. But if it had been a full-length tragedy plodding glumly through the seven drownings one after another, the audience would have been helpless with unsympathetic laughter long before it was over. The principle of repetition as the basis of humor both in Jonson's sense and in ours is well known to the creators of comic strips, in which a character is established as a parasite, a glutton (often confined to one dish), or a shrew, and who begins to be funny after the point has been made every day for several months. Continuous comic radio programs, too, are much more amusing to habitués than to neophytes. The girth of Falstaff and the hallucinations of Quixote are based on much the same comic laws. Mr. E. M. Forster speaks with disdain of Dickens's Mrs. Micawber, who never says anything except that she will never desert Mr. Micawber: a strong contrast is marked here between the refined writer too finicky for popular formulas, and the major one who exploits them ruthlessly.

The humor in comedy is usually someone with a good deal of social prestige and power, who is able to force much of the play's society into line with his obsession. Thus the humor is intimately connected with the theme of the absurd or irrational law that the action of comedy moves toward breaking. It is significant that the central character of our earliest humor comedy, *The Wasps*, is obsessed by law cases: Shylock, too, unites a craving for the law with the humor of revenge. Often the absurd law appears as a whim of a bemused tyrant whose will is law, like Leontes or the humorous Duke Frederick in Shakespeare, who makes some arbitrary decision or rash promise: here law is replaced by "oath," also mentioned in the *Tractatus*. Or it may take the form of a sham Utopia, a society of ritual bondage constructed by an act of humorous or pedantic will, like the academic retreat in *Love's Labor's Lost*. This theme is also as old as Aristophanes, whose parodies of Platonic social schemes in *The Birds* and *Ecclesiazusae* deal with it.

The society emerging at the conclusion of comedy represents, by contrast, a kind of moral norm, or pragmatically free society. Its ideals are seldom defined or formulated: definition and formulation belong to the humors, who want predictable activity. We are simply given to understand that the newly-married couple will live happily ever after, or that at any rate they will get along in a relatively unhumorous and clear-sighted manner. That is one reason why the character of the successful hero is so often left undeveloped: his real life begins at the end of the play, and we have to believe him to be potentially a more interesting character than he appears to be. In Terence's *Adelphoi*, Demea, a harsh father, is contrasted with his brother Micio, who is indulgent. Micio being more liberal, he leads the way to the comic resolution, and converts Demea, but then Demea points out the indolence inspiring a good deal of Micio's liberality, and releases him from a complementary humorous bondage.

Thus the movement from *pistis* to *gnosis*, from a society controlled by habit, ritual bondage, arbitrary law and the older characters to a society controlled by youth and pragmatic freedom is fundamentally, as the Greek words suggest, a movement from illusion to reality. Illusion is whatever is fixed or definable, and reality is best understood as its negation: whatever reality is, it's not *that*. Hence the importance of the theme of creating and dispelling illusion in comedy: the illusions caused by disguise, obsession, hypocrisy, or unknown parentage.

The comic ending is generally manipulated by a twist in the plot. In Roman comedy the heroine, who is usually a slave or a courtesan, turns out to be the daughter of somebody respectable, so that the hero can marry her without loss of face. The *cognitio* in comedy, in which the characters find out who their relatives are, and who is left of the opposite sex not a relative, and hence available for marriage, is one of the features of comedy that have never changed much: *The Confidential Clerk* indicates that it still holds the attention of dramatists. There is a brilliant parody of a *cognitio* at the end of *Major Barbara* (the fact that the hero of this play is a professor of Greek perhaps indicates an unusual affinity to the conventions of Euripides and Menander), where Undershaft is enabled to break the rule that he cannot appoint his son-in-law as successor by the fact that the son-in-law's own father married his deceased wife's sister in Australia, so that the son-in-law is his own first cousin as well as himself. It sounds complicated, but the plots of comedy often are complicated because there is something inherently absurd about complications. As the main character interest in comedy is so often focussed on the defeated characters, comedy regularly illustrates a victory of arbitrary plot over consistency of character. Thus, in striking contrast to tragedy, there can hardly be such a thing as inevitable comedy, as far as the action of the individual play is concerned. That is, we may know that the convention of comedy will make some kind of happy ending inevitable, but still for each play the dramatist must produce a distinctive "gimmick" or "weenie," to use two disrespectful Hollywood synonyms for *anagnorisis*. Happy endings do not impress us as true, but as desirable, and they are brought about by manipulation. The watcher of death and tragedy has nothing to do but sit and wait for the inevitable end; but something gets born at the end of comedy, and the watcher of birth is a member of a busy society.

The manipulation of plot does not always involve metamorphosis of character, but there is no violation of comic decorum when it does. Unlikely conversions, miraculous transformations, and providential assistance are inseparable from comedy. Further, whatever emerges is supposed to be there for good: if the curmudgeon becomes lovable, we understand that he will not immediately relapse again into his ritual habit. Civilizations which stress the desirable rather than the real, and the religious as opposed to the scientific perspective, think of drama almost entirely in terms of comedy. In the classical drama of India, we are told, the tragic ending was regarded as bad taste, much as the manipulated endings of comedy are regarded as bad taste by novelists interested in ironic realism.

The total *mythos* of comedy, only a small part of which is ordinarily presented, has regularly what in music is called a ternary form: the hero's society rebels against the society of the *senex* and triumphs, but the hero's society is a Saturnalia, a reversal of social standards which recalls a golden age in the past before the main action of the play begins. Thus we have a stable and harmonious order disrupted by folly, obsession, forgetfulness, "pride and prejudice," or events not understood by the characters themselves, and then restored. Often there is a benevolent grandfather, so to speak, who overrules the action set up by the blocking humor and so links the first and third parts. An example is Mr. Burchell, the disguised uncle of the wicked squire, in *The Vicar of Wakefield*. A very long play, such as the Indian *Sakuntala*, may present all three phases; a very intricate one, such as many of Menander's evidently were, may indicate their outlines. But of course very often the first phase is not given at all: the audience simply understands an ideal state of affairs which it knows to be better than what is revealed in the play, and which it recognizes as like that to which the action leads. This ternary action is, ritually, like a contest of summer and winter in which winter occupies the middle action; psychologically, it is like the removal of a neurosis or blocking point and the restoring of an unbroken current of energy and memory. The Jonsonian masque, with the antimasque in the middle, gives a highly conventionalized or "abstract" version of it.

We pass now to the typical characters of comedy. In drama, characterization depends on function; what a character is follows from what he has to do in the play. Dramatic function in its turn depends on the structure of the play; the character has certain things to do because the play has such and such a shape. The structure of the play in its turn depends on the category of the play; if it is a comedy, its structure will require a comic resolution and a prevailing comic mood. Hence when we speak of typical characters, we are not trying to reduce lifelike characters to stock types, though we certainly are suggesting that the sentimental notion of an antithesis between the lifelike character and the stock type is a vulgar error. All lifelike characters, whether in drama or fiction, owe their consistency to the appropriateness of the stock type which belongs to their dramatic function. That stock type is not the character but it is as necessary to the character as a skeleton is to the actor who plays it.

With regard to the characterization of comedy, the *Tractatus* lists three types of comic characters: the *alazons* or imposters, the *eirons* or self-deprecators, and the buffoons (*bomolochoi*). This list is closely related to a passage in the *Ethics* which contrasts the first two, and then goes on to contrast the buffoon with a character whom Aristotle calls *agroikos* or churlish, literally rustic. We may reasonably accept the churl as a fourth character type, and so we have two opposed pairs. The contest of *eiron* and *alazon* forms the basis of the comic action, and the buffoon and the churl polarize the comic mood.

We have previously dealt with the terms *eiron* and *alazon*. The humorous blocking characters of comedy are nearly always impostors, though it is more frequently a lack of self-knowledge than simple hypocrisy that characterizes them. The multitudes of comic scenes in which one character complacently soliloquizes while another makes sarcastic asides to the audience show the contest of *eiron* and *alazon* in its purest form, and show too that the audience is sympathetic to the *eiron* side. Central to the *alazon* group is the *senex iratus* or heavy father, who with his rages and threats, his obsessions and his gullibility, seems closely related to some of the demonic characters of romance, such as Polyphemus. Occasionally a character may have the dramatic function of such a figure without his characteristics: an example is Squire Allworthy in *Tom Jones*, who as far as the plot is concerned behaves almost as stupidly as Squire Western. Of heavy-father surrogates, the *miles gloriosus* has been mentioned: his popularity is largely due to the fact that he is a man of words rather than deeds, and is consequently far more useful to a practising dramatist than any tight-lipped hero could ever be. The pedant, in Renaissance comedy often a student of the occult sciences, the fop or coxcomb, and similar humors, require no comment. The female *alazon* is rare: Katharina the shrew represents to some extent a female *miles gloriosus*, and the *précieuse ridicule* a female pedant, but the "menace" or siren who gets in the way of the true heroine is more often found as a sinister figure of melodrama or romance than as a ridiculous figure in comedy.

The *eiron* figures need a little more attention. Central to this group is the hero, who is an *eiron* figure because, as explained, the dramatist tends to play him down and make him rather neutral and unformed in character. Next in importance is the heroine, also often played down: in Old Comedy, when a girl accompanies a male hero in his triumph, she is generally a stage prop, a *muta persona* not previously introduced. A more difficult form of *cognitio* is achieved when the heroine disguises herself or through some other device brings about the comic resolution, so that the person whom the hero is seeking turns out to be the person who has sought him. The fondness of Shakespeare for this "she stoops to conquer" theme needs only to be mentioned here, as it belongs more naturally to the *mythos* of romance.

Another central *eiron* figure is the type entrusted with hatching the schemes which bring about the hero's victory. This character in Roman comedy is almost always a tricky slave (*dolosus servus*), and in Renaissance comedy he becomes the scheming valet who is so frequent in Continental plays, and in Spanish drama is called the *gracioso*. Modern audiences are most familiar with him in Figaro and in the Leporello of *Don Giovanni*. Through such intermediate nineteenth-century figures as Micawber and the Touchwood of Scott's *St. Ronan's Well*, who, like the gracioso, have buffoon affiliations, he evolves into the amateur detective of modern fiction. The Jeeves of P. G. Wodehouse is a more direct descendant. Female confidantes of the same general family are often brought in to oil the machinery of the well-made play. Elizabethan comedy had another type of trickster, represented by the Matthew Merrygreek of *Ralph Roister Doister*, who is generally said to be developed from the vice or iniquity of the morality plays: as usual, the analogy is sound enough, whatever historians decide about origins. The vice, to give him that name, is very useful to a comic dramatist because he acts from pure love of mischief, and can set a comic action going with the minimum of motivation. The vice may be as light-hearted as Puck or as malignant as Don John in *Much Ado*, but as a rule the vice's activity is, in spite of his name, benevolent. One of the tricky slaves in Plautus, in a soliloquy, boasts that he is the *architectus* of the comic action: such a character carries out the will of the author to reach a happy ending. He is in fact the spirit of comedy, and the two clearest examples of the type in Shakespeare, Puck and Ariel, are both spiritual beings. The tricky slave often has his own freedom in mind as the reward of his exertions: Ariel's longing for release is in the same tradition.

The role of the vice includes a great deal of disguising, and the type may often be recognized by disguise. A good example is the Brainworm of Jonson's *Every Man in His Humour*, who calls the action of the play the day of his metamorphoses. Similarly Ariel has to surmount the difficult stage direction of "Enter invisible." The vice is combined with the hero whenever the latter is a cheeky, improvident young man who hatches his own schemes and cheats his rich father or uncle into giving him his patrimony along with the girl.

Another *eiron* type has not been much noticed. This is a character, generally an older man, who begins the action of the play by withdrawing from it, and ends the play by returning. He is often a father with the motive of seeing what his son will do. The action of *Every Man in His Humour* is set going in this way by Knowell Senior. The disappearance and return of Lovewit, the owner of the house which is the scene of *The Alchemist*, has the same dramatic function, though the characterization is different. The clearest Shakespearean example is the Duke in *Measure for Measure*, but Shakespeare is more addicted to the type than might appear at first glance. In Shakespeare the vice is rarely the real *architectus*: Puck and Ariel both act under orders from an older man, if one may call Oberon a man for the moment. In *The Tempest* Shakespeare returns to a comic action established by Aristophanes, in which an older man, instead of retiring from the action, builds it up the stage. When the heroine takes the vice role in Shakespeare, she is often significantly related to her father, even when the father is not in the play at all, like the father of Helena, who gives her his medical knowledge, or the father of Portia, who arranges the scheme of the caskets. A more conventionally treated example of the same benevolent Prospero figure turned up recently in the psychiatrist of *The Cocktail Party*, and one may compare the mysterious alchemist who is the father of the heroine of *The Lady's Not for Burning*. The formula is not confined to comedy: Polonius, who shows so many of the disadvantages of a literary education, attempts the role of a retreating paternal *eiron* three times, once too often. *Hamlet* and *King Lear* contain subplots which are ironic versions of stock comic themes, Gloucester's story being the regular comedy theme of the gullible *senex* swindled by a clever and unprincipled son.

We pass now to the buffoon types, those whose function it is to increase the mood of festivity rather than to contribute to the plot. Renaissance comedy, unlike Roman comedy, had a great variety of such characters, professional fools, clowns, pages, singers, and incidental characters with established comic habits like malapropism or foreign accents. The oldest buffoon of this incidental nature is the parasite, who may be given something to do, as Jonson gives Mosca the role of a vice in *Volpone*, but who, *qua* parasite, does nothing but entertain the audience by talking about his appetite. He derives chiefly from Greek Middle Comedy, which appears to have been very full of food, and where he was, not unnaturally, closely associated with another established buffoon type, the cook, a conventional figure who breaks into comedies to bustle and order about and make long speeches about the mysteries of cooking. In the role of cook the buffoon or entertainer appears, not simply as a gratuitous addition like the parasite, but as something more like a master of ceremonies, a center for the comic mood. There is no cook in Shakespeare, though there is a superb description of one in the *Comedy of Errors*, but a similar role is often attached to a jovial and loquacious host, like the "mad host" of *The Merry Wives* or the Simon Eyre of *The Shoemakers Holiday*. In Middleton's *A Trick to Catch the Old One* the mad host type is combined with the vice. In Falstaff and Sir Toby Belch we can see the affinities of the buffoon or entertainer type both with the parasite and with the master of revels. If we study this entertainer or host role carefully we shall soon realize that it is a development of what in Aristophanic comedy is represented by the chorus, and which in its turn goes back to the *komos* or revel from which comedy is said to be descended.

Finally, there is a fourth group to which we have assigned the word *agroikos*, and which usually means either churlish or rustic, depending on the context. This type may also be extended to cover the Elizabethan gull and what in vaudeville used to be called the straight man, the solemn or inarticulate character who allows the humor to bounce off him, so to speak. We find churls in the miserly, snobbish, or priggish characters whose role is that of the refuser of festivity, the killjoy who tries to stop the fun, or, like Malvolio, locks up the food and drink instead of dispensing it. The melancholy Jacques of *As You Like It*, who walks out on the final festivities, is closely related. In the sulky and self-centered Bertam of *All's Well* there is a most unusual and ingenious combination of this type with the hero. More often, however, the churl belongs to the *alazon* group, all miserly old men in comedies, including Shylock, being churls. In *The Tempest* Caliban has much the same relation to the churlish type that Ariel has to the vice or tricky slave. But often, where the mood is more light-hearted, we may translate *agroikos* simply by rustic, as with the innumerable country squires and similar characters who provide amusement in the urban setting of drama. Such types do not refuse the mood of festivity, but they mark the extent of its range. In a pastoral comedy the idealized virtues of rural life may be represented by a simple man who speaks for the pastoral ideal, like Corin in *As You Like It*. Corin has the same *agroikos* role as the "rube" or "hayseed" of more citified comedies, but the moral attitude to the role is reversed. Again we notice the principle that dramatic structure is a permanent and moral attitude a variable factor in literature.

In a very ironic comedy a different type of character may play the role of the refuser of festivity. The more ironic the comedy, the more absurd the society, and an absurd society may be condemned by, or at least contrasted with, a character that we may call the plain dealer, an outspoken advocate of a kind of moral norm who has the sympathy of the audience. Wycherley's Manly, though he provides the name for the type, is not a particularly good example of it: a much better one is the Cléante of *Tartuffe*. Such a character is appropriate when the tone is ironic enough to get the audience confused about its sense of the social norm: he corresponds roughly to the chorus in a tragedy, which is there for a similar reason. When the tone deepens from the ironic to the bitter, the plain dealer may become a malcontent or railer, who may be morally superior to his society, as he is to some extent in Marston's play of that name, but who may also be too motivated by envy to be much more than another aspect of his society's evil, like Thersites, or to some extent Apemantus.

In tragedy, pity and fear, the emotions of moral attraction and repulsion, are raised and cast out. Comedy seems to make a more functional use of the social, even the moral judgement, than tragedy, yet comedy seems to raise the corresponding emotions, which are sympathy and ridicule, and cast them out in the same way. Comedy ranges from the most savage irony to the most dreamy wishfulfilment romance, but its structural patterns and characterization are much the same throughout its range. This principle of the uniformity of comic structure through a variety of attitudes is clear in Aristophanes. Aristophanes is the most personal of writers, and his opinions on every subject are written all over his plays. We know that he wanted peace with Sparta and that he hated Cleon, so when his comedy depicts the attaining of peace and the defeat of Cleon we know that he approved and wanted his audience to approve. But in *Ecclesiazusae* a band of women in disguise railroad a communistic scheme through the Assembly which is a horrid parody of a Platonic republic, and proceed to inaugurate its sexual communism with some astonishing improvements. Presumably Aristophanes did not altogether endorse this, yet the comedy follows the same pattern and the same resolution. In *The Birds* the Peisthetairos who defies Zeus and blocks out Olympus with his Cloud-Cuckoo-Land is accorded the same triumph that is given to the Trygaois of the *Peace* who flies to heaven and brings a golden age back to Athens.

Let us look now at a variety of comic structures between the extremes of irony and romance. As comedy blends into irony and satire at one end and into romance at the other, if there are different phases or types of comic structure, some of them will be closely parallel to some of the types of irony and of romance. A somewhat forbidding piece of symmetry turns up in our argument at this point, which seems to have some literary analogy to the circle of fifths in music. I recognize six phases of each *mythos*, three being parallel to the phases of a neighboring *mythos*. The first three phases of comedy are parallel to the first three phases of irony and satire, and the second three to the second three of romance. The distinction between an ironic comedy and a comic satire, or between a romantic comedy and a comic romance, is tenuous, but not quite a distinction without a difference.

The first or most ironic phase of comedy is, naturally, the one in which a humorous society triumphs or remains undefeated. A good example of a comedy of this type is *The Alchemist*, in which the returning *eiron* Lovewit joins the rascals, and the plain dealer Surly is made a fool of. In *The Beggar's Opera* there is a similar twist to the ending: the (projected) author feels that the hanging of the hero is a comic ending, but is informed by the manager that the audience's sense of comic decorum demands a reprieve, whatever Macheath's moral status. This phase of comedy presents what Renaissance critics called *speculum consuetudinis*, the say of the world, *così fan tutte*. A more intense irony is achieved when the humorous society simply disintegrates without anything taking its place, as in *Heartbreak House* and frequently in Chekhov.

We notice in ironic comedy that the demonic world is never far away. The rages of the *senex iratus* in Roman comedy are directed mainly at the tricky slave, who is threatened with the mill, with being flogged to death, with crucifixion, with having his head dipped in tar and set on fire, and the like, all penalties that could be and were exacted from slaves in life. An epilogue in Plautus informs us that the slave actor who has blown up in his lines will now be flogged; in one of the Menander fragments a slave is tied up and burned with a torch on the stage. One sometimes gets the impression that the audience of Plautus and Terence would have guffawed uproariously all through the Passion. We may ascribe this to the brutality of a slave society, but then we remember that boiling oil and burying alive ("such a *stuffy* death") turn up in *The Mikado*. Two lively comedies of the modern stage are *The Cocktail Party* and *The Lady's Not for Burning*, but the cross appears in the background of the one and the stake in the background of the other. Shylock's knife and Angelo's gallows appear in Shakespeare: in *Measure for Measure* every male character is at one time or another threatened with death. The action of comedy moves toward a deliverance from something which, if absurd, is by no means invariably harmless. We notice too how frequently a comic dramatist tries to bring his action as close to a catastrophic overthrow of the hero as he can get it, and then reverses the action as quickly as possible. The evading or breaking of a cruel law is often a very narrow squeeze. The intervention of the king at the end of *Tartuffe* is deliberately arbitrary: there is nothing in the action of the play itself to prevent Tartuffe's triumph. Tom Jones in the final book, accused of murder, incest, debt, and double-dealing, cast off by friends, guardian, and sweetheart, is a woeful figure indeed before all these turn into illusions. Any reader can think of many comedies in which the fear of death, sometimes a hideous death, hangs over the central character to the end, and is dispelled so quickly that one has almost the sense of awakening from nightmare.

Sometimes the redeeming agent actually is divine, like Diana in *Pericles;* in *Tartuffe* it is the king, who is conceived as a part of the audience and the incarnation of its will. An extraordinary number of comic stories, both in drama and fiction, seem to approach a potentially tragic crisis near the end, a feature that I may call the "point of ritual death"—a clumsy expression that I would gladly surrender for a better one. It is a feature not often noticed by critics, but when it is present it is as unmistakably present as a stretto in a fugue, which it somewhat resembles. In Smollett's *Humphry Clinker* (I select this because no one will suspect Smollett of deliberate mythopoeia but only of following convention, at least as far as his plot is concerned), the main characters are nearly drowned in an accident with an upset carriage; they are then taken to a nearby house to dry off, and a *cognitio* takes place, in the course of which their family relationships are regrouped, secrets of birth brought to light, and names changed. Similar points of ritual death may be marked in almost any story that imprisons the hero or gives the heroine a nearly mortal illness before an eventually happy ending.

Sometimes the point of ritual death is vestigial, not an element in the plot but a mere change of tone. Everyone will have noted in comic actions, even in very trivial movies and magazine stories, a point near the end at which the tone suddenly becomes serious, sentimental, or ominous of potential catastrophe. In Aldous Huxley's *Chrome Yellow*, the hero Denis comes to a point of self-evaluation in which suicide nearly suggests itself: in most of Huxley's later books some violent action, generally suicidal, occurs at the corresponding point. In *Mrs. Dalloway* the actual suicide of Septimus becomes a point of ritual death for the heroine in the middle of her party. There are also some interesting Shakespearean variations of the device: a clown, for instance, will make a speech near the end in which the buffoon's mask suddenly falls off and we look straight into the face of a beaten and ridiculed slave. Examples are the speech of Dromio of Ephesus beginning "I am an ass indeed" in the *Comedy of Errors*, and the speech of the Clown in *All's Well* beginning "I am a woodland fellow."

The second phase of comedy, in its simplest form, is a comedy in which the hero does not transform a humorous society but simply escapes or runs away from it, leaving its structure as it was before. A more complex irony in this phase is achieved when a society is constructed by or around a hero, but proves not sufficiently real or strong to impose itself. In this situation the hero is usually himself at least partly a comic humor or mental runaway, and we have either a hero's illusion thwarted by a superior reality or a clash of two illusions. This is the quixotic phase of comedy, a difficult phase for drama, though *The Wild Duck* is a fairly pure example of it, and in drama it usually appears as a subordinate theme of another phase. Thus in *The Alchemist* Sir Epicure Mammon's dream of what he will do with the philosopher's stone is, like Quixote's, a gigantic dream, and makes him an ironic parody of Faustus (who is mentioned in the play), in the same way the Quixote is an ironic parody of Amadis and Lancelot. When the tone is more light-hearted, the comic resolution may be strong enough to sweep over all quixotic illusions. In *Huckleberry Finn* the main theme is one of the oldest in comedy, the freeing of a slave, and the *cognitio* tells us that Jim had already been set free before his escape was bungled by Tom Sawyer's pedantries. Because of its unrivalled opportunities for double-edged irony, this phase is a favorite of Henry James: perhaps his most searching study of it is *The Sacred Fount*, where the hero is an ironic parody of a Prospero figure creating another society out of the one in front of him.

The third phase of comedy is the normal one that we have been discussing, in which a *senex iratus* or other humor gives way to a young man's desires. The sense of the comic norm is so strong that when Shakespeare, by way of experiment, tried to reverse the pattern in *All's Well*, in having two older people force Bertram to marry Helena, the result has been an unpopular "problem" play, with a suggestion of something sinister about it. We have noted that the *cognitio* of comedy is much concerned with straightening out the details of the new society, with distinguishing brides from sisters and parents from foster-parents. The fact that the son and father are so often in conflict means that they are frequently rivals for the same girl, and the psychological alliance of the hero's bride and the mother is often expressed or implied. The occasional "naughtiness" of comedy, as in the Restoration period, has much to do, not only with marital infidelity, but with a kind of comic Oedipus situation in which the hero replaces his father as a lover. In Congreve's *Love for Love* there are two Oedipus themes in counterpoint: the hero cheats his father out of the heroine, and his best friend violates the wife of an impotent old man who is the heroine's guardian. A theme which would be recognized in real life as a form of infantile regression, the hero pretending to be impotent in order to gain admission to the women's quarters, is employed in Wycherley's *Country Wife*, where it is taken from Terence's *Eunuchus*.

The possibilities of incestuous combinations form one of the minor themes of comedy. The repellent older woman offered to Figaro in marriage turns out to be his mother, and the fear of violating a mother also occurs in *Tom Jones*. When in *Ghosts* and *Little Eyolf* Ibsen employed the old chestnut about the object of the hero's affections being his sister (a theme as old as Menander), his startled hearers took it for a portent of social revolution. In Shakespeare the recurring and somewhat mysterious father-daughter relationship already alluded to appears in its incestuous form at the beginning of *Pericles*, where it forms the demonic antithesis of the hero's union with his wife and daughter at the end. The presiding genius of comedy is Eros, and Eros has to adapt himself to the moral facts of society: Oedipus and incest themes indicate that erotic attachments have in their undisplaced or mythical origin a much greater versatility.

Ambivalent attitudes naturally result, and ambivalence is apparently the main reason for the curious feature of doubled characters which runs all through the history of comedy. In Roman comedy there is often a pair of young men, and consequently a pair of young women, of which one is often related to one of the men and exogamous to the other. The doubling of the *senex* figure sometimes gives us a heavy father for both the hero and the heroine, as in *The Winter's Tale*, sometimes a heavy father and benevolent uncle, as in Terence's *Adelphoi* and in *Tartuffe*, and so on. The action of comedy, like the action of the Christian Bible, moves from law to liberty. In the law there is an element of ritual bondage which is abolished, an element of habit or convention which is fulfilled. The intolerable qualities of the *senex* represent the former and compromise with him the latter in the evolution of the comic *nomos*.

With the fourth phase of comedy we begin to move out of the world of experience into the ideal world of innocence and romance. We said that normally the happier society established at the end of the comedy is left undefined, in contrast to the ritual bondage of the humors. But it is also possible for a comedy to present its action on two social planes, of which one is preferred and consequently in some measure idealized. At the beginning of Plato's *Republic* we have a sharp contrast between the *alazon* Thrasymachus and the ironic Socrates. The dialogue could have been stopped there, as several of Plato's dialogues do, with a negative victory over a humor and the kind of society he suggests. But in the *Republic* the rest of the company, including Thrasymachus, follow Socrates inside Socrates's head, so to speak, and contemplate there the pattern of the just state. In Aristophanes the comic action is often ironic, but in *The Acharnians* we have a comedy in which a hero with the signficant name of Dicaeopolis (righteous city or citizen) makes a private peace with Sparta, celebrates the peaceful festival of Dionysos with his family, and sets up the pattern of a temperate social order on the stage, where it remains throughout the play, cranks, bigots, sharpers, and scoundrels all being beaten away from it. One of the typical comic actions is at least clearly portrayed in our earliest comedy as it has ever been since.

Shakespeare's type of romantic comedy follows a tradition established by Peele and developed by Greene and Lyly, which has affinities with the medieval tradition of the seasonal ritual-play. We may call it the drama of the green world, its plot being assimilated to the ritual theme of the triumph of life and love over the waste land. In *The Two Gentlemen of Verona* the hero Valentine becomes captain of a band of outlaws in a forest and becomes converted. Thus the action of the comedy begins in a world represented as a normal world, moves into the green world, goes into a metamorphosis there in which the comic resolution is achieved, and returns to the normal world. The forest in this play is the embryonic form of the fairy world of *A Midsummer Night's Dream*, the Forest of Arden in *As You Like It*, Windsor Forest in *The Merry Wives*, and the pastoral world of the mythical sea-coasted Bohemia in *The Winter's Tale*. In all these comedies there is the same rhythmic movement from normal world to green world and back again. In *The Merchant of Venice* the second world takes the form of Portia's mysterious house in Belmont, with its magic caskets and the wonderful cosmological harmonies that proceed from it in the fifth act. We notice too that this second world is absent from the more ironic comedies *All's Well* and *Measure for Measure*.

The green world charges the comedies with the symbolism of the victory of summer over winter, as is explicit in *Love's Labor's Lost*, where the comic contest takes the form of the medieval debate of winter and spring at the end. In *The Merry Wives* there is an elaborate ritual of the defeat of winter known to folklorists as "carrying out Death," of which Falstaff is the victim; and Falstaff must have felt that, after being thrown into the water, dressed up as a witch and beaten out of a house with curses, and finally supplied with a beast's head and singed with candles, he had done about all that could reasonably be asked of any fertility spirit.

In the rituals and myths the earth that produces the rebirth is generally a female figure, and the death and revival, or disappearance and withdrawal, of human figures in romantic comedy generally involves the heroine. The fact that the heroine often brings about the comic resolution by disguising herself as a boy is familiar enough. The treatment of Hero in *Much Ado*, of Helena in *All's Well*, of Thaisa in *Pericles*, of Fidele in *Cymbeline*, of Hermione in *The Winter's Tale*, shows the repetition of a device in which progressively less care is taken of plausibility and in which in consequence the mythical outline of a Proserpine figure becomes progressively clearer. These are Shakespearean examples of the comic theme of ritual assault on a central female figure, a theme which stretches from Menander to contemporary soap operas. Many of Menander's plays have titles which are feminine participles indicating the particular indignity the heroine suffers in them, and the working formula of the soap opera is said to be to "put the heroine behind the eight-ball and keep her there." Treatments of the theme may be as light-hearted as *The Rape of the Lock* or as doggedly persistent as *Pamela*. However, the theme of rebirth is not invariably feminine in context: the rejuvenation of the *senex* in Aristophanes' *The Knights*, and a similar theme in *All's Well* based on the folklore motif of the healing of the impotent king, come readily to mind.

The green world has analogies, not only to the fertile world of ritual, but to the dream world that we create out of our own desires. This dream world collides with the stumbling and blinded follies of the world of experience, of Theseus' Athens with its idiotic marriage law, of Duke Frederick and his melancholy tyranny, of Leontes and his mad jealousy, of the Court Party with their plots and intrigues, and yet proves strong enough to impose the form of desire on it. Thus Shakespearean comedy illustrates, as clearly as any *mythos* we have, the archetypal function of literature in visualizing the world of desire, not as an escape from "reality," but as the genuine form of the world that human life tries to imitate.

In the fifth phase of comedy, some of the themes of which we have already anticipated, we move into a world that is still more romantic, less Utopian and more Arcadian, less festive and more pensive, where the comic ending is less a matter of the way the plot turns out than of the perspective of the audience. When we compare the Shakespearean fourth-phase comedies with the late fifth-phase "romances," we notice how much more serious an action is appropriate to the latter: they do not avoid tragedies but contain them. The action seems to be not only a movement from a "winter's tale" to spring, but from a lower world of confusion to an upper world of order. The closing scene of *The Winter's Tale* makes us think, not simply of a cyclical movement from tragedy and absence to happiness and return, but of bodily metamorphosis and a transformation from one kind of life to another. The materials of the *cognitio* of *Pericles* or *The Winter's Tale* are so stock that they would be "hooted at like an old tale," yet they seem both far-fetched and inevitably right, outraging reality and at the same time introducing us to a world of childlike innocence which has always made more sense than reality.

In this phase the reader or audience feels raised above the action, in the situation of which Christopher Sly is an ironic parody. The plotting of Cleon and Dionyza in *Pericles*, or of the Court Party in *The Tempest*, we look down on as generic or typical human behavior: the action, or at least the tragic implication of the action, is presented as though it were a play within a play that we can see in all dimensions at once. We see the action, in short, from the point of view of a higher and better ordered world. And as the forest in Shakespeare is the usual symbol for the dream world in conflict with and imposing its form on experience, so the usual symbol for the lower or chaotic world is the sea, from which the cast, or an important part of it, is saved. The group of "sea" comedies includes *A Comedy of Errors, Twelfth Night, Pericles,* and *The Tempest*. *A Comedy of Errors*, though based on a Plautine original, is much closer to the world of Apuleius than to that of Plautus in its imagery, and the main action, moving from shipwreck and separation to reunion in a temple in Ephesus, is repeated in the much later play of *Pericles*. And just as the second world is absent from the two "problem" comedies, so in two of the "sea" group, *Twelfth Night* and *The Tempest*, the entire action takes place in the second world. In *Measure for Measure* the Duke disappears from the action and returns at the end; *The Tempest* seems to present the same type of action inside out, as the entire cast follows Prospero into his retreat, and is shaped into a new social order there.

These five phases of comedy may be seen as a sequence of stages in the life of a redeemed society. Purely ironic comedy exhibits this society in its infancy, swaddled and smothered by the society it should replace. Quixotic comedy exhibits it in adolescence, still too ignorant of the ways of the world to impose itself. In the third phase it comes to maturity and triumphs; in the fourth it is already mature and established. In the fifth it is part of a settled order which has been there from the beginning, an order which takes on an increasingly religious cast and seems to be drawing away from human experience altogether. At this point the undisplaced *commedia*, the vision of Dante's *Paradiso*, moves out of our circle of *mythoi* into the apocalyptic or abstract mythical world above it. At this point we realize that the crudest of Plautine comedy-formulas has much the same *structure* as the central Christian myth itself, with its divine son appeasing the wrath of a father and redeeming what is at once a society and a bride.

At this point too comedy proper enters its final or sixth phase, the phase of the collapse and disintegration of the comic society. In this phase the social units of comedy become small and esoteric, or even confined to a single individual. Secret and sheltered places, forests in moonlight, secluded valleys, and happy islands become more prominent, as does the *penseroso* mood of romance, the love of the occult and the marvellous, the sense of individual detachment from routine existence. In this kind of comedy we have finally left the world of wit and the awakened critical intelligence for the opposite pole, an oracular solemnity which, if we surrender uncritically to it, will provide a delightful *frisson*. This is the world of ghost stories, thrillers, and Gothic romances, and, on a more sophisticated level, the kind of imaginative withdrawal portrayed in Huysmans' *À Rebours*. The somberness of Des Esseintes' surroundings has nothing to do with tragedy: Des Esseintes is a dillettante trying to amuse himself. The comic society has run the full course from infancy to death, and in its last phase myths closely connected psychologically with a return to the womb are appropriate.

Comedy and Laughter*

Benjamin Lehmann

The student of literature, reviewing what has been written about comedy, may well be dismayed. For what has been written about the subject is, except for incidental insights, not about comedy. It is about satire. There are indeed studies of individual comedies, of comic devices, of a single writer's practices, and of comedy in a period or in a tradition. But these also more or less involve themselves, without due distinction of terms, with satire. And with an incidental exception or two when a general view of comedy is undertaken, attention is fixed upon the ludicrous, the absurd, the ridiculous. Laughter is said to be provoked by these human manifestations. The laughter, it is said, is corrective; we are invited to believe that the chief end of comedy is to reform manners and dispositions. Laughter itself has been inquired into; its bases in physiology, in psychology, and in group reaction have been explored, not without illumination. The illumination falls, however, not on comedy; it is shed on satire and on the comic, those fragments of action and utterance which beget the flash of a laugh. It does not fall on the work of literary art all consent to call comedy, whether for audiences in a theater or for readers by a fireside.

Yet the literary mode called comedy is an ancient one, and in our time of remarkable vitality. Epic, we often hear, is no longer possible; lyric, we are told, is now for a special audience; of tragedy, it is said, the essentials no longer exist in our world view. Comedy prospers. We may set aside as childish the notion that the age seeks merely to be amused; it seeks recreation, an honorable seeking which the arts are intended to foster. In design and color, in tone and implication, comedy seems now even more than in other times to meet a need, to correspond to a primary and universal intuition of life and the world. Is it not possible to examine the comedies, to discover that intuition of life and the world which so persistently captivates the human spirit? The incongruities and all the rest of which the critics speak are in the service of a vision of reality the average man takes daily for granted and delights to see illustrated and affirmed. In the service of that vision are also the mistaken identities, disguises, the eavesdropping, the non-sequiturs, the famous mechanical incrustation of vitality; even the wisecrack and the pratfall, for which the average man invented words.

At the outset, we must observe that though we laugh at actions and utterances in comedy, we do not laugh at the comedy as a whole. For the comedy as a whole is serious work, making an affirmation about life that chimes with our intuitive sense of how things are and with our deep human desire to have the nec-

* Benjamin Lehmann, "Comedy and Laughter," in *University of California Publications. English Studies*, Vol. 10 (University of California Press, 1954), pp. 81–101.

essary and agreeable prevail and our even deeper human desire to arrest before our minds a condition of things pleasant in itself and completely free from the threat of time and of disruption. For time brings the aftermath, in which the seeds of disruptive forces will sprout, in which decay will set in, and the whole process of making the necessary and agreeable secure will have to start over. That golden lads and girls must like chimney sweepers come to dust is not the stuff of comedy; it is a comment from beyond comedy's world on that world, and so appalling that its truth must be obscured by a pun. Never in comedy are we without love, and almost never without lovers. Comedy fixes the lads and girls forever in their brilliant moment; it usually contrives to close our minds to what lies ahead. This is not from any desire to deny life all its stages. We know it would be no true bliss that was bliss always, and that this enchanting hour is itself possible because of the not entirely comfortable growth that preceded it. Ambivalently perhaps, but certainly, though we desire for these lovers and for ourselves all the stages of life, it is yet pleasant, it agrees with the feeling we have of valuable things, to put a period here where the mates are free of all save their own inner commitment. That commitment is of course one in which we have a vicarious refreshment of old innocence, or if we are very young, a veiled prevision of an hour when innocence will be lost. But it is more than that. It reassures us about life and its continuation—the more so, that these lovers are so young, so beautiful or so charming, if also so compelled. We do not laugh at all this. We are delighted; we are content. The folk have a phrase for it: all the world loves a lover, they say.

But the folk have another phrase: the course of true love never runs smooth, they also say. If this saying is large enough to include postmarital trials, that is as it should be, for comedy, in putting a period at mating, does not deny the aftermath; it simply ignores it for these lovers. The course of true love that does not run smooth is in comedy the preceding course. In that phase, these are difficulties. They arise at many points and from many causes in human nature and human circumstance: social prejudice, finances, an older generation that has forgotten its youth, even conflicts within the lovers that for a while thwart their profound instinctive sense that they can, in the mysterious way of things, complete one another. Against that prevision of completeness nothing can prevail: not poverty, not social barriers, not advice, not even upon occasion a glimpsing foresight that life may be one long bickering. The elements, within and around lovers, which stand in the way of their fulfilling themselves and their biological function, are in comedy usually treated with sympathetic derision. It is folly to oppose this compulsion to mate, and what opposes properly falls under a derisive light.

The forces that oppose lovers, however, are themselves constituted in the nature of things. All these exasperating parents, these crotchety uncles and spinster aunts with lapdogs and money, these competing lovers, jealous, irresponsible, full of devious plans, these group attitudes regarding social status, race, religion, culture—these too have come into existence as inevitable as the lovers' promptings. The manners and the morals of the group, and the members of the group themselves, are manifestations of the freedom of all things to be what they are, to improve such opportunities as exist for realizing the never ceasing activity of becoming what further they may become. Consequently in the world of comedy the greatest diversity of being and of morals is deployed, and it is granted that those who seek to frustrate our lovers have a right to be what they are. Yet since not all possibilities of being can happily exist together, some must be sacrificed, some must be defeated. Social homogeneity, or true unity, cannot be always maintained; there is bound to be schism. But the sacrificed will be gently discarded, after being duly wrapped in derision, away from our complete sympathy; and the mutually opposed parties will fuse once more in a firm social unity.

The vision of comedy, then, keeps its eye on lovers, its foresight upon their prosperous mating and on implied procreation. And it consents heartily that the world they live in shall be populated by a richly diverse humanity, some for and some against the desired consummation, provided only all these illustrate the variety of the possibilities of being, generous or crabbed, fulfilled or thwarted, and provided further that the crabbed and the thwarted exhibit to us within their limits the best realization of their meager possibilities and, when necessary, yield duly to clear the way for fuller, better-natured possibilities. The vision of comedy fixes its eye on separateness, on diversity, even on oppositions, but it insists at last on togetherness for lovers and on the restored social fabric, on solidarity for the group. From its world are excluded insurmountable barriers, unassimilable evils, and suffering that strikes at the core or is irremediable. In that world all is tipped toward life, abundance, health, energy, companionship, respect, and admiration. Song, music, dance, feasting belong in it. Whatever within the range of vision is otherwise will be minimized by laughter, though it is understood it cannot be abolished from the world, and that all will end happily for human beings, not merely for human minds.

Historically, what is called comedy grew out of carnival and the secrets of carnival are masquerade, fellow feeling, and such immersion in being that the sense of impermanence vanishes. Originally the carnival was dedicated to the continuity of life; in its beginnings comedy was involved with the fertility of the species, and with that animality which puritans might condemn but could only advertise. That nothing lasts, that we may as well be ourselves, that when we are ourselves the mask is thrown off and primal forces emerge in us, these ancient intuitions in the circumstances of carnival call out gaiety and joyousness. The sense of human isolation is dissolved by the communal activity and the sense of impermanence is annihilated by the promised projection of life. The participants seem to say, we are not only solidly here in this company, but in time to come there will also be others. Birth, maturity, mating—though these are not the ecclesiastical sacraments, for life they are sacramental, and they are ceremonially so recognized in all religions. Comedy, from this point of view, is seen, once again, to deal with mating and marriage, with maturity which is their condition, and birth which is their consequence.

Seeing things as they are, however, involves more than a clear gaze at the agents of the life-stream. Though these agents are rarely left out of the picture, and though they are sometimes exhibited in a more advanced phase, shown for example as married and readjusting with the passing years and the changing natures, often they constitute a contrapuntal design in a picture of the diversely populated world, or a reassuring frame for the picture of that world. If from Menander to our own day we can follow the tradition the folk has summarized in the sayings that all the world loves a lover and that the course of true love never runs smooth, we can also from Aristophanes to Shaw follow another tradition. In it derision, verging on half affectionate raillery, is played upon human instances and patterns of behavior that appear to prevent free fulfillment of any

kind whatsoever. Long ago Wilamovitz made clear that Aristophanic comedy
was not intended to improve morals of the audience, and Werner Jaeger has in
recent years and in a larger context taken the same position. What an unbiased
reading of the comedies of Aristophanes shows us is that, except when—as in his
invective against Cleon—he is a bitter satirist, he stands for freedom. The freedom he stands for is sometimes the freedom of the immediate past, but it is always the freedom of man to be and to become what it lies in him to be and to
become, unhampered by the community, by the mob, by law, by too much or
too little money, by the newfangled and the restricting old-fashioned. "Freedom
to *be*" is the motto, freedom from disorder, lust, cruelty, war. The image is
Cloud-Cuckoo-Land where all the hampering forces are abolished, where not
only lovers but every man is free and winged, subject only to those self-decep-
tions which are harmless because they are in the nature of things and laughable
because they are harmless. Cloud-Cuckoo-Land comes through into our day in
such plays as *Harvey, Arsenic and Old Lace*, and in the Wonderland of Alice. It
is not love of others but love of humanity's best and most various possibilities
which is the spirit of this comedy. Such comedy realizes the insight of certain
Pythagoreans and of Plato that civilization should foster the fulfillment of the
real individual both in himself and in his natural affiliations. The freedom desired is beyond any conceived in political and economic utopias and would of
course be impossible under political or economic despotism. Under despotism,
deviation from the prescribed would be the object of unmitigated ridicule and
invective, what we call satire. It is in democracy that comedy particularly prospers, for true democracy and true comedy are of an immense hospitality and
have respect for all men. That Molière, for example, lived under a sort of despotism does not alter the case. An era is not despotic about everything: about the
forms Molière chiefly explored and exhibited, his era was not despotic; when he
moved into the areas of supposed unalterable truth he was forced to recast his
work. Straight satire, in fact, is itself despotic; it assumes the absolute validity of
the satirist's values and is intolerant; it judges without misgiving; it does more
than condemn, it excludes. Aristophanes and Molière, thus, show themselves despotic in behalf of freedon when they are primarily satirists.

    At its truest, comedy of the Aristophanic kind is devoted to the free matur-
ing of diverse and even of eccentric possibilities. Like the comedy of lovers, this
is a serious affirmation of life, delightedly asserted, joyously accepted, and often-
est with laughter. The fullest comedy, at all events, intuitively rendering unity in
diversity, now and in time to come, views the world simultaneously in both the
Aristophanic and the Menanderian modes. When it does not, the boy-gets-girl
fable will seem trite and perhaps trivial, for it will lack reference, relation, affiliation. It will be what we call romance. In romance life has ceased to be a forest;
it has become a park. The underbrush has been cleaned out, the windfalls and
the deadfalls have been cleaned up, and nature's way of enriching herself by her
own decay is lost to us. On the other hand, without the lovers the satiric practice
which derides the old-established morals in the hope of destroying them will
seem, if not heartless, at least without a sufficient symbol of dedication; and all
observations of human nature will seem too intellectual not because there is too
much intellect in the observation but because it is observation without love of
life. Phenomenal mental energy, expressed in notable wit, may conceal this
truth, as it sometimes does in Aristophanes and in Shaw and in Ben Jonson.

    By glancing now at individual works, we can perhaps at once test the validity of the general position here set forth and take note of some of the special ways in which comedy employs congenial attitudes and convenient devices, of what may be called the practice of comedy, as distinguished from comic vision. We can also by proceeding in this way suggest the complexity which is characteristic of a wholly achieved work of literary art in this genre, the more readily if we include among our instances some works which though deficient as works of art have proved persuasive for large audiences.

Between the mating young and the old lies family life and the commitments of the social group. In *Abie's Irish Rose*, finanical considerations and the blood feud between Jew and non-Jew, presented in stereotypes, are treated as barriers. The Rabbi and the Priest are of a most sweet broadmindedness, conditioned no doubt by the professional sense of sacramental marriage and by a professional belief that it is better to marry than to burn, learned from St. Paul who is of the race of the Rabbi and of the church of the Priest. The lovers are young moderns who have to bring their own intelligences to bear in order to support their natural promptings against their conditioned reluctances about miscegenation. The capitulation of both their fathers when they become grandfathers—in the presence of twins—is both touching and laughable: we have in that future generation not only a boy and a girl, but it may be a Jew and a Catholic. All this, and also the acceptance of roast pork—which enlarges the range of festive feeding—and of Christmas, which commemorates the birthday of a glorious figure of the race of one family and the religion of the other. In the most popular of modern comedies, fusion and unity are achieved without neglect of the lifestream and with persuasive setting aside of commitments. Yet it is shallow stuff, true only in a single plane, the possibilities not realized. In *Ah, Wilderness*, we are not taken so far into the future, but we go deeper. Reciprocally in the world of the family Miller, everyone is loved not alone for himself but for his idiosyncrasies. In regard to the adolescent, that means "keeping up," since adolescents spawn new idiosyncrasies in a day: the man you say good night to is not the child you greeted at breakfast; he may well for the time being have grown unbearable. But it is not otherwise with grown-ups when they have let liquor have its way, and if as with Sid Davis this is a recurrent phenomenon, it frustrates love and life. Yet the family before us is so firmly on its feet, the group so inwardly attuned by time and custom, that this frustration is ameliorated; it becomes, almost, a nostalgia for something once had and lost rather than for something dreamed of and never had. And at the close, in young Richard, the dream—on the piazza, until the moon sets—is a forecast upon that fate which nature has decreed for all who live, though some miss it. Not, however, before we have seen that young Richard has an inkling that it has been so before his time, and incidentally that those old people, his parents, were young once. He learns not to forget that way back then the moon was the same—"and everything." Everything—the freshness, the discovery, the magic, the love. The threatened break of the texture of family life is avoided, and there is a creating future.

Comic vision sometimes presents us these characteristic matters not in a city milieu but in the country, among those nearer the earth, where the procreative is in the daily visible round. In *Tobacco Road*, Jeeter is a hungry man, haunted by a kind of negative feasting, but his greatest hunger is to till the soil, to plant a crop and, when it appears for a short time that they may be given seed for a crop, even the selfish and rebellious Dude helps to burn off the fields. Framed by an illusory sense of Earth's harvest, the drive to beget runs wild, coming to little as civilization counts, but never coming to nothing. Pearl was clearly meant to beget her kind and, escaping, doubtless will do so. Ellie May, harelipped and urgent, goes to cook for Lov and, who can doubt, to bear him children, out of wedlock probably. Dude is a born father, though he may postpone the time. It is a world without conventions; so far as it has any mores, they are in the service of life. Millions have been delighted to see it so. In *They Knew What They Wanted,* upon the land thriftily husbanded, Tony, who loves eating, drinking, all the good physical things, who has affection for children and for men and women in general, accepts a child for his child. That his stand-in as father is his hired man, that the circumstances from his point of view appear to violate all the loyalties, releases a berserk fury in him, when he is informed of the facts. However, with his country-bred sense of such things, he is easily calmed, and the child and mother fall in with all the festive elements that make his life. That the hired man goes his way is in nature, too, for paternity is accidental and in nature, not generally responsible. That in *Tobacco Road* the impoverished picture rendered for us provokes more laughter than one might expect of an audience setting so great store by "more things for more people" at a play in which a superannuated mother is killed by one of those "things" would surprise us if we did not realize that, when we laugh, we are affirming ancient truths about humanity. That we laugh at all before the intensities of *They Knew What They Wanted* would surprise us, too, if it were not intimated to us by the title that this is a comedy of fulfillment.

In Restoration comedy, the tone and the practice are both largely those of satire, that is, derision of pretense, of sterility, of form without matter, of what is not directed lifeward. Nonetheless, by its gusto, its tolerant consent that it shall seem in the nature of its creatures so to pervert nature, and by its recognition that conflicts are resolved in marriages and in reconciliations among the married, satire is given comic values. Our general impression is that life in its essential force cannot be annihilated even by these manners that are satirized. In the finest of Restoration comedies, indeed, we are presented with two people in whom natural promptings served by brilliant gifts attain their true destiny by manipulating the trivialities and irrelevances of upper-class life. In *The Way of the World* mating is central, and marriage, though basely illustrated by others, is richly conceived by the lovers. Mirabell converts the looseness of his philandering ways into premarital experience and Millamant transmutes her coquetry, so that these two at last stand as peerless examples of human beings using their environment for their love. Early in the play Mirabell says of Lady Wishfort that she lets "posterity shift for itself, she'll breed no more." Throughout, it reverberates to our sense that this society is in every way sterile, but it is steadily made clear that for our lovers it is and will be fruitful. In a passage of shining wittiness, they speak of the children they will have, of pregnancy, and of domestic routine. Millamant acts to preserve her wealth as the condition of a good life for children and parents. This is a recognition that their life is to be lived in their accustomed way. The glitter that surrounds them is bedizenment; it does not come from life within, warm and bright, from life tended, kept fresh. In the last of their swift interchanges, they see in the inevitable repetitions of conjugal life an opportunity. They will give themselves "over and over again." Thus, whereas in *The Country Wife* the ignorant naturalness of Margery accents the satire of a sophisticated unnatural society, in *The Way of the World* that society is exhibited to reveal how those duly endowed may live life truly. In nothing are these brilliant lovers so brilliant as in the attainment of that triumph which is ideally possible to all.

From *They Knew What They Wanted,* where the subject is "played straight," without derision, to *The Way of the World,* where derision is neatly balanced by approvals, in these instances no pain is irremediable. That, we ventured, is the condition of comic vision. Yet there are works in which this condition is barely met, and others in which it is aimed at but missed. In *Pride and Prejudice,* a wonderful skill just prevents Mr. Bennet from being the object of our pity. Had he not the sanctuary of his library, delight in the gentle taunt, happy communication with his daughter Elizabeth, his predicament would strike us as painful. As it is, his story encloses the matchmaking that is the chief matter, and gives the book an extra dimension. The daughters of Mr. and Mrs. Bennet are ready for marriage, or in the case of Lydia for a mate. Pursuit of a husband or a mate is exhibited in great variety. Beset by caste snobberies and by personal snobberies, the girls may not be able to marry according to the promptings of their natures, and that will be bad; but if they should succeed in doing so,—well, look at what happened to father. Mr. Bennet had married Mrs. Bennet for herself alone; she had a negligible fortune, she had negligible intelligence, but she had what was required to enmesh her man. She thereupon bore him five daughters, trying for the son who would lift the entail. Now, with luck, the girls will be off his hands, and one day Mr. Bennet will live in an empty house with Mrs. Bennet, until he dies and leaves Mrs. Bennet a propertyless nuisance in the house of a son-in-law. Yet while he lives there will be his daughter Elizabeth to correspond with, to visit; there will be seclusion with books; there will be the gibes at Mrs. Bennet for safety valve. At least two of the daughters will marry fortunes. Life is not quite sweet; it has more flavor than that; it is bittersweet. Jane Austen, then, just prevents our pain.

Whether Shakespeare did so in *Twelfth Night* is debatable, a matter of how we read the play, or how it is directed. It is a question of the intonation of Olivia's final speeches, of the compassion and warmth she shows toward a tried though illuded retainer. If the derision of Malvolio is reserved to Sir Toby Belch and Sir Andrew Aguecheek and Maria, comedy is safe; if it is Shakespeare deriding a puritan, our pain is past remedy. For Malvolio is also himself, showing a quite human aspiration, however inappropriate. And in any case it is clear that he will be continued in Olivia's household, where we might well have seen him, earlier, under other circumstances, competent, apt, a careful steward, dignified and even decorative as the house of a great lady requires. Shylock takes us, in our day, out of the world comedy appears to prescribe for itself. Even if he were not deprived of his loved property and if his Jessica were not hedged away from him, he is clearly no kinsman of Solomon Levy in *Abie's Irish Rose,* and he can therefore not bear that the flesh of his flesh shall feast on pork and submit to wedding outside the synagogue. For him, whom we see last in the courtroom, there is no resumption of anything at all. He stands alone before the bar of justice, he leaves alone. His house, bereft of daughter and of wealth, is no home. Since for our day he is too grounded in his humanity to be a derided figure of greed, he is painful. Not all the delectable goings on at Portia's villa on the Brenta can reassure us, after he goes. With Falstaff, as we last see him, it is different. The King may not know the old man. The best of fellows, and of audience, is lost, but Falstaff will make the best of what is left.

... go with me to dinner.
Come, Lieutenant Pistol; come, Bardolph. I shall
be sent for soon at night.

The group is not intact, but it is still a group; there will be festivity, and—who knows?—later an account, pure fabrication and wonderfully acted, of being introduced into King Henry's chamber by palace backways and of having caroused with a prince who for an hour threw off affairs of state. Banishment of them all to the Fleet till their conversation appear more wise and modest to the world is only for an interval, we feel. The pain is just not too much, because the life in Falstaff is just enough and because he is not deprived of what to him is indispensable—fellowship.

Comic practice, we said, views with half-affectionate derision the unfruitful, the incomplete, and the contrived, when they seek to frustrate vitality and fulfillment, and, when they merely exist in the neighborhood, presents such to us as examples of the rich variety in the human scene. Though comic vision is devoted to spontaneous and fulfilling expression, it knows that fulfillment is not always possible. Then comic practice shows us how the wise keep their heads down. Shandean comedy exhibits the disparity between the dreams that are enclosed in such words as love, war and glory, reason, and the world of fact. Love and war, in *Tristram Shandy*, are exhibited not in their glamorous phases but in their tawdry aftermaths as demonstrations of that inevitable coming to earth of which Yorick warns us. Reason, which in man is thought so ennobling, is reduced by a battery of non-sequiturs endlessly replenished from the associative faculty. The manifestation of the life-force itself sets the pattern of non-sequitur, for Tristram is the son in the flesh of a woman who cannot catch an implication and a man who tortures all reality to fit hypothesis—Tristram who has a genius for implication and who had the intuition to find that the reality of the world is what it is, that if you keep expanding a hypothesis to fit the facts you presently have no hypothesis at all, moral or intellectual or scientific: you have only nature. The Shandean way is to disclose nature's secret and bid us go along with it. The secret is that, as man imagines possibilities, nothing is complete or enduring, and our dreams are inordinate. Yorick and all the jesters have told us so; thus they safeguard the human, preserve it from pain. They say, when aspiration is incommensurate with reality, it is wise in human beings to cut aspiration back. There is no absolute freedom of being.

At least not in this world. In *Man and Superman* it is only in another world—in a dream hell—that John Tanner masquerading as Don Juan can assert without desperation that it is the role of mind to steer nature, not to drift with her. In that other world of dream, he leaves hell to find his way to heaven where he may fulfill "Life's incessant aspiration to higher organization, wider, deeper, intenser self-consciousness, and clearer self-understanding," where only human perfection will be worth dying for. But he does not get to heaven. He wakes up. And waking he takes the sober view that he has been dreaming damnably. And so he has. For he now confronts once more the world where Life's incessant determination that there shall be more life grips him, in the interest of a household and a family. In *Man and Superman*, in a little imagined universe diversely enough populated, man's highest and most articulate aspiration is brought to earth. Man's greatest freedom, as woman's too, is only to be oneself, so far as one may. Jack Tanner ends asking Anne a curious pair of questions: "What have you grasped in me? Is there a father's heart as well as a mother's?" In his half-century exploitation of a form that combines the Platonic dialogue with the operatic fable, Shaw sought to help man be a free, a winged creature by showing how desirable it is to abolish ignorance, disease, poverty, war and—some would say—marriage. But the abolition of marriage would not get to the heart of the matter. Men and women would still be biological entities. Tanner gives up.

So men view the world, Laurence Sterne by intuition and Shaw by intelligence, but all men somehow or other, it appears. Unphrased intuition or that wordless understanding we call common sense creates the enormous audience for Dickens' Pickwickian world. That world is as profuse an array of the possibilities of being as can be imagined, and it extends from the *Pickwick Papers* to the last of the novels, through all of which it refreshes itself, no matter how melodramatic the story. For author, for reader, and for the creatures themselves it is infused with the faith that life in all its infinite variety is made livable through the constant, vigilant application of the generous, the humane impulses that arise in most people most of the time, and is made secure by troops of children. Even in the presence of deprivations that forbid laughter, the ancient ingenuity of pure being—its exuberance and resilience—calls for delight, and the lower classes from which Dickens' imagination always reluctantly turned afford us a greater sense of richness and variety, because in the lower classes "good form" has made fewer prescriptions and nature is freer to exhibit her fertility.

It is such a vision of the richness and variety in nature, rather than the necessity to complicate an action, that brings the lower classes into Shakespeare's comic world. It is of course at its freest within Forest, in the Dream, or on the Magic Island. That comic world as it is rendered in his earlier comedies is exactly as we should expect it from an imagination that was almost without party or class bias. The activities of lovers prosper and are utterly delightful. The desirability of progeny is implicit in their good looks, their charm, their power to rejoice. The socal fabric, however rent by usurpation, or illusions pursued, or foolhardy commitments, it restored. The more so, because those who cannot partake of the golden last state of things give their approval. In that world who would not sing or listen to music? Who would not dance or look on at dancing? Who would not sit down heartily to feast or serve the feast?

Yet from the earliest Shakespearean comedies, there is also a troubled note. Winter as well as spring sounds at the close of *Love's Labour's Lost;* in *A Midsummer Night's Dream* the wonderful spoofing covers but does not conceal the sadness of Pyramus' and Thisbe's fate; in *Much Ado* brother John's punishment is merely postponed till tomorrow; Jacques is alone, Feste is alone, finally. And from *Troilus and Cressida* through *The Winter's Tale* there is enough of the pain of the world to make us doubt the well-being possible to mortals. The bitter is often not overbalanced by the sweet, until in *The Tempest* the golden state of things is once more raised before us. And then not by an affirmative love of life operating directly. In *The Tempest* only magic can procure the condition of delight, joy, and peace. From *Troilus and Cressida* to *The Winter's Tale*, Shakespeare, though he continues to employ the devices of comic practice, appears to be reaching for a form that several centuries later came to be called the problem play. For the problem play exhibits those human predicaments out of which we cannot escape by death and an accompanying sense of enlarged understanding, as in tragedy, or by mating and thinking well of life in limited areas because so much of it is clearly a positive good, humanity being what it is. Such plays do not invite us to immerse ourselves in life, nor do they spark in us impulses to transcend life in ultimate ways.

Molière appears sometimes to have been caught by the same aspect of things. In *The Misanthrope* society is brilliantly satirized in the interest of something which is not satirized but approved—the love of man and a woman. Philinte could sacrifice his life and soul for the hand of Eliante, he says. But for Célimène Alceste will not sacrifice even his opinions, at least not yet, though Philinte's final speech suggests they may bring him around. Molière's animus has counterpoised against the artificiality of society an unnaturalness in Alceste which we do not see brought back to nature. Yet he is clearly under Célimène's spell, and the example of the other pair of lovers shows us how these things should be. In *Tartuffe*, too—in Molière's final version—the interplay of a great hypocrite and a great fool is mercilessly satirized in the interest of preserved property and a sweet union of lovers. As in *The Miser*, as also often in Ben Jonson—*Volpone*, for example—so also in *Tartuffe*, the obstacles to decency, to good human promptings bulk too large; they present a problem which no marriages of the innocent, no social fabric renewed can overcome. When Philinte compares the rogues to vultures, the unjust to mischievous apes, and the selfish to fury-lashed wolves, he misunderstands the nature of men and animals alike; and it is not clear that Molière in a troubled hour is not failing in the same way. At all events, these plays exhibit the limits rather than the powers of humanity, they fix our attention on human destructiveness rather than creativeness, without consolation, on the perversion of the promptings rather than on their expression. They are not, then, true comedies, for in them the practices of comedy are brought to bear upon insoluble human problems which are not susceptible to comic vision. Elsewhere, Molière for the most part avoided such painful cases. The preservation of property for those who will know how to enjoy it, the even-handed revelation of fidelity and infidelity, the just exhibition of ignorance and comprehension, the unsealing of blind eyes, the sound countrybred sense of servants —in play after play all flow into one channel. Through the symbol of mating lovers or of lovers reunited they become an affirmation of life as it is, and are presented with a witty poetry that arises directly from the affirmation. Laughter is provoked by the witty utterance and the witty situation in Molière always, but we cannot say the *The Miser* and *Tartuffe* reassure us, or that in the presence of *The Misanthrope* our joy is unqualified.

Of course, the reassurance which comedy gives us may be less than total, and it may be involved with the tragic, or with those phenomena which we call problems. For example, midway in *Madame Bovary*, itself a tragic work, Flaubert remarks:

> Never had Madame Bovary been so beautiful as at this period; she had that indefinable beauty that comes from joy, from enthusiasm, from success, and that is only the harmony of temperament with circumstances. Her desires, her sorrows, the experience of pleasure, and her ever-young illusions had, as manure, rain, winds and the sun make flowers grow, gradually developed her; she had at length blossomed in all the plentitude of her nature.

At the moment Emma Bovary herself is figure comedy could delight in. She is, however, not a figure of comedy because, that she might become what she then was, the social fabric had to be broken beyond repair. In *High Noon* the hero and heroine are figures of comedy, suspended between social obligation and their own promptings to fufillment; but the people of the town in the emergency, huddled in their church and their saloon, withhold their hand from the community good. Hence, we have at best comedy in a minor key, for, though all these townfolk are behaving characteristically and the threats to personal fulfill-ment and to the continuing of life are removed, the lovers are alone. They will have to find their social fabric elsewhere. The failure of solidarity is symbolized by the empty streets, is accented by the uneasy huddles at altar and at bar, and counterpointed by the couples seen in rooms here and there. In *Come Back, Little Sheba* the matter of comedy is barely asserted, as contrast, by the young girl married at the end and by the doubly anonymous men from Alcoholics Anony-mous entering the picture. The story is a tragic instance of biological necessity betrayed by biological necessity itself, and the husband and wife though restored to one another are bitterly without affiliation, for his parents are dead and hers are alienated; they are without friends, and will be without children. In these in-stances, from novel and from motion picture, there is a remarkable absence of the festive and the convivial, which increases our sense that no matter what laughter is provoked from moment to moment all is not well with life. A way of life has been attained, reasonable no doubt but not what reason would approve in an ideal world or what our intuition of nature yearns for. We are confronted with a problem, with which two people have learned to live in reconciliation.

Reason is a function much spoken of in connection with comedy. Some-times it is made the heart of the matter. In that case we observe a snobbery of the self-valuing intelligence; more often we are in the presence of a failure to understand the role reason plays in human affairs. Reason, when it shows to a degree at which it may be separately designated, sees the many diverse claims made upon our imagination, our loyalties, our sympathies, our energy, or our time. It may sometimes appear to make a choice among these diverse claims. But reason is not really free. Were it not tied to the needs of the body and the demand of events, it would still be the creature of the nervous system, at the very least enslaved by accustomed ways of being reasonable. To be natural, which we are by virtue of being alive, and to be rational is to be confronted from hour to hour not so much by choice, as by the necessity for adapting, for making the best of it, as we say, even perhaps for throwing reason out. Reason is not the instrument of comic vision. It is part of the material upon which comic vision gazes.

Here we have the overreaching incongruity, which all other incongruities are lighted by. There are many others. Under the most fortunate circumstances it is incongruous that mind should see clearly and sometimes soar but the body should feed and sleep; that the human spirit should feel perennial and the matter of which spirit is a function should be changing always; that the state of being whose nature it is to pledge itself eternally should be so fragilely grounded, so briefly possible; and it is incongruous that the freedom lovers find to commit themselves should at once deprive them of their freedoms. Since nothing re-mains as it is, it is inconsistent to take satisfaction in an arrived-at solidarity, for it too will be destroyed and succeeded by another, different, whether better or worse. The freedom Aristophanes desired would be procured at the cost of freedom to other entities to be themselves. All other incongruities arise from these, and illustrate these, actually or typically or symbolically.

Comedy did not invent incongruity, it discovered it. Long before psychiatry formulated analogous concepts, comedy discovered the masque, the disguise, mistaken identity. Comedy found them what we call laughable, but on the deeper level felt them as symbolic expression. It recognized in non-sequiturs the verbal symbol of those minor derangements in the sequence of events which are always present when we view reality with preconceptions. It found in wit—the surprising juxtaposition, implied or expressed and happily phrased—the verbal suggestion of the infinite possibilities of being and of connection. In those unillusioned judgments made with love, what we call humor, it found the manner of consent to all possible being and all possible connection. In puns, which begin with one meaning and end with another, it found the verbal means of rendering those random collisions of phenomena which both do, and do not, make sense. And each of these, perceived, may make us laugh; but their doing so is incidental to another effect which is a delight too deep for laughter, a joy too persuasive for laughter. That effect is a felt affirmation about life which chimes with our intuitive sense of how things are and with our deep human desire to be recreated by seeing true humanness prevail, against the frightening altitudes of aspiration, against the set mechanism of the habitual and conventional, against the threat of corruption and of time.

III
THE
CHARACTERISTICS
OF COMEDY

The Sense of Regain:
A Theory of Comedy*

Harold H. Watts

Aristotle is silent. Discussions of the nature of comedy lack the peak which dominates all journeys exploring the nature of tragedy. Such journeys can be measured by the distance which lies between them and the sacred mountain; speculations about comedy cannot be. An effort to trace the psychological effects of comedy is—one may as well confess—chiefly a product of one age. When one writes about comedy—indeed, when one *writes* comedy—he should know that he can no more than touch or assess current risibilities. The comic dramatist, at least, does not dream of making bold claims for his work. The teller of the *grants douleurs* of Tristan and Iseut might boast that their grief speaks to unknown times. Indeed, modesty may not be one of the chief virtues; and it is certainly not the virtue of the tragic poet. But modesty of a particular kind dominates the mind of a man who writes comedy, and this even though his play be as gross and immodest as the symbol of Priapus.

II

A sort of modesty, then, is the *vade mecum* of the comic playwright. He may or may not be aware of its presence; but so long as he writes comedy, it guides him. It does not hold him from bold judgment of the vices and follies of his time; it lets him speak boldly in the forum. But it keeps him in the forum; that is the clue to this sort of modesty. The comic writer may not leave the market-place; to ascend the hill, to address Capitoline Jove in eternal accents is not permitted him. His modesty constrains him for making assertions that the tragic poet *must* make if, indeed, he is to be a tragic poet. The tragic poet supposes that he sees truly and profoundly as concerns the will of the gods, human greatness and vileness, and the ties that link man with man. The tragic poet reports little or nothing of how people dress and amuse themselves, how they make their living, and how they consult one soothsayer after another. Not his concern is man's stubborn refusal to understand his fellows—and, for that matter, his even more stubborn timidity which keeps him from pushing to bloody extremes the results of his misunderstanding. These things lie in the province of the comic writer.

Again, as the tragic writer tells of the love of Tristan and Iseut, he should (we feel) keep at a minimum his accounts of tapestries and table-manners. This

* Harold H. Watts, "The Sense of Regain: A Theory of Comedy," *University of Kansas City Review*, Vol. xiii, No. 1 (Autumn, 1946), pp. 19–23.

same feeling is at work in the production we give to an old tragic drama. We suppress antiquarian clutter; we aim at a style of acting that is simple and eternal. All this indicates our belief that enjoyment of great tragedy ought to be natural and immediate—and that, if we do not, the fault is ours and not the tragic poet's. It is some imperfection of our own that holds us back from the complete identification that the dead poet confidently expected.

It is true that we may also fail to come to grips with the comedy of another age, Goldoni's or Marivaux's or Sheridan's. But here we do not feel ashamed. Why *this* failure does not trouble us, we perhaps may not formulate; but we admit our incapacity cheerfully. Scrutiny suggests that the "fault" lies in the very nature of comedy itself. It is a by-product of that modesty which kept the comic writer strolling in the public square and which forbade him to have traffic with holy places, be they temples or churches, synagogues or chapels. Usually, we are content to say that an old comedy is too quaint; it is our right to be ignorant of the sedan-chairs and the pomades of another time. But perhaps we do not see that these objects, which once cluttered the foreground of men's minds, are a sign-manual, the expression of the particular modesty which pervades all comedy. This modesty is likely to inhibit profound insight; it certainly encourages *reportage*.

This barrier of facts observed at a particular moment in a particular street or chamber bars the way to the reader of an old comedy. Sometimes it will seem that the old play is *all* reportage and our reading of it bootless. This we distinctly feel in reading certain comic scenes of Shakespeare, even though we have realized that comedy, of its very nature, permits scenes that are no more than a tissue of reportage. In fact, the opposite is non-existent: comic scenes devoid of reportage. For we cannot imagine Maria and Sir Toby Belch and Malvolio sitting at any other board than one of Jacobean oak; we cannot fancy Lady Teazle hiding behind a screen covered with anything else than scenic paper. In short, to enjoy old comedy, we must in the first place cultivate antiquarian enthusiasm: the sort of emotion that impels us to exclaim with amusement, when we are at a museum, "Did they actually ride in such carriages!"

Only this acquired taste will get us over the initial barricade thrown up by the modesty of the old comic writer. Even if he had had foresight, he could not have freed himself of these imperfections, this excess of reporting. Had he tried, he would have moved away from the public area; he would have ceased to write comedy.

From this, it is plain that the only comedy for which we can have spontaneous enthusiasm is the comedy of our own day. Comedy never intends to speak across the years; it is a dramatic representation addressed to *us*. We frequent certain places of business and amusement, we read certain books, and (unlike our forbears) we pronounce *tea* to rhyme with *bee*. A comedy must be written in a certain year of grace; as Maugham has observed, it cannot hope to have a natural, easy existence for more than ten or twenty years.

These observed circumstances point to the psychological values of comedy, which are in sharp contrast to the better known ones of tragedy. Further, the truth of any assertion one makes about comedy can be verified only in the comedy of our own period, of our own market-place. Other comedy can offer but halting evidence. We can *suspect* that comedy had, in another age, certain psychological functions; we cannot declare.

III

Comedy of our own day—comedy which does not demand spadework, comedy to which we can give a response naive and true—gives us two immediate pleasures: (1) that of recognition; and (2) that of applying a limited scale of human truth. These separate pleasures are found together; they produce, almost, a single effect—they call forth what one may call a sense of regain. What this sense is we cannot justly state until we study in isolation each pleasure that stimulates it.

Recognition is the pleasure given us by certain objects and ideas which we find in the comedy of our own period. They are the very ideas and objects which will challenge the antiquary and discourage the student of time to come. But their griefs do not concern us. We only feel (rather than know) that, in today's comedy, the characters must lead the kind of lives we lead, or at least the kind of lives led by certain of our acquaintance. The characters must follow a modern schedule of living, depending on the appliances and catch-words we depend on. They must make their living—and their often silly economies—as we make ours. They must be guilty of the same false emphasis that our neighbors make today and that we (alas, for our folly!) made yesterday. We go to the theatre determined to encounter the mental and material bric-a-brac of our stretch of time.

From this it should be plain—the list of items asserts it—that this process of recognition is not the same as the process of identification (complete or partial) which tragedy demands. If we "recognize" with anything but calm or lively pleasure, the dramatist has ceased to be comic, has stepped into the shadow of a nearby temple. For recognition is always made with a crucial reservation: Here is something that is a part of my experience, *but not an immediate part.* Even when we recognize ourselves in a comedy, it is ourselves as we were some years since, not as we now are. (Tragedy, of course, directs our gaze to our present moral nature.) Thus, a collection of peccadilloes that *were* ours moves us no more deeply than the sight of our faces in an old picture or the sound of our voices on a recording machine. Even as we acknowledge the likeness, we privately repudiate it: the real, essential ego has escaped the comic arrow. The egos that do not escape really rough handling (hence our delight) are those of our dear friends and relatives. Their folly we have always suspected, and now the dramatist has put it in a revealing light. That the dramatist's models do not see what has happened to them adds the final, ironical spice to the act of recognition.

IV

In actuality, this pleasure intertwines with the other delight which a comic dramatist gives: that of exercising an extremely limited scale of values, of saying glibly, "How true to human nature!" This pleasure, admittedly, still lurks for us, behind the reportage of old comedies. But it exists immediate and delicious in a comedy of our own age. Our reaction is so "natural," so keen in our joy at having certain of our values affirmed, that we are blind as to what has really taken place. In the first place, the dramatist has, by surprise and contrast, forced the "natural" exclamation from us; further, his ingenuity conceals from us that no comedy is true to human nature as we seriously know it. It is true to human nature only as we (with the dramatist for cicerone) know it from our walks in public places. It has nothing to say of that nature when it is really most human; that is, private, retired, tragic. It is the trick of comedy to confirm all our superficial judgments; it must make us ignore those which we regard as profound and eternal.

Our superficial judgments, we see when we inspect them—a scrutiny the comic dramatist discourages—are those which we hold in common with our fellows, with those who are of like background and education. In the sixteenth century, it was a belief in the humors and their power to shape folly. In the eighteenth century, it was belief in good sense and its power to avert folly. We of the twentieth share, perhaps, a belief in complete relativity and its power maliciously to illuminate all firm adherences, whether to outworn traditions or to new dogma. Such held beliefs enable us to live at peace with our neighbors and, quite often, in ignorance of what we as individuals are. When we participate in comedy, we are spared asking how much we decline from, how much we overshoot the normal beliefs of our age. Comedy fully enjoyed reiterates that these beliefs are the only ones worth pursuing; comedy indicates deftly the folly of men who ponder a measure of vice and virtue different from the pat discriminations which stabilize affairs of state, of the counting-house, and (even) of the heart. Malvolio may be own cousin to Hamlet, but since he figures in a comedy, we join Maria and Sir Toby in reassuring laughter.[1] Likewise, we are glad to see that Lydia Languish decides that the nameless stirrings in her breast are indeed vapors. And we are grateful to a playwright like Mr. Maugham who assures us that efforts to discover and comply with laws of behavior are no more than "stuffy"; for we have moments when we suspect that all life is not just a flux, jolly and formless.

Tragedy, more or less great, does the opposite of confirming us in a conventional set of values. It gives us Hamlet for Malvolio, a Chekhov woman for Lydia Languish, and—or so Mr. O'Neill supposes—Nina Leeds for a Maugham heroine. And these are gifts that the human spirit can only at its peril reject, since all of them—well or less well—point to that within us which rejects the values that have forum-currency. Tragic figures affect us entirely otherwise than do comic. They stir us to thought which is inconvenient in the marketplace (and in the comedy) of any age. The true relation of man to the gods (or God), the duty of man to himself, the validity of all concepts of good and evil—these are the stuff of tragedy, and they are the stuff of that life of our own which is secret and often—thanks to comedy and our participation in it—most ignored. We are content to recognize, we are glad to cry a facile *Hail* to truth of a sort. We are eager to find an abiding place in the type of universe the comic dramatist provides for us. It is a universe compact of familiar objects and painless ideas. To reside there is to be cradled, to forego mental and spiritual growth in favor of a lively jounce.

V

But too often we, like the greatest comic dramatists, slip unwillingly into tragedy. With them and with the professedly tragic writers, we wander toward the sacred hill which rises above trade and gaiety. Yet, since we are quite limited beings—not tragic poets—we must retreat from the precipices where one stands to talk to the gods. It is the comic writer who shows us how to retreat, who recalls

---

[1] This after *reportage* is penetrated, to be sure.

us "to ourselves," as the saying goes. To our relief, he offers us recognition and a commonplace set of values. He provides a mediocre kind of sanity in place of the destructive truth which tragedy and the secret parts of our own nature contain. He stirs in us, for evil or for good, a sense of regain. The familiar objects reproduced, the current platitudes buttressed—it is these that give us a sense of regaining what the more cowardly part of our natures had feared might be gone forever. It is, to be accurate, a repossession of objects that some part of our being should say farewell to without a sigh.

But few of us are ready to say farewell without a sigh. We do not desire to turn to a deep, consistently tragic view of man's life. When this view threatens to dominate our minds, then do we welcome the power of comedy to stir in us a sense of return, of a restored "sense of balance." We are willing to overlook the fact that balancing involves cancellation. We do not care what we strike out; simply we pant to walk in the public place again, to be repatriated in the world of mediocrity from which tragedy and our own self-knowledge have drawn us away.

In tragedy (and in religion) we come to see man's character as it is. In the facile and compromising world of comedy we learn how to be content with man's nature as it seems to be. One must note that the person who wills to live in no other world has confessed that for him no other attitude is possible. Perhaps, however, there persist in him impulses maimed and unfruitful. One need not be an enemy of comedy to observe that for such a lack the brightness and unimplemented scepticism of modern comedy is no anodyne.

The Subject Matter of Comedy*

L. J. Potts

I

I began this book by saying that comedy depends on the eye of the beholder, not on the character of the object he has in view; that nothing in nature is categori-cally comic—whether it is so or not depends on what you make of it. It would seem to follow that anything or everything is suitable subject matter for comedy. From a strictly philosophical point of view, that is so. But comedy is a tradition as well as an idea; and to the writer and reader of comedy the selection of sub-ject matter and setting is as important as abstract notions about art, if not more so. Of course, in making his selection, the writer will be influenced consciously or unconsciously by the ideal character of his art, or at least by his opinions about it.

He is trying to present a social point of view; to measure human conduct against a norm rather than an ideal. He is, or should be, actuated always by a sense of proportion. What he depicts—his subject matter—may therefore be de-fined as the abnormal. He may include some normal characters in his work, to serve as a kind of yard-stick; but for the most part he will leave his public to de-duce his norm from the way he depicts the clash and contrast of varied abnor-malities. In any case, far the greater part of his matter must inevitably be abnor-mal.

This indicates another difference between tragedy and comedy. It has been argued convincingly that the characters and even the events in a tragedy must be normal if we are to feel the full tragic effect. But can the character and be-haviour of Macbeth, for example, be called normal? A clear distinction must be drawn between the *normal* and the *usual*. Tragedy of course deals with unusual situations and consequently with unusual states of mind; but we should always feel that the situation is one in which we might have been placed, and that in similar circumstances we should, or at least very probably might, have felt as the characters of the tragedy do. We should be able to identify ourselves with them for the time being. The problem for the tragic writer is to bridge the gap be-tween the terrible and the normal: to show us, for example, a murderer like Macbeth or a madman like Lear, who yet retain the deepest and sanest human feelings. He does this, not by stressing normality, but by making us feel it as an undertone in the situation: by speeches like Macbeth's

* L. J. Potts, "The Subject Matter of Comedy," in *Comedy* (Hutchinson's University Library, Lon-don, 1950), pp. 45–63.

> If thou couldst, doctor, cast
> The water of my land, find her disease,
> And purge it to a sound and pristine health,
> I would applaud thee to the very echo,
> That should applaud again;

or Lear's

> Poor naked wretches, wheresoe'er you are
> That bide the pelting of this pitiless storm,
> How shall your houseless heads and unfed sides,
> Your loop'd and window'd raggedness, defend you
> From seasons such as these?

It may be said that whereas tragedy deals with the unusual but normal, comedy deals with the abnormal but not unusual. The abnormality of comic characters is not absolute; we should feel that they are capable of behaving normally if they would. But it is the main concern of the comic writer to discriminate between what is normal and abnormal in human behaviour; he is detached from his subject matter in a sense in which other artists are not. He needs not merely a strong feeling for normality, but also a clear notion of it. It is therefore necessary for him to be in some measure a moral philosopher; for the norm is a philosophical concept. The usual, or average, is not; it can be calculated statistically from observed facts. But normality, like the cognate concepts of health and sanity, is not a fact, nor a complex of facts, nor even a simplification of facts; it is an idea, and exists only in the mind that has brought itself to bear on all the relevant facts. There is not one norm of human behaviour, but many: some of them widely divergent and even contradictory. Jane Austen's norm differs drastically in some respects from Chaucer's or Fielding's. But all comic writers must have a norm in view. To detect eccentricity you must have a centre: that is to say a consistent, if not consciously worked out, standard of character and conduct.

From these considerations it might be deduced that the world of comedy would be a realistically depicted world peopled by eccentric characters. This formula fits some comic writers: Fielding and Jane Austen in particular. It was also the formula laid down by Ben Jonson and in the main followed by him. But as a general definition it is too narrow, and also radically misleading. Meredith puts his finger on the error contained in it, in the passage I have quoted previously comedy *may be taken for* a slavish reflex of real life, *until its features are closely studied.* There is always an element of caricature in comedy, the caricature being so designed as to stress the eccentricity of the individual. Everyone, however nearly normal, has his foibles, however slight. But this, perhaps, is obvious.

A more serious objection to this formula is that comedy is not necessarily at all realistic in technique. None of Shakespeare's comedies are: even *Measure for Measure*, which is often classed as a realistic play, is strange and remote—suffused in "the light that never was on sea or land". The Fable (as used by Aesop, for example) is one of the earliest and most efficient vehicles for comedy, and it is quite unrealistic. Even allegory, which is more unrealistic still, adapts itself well and easily to comic purposes: the vice in the late medieval morality plays was a comic figure, and probably the literary ancestor of Shakespeare's Falstaff. Even in so tedious an allegory as the *Roman de la Rose* the character of Fals-

Semblant is fully developed comedy; it provided Chaucer with the outline of the character of his Pardoner. Chaucer himself took his first exercises in comedy in *The House of Fame* and *The Parliament of Fowls* (an allegory and a fable). I have already called attention to the technique of the Bottom-Titania scene in *A Midsummer Night's Dream*, which is unrealistic and close to allegory. The best plays of the first great European comic writer, Aristophanes, are all fantasies, although the central character in an Aristophanic comedy is usually a realistically conceived middle-aged and middle-class Athenian citizen. There is a similar blend of realism and fantasy in the greatest of all European comedies, *Don Quixote;* and there is comedy, both realistic and unrealistic, in Bunyan's *Pilgrim's Progress*, the general structure of which is allegorical.

Even this cursory survey shows that comedy demands the utmost latitude in its choice of setting and in the form of its subject matter; and that its bias is away from rather than towards, a close imitation, or as Meredith puts it, a slavish reflexion, of real life.

II

In the prologue to *Every Man in his Humour*, Ben Jonson professed to "sport with human follies, not with crimes"; and perhaps there is little more to be said about the subject matter of comedy. According to the gentler Congreve, natural folly (being incurable) is not a fit subject for comedy; it is unseemly to mock at it; he therefore took affectation for the theme of his masterpiece, *The Way of the World*. This seems on the whole to have been Shakespeare's practice also. It is a more attractive, and perhaps profounder, notion than Jonson's (though, by the way, affectation was one of the main follies Jonson ridiculed). But Congreve's scruples limit comedy rather too drastically. Even in *The Way of the World* one has to strain the definition of affectation to the utmost if it is to cover the criminal folly of Mrs. Marwood and the criminal cunning of Fainall; though if duplicity may be regarded as a crude form of affectation the formula will work. There are advantages in Jonson's wider formula. He himself certainly did not regard folly as either natural or incurable. And if the stress is laid on folly, rather than wickedness on the one hand or misfortune on the other, it follows that the comic situation is involuntary but avoidable, whereas the tragic hero deliberately (if blindly) presses on to an inevitable doom. This is very generally true.

But Jonson's formula does not tell us very much. For one thing, folly can be tragic without being actually criminal, as in Lear, and perhaps also some of Shakespeare's other heroes. Further, both Jonson and Congreve seem to assume that comic situations arise solely from flaws in character. This is not so. They can arise between quite healthy people (like Higgins and Eliza in *Pygmalion*) as the result of natural or accidental misunderstanding; though unless they are to be merely farcical, character must play a part in them. The situation need not be caused by character, but it must reveal character. Perhaps the subject matter of comedy might be defined as "curable or manageable faults or maladjustments". The disturbances with which comedy deals are not always curable; but if they cannot be cured, then their ill-effects are strictly circumscribed; they do not ultimately cause widespread damage to the society in which they occur, and when they are finally isolated in the lives of one or two people, they do not prevent even those people from finding a *modus vivendi*. The situation in Molière's *Misanthrope* is of that kind. On the other hand, where the disturbance leads to or results from the widespread maladjustments of a whole group of people, it must be such as to work itself out to a cure. That would describe the situation in *Tom Jones*.

Is comedy then essentially trivial? In one sense, yes.

> Great things are done when men and mountains meet;
> This is not done by jostling in the street.

These two lines of Blake's are good symbols for tragedy and comedy. But what happens as we jostle against each other in our homes and businesses and villages and towns is perhaps by accumulation more important than the "great things" in determining human happiness and unhappiness, and even in determining the way of the world.

It is not therefore surprising that easily the favourite topic of comedy is sex. In no other department of life is there more "jostling". And nowhere else can we *all* be said to be eccentric; but here we can. All women appear abnormal to all men, and all men to all women; and rightly, for sex carries with it specialisation and so a departure from the *common* human pattern. This departure is accentuated in civilised life. There is a wide gap between the impulses that precede and accompany human mating, and the codes of manners and sentiment between men and women that prevail from time to time. Such widely different works as Chaucer's *Troilus and Criseyde*, Fielding's *Tom Jones*, and Mr. Shaw's *Candida*, all make comedy out of the clash between sentiment and behaviour, the ideal and the real. It is this inconsistency in almost all civilisations and almost all people that makes the comic writers choose sex for one of their main themes, and also makes comedy the best, perhaps the only really humane, attitude to sex. For comedy denies neither the romance and delicacy that has in some odd way become a second nature in civilised men and women, nor the primitive chase, enticement, conquest, and yielding that we share with other animals.

And lastly the mere fact that no other human relationship is so natural as this one; that the survival of the race depends on it; and that it is the commonest disturbing influence to which human nature and social life are subject—this ensures that it should be the most persistent theme of comedy.

And so, in fact, it is: in Chaucer and Shakespeare, in Restoration Comedy, in Fielding and Sterne, Sheridan and Goldsmith, Jane Austen and Mr. Bernard Shaw.

But, alas, comedy has given the most widespread and bitter offence by its attitude to sex. It seems that whatever the comic writer does some one will complain loudly. Jane Austen writes within the strictest bounds of propriety; so she is charged with prudishness. She has her "centre" from which to judge what is or is not socially normal; and from it she utterly condemns all licence between men and women. Moreover, as an artist, she "quits such odious subjects as soon as she can". I do not think that even the fanatics of literary criticism insist that she ought to *approve* of licentiousness; but they do complain that she leaves the unruly workings of passion out of her books. It may be replied to this complaint that she is under no obligation to depict erotic passion; but that if it could be proved that she ignores it or pretends that it does not exist, she might be charged with prudishness. It cannot be proved; and the contrary can be proved. It is the impact of Lydia's seduction on *Pride and Prejudice* that shocks the characters of the story out of their unreally trivial life. In *Mansfield Park* loose conduct is analysed (though not depicted) in some detail in the characters of Henry and Mary Crawford, who are condemned not for the strength of their passions, but for shallowness and lack of sensibility. The main theme of *Persuasion* is the danger of allowing one's feelings to be swayed overmuch by prudence and the worldly advice of one's seniors. And let those who think that Jane Austen handles sex timidly, read this passage from *Sanditon:*

> Sir Edward's great object in life was to be seductive. With such personal advantages as he knew himself to possess, and such talents as he did also give himself credit for, he regarded it as his duty. He felt that he was formed to be a dangerous man—quite in the line of the Lovelaces. The very name of Sir Edward, he thought, carried some degree of fascination with it. To be generally gallant and assiduous about the fair, to make fine speeches to every pretty girl, was but the inferior part of the character he had to play. Miss Heywood, or any other young woman with any pretensions to beauty, he was entitled (according to his own views of Society) to approach with high compliment and rhapsody on the slightest acquaintance; but it was Clara alone on whom he had serious designs; it was Clara whom he meant to seduce. Her seduction was quite determined on. Her situation in every way called for it. She was his rival in Lady Denham's favour, she was young, lovely and dependent. He had very early seen the necessity of the case, and had now been long trying with cautious assiduity, to make an impression on her heart, and to undermine her principles. Clara saw through him, and had not the least intention of being seduced; but she bore with him patiently enough to confirm the sort of attachment which her personal charms had raised. A greater degree of discouragement, indeed, would not have affected Sir Edward. He was armed against the highest pitch of disdain or aversion. If she could not be won by affection, he must carry her off. He knew his business. Already had he had many musings on the subject. If he *were* constrained so to act, he must naturally wish to strike out something new, to exceed those who had gone before him, and he felt a strong curiosity to ascertain whether the neighbourhood of Tombuctoo might not afford some solitary house adapted for Clara's reception; but the expense, alas! of measures in that masterly style was ill-suited to his purse, and prudence obliged him to prefer the quietest sort of ruin and disgrace for the object of his affections to the more renowned.

It is not however by squeamishness that comedy most often gives offence, but by licentiousness or obscenity. The two charges are usually confused or combined, but they are really quite different; it is one thing to advocate lax conduct, and quite a different thing to display in the open matters over which politeness draws a veil. The former concerns morality; the latter good taste. Let us therefore treat the first as a moral question and the second as an aesthetic question.

In its historical beginnings comedy was a species of authorised licence. That does not mean that it was an attack on morality, good manners, or social discipline; in fact, Aristophanes (the only dramatist of this phase whose works have survived in bulk) had and expressed strict views about conduct, and in the *Frogs* he takes Euripides to task for laxity of principle about many matters, including sex. Aristophanes is far from primitive in his dramatic art, indeed he was the very last writer of the Attic Old Comedy; but his plays belong to the licentious class. What this means is that the comedy was a safety-valve or outlet for disorderly passions, including erotic passions; and by treating them in an unserious spirit it rendered them less dangerous socially. How far this has remained a deliberate purpose of comic writers is very doubtful. It seems to have been in Fielding's mind when he wrote *Tom Jones;* Tom's frequent falls from grace are upon the whole treated as a joke, for two reasons. Fielding does not wish to approve of them, but at the same time he wishes to insist that natural faults are curable, and far less serious than cold-blooded selfish dishonesty, as exemplified in Tom's foil, Blifil. I think almost any scene in *Tom Jones* makes Fielding's attitude clear; this passage from Chapter 10 of the Fifth Book will do as well as any:

Jones retired from the company in which we have seen him engaged, into the fields, where he intended to cool himself by a walk in the open air before he attended Mr. Allworthy. There, whilst he renewed those meditations on his dear Sophia which the dangerous illness of his friend and benefactor had for some time interrupted, an accident happened, which with sorrow we relate, and with sorrow, doubtless, will it be read; however, that historic truth to which we profess so inviolable an attachment obliges us to communicate it to posterity.

It was now a pleasant evening in the latter end of June, when our hero was walking in a most delicious grove, where the gentle breezes fanning the leaves, together with the sweet trilling of a murmuring stream, and the melodious notes of nightingales, formed all together the most enchanting harmony. In this scene, so sweetly accommodated to love, he meditated on his dear Sophia. While his wanton fancy roved unbounded over all her beauties, and his lively imagination painted the charming maid in various ravishing forms, his warm heart melted with tenderness, and at length, throwing himself on the ground by the side of a gently murmuring brook, he broke forth into the following ejaculation:

"O Sophia, would Heaven give thee to my arms, how blest would be my condition! Curst be that fortune which sets a distance between us! Was I but possessed of thee, one only suit of rags thy whole estate, is there a man on earth whom I would envy? How contemptible would the brightest Circassian beauty, drest in all the jewels of the Indies, appear to my eyes! But why do I mention another woman? Could I think my eyes capable of looking at any other with tenderness, these hands should tear them from my head. No, my Sophia, if cruel fortune separates us for ever, my soul shall doat on thee alone. The chastest constancy will I ever preserve to thy image. Though I should never have possession of thy charming person, still shalt alone have possession of my thoughts, my love, my soul. Oh! my fond heart is so wrapt in that tender bosom, that the brightest beauties would for me have no charms, nor would a hermit be colder in their embraces. Sophia, Sophia alone, shall be mine. What raptures are in the name! I will engrave it on every tree."

At these words he started up, and beheld—not his Sophia—no, nor a Circassian maid richly and elegantly attired for the grand signior's seraglio. No; without a gown, in a shift that was somewhat of the coarsest and none of the cleanest, bedewed likewise with some odoriferous effluvia, the produce of the day's labour, with a pitchfork in her hand, Molly Seagrim approached. Our hero had his penknife in his hand, which he had drawn for the before-mentioned purpose of carving in the bark; when the girl, coming near him, cried out with a smile, "You don't intend to kill me, squire, I hope?" "Why should you think I would kill you?" answered Jones, "Nay," replied she, "after your cruel usage of me when I saw you last, killing me would, perhaps, be too great kindness for me to expect."

Here ensued a parley, which, as I do not think myself obliged to relate, I shall
omit. It is sufficient that it lasted a full quarter of an hour, at the conclusion of
which they retired into the thickest part of the grove.

But in other writers, such as Chaucer, there seems no such motive, or if it is
present it is very slight. The "swiving" of the Miller's wife and daughter in the
Reeve's Tale is described with the most light-hearted high spirits; for the girl it
was perhaps a piece of pleasure and kindness that had rarely come her way in a
home presided over by such unpleasant parents (Chaucer may not have meant to
imply this, but he certainly implies that she enjoyed her night with the young
man); for the parents it was a comic punishment of their self-importance and of
the miller's dishonesty. In *Troilus and Criseyde*, the detailed description of Criseyde's seduction, and particularly Pandarus's part in it, serves a different purpose. Partly it brings out a contrast between the characters of Pandarus and Criseyde on the one hand and Troilus on the other; and partly it reveals the divided
impulses in Troilus himself, for the main theme of the poem is the inconsistency
of feeling and motive in which he is involved (like all decent and natural young
lovers) between plain physical desire and respect for the feelings and interests of
the woman. The convention of courtly love was one of those codes of sentiment
for civilising sex of which I have spoken; it is not to be despised, nor does Chaucer despise it; the despairs and scruples of Troilus are by no means unnatural and
have their counterpart even in enlightened (or cynical) ages like the present. But
love is desire as well as sentiment; Chaucer's Troilus was a flesh-and-blood
young man, not a mere collection of ideals; he wanted to possess Criseyde and he
was human enough to enjoy possessing her. The truth to life of this great love
story demanded that every side of Criseyde's seduction should be fully revealed.
Yet although Chaucer included *Troilus and Criseyde* among the sinful works of
which he repented in his famous retraction at the end of the *Canterbury Tales*,
it is not in the least an immoral work. The love-affair comes to grief because of
faults in all the three main characters; but chiefly because Pandarus, by his well-
meaning but unprincipled interference, degraded it into a mere fornication.

But there are comic works that are more reasonably accused of advocating
licence. All our Restoration comedies, from Etherege to Farquhar, take seduction for granted as a normal form of sport, which indeed upon the whole it was
for Charles II and his courtiers. The mere fact that they take it *for granted* par-
tially acquits them of advocating it; and Wycherley, who has the worst reputation of them all, was obviously unhappy about its results and implications—so
much so that *The Country Wife*, in which he accepts it and exploits its comic
possibilities without reserve, is a far healthier and therefore more moral play
than *The Plain Dealer*, in which he is both fiercely satirical and morbidly sentimental. *The Country Wife*, indeed, has a moral, and a sound one: that the husband who mistrusts his wife and tries to keep her from other men will merely
stimulate her desires and teach her to deceive him, however ill-equipped she is
with natural cunning. This is in accord with the rationalism of the period. The
comic dramatists of the late Seventeenth Century treat sex as an opportunity for
pleasure but a potential source of trouble; and their norm of conduct it to get a
fair share of the pleasure with the least possible distress to all concerned. For the
most part their men and women are of the same class, and treat each other as
equals; and in one respect their morality compares favourably with the average
Victorian morality, for they have roughly the same standards for men as for

women. The Victorian code (both legal and social) was that whereas a wife should forgive her husband's infidelity if he asked her to, a husband was under no obligation to forgive his wife's. In the Seventeenth Century, divorce could only be obtained by an *ad hoc* Act of Parliament; it was therefore very rare, and perhaps for that very reason there was greater mutual tolerance among civilised people though of course they were often very unhappy, as is made clear by Halifax's *Advice to a Daughter*. And there were husbands who literally locked their wives up, though public opinion censured that kind of behaviour. A cynic might say that there was an obvious reason for the censure: that every man was interested in having his neighbour's wife at large and accesible. But the cynicism would not be altogether justified; cynicism seldom is. The Restoration with, however little respect they had for the Seventh Commandment, were upon the whole humane towards women and respected them as equals. There were among them notorious rakes, such a Rochester; but the general feeling was against the extremes of debauchery. That is at any rate the standpoint of Etherege, Congreve and Vanbrugh. Wycherley's Horner is not a typical Restoration gentleman; he is a comic rogue, comparable on a different plane to Shakespeare's Autolycus or Ben Jonson's Volpone; his function is to expose the other characters and keep the plot in motion.

But for the moralist to condemn any comedy because of its subject matter is an error of judgement. It is not the business of comedy to inculcate moral doctrine. Its business is to satisfy a healthy human desire; the desire to understand the behaviour of men and women towards one another in social life, and to judge them according to their own pretensions and standards. So far as it does this well and truly it makes for righteousness. We may, and probably most of us do, dissent from the moral standards of Etherege or Wycherley, at least in part; but unless our morality is of the kind that needs wrapping up in cotton wool, we need not be protected against their plays. I will go further than this: even assuming that the moral standards of Restoration Comedy are utterly bad, we ought to be able to enjoy the comedies themselves, and to do so will strengthen rather than weaken our moral fibre, provided always that we have grown out of the cotton wool stage. All we are justified in asking of the comic writer is that his standards should be consistent; not that they should be right. The whole question is part of a wider quarrel between moralists and artists. But let me make it clear that I am not on the side of the artist *against* the moralist; I believe myself to be on the side of morality *and* art, as Milton was in *Areopagitica* and Shelley in his *Defence of Poetry*.

With the other charge, of obscenity, as it is much less serious, I will be very brief. There are people who object to many comedies, and particularly all Restoration comedies on the ground that they are indecent. It is difficult, and perhaps futile, to argue about questions of taste such as this. We can only state our own tastes and plead for some tolerance on both sides of the question. Sex is a nuisance; we all sometimes wish we could dispense with it. But there it is; and just as the poets have paid tribute to its noblest and most beautiful manifestations and also reviled it for cruelties and humiliations, so let the comic writers enjoy it as the greatest of eternal jokes. But let them do it with a certain discretion of speech. I cannot see the objection to innuendo. It offends some people, who feel it to be cowardly; if we are to have filth, they say, let us have frank filth. But this use of the word filth is equivocal; and it is begging the question to equate coarseness with frankness. In literature and drama, surely the crude and limited vocabulary of the navy and that of the clinical lecture-room are equally out of place—and they are the only two perfectly plain vocabularies available for use in this connexion. It is true that the point of an innuendo can be missed, if one is not on the look-out; but on this, of all subjects, it is proper to make jokes with a certain finesse.

The most daring and notorious joke in Restoration Comedy occurs in Act IV, Scene 3 of *The Country Wife*, where Wycherley comes as near as possible to depicting "the lineaments of gratified" (and ungratified) "desire" by a very clever innuendo.

> *Re-enter Lady Fidget with a piece of china in her hand, and Horner following.*

LADY FIDGET (*to Mrs Squeamish*) . . . I have been toiling and moiling, for the prettiest piece of china, my dear.

HORNER Nay, she had been too hard for me, do what I could.

MRS SQUEAMISH Oh lord, I'll have some china too. Good Mr Horner, don't think to give other people china, and me none; come in with me too.

HORNER Upon my honour, I have none left now.

MRS SQUEAMISH Nay, nay, I have known you deny your china before now, but you shan't put me off so, come—

HORNER This lady had the last there.

LADY FIDGET Yes, indeed, Madam, to my certain knowledge, he had no more left.

MRS SQUEAMISH O, but it may be he may have some you could not find.

LADY FIDGET What, d'ye think if he had had any left, I would not have had it too? for we women of quality never think we have china enough.

HORNER Do not take it ill I cannot make china for you all; but I will have a roll-wagon for you too, another time.

MRS SQUEAMISH Thank you, dear toad.

The disguise is purely verbal and scenic; there can be no doubt of what the characters are talking about. The question, and it is merely a question of taste, is whether it should be talked about so openly on the stage. The answer will depend mainly on whether the situation is comic, or only coarse; and comic it certainly is in this scene. But any one who is squeamish had better not go to see *The Country Wife* without first reading it.

III

Comedy depicts men and women in society. Meredith stresses this point; and it leads him to the questionable conclusion that the setting of comedy should be urban and that Shakespeare's characters, being "creatures of the woods and wilds", are "subjects of a special study in the poetically comic." It is true that Shakespeare's comedy is unique, because of his apparent inability to write with his imagination at less than full stretch: he was *incapable* of realism. But it is not clear, without better reasons than Meredith gives, that pure comedy cannot be staged in a fairy-tale setting as successfully as in Paris or London. Meredith seems to have been misled by the special narrow use of the word society in the Victorian and Edwardian periods, and indeed to have been obsessed by the idea of Society with a capital S: a select class of wealthy and leisured persons, speaking an artificial language of their own and spending all their time and energy in entertaining themselves and one another. Certainly that kind of society provides a good setting for comedy; but to *limit* comedy to it is simply to fly in the face of the facts.

Characters like Bottom were too close to nature for Meredith's strict notion of comedy; and Titania, a "creature of the woods and wilds", was quite outside his pale. But no particular class of person or environment is in itself either comic or un-comic; it is the imagination of the writer or spectator that makes them so. Meredith's argument is parallel to the orthodox renascence convention of dramatic propriety, according to which a king or a statesman should not be made ridiculous or contemptible. Dr. Johnson met this pedantry with a common sense if not completely conclusive rejoinder:

> Shakespeare always makes nature predominate over accident; and if he preserves the essential character, is not very careful of distinctions superinduced and adventitious. His story requires Romans or Kings, but he thinks only on men. He knew that Rome, like any other city, had men of all dispositions; and wanting a buffoon he went into the Senate-house for that which the Senate-house would certainly have afforded him. He was inclined to shew an usurper and a murderer not only odious but despicable, he therefore added drunkenness to his other qualities, knowing that kings love wine like other men, and that wine exerts its natural power upon kings. These are the petty cavils of petty minds; a poet overlooks the casual distinctions of country and condition, as a painter, satisfied with the figure, neglects the drapery.

As for Meredith's thesis, it is probably true that man in his urban environment lends himself more readily to comedy; and certainly true that comedy is essentially concerned with men and not with fairies. But all art is in greater or less degree symbolic: as Johnson said, imitations convince not because they are mistaken for realities, but because they bring realities to mind. Surely even in the strictest sense, rustics can be comic, and not only rustics but animals and even vegetables; and not only things in nature, but purely imaginary creatures like Titania. In transporting Bottom into fairy-land Shakespeare knew very well what he was doing, and was well within his rights as a comic dramatist. The situation of course is unrealistic and dreamlike; but any one who has himself dreamed will know how much richer in comedy the world of dreams is than the circumspect world of every-day working reality.

Society in the proper sense—or at least in the sense in which the word defines the setting of comedy—stands for an idea rather than a particular set of persons. It stands for coherence; for a common body of opinions and standards and a disposition to co-operate. It can be contracted to a very small class living together in a small area; it can be extended to the whole of humanity or even beyond the limits of the human species. Its extent will depend partly on the power of statesmen, philosophers, and artists to impose unity on apparently heterogeneous material; partly on the social conditions of the time and place in which they are living; partly on the purpose they have in view. To the mind of Shakespeare and his fellow-Elizabethans the universe was more homogeneous than it is to us; for our moral ideas lag behind the lessons of modern physics and economics. Shakespeare did not therefore need to restrict his setting at all. The distinctions between man, beast, and spirit, which our minds can only surmount by a change of gear and often a very violent one, did not trouble him; Prospero, Ariel, and Caliban are all members of one society. For Chaucer it was the same. His range was somewhat narrower; but that was because his imagination, powerful and adventurous though it was, had not quite the range of Shakespeare's, not because the medieval world was in any except the strictly material sense narrower than the Elizabethan. Chaucer's comic world contains Chantecleer, and the Eagle in the *House of Fame;* January and May in the *Merchant's Tale* (the story is an allegory, though a very realistic one); the Prioress and the Wife of Bath; Troilus, Criseyde, and Pandarus. It is a world at least as varied, if not quite so cosmic, as Shakespeare's.

But about the beginning of the Seventeenth Century the outlook of the educated Englishman changed; not in a single generation, but with the rapidity of a revolution. Men's eyes turned towards the material world in which they lived; and in this movement towards materialistic rationalism Ben Jonson was the central literary figure, as he was also the founder of modern comedy. There were to be no more fairies in comedy. Into the merits of the controversy about realism I will not go here. One can only be thankful that Jonson was in the field a few years later than Shakespeare, and not a few years earlier. But probably the reaction was both inevitable and salutary. Fletcher's realistic comedies are altogether superior to *The Faithful Shepherdess* and the romantic tragedies and tragi-comedies that earned him from Dryden the disparaging description, "a limb of Shakespeare." Be this as it may, Jonson narrowed the field to particular time and place. But his own comedy was still very wide in range. Society for him was still at least as wide as human nature, though his imagination was only at its ease in the underworld of London. The test his characters have to submit to—the standard they have to satisfy—is a hard but crude one. They have to survive in the world of *Bartholomew Fair.*

Later writers, lacking the large ideal vision of Shakespeare and Chaucer, and the robust digestion of Jonson, have discovered an excellent convention which is sometimes called the Comic Microcosm. They take for the setting of their comedy a "little world," a strictly limited society with fairly homogeneous traditions, standards, and habits. In such a world, where the rules of the game of life are the same for everybody, where all know the rules and accept them in theory at least, it is easy to measure men and women against each other fairly, and to pick out the good and the bad mixers, at the same time depicting even in the good mixers those faults of temperament and foibles of the intellect that cause both the graver irritations and the pleasant smaller frictions provocative of nothing worse than a smile. The first very clear example of the Comic Microcosm in our literature is the world of Restoration comedy. Perhaps Etherege, the earliest of the Restoration comic dramatists, deserves the credit of discovering it; but he did not invent it, he saw it around him. How closely he followed in his plays the pattern of a real little world in which he lived may be seen from his letters. I have said something of the standards of this society, and it only remains to repeat that for the purpose of comedy (as outlined in the third sentence of this paragraph) it does not matter so much that they should be morally sound as that they should be consistent, clearly understood, and generally accepted within the society.

The world of Restoration comedy, small and never very important historically, soon melted away. In the Eighteenth Century English civilisation broke up into innumerable units centered in the home. This decentralisation gave birth to *The Spectator;* and Addison created around Sir Roger de Coverley a kind of domestic comedy new to English literature, unless it had been foreshadowed by the country seat of Mr. Justice Shallow in Shakespeare's *Henry IV*. In a nation alive with vigorous and self-centred homes the domestic world offers an obvious microcosm to the comic writer. In the early days of our literature, Chaucer had used it for many of his best Canterbury Tales. In Eighteenth Century England domestic comedy revived. By a charming irony it was a homeless Irish wanderer, Goldsmith, who wrote the best of all our domestic plays, *She Stoops to Conquer;* I wish I could rank his even more domestic novel *The Vicar of Wakefield* as highly, but it is too unequal, ill-constructed, and heterogeneous to be quite successful as a comedy or anything else. I suppose the most *remarkable* of all domestic microcosms is Shandy Hall, the setting of one of the greatest and most sustained flights of comic imagination in our literature. But a single home is rather small to allow comedy to display its full powers; *Tristram Shandy* is a tour-de-force, and Sterne himself is rather too much of a virtuoso—even an exhibitionist—to keep consistently within the bounds of comedy. Jane Austen saw what was wanted; her "three or four families in a country village" provided the most successful, and famous, of all English comic microcosms.

No later writer has created comedy to equal hers. Trollope's Barsetshire is a convincing little world and offers some high moments of comedy: the death of Mrs. Proudie, for instance. Unfortunately it is not a purely *comic* microcosm; Trollope sacrifices too many of his characters to the demons of sensationalism and sentimentality. Meredith's "Society" is too unreal to serve convincingly as a measure of character. Mr. Shaw has not chosen to use any consistent convention for his settings; they are varied, and all of them more or less fantastic even when they appear most realistic. Since his comedy is a comedy of ideas its material setting has little importance except for theatrical purposes. He has a sort of intellectual microcosm: the world of self-conscious middle-class ideas which flourished at the end of the Nineteenth Century. One is conscious in his plays of a consistent milieu, in which the mental habits of his characters can be accurately measured against each other. Lastly, James Joyce's Dublin is a little world within which he achieved a masterpiece; but *Ulysses* is more than a comedy, it is what he intended it to be, an epic.

From **Problems of the Theatre**[*]

Friedrich Duerrenmatt

In theories of the drama a difference is made between a tragic hero, the hero of tragedy, and a comic hero, the hero of comedy. The qualities a tragic hero must possess are well known. He must be capable of rousing our sympathy. His guilt and his innocence, his virtues and his vices must be mixed in the most pleasant and yet exact manner, and administered in doses according to well-defined rules. If, for example, I make my tragic hero an evil man, then I must endow him with a portion of intellect equal to his malevolence. As a result of this rule, the most sympathetic stage character in German literature has turned out to be the devil. The role of the hero in the play has not changed. The only thing that has changed is the social position of the character who awakens our sympathy.

In ancient tragedy and in Shakespeare the hero belongs to the highest class in society, to the nobility. The spectators watch a suffering, acting, raving hero who occupies a social position far higher than their own. This still continues to impress audiences today.

Then when Lessing and Schiller introduced the bourgeois drama, the audience saw itself as the suffering hero on the stage. But the evolution of the hero continued. Büchner's Woyzeck is a primitive proletarian who represents far less socially than the average spectator. But it is precisely in this extreme form of human existence, in this last, most miserable form, that the audience is to see the human being also, indeed itself.

And finally we might mention Pirandello who was the first, as far as I know, to render the hero, the character on the stage, immaterial and transparent just as Wilder did the dramatic place. The audience watching this sort of presentation attends, as it were, its own dissection, its own psycho-analysis, and the stage becomes man's internal milieu, the inner space of the world.

Of course, the theatre has never dealt only with kings and generals; in comedy the hero has always been the peasant, the beggar, the ordinary citizen—but this was always in comedy. Nowhere in Shakespeare do we find a comic king; in his day a ruler could appear as a bloody monster but never as a fool. In Shakespeare the courtiers, the artisans, the working people are comic. Hence, in the evolution of the tragic hero we see a trend towards comedy. Analogously the fool becomes more and more of a tragic figure. This fact is by no means without significance. The hero of a play not only propels an action on, he not only suffers a certain fate, but he also represents a world. Therefore we have to ask ourselves how we should present our own questionable world and with what sort of heroes.

[*] Friedrich Duerrenmatt, "Problems of the Theatre." Translated by Gerhard Nellhaus (Grove Press, 1964 and Jonathan Cape Limited).

We have to ask ourselves how the mirrors which catch and reflect this world should be ground and set.

Can our present-day world, to ask a concrete question, be represented by Schiller's dramatic art? Some writers claim it can be, since Schiller still holds audiences in his grip. To be sure, in art everything is possible when the art is right. But the question is if an art valid for its time could possibly be so even for our day. Art can never be repeated. If it were repeatable, it would be foolish not just to write according to the rules of Schiller.

Schiller wrote as he did because the world in which he lived could still be mirrored in the world his writing created, a world he could build as an historian. But just barely. For was not Napoleon perhaps the last hero in the old sense? The world today as it appears to us could hardly be encompassed in the form of the historical drama as Schiller wrote it, for the reason alone that we no longer have any tragic heroes, but only vast tragedies staged by world butchers and produced by slaughtering machines. Hitler and Stalin cannot be made into Wallensteins. Their power was so enormous that they themselves were no more than incidental, corporeal and easily replaceable expressions of this power; and the misfortune associated with the former and to a considerable extent also with the latter is too vast, too complex, too horrible, too mechanical and usually simply too devoid of all sense. Wallenstein's power can still be envisioned; power as we know it today can only be seen in its smallest part for, like an iceberg, the largest part is submerged in anonymity and abstraction. Schiller's drama presupposes a world that the eye can take in, that takes for granted genuine actions of state, just as Greek tragedy did. For only what the eye can take in can be made visible in art. The state today, however, cannot be envisioned, for it is anonymous and bureaucratic; and not only in Moscow and Washington, but also in Berne. Actions of state today have become *post-hoc* satyric dramas which follow the tragedies executed in secret earlier. True representatives of our world are missing; the tragic heroes are nameless. Any small-time crook, petty government official or policeman better represents our world than a senator or president. Today art can only embrace the victims, if it can reach men at all; it can no longer come close to the mighty. Creon's secretaries close Antigone's case. The state has lost its physical reality, and just as physics can now only cope with the world in mathematical formulae, so the state can only be expressed in statistics. Power today becomes visible, material only when it explodes as in the atom bomb, in this marvellous mushroom which rises and spreads immaculate as the sun and in which mass murder and beauty have become one. The atom bomb cannot be reproduced artistically since it is mass-produced. In its face all man's art that would recreate it must fail, since it is itself a creation of man. Two mirrors which reflect one another remain empty.

But the task of art, in so far as art can have a task at all, and hence also the task of drama today, is to create something concrete, something that has form. This can be accomplished best by comedy. Tragedy, the strictest genre in art, presupposes a formed world. Comedy—in so far as it is not just satire of a particular society as in Molière—supposes an unformed world, a world being made and turned upside down, a world about to fold like ours. Tragedy overcomes distance; it can make myths originating in times immemorial seem like the present to the Athenians. But comedy creates distance; the attempt of the Athenians to gain a foothold in Sicily is translated by comedy into the birds undertaking to create their own empire before which the gods and men will have to capitulate. How comedy works can be seen in the most primitive kind of joke, in the dirty story, which, though it is of very dubious value, I bring up only because it is the best illustration of what I mean by creating distance. The subject of the dirty story is the purely sexual, which because it is purely sexual, is formless and without objective distance. To give form the purely sexual is transmuted, as I have already mentioned, into the dirty joke. Therefore this type of joke is a kind of original comedy, a transposition of the sexual on to the plain of the comical. In this way it is possible today, in a society dominated by John Doe, to talk in an accepted way about the purely sexual. In the dirty story it becomes clear that the comical exists in forming what is formless, in creating order out of chaos.

The means by which comedy creates distance is the conceit. Tragedy is without conceit. Hence there are few tragedies whose subjects were invented. By this I do not mean to imply that the ancient tragedians lacked inventive ideas of the sort that are written today, but the marvel of their art was that they had no need of these inventions, of conceits. That makes all the difference. Aristophanes, on the other hand, lives by conceits. The stuff of his plays are not myths but inventions, which take place not in the past but the present. They drop into their world like bomb-shells which, by throwing up huge craters of dirt, change the present into the comic and thus scatter the dirt for everyone to see. This, of course, does not mean that drama today can only be comical. Tragedy and comedy are but formal concepts, dramatic attitudes, figments of the aesthetic imagination which can embrace one and the same thing. Only the conditions under which each is created are different, and these conditions have their basis only in small part in art.

Tragedy presupposes guilt, despair, moderation, lucidity, vision, a sense of responsibility. In the Punch-and-Judy show of our century, in this back-sliding of the white race, there are no more guilty and also, no responsible men. It is always, 'We couldn't help it' and 'We didn't really want that to happen.' And indeed, things happen without anyone in particular being responsible for them. Everything is dragged along and everyone gets caught somewhere in the sweep of events. We are all collectively guilty, collectively bogged down in the sins of our fathers and of our forefathers. We are the offspring of children. That is our misfortune, but not our guilt: guilt can exist only as a personal achievement, as a religious deed. Comedy alone is suitable for us. Our world has led to the grotesque as well as to the atom bomb, and so it is a world like that of Hieronymus Bosch whose apocalyptic paintings are also grotesque. But the grotesque is only a way of expressing in a tangible manner, of making us perceive physically the paradoxical, the form of the unformed, the face of a world without face; and just as in our thinking today we seem to be unable to do without the concept of the paradox, so also in art, and in our world which at times seems still to exist only because the atom bomb exists: out of fear of the bomb.

But the tragic is still possible even if pure tragedy is not. We can achieve the tragic out of comedy. We can bring it forth as a frightening moment, as an abyss that opens suddenly; indeed, many of Shakespeare's tragedies are already really comedies out of which the tragic arises.

After all this the conclusion might easily be drawn that comedy is the expression of despair, but this conclusion is not inevitable. To be sure, whoever realizes the senselessness, the hopelessness of this world might well despair, but this despair is not a result of this world. Rather it is an answer given by an individual to this world; another answer would be not to despair, would be an individual's decision to endure this world in which we live like Gulliver among the giants. He also achieves distance, he also steps back a pace or two who takes measure of his opponent, who prepares himself to fight his opponent or to escape him. It is still possible to show man as a courageous being.

In truth this is a principal concern of mine. The blind man, Romulus, Übelohe, Akki, are all men of courage. The lost world-order is restored within them; the universal escapes my grasp. I refuse to find the universal in a doctrine. The universal for me is chaos. The world (hence the stage which represents this world) is for me something monstrous, a riddle of misfortunes which must be accepted but before which one must not capitulate. The world is far bigger than any man, and perforce threatens him constantly. If one could but stand outside the world, it would no longer be threatening. But I have neither the right nor the ability to be an outsider to this world. To find solace in poetry can also be all too cheap; it is more honest to retain one's human point of view. Brecht's thesis, that the world is an accident, which he developed in his *Street Scene* where he shows how this accident happened, may yield—as it in fact did—some magnificent theatre; but he did it by concealing most of the evidence! Brecht's thinking is inexorable, because inexorably there are many things he will not think about.

And lastly it is through the conceit, through comedy, that the anonymous audience becomes possible as an audience, becomes a reality to be counted on, and also one to be taken into account. The conceit easily transforms the crowd of theatre-goers into a mass which can be attacked, deceived, outsmarted into listening to things it would otherwise not so readily listen to. Comedy is a mousetrap in which the public is easily caught and in which it will get caught over and over again. Tragedy, on the other hand, predicated a true community, a kind of community whose existence in our day is but an embarrassing fiction.

Comedy*

Arthur Koestler

Most of the devices employed in comedy have already been analysed in previous chapters. It was once usual to classify comedies into those relying on the comic of situations, manners, and character; and though all such classifications are of small value, they may serve as an approximate guide.

In his discussion of the comic of situations, Bergson came nearest to the essence of the comic itself: "A situation is always comic," he writes, "if it participates simultaneously in two series of events which are absolutely independent of each other, and if it can be interpreted in two quite different meanings." One is tempted to cry "Fire!" but a couple of pages further on Bergson has dropped the clue and gone back to his metaphysical hobby; the interference of two independent series in a given situation is merely a further example of the "mechanisation of life."

In fact the interference of series in its many variations—coincidence, mistaken identity, and so forth—is the clearest example of bisociated contexts. Any attempt at enumerating the various patterns of the comic of situations (disguise, confusion of time and occasion, and so on) would be tedious and repetitive. Similarly the main techniques of the comedy of manners have been discussed under the headings of Satire, Irony, and Caricature, and need no further elaboration. Our concluding remarks concern the comic of *character*.

A good history of literature could be written which would use as leitmotif the gradually growing realization of the complexities of character, its internal contradictions, its simultaneous existence on several planes. There are ups and downs on this curve according to the rise and fall of civilizations, but if we could draw the average curve, it would probably show that, as far as literature can be said to "progress," it progresses in the direction of growing insight into the complexities of the human condition. Masterpieces are produced in each peak period, but they are relative peaks on a steadily mounting tide and can only be appreciated by an attitude of (not necessarily deliberate or conscious) regression to an earlier level. Hence the impossibility of copying their method and approach, even if we are taught to regard them as immortal models of perfection; they are perfect only relative to their own level of complexity.

This development can easily be demonstrated in the progress from the comic "type" to the comic "character." The type is a caricature in which exaggeration and simplification of one feature are carried almost to the point of abstrac-

* Arthur Koestler, "Comedy," in *Insight and Outlook* (The Macmillan Company, 1949), pp. 102–104. Reprinted with the permission of The Macmillan Company and A. D. Peters & Company Ltd. © 1977 by Arthur Koestler.

tion—the miser, the glutton, the misanthropist, the cuckold, and so forth. The mechanism of the comic resulting from this technique has been analysed before, and needs no further comment. Equally obvious is the marked increase of complexity in the characters of modern comedy—in Tchekhov, Wilde, Shaw, or even Sacha Guitry.

A parallel development, and directly dependent on the first, is the gradual displacement of character features and of the situations deriving from them, from the comic towards the tragic end of the spectrum. Timidity, adolescent gaucherie, clumsiness in athletic games have moved from the sphere of the ludicrous to that of the psychological novel and self-pitying autobiography. Cuckoldry is no longer comic; the classic triangle has migrated from the vaudeville stage to the waiting room of the psychoanalyst. Harpagon's pedantry and meanness are aspects of his anal-erotic fixation; the bearded Jew is recognized as a scapegoat for irrational aggression; obesity and thinness, the deformities of body or mind are objects of sympathy. The turning point can be clearly seen where Shakespeare's figures change from comic into tragic characters: Shylock, the clown in Lear, Caliban, Falstaff at the end of *Henry V*. Growing insight into the complexities of human character, including one's own, has as its inevitable consequence sympathy and identification with the weaknesses and foibles of others. Hence the modern comedy has increasingly to rely for its effects on a change from caricature to witticism, from the comic of situations to brilliant dialogue. But while individual aggression is in steady retreat and leads to the decline of the types of comic based on it, collective social aggressiveness against institutions, between classes and nations increases, and so, in consequence, does social satire on the stage, in novels, and cartoons. The old character types, the miser and cuckold, are replaced by social types: Blimp, the fox-hunting squire, the long-haired aesthete. With the crumbling of sex taboos, the sexy joke becomes increasingly sophisticated and implicit, sometimes almost a riddle, as in Peter Arno's cartoons. The general increase in education and sophistication furthers the tendency towards the dry, allusive wisecrack and the apparent nonsense joke. Charlie Chaplin marked the end of an era of social sentimentality towards the Little Man, the timid and downtrodden; the Marx Brothers are a mixture of buffoonery in a crazy, disintegrating world, with a kind of surrealistic logic—the twisted laws and curved spaces of the non-Euclidean geometries.

IV
THE NATURE
OF COMEDY

Comedy Now[*]

Walter Kerr

Comedy cannot help finding the flaw in free, proud, vaulting activity. Its eyes are trained in that direction, its habits of mind are compulsive. Let a clown loose anywhere and he will unerringly detect the least trace of spuriousness in an otherwise confident posture. The clown cannot help himself; he was born to bring ambition down. He will do it to his own mother, he will quickly be caustic about the children he loves, he will put his own body on the firing line if he has to. His pessimism is reflexive, unpremeditated, uncontrollable. In the presence of Michelangelo's David, he will see only the idealized pubic hair. With a quick and gleeful whoop, he will make use of the single subterfuge he has seen to call the whole vast image into question. He focuses exclusively upon the prettying-up that can be ridiculed and makes the rest of the soaring architecture a mere appendage to the tiny pretense he has pointed out. He devalues by instinct, and his inverted vision is 20–20.

Yet he detests his own accuracy and secretly wishes, in great anguish, that his eye could be proved false. He really keeps at his work in the hope that one day he *will* be proved mistaken. He yearns, with all his heart, for the perfection he is constantly exploding. One day, one day perhaps, he will cast his cunning eye on an image of aspiration that will defy him; the blemish will not be there, he will look feverishly and not find it, he will feel his talent is failing him. That is his unacknowledged hope, the hidden affinity for greatness that keeps him working so hard, the secret of his tagging forever after the tragic hero whose failures he taunts. He keeps close on the heels of the man-god he has long since disposed of. He has had so many successes in ridiculing this pretentious fellow that he might well have washed his hands of him, long since. But he hasn't. He doesn't now. With the expression of an anxious spaniel, he begs to be permitted to come along on the journey. He will be a nuisance on the journey, he will mock it and make a mess of it; but he wants to be there. He is driven by his need to demoralize; he is also driven by the same ideal of perfection—future perfection, possible perfection, somewhere, somehow—that animates the tragic man he doubts so. He has inherited his furtive, constantly denied, dream of perfection from the tragic hero because he has inherited his very being from the tragic hero. It is just his bad luck that he happens to notice, all of the time, the stupid impediments the tragic hero is trying to forget. He really hates himself for his own perceptiveness.

Thus, there is always an element of exasperation with *self* in the clown, in comedy. A comedian is rarely exasperated by the situation in which he finds himself. He rarely permits himself to be too much exasperated by others; that would suggest bitterness, anger, those qualities that unfailingly turn comedy sour. What fills the clown with occasional, usually briefly displayed, disgust is not the fact of hurricanes in the sky or haplessness in other people's conduct, but his intense awareness of his own nature. He is the dour one who *sees* what is wrong. He is the advocate of impediments. He can find something inadequate in everyone he meets, in everything he touches. And because he has doggedly hoped all along to find someone or something that would not yield to his iconoclastic investigations, that would not further encourage his doubts, he becomes— now and again, and very slightly—fed up. He becomes fed up, as we all do, with a mind that functions in only one way, however effectively.

He does not let us see this impatience with his own nature too often. He does not want to betray an underlying streak of futile optimism that his own talents are committed to denying and destroying; he must not give more than an inch to the affirmative temperament of the tragic hero, it is not his business to do so. Yet the streak sometimes shows, in the form of contempt for his own task. It is there in the strange little gasp, accompanied by a rattled shake of the head, that Buster Keaton permits himself perhaps once in each film. He wants to say something else, and can't. He wants himself to be better, and cannot quite bear the knowledge that he never, never will be. The streak is present at once in Feste, whose very first words are "Let her hang me," when he hears that his mistress is angry with him for being dilatory about his fooling; it is covered over with great effort by the nearly exhausted clown during the rest of the play. It is defined without evasion by Jaques. "They say you are a melancholy fellow" is Rosalind's greeting to him in the forest. "I am so," Jaques replied, "I do love it better than laughing." When Rosalind quickly points out that the extremes of gaiety and melancholy are both to be avoided, Jaques stands his sorry ground.

> "Why, 'tis good to be sad and say nothing."
> "Why, then, 'tis good to be a post."
> "I have neither the scholar's melancholy, which is emulation; nor the musician's, which is fantastical; nor the courtier's, which is proud; nor the soldier's, which is ambitious; nor the lawyer's, which is politic; nor the lady's, which is nice; nor the lover's, which is all of these: but it is a melancholy of mine own, compounded of many simples, extracted from many objects; and indeed the sundry contemplation of my travels, in which my often rumination wraps me in a most humorous sadness."
> "A traveller! By my faith, you have great reason to be sad. I fear you have sold your own lands to see other men's. Then, to have seen much, and to have nothing, is to have rich eyes and poor hands."
> "Yes, I have gained my experience."

Jaques' experience, his use of his eyes, has robbed him of Touchstone's exuberant animation and left him both cynic and introvert. The strain, almost a strain of madness, erupts as W. C. Fields slashes out with his stick in undisguised fury, not bothering for the sudden second to keep himself attractive, or as Bert Lahr, in a burlesque sketch, fiercely snatches from a woman a package of pork chops he doesn't want. For this woman's purposes, and for comedy's, he has had to descend into feigned, but nearly real, madness, in order to pursue the matter of who is going to pay for the pork chops. When he snatches them away he does so abruptly, with his teeth set and with a kind of moral perspiration showing plainly on his forehead; he wishes to terminate violently the playful nonsense that has supported him as a clown. Groucho Marx lurches to the footlights in the middle of a sequence to look directly at the audience and remark, "Well, you can't expect all the jokes to be funny." The remark itself becomes funny in the circumstances. It is not a snarl. But it is the candor that short-circuits a snarl by anticipating it. The clown is here absolving himself of his own hatred for his work. Similarly, Groucho must insist, as a professional comedian, that the figure in the wheel chair headed directly for a stone wall must be a real old lady. The clown feels a meanness inside himself that can only be exorcised by being acknowledged. "You think I'm kidding," the clown says. "I'm *not*."

The clown suffers deeply for the meanness his work entails. We pay virtually no attention to the problem of suffering in comedy, largely because the moment we think of "suffering" we think of tragedy. We quite forget that the comic miser who has lost his money is genuinely racked with a pain that is to him intolerable, that the comedy coward dies a thousand times each time he fails to fight, that even at the lightest level the thwack of a slapstick *hurts*. In *The School for Wives*, one of the most artificial of great comedies, the old fool who has carefully reared a girl to be as stupid as possible so that she will not hesitate to marry him is presented throughout as an obvious, though incredibly ingenious, fool. He earns no sympathy from us; we want to see him hoodwinked and despoiled. Yet there comes a moment—one only—in the play when this man reveals the hurt that has lodged all along inside him. The girl is still his prisoner. He can have her. But he is, in a burst of unlooked-for anguish, suddenly beside himself. He can no longer repress the *self* that he simultaneously coddles and despises:

> Look at me; see the torture in my face;
> . . . no love can match the love I offer.
> Ingrate, what is the proof you ask of me?
> You want to see me weep? And beat my breast?
> You want to have me tear out half my hair?
> Or shall I kill myself? Is that what you want?
> Oh, cruel girl, I'm ready to prove it so.

Shylock suffers so deeply that we still cannot decide whether he is a comic figure or a tragic figure or possibly a playwright's mistake. The fact of the matter is that the central contest of *any* play—comic or tragic—engages its principals in a kind of agony; Sir Giles Overreach, in what is certainly a comedy, suffers so much that he does go mad.

Pain is common to both forms and is so far from being a distinguishing mark between them that it actually attests to their close relationship. The contest that is going on in a play—its *agon*—is an agony whether in a comedy or a tragedy. It so happens that the theatrical use of the term *agon* derives from comedy rather than tragedy.

But the pain of comedy is possibly more protracted and more frustrating than that of tragedy, because it does not know how to expel itself. Tragedy's pain is productive; it comes of the abrasiveness of moving forward toward transformation. Comedy, making capital of the absurdity of seeking transformation, must forever contain its pain. By denying freedom it denies release. Tragedy *uses* suffering; comedy can only live with it. Comedy can only live with it, that is to say, against the possible day when tragedy, in an ultimately successful transformation, frees them both. Comedy, hugging the fox to its breast, stays close to tragedy against that possible, eternally doubted, day.

But this interior anguish of comedy, this intense impatience and exasperation with self, in itself becomes an energy. Dissatisfaction with self is a goad, perhaps the most powerful goad man knows. The tragic hero courageously, sometimes presumptuously or even wrongly, takes up arms to advance the self; the clown, holding back as he must if he is to be a clown, retains the dissatisfaction as a canker which can neither be expelled nor quieted. Impatience kicks and thrashes inside the clown, like a violent baby in the womb that cannot bring itself to term.

It is just this powerful agitation that is, in the end, comedy's strongest assurance of survival. Detesting its work while half despising itself for being so good at it, finding its limited situation intolerable even while it is being applauded for the hilarity it provokes in so accurately describing the situation, comedy burns with a fever that may prove unquenchable. Transforming anger into laughter abates the anger temporarily, slightly; it does not remove its causes. The causes fester, seek expression in any which way, generate activity. If we have seen comedy cropping up on all sides in all hues in our time, willing to offer itself as a sacrifice to seriousness or to paint itself black where it was once too carelessly thought to be a painter of rainbows, it is because it can never be content to lie fallow in the face of the contempt it feels for itself. Comedy may keep kicking, because it cannot help kicking out at itself. And because it owes everything to tragedy, both the original gift of a thing to be parodied and also the only ultimate promise of a new state of being in which all private exasperations and secret despairs will be melted away in the annealing passage through time and space, it must keep kicking to see if it can kick tragedy awake.

The clown screams at his sleeping companion. He wants him up and on with it. Once he has got him up, if he ever succeeds, he will of course tell him that his activity is absurd. But he wants it to be absurd. Only the tragic absurdity is capable of transcending itself.

What a good man the clown is, to endure so much, to survive so relentlessly, to keep us company in all weathers, to provide us with a way of looking at the worst that enables us to take a temporary joy in the worst! For that is what he does: he stands horror on its head to keep us tolerably happy against the day when tragedy will look horror straight in the eye and stare it down.

He knows what it is that he secretly wants, and he is wonderfully ingenious about doubling us up as he displays his—and our—combined anguish and desire. Chekhov's Platonov is a marvelously wretched fool: he is so naturally attractive to women that he has quite exhausted himself in the process of satisfying the lovely, predatory creatures. Fighting off the latest swarm of conquests that have so conquered him, he turns in desperation to his wife, the wife he has endlessly betrayed. She, however, has had her fill of his revelry and is leaving him.

"Sacha, stay here!" he cries out in mortal pain. "I don't want happiness. I just want you."

That is what comedy is forever saying to tragedy. And that is its funny way of saying it.

The World as Comic Realm*

Robert Bechtold Heilman

Comic vs. Tragic Realms

Balzac both defined the realm of comedy and revealed the inclusiveness of comedy when he called his immense novelistic panorama "La Comédie humaine": not the divine comedy, this, but the total picture of the way things go in this world. Yet despite its inclusiveness Balzac's phrase does some cutting back that will help us make distinctions: it eliminates, for instance, the transcendent and the eschatological, either of which may have a literal or a symbolic role in tragedy. The comic embrace of the world is in contrast with the rejection of it in the Book of Common Prayer, which identifies antispiritual life in familiar trinitarian terms: "the world, the flesh, and the devil." ("The world" invariably means "this world," not "the other world.") In this formulation the world—secular life—is really narrower than it is in comedy, for by definition it includes only the unworthy bound to be lost; in comedy, however much may be lost, there are always immanent possibilities of salvation—for instance, by personal or institutional good sense. If we go behind the Prayer Book into scriptural sources, we find in Matthew and Mark the familiar overt distinction between the world and other realities: in Mark's phrasing, "What shall it profit a man, if he shall gain the whole world, and lose his own soul?" Someone might be inclined to rephrase, "If he succeeds in comedy but loses in tragedy." Actually, however, "gain the whole world" is hardly what characters in comedy are up to; they may endeavor to snatch a little more of it than is their due—Malvolio of love, Hotspur of glory, Alceste of power, Jack Tanner of freedom—but graspingness is not the only form of error. In *She Stoops to Conquer* Marlow has to be tricked into taking a willing girl, and Hastings through an excess of anxiety might well lose his girl; their error would be not gaining an available world. One may err in the world by being recessive as well as by being aggressive, loose-handed as well as strong-armed. Gaining the whole world better describes the ambition of a Faustus or a Macbeth, and losing his soul the fate of either; such a pursuit and such a stake are the heart of tragedy.

   Mark's metaphor speaks of the world as a totality (coveted by the mistaken, fled by the true). If, by way of instructive anticlimax, we throw Mark into juxtaposition with a mistress of Louis XIV, we get a different extreme. In W. S. Landor's *Imaginary Conversations* there is an ironic dialogue between the Duchess de Fontanges and Bishop Bossuet, who is to be her confessor. "Do you hate the

*Robert Bechtold Heilman, "The World as Comic Realm," *The Ways of the World: Comedy and Society* (University of Washington Press, Seattle, WA., 1978).

world, mademoiselle?" he asks, and she replies, "A good deal of it: all Picardy for example, and all Sologne: nothing is uglier—and, oh my life! what frightful men and women!" To the Duchess the world is the unpleasant parts of familiar territory, a smallish space for comic purposes, and, what is more, she rejects it. While Mark describes a tragic relationship to the world, the Duchess enacts a satirical one. But this unconscious satirist is herself viewed comically: the Conversation does not approve or disapprove her rejection, but lets it stand as a piece of ingenuous literalness charmingly deployed against a metaphor so conventionalized as to have become a rather faded concrete universal.

Here I am not defining the rejection of the world—that issue is related to "acceptance," the major point of the next chapter—but looking at some of the ways of defining the world implicit in rejective statements. The realm of the human comedy is obviously something between the vast complex of material, secular, godless existences whose essence is spiritual peril ("the world" in Christian terms), and parochial areas too restricted to be representative (Picardy and Sologne). Again, it is something between the corrupt and depraved condition which appears to call for an Inquisition, a Terror, a Flood, or an Inferno, and the life of spiritual struggle in which guilt may be the penalty for the courses that an individual does pursue or needs or is driven to pursue. The life of spiritual struggle is what Eliot dramatizes in Celia in *The Cocktail Party*, and what he balances against it is not an opposite extreme of callousness and vice, but rather that middling life, neither diabolical nor saintly, in which the ordinary Chamberlaynes find a social adjustment to their circumstances and their natures. Eliot's comedy, then, is about comic and tragic modes; that is, in employing the comic mode—the discovery of working personal relationships in the world—he uniquely transcends the mode by presenting another option in which the vital decisions lead into a nonworldly mode of action. Comedy characteristically ignores this option.[1]

The Inner World as Tragic Stage

All the world's a comic stage, we might say. The tragic stage is the inner one in which the conflict is between elements in the personality or in the mind of the psyche of the protagonist.[2] It would be wrong to think of Celia as an achieved

[1]Thomas McFarland argues, however, that pastoral comedy is an "alliance [which] realizes what neither mode [i.e., pastoral and comedy] could adequately achieve by itself: the representation of paradise" (*Shakespeare's Pastoral Comedy*, p. 37).

[2]Discussing Eliot's *Confidential Clerk*, Bonamy Dobrée makes some observations relevant to the distinction which I have proposed: "Comedy deals with the relation of people to each other in society, or with their place in society, with their interactions in a social milieu; tragedy deals with the relation of man to God—or whatever name he may be called by. . . . But whereas the moral of comedy is usually 'Fit yourself into society,' here it is 'Follow the indication that God has given you of the sort of life you ought to lead, the sort of person you ought to be.' [*The Confidential Clerk*] is, in fact, as some have called it, 'a religious farce'" ("*The Confidential Clerk*," *Sewanee Review*, 62 [1954]: 128–29).

However, Benn W. Levy's skillful *The Devil: A Religious Comedy* (London: Martin Secker, 1930) seems on the face of it to merge the two areas. In this modern reinterpretation of the Faust myth, several English people—artists, writers, an actress, a clergyman—play Faust to the Mephistopheles of the Rev. Nicholas Lucy (Old Nick, Lucifer), who seems able to gratify their various publicly expressed desires for passion, success, fame etc. Each person can choose between gratifying his desire at a known price such as Faust paid (here, dishonesty, infidelity, etc.) and living more honorably but less glamorously (as Macbeth too might have done). But Nicholas Lucy, the tempter with mysterious

tragic figure; rather, she receives the kind of portrayal that characteristically occurs in the realm of tragedy. When Reilly says of his patients that "usually they think that someone else is to blame," Celia replies, "I at least have no one to blame but myself." Later she says that she has a "sense of sin," of "failure / Towards someone, or something, outside of myself" (II). That is, she takes responsibility for what she does; she has the capacity for self-judgment. Yet, as we come to see, Celia has not really committed the tragic act that has a catastrophic outcome; like Beckett in *Murder in the Cathedral* and Harry in *The Family Reunion*, Celia has a fear and a consciousness of wrong action greater than her capacity for it. The complete tragic hero is likely to fall into action first and come into an awareness of truth later. But the time relationship between action and knowledge is not a constant; either may precede, or they may coincide; when knowledge comes is less important than the capacity for knowledge, knowledge of self and of the deed done. Knowledge means judgment, and judgment reflects the felt moral standard which, in acting, one has ignored or thought to circumvent or forced into a temporary subsurface oblivion where it cannot determine conduct. Conduct comes from one source of energy, judgment from another. A person acts from bounding ambition, delusions of invulnerability, unmanageable passion, a conviction that seems to take precedence over all other guides to action—all the outbreaks of self into the active arrogance for which the traditional term is *hubris*. Yet he knows, or comes to know, or is able to know, the nature of what he has done and to place himself as the doer. His conflict is between need, passion, drive, will, or illusion on the one hand, and, on the other, whatever sense of right or principle or obligation or authority would have a restraining effect or impel one to a different mode of conduct. Faustus and Macbeth both know what they are up to when they embark on their grand enterprises; Oedipus comes to see what he has been up to in the past.

For the opposite poles of influence upon divided man a convenient pair of terms is *impulse* and *imperative; impulse* as the whole range of self-aggrandizing forces and motives, *imperative* as the range of sanctions—religious, traditional, community—that, acting through conscience, both morally restrain and morally commit. The terms indicate tendencies rather than absolutes, and the opposites can even move toward each other. Further, there can be a paradoxical conflict of two imperatives that seem equally valid. Orestes cannot avenge his father without killing his mother, and Hamlet's situation is fascinatingly similar; Antigone, of course, is the archetypal figure caught in a conflict of imperatives, the familial and the civic (some critics tend to diminish the stature of the drama by treating the civic imperative as no more than callous arbitrariness by Creon). Two protagonists in modern dramas of political life agonize in similar conflicts. In Arthur Koestler's *Darkness at Noon* (1941, dramatized by Sidney Kingsley, 1951) Rubashov is caught between loyalty to the Party as it actually exists and loyalty to the ideals that created it; in Carl Zuckmayer's *The Devil's General*

---

power, is strictly a Goethean Mephistopheles who "seeks the bad but works the good": these Fausts opt for a decent mediocrity instead of paying the huge price for an imagined power and glory (we are not sure, finally, whether Lucy is an ironically disguised divine agent who succeeds, or a demonic figure who fails, in his assignment). In generic terms, the crucial actions take place in the inner arena of tragedy, but the nature of the final action is comic: the characters accept an imperfect world. Hence "religious comedy": a supramundane agent helps define destiny as an accommodation to the actual. Cf. Harcourt-Reilly and the Chamberlaynes in *The Cocktail Party*.

(1946) General Harras is loyal to Germany at war, though this also leads to collaboration with the Nazi regime that he detests.

This hasty survey of the modes of tragic action is meant only to make concrete the generalization that I have introduced several times—that the essential action of tragedy occurs on an inner stage: everything flows from the conflict in the divided personality.[3] If Macbeth did not know what he was up to, or Lear was incapable of finding out, they would be less significant personalities, and the plays about them would be relatively unsubtle, and quite untragic, dramas of aggression and disaster. This does not mean that the inner struggle is sealed within a private chamber that shuts off all possibilities of outer resonance. Only in Marlowe's *Doctor Faustus* is the conflict so internalized that it has no tangible impact on the society in which the hero lives. In most tragedies, indeed, the hero is a principal figure in a realm or community that is vitally marked by his private choices—the Thebes of Oedipus, the Britain of Lear, the Scotland of Macbeth; the tragedy of the hero is the disaster of the state. But the dramas do not focus our attention upon the disaster as such; the disasters function as the public echoes of the crucial private acts. There is plenty of action in the public world, but the restoration of well-being to the political realms is secondary to the resolution of the conflict within the personality of the political head.

The World as Comic: Implications

Tragedy is not our business, however, and it enters the discussion only temporarily to help establish and clarify limits of the comic realm. To say that comedy is of the world, then, is to say that it is of this world, not of the other, or some other, world; that it is not of that inner domain in which the human being struggles among diverse impulses and imperatives. Not that comedy forbids a confronting of self: a new opening up of common sense may make a character criticize his earlier lack of it, as is true of both Honeywood and Lofty in *The Good-Natured Man.* Mandryka in Hugo von Hofmannsthal's *Arabella* (1928; 1933) can exclaim, "Fool, fool that I am! / How should she ever pardon me for this, / unable as I am to pardon myself for it?" (III). In Peter Nichols' *A Day in the Death of Joe Egg* (1967) the wife, Sheila, can say, "It was my fault. I've been asking too much," and the husband, Bri, can acknowledge his immaturity (II). But three comments are in order here. First, such passages are less moral judgments than acknowledgments of tactical errors or practical missteps; second, they are incidents of the dramatic movement rather than the resolution of long struggles; third, the comic tone can survive even the ill-temper of a man who clings to his grievances rather than acknowledges his part in them, for example, Malvolio's final exit line in *Tuelfth Night*, "I'll be reveng'd on the whole pack of you" (V.i. 386).

For comic character there is one very important implication in viewing "the world" as primarily the realm of relationships with others, as the actual working out of situations by participants who face each other with difficulties and differences to adjust, cross-purposes to reconcile, clashing interests and in-

---

[3] The effect is fully discussed in my *Tragedy and Melodrama: Versions of Experience* (Seattle and London: University of Washington Press, 1968), pp. 7–18, 97, and in Chapter 2 of my *The Iceman, the Arsonist, and the Troubled Agent: Tragedy and Melodrama on the Modern Stage* (Seattle: University of Washington Press, and London: Allen and Unwin, 1973), pp. 22–62.

tentions to be mediated. In these relationships the characters cannot be significantly troubled by inner splits, which simply by being present would have to take the drama off in different direction. Unlike the tragic figure, the comic figure is to all intents and purposes undivided; that is, he is not caught in a basic cross-fire of desires and values that makes the primary demand upon his psychic energy and hence upon ours. Not that he is really free of uncertainties, inconsistencies, and alternatives; to take several almost too clear-cut examples. Mrs. Erlynne has to choose between pressing on with her campaign to re-enter society and repressing her daughter's intended exit from it, and Sir Colenso Ridgeon has to choose which of two patients he will try to save. But the choices are not between a right and a wrong; hubris is not a key element; and the choosing itself is not an agonizing affair which would have to become central in the drama. Each chooser acts, finally, as if there were only one real course, and he pursues it, not dividedly, but with "wholeness."

The comic choice characteristically turns on what is suitable, sensible, feasible; it does not often forget the convenient and the pragmatic. To Peachum and Lockit in Gay's *The Beggar's Opera* (1728) there is only one course to pursue with Macheath, however that course may impinge upon the tender hearts of their daughters; and vis-a-vis the daughters, Macheath strives for a comic both-and rather than a romantic either-or. In Synge's *Playboy of the Western World* (1907) Pegeen Mike fluctuates in her attitude to the playboy; the drama is based not on her struggle, however, but on the thoroughness of her pursuit, and then of her disenchantment with him, and finally of her sense of loss. Those somewhat similar trainers of women, Petruchio and Henry Higgins, could imaginably be split between the disciplinarian and the humanitarian, or between the professional and the man, but in fact there is no such split even when there is every *a priori* reason for us to expect one. Thus the comic management of the situation. In Petruchio, of course, the dual functions are integrated in a seamless garment of personality; in that sense his wholeness is more complex than that of Henry Higgins, in whom the trainer becomes virtually the whole man. Indeed, Petruchio provides a good, almost too good, pattern of the comic personality. If he were tragic, he would be split between loving and a need to dominate; as it is, temporary domination is the means of securing two independences that make possible a genuine mutuality. Likewise Congreve's Mirabell acts as a man of fashion, as a devoted lover, and as an independent man; the comic achievement is the integration of all elements in action rather than the domination of one element in the self which leads to the rebound of another neglected one, as in tragedy.

In the world, then, people meet each other as whole or as-if whole;[4] either their wholeness is actual, or it is secured as a comic necessity by the ignoring of any element from which an anticomic dividedness might spring. (Aristophanes, for instance, does not let Lysistrata, an opponent of war, be troubled by any suspicion that people are inalienably warlike, for her having such a fear would inevitably reorder the drama into a conflict of fact and desire, or ideal and actual.) The wholeness, whether intrinsic or pragmatic, is essential to a drama of relationships that are to lead neither to failure nor to an impasse; a person acting for only a part of himself would establish relationships of an abortive, unbalanced,

---

[4] For more detailed discussion of the variations of "wholeness" (in contrast with dividedness) in tragedy and other forms, see my *Tragedy and Melodrama*, pp. 16–17, 79, 84–86, 97–100.

or distorted kind that could scarcely produce even a temporary, not to mention a permanent, accommodation of moot issues or of adversaries. Ibsen's men—Solness and Rosmer, for instance—tend to remedy unsatisfying lives by taking up with alluring demonic women, but the relationship corresponds to only part of their unintegrated natures and hence leads to disaster. These men, that is, are not conceived comically.

So much for these various ways of outlining, circumscribing, and giving substance to "the world" which is the scene of comedy; an immediate world—solid, populated, representative—where the conflicts are not between impulses and imperatives that are elements of the psyche, but between individuals who are elements of society; where public events, whether political or social or familial, are primary, and not, as in tragedy, the aftermath of private moral actions; where the issue is not an individual's coming to spiritual terms with himself but his coming to working terms with other persons or groups of persons; where the individual may not have to engage in self-criticism at all but where, if he does, it takes the form "I have been foolish" or "I have made a practical mistake" rather than "I have been morally at fault"; where the actors are characterized, not by the dividedness of tragedy, but by an essential or working wholeness that equips them for all the tactics, bargaining, and even scheming that are the expectable currency of dealings in a scene where men and the shape of things are something less than perfect and yet not hostile to betterment for, or achievement by, those equipped for it. Comic action is outer, public, relational, social, comprising all the modes of intercourse in which accommodation—the end-product of struggling, jockeying, compromising, giving as well as taking—is made possible by the relative equality, instead of the excessive strength or weakness, of those concerned.

Types of Comedy[*]

J. L. Styan

The recognized theories of comedy do not help us any the more to understand the characteristic drama of the twentieth century. Ideas about the comic have never been expressed as abundantly as those about tragedy, both because the seriousness of comedy has not been as evident to writers as its more impressive high-toned counterpart, and because the ways and intentions of comedy may be more tiresome to explain. Up to the beginning of this century, comedy suffered a hardening in its arteries and its critics had grown further and further away from the practice on the stage. Certainly, no theorist seemed capable of putting forward an explanation sufficiently all-embracing, and the philosophical and the psychological approaches have both been wanting.

The diagnosis of comedy presents many difficulties. Laughter, a recurring and therefore an evidently important ingredient, seems to arise from a great variety of sources: we laugh at other people's bad luck, or at relief from embarrassment, or at a little flattery, or even when we do not want to laugh. We laugh heartily, or smile gently, or at some comedy we may not laugh at all. There are so many uses to which laughter can be put, from the promotion of a cold vindictive sarcasm to that of the empty gaiety of knock-about. There is considerable discrepancy between the things we find comic in life and those contrived on the stage: a man falling on his face in the street may be an object of pathos, but on the stage an object of derision. There is confusion between the techniques of comedy designed to raise laughter and the use to which the laughter is put: why should an anticlimax make us happy, or a clown make us sad? There are too many 'types' of the comic, and we plague ourselves by trying to sort comedy from burlesque, satire and farce, notwithstanding that in Shakespearian comedy elements of each seem to be present, and the points where they overlap are none too clearly defined. We are often at a loss to assess a total impression: even where in Molière the play's parts have been largely sweet and farcical, the whole when swallowed can leave a bitter taste in the mouth.

We find that when a joke is dissected, it abruptly ceases to be funny, which is disconcerting to say the least. It is also notorious that a 'sense of humour' is an unreliable quality, and what will seem laughable to an English audience will not necessarily seem so to a Scottish. As a psychologist has written, 'If members of a social group observe that their own objects of laughter do not produce laughter in another social group they are inclined to express this fact by saying that the

[*] J. L. Styan, "Types of Comedy," in *The Dark Comedy* (Cambridge University Press, 1962), pp. 42–58. [The footnotes in this selection have been renumbered.]

second group has "no sense of humour" '.[1] From the world of the theatre we might add that what will seem laughable on Monday may be damned on Tuesday. It is, moreover, a nuisance that what is comic to one age is not to another: Shylock was a butt for the Elizabethans, but not for the Victorians; Richard III was played for comedy by Irving, but for pathos by Olivier. Fashions in laughter change too readily, and we are in some doubt today whether to laugh at or sympathize with a Falstaff or a Tartuffe or a Sir Peter Teazle, Furthermore, should we begin by studying crowd psychology or the particular successes of a particular writer? And if we are to set our standards by one author, who shall it be?— Aristophanes, Shakespeare, Molière, Shaw?

For Hazlitt[2] the essence of the laughable was 'the incongruous', a distinction between 'what things are and what they ought to be'. This happily enough explains what we may call 'satirical' laughter, the laughter by which the spectator refuses to acknowledge the propriety of the fop and the coquette in Restoration comedy, when he recognizes the affectation in their gesture and speech, or by which he knows to ridicule the seriousness with which the characters in *The Importance of Being Earnest* pursue their absurd ends. But Hazlitt lets fall a damning admission: 'It is perhaps the fault of Shakespeare's comic muse that it is too good-natured and magnanimous. We sympathize with his characters more often than we laugh at them.' It is a *fault!*

For Meredith[3] 'the test of true Comedy is that it shall awaken thoughtful laughter', but he too can only comfortably explain the *raison d'être* of the 'high' comedy of intellect: 'The laughter of Comedy is impersonal and of unrivalled politeness. . . . It laughs through the mind, for the mind directs it.' And though in another place he suggests, attempting to distinguish between comedy and humour, 'The stroke of the great humourist is world-wide, with lights of Tragedy in his laughter', he will not admit that this quality can also appear in the greatest forms of comedy. Shakespeare is again the stumbling-block: because Shakespeare paints 'humanity' rather than 'manners', he does not begin to explain Shakespeare's eye for the comic. 'Jaques, Falstaff and his regiment, the varied troop of Clowns, Malvolio, Sir Hugh Evans and Fluellen—marvellous Welshmen!—Benedick and Beatrice, Dogberry, and the rest, are subjects of a special study in the poetically comic.' So we move on to safer ground with Molière, some of whose success he can account for.

After Meredith has named this glittering variety of the ostensibly comic, should he not have tried to understand them? Neither Hazlitt nor Meredith can explain the warm comic success of these and others like Rosalind and Touchstone and Quinee and Bottom and that great host of Shakespeare's comic creation which reflects so closely the 'English' sense of humour. Moreover, they cannot help us to sense the nature of the achievement in plays like *The Wild Duck, The Cherry Orchard, Major Barbara* and *Waiting for Godot*, ambiguous plays of the modern theatre which challenge our laughter, as we shall see.

Bergson[4] with every good intention turned to example after example to establish his precepts, but concerned himself too much with first causes and with

---

[1] R. H. Thouless, *General and Social Psychology* (London, 2nd ed., 1937), p. 209.
[2] Hazlitt, Introduction to *The English Comic Writers* (1818).
[3] Meredith, 'On the Idea of Comedy and of the Uses of the Comic Spirit,' a lecture delivered in 1877.
[4] Bergson, *Laughter, an Essay on the Meaning of the Comic*, trans. C. Brereton and F. Rothwell (London, 1921), first French ed. 1889.

the detail of technique rather than the odd results produced in the theatre. He further remained rather parochial in drawing too much on the kind of comedy which has so admirably set the standard for the French comic stage, that of Molière. It is noticeable that his examples are drawn chiefly from the farces and farcical moments of Molière and Labiche (author of such plays as *Le Voyage de M. Perrichon* and *Un Chapeau de paille d'Italie*) or the comical absurd of such works as *Don Quixote*. He diagnoses comedy as arising from the incongruity of 'something mechanical encrusted on the living': 'the attitudes, gestures, and movements of the human body are laughable in exact proportion as that body reminds us of a mere machine'. He thus cites as laughable the forms and movements of the puppet, and in the same way Molière's Sganarelle and his kind. Sganarelle, *The Doctor in Spite of Himself,* is enjoying his newfound power as a man of medicine, when he is accused by Géronte of reversing the position of the heart and the liver:

> GÉRONTE . . . the heart should be on the left side, and the liver on the right.
> SGANARELLE Yes, it used to be so, but we have changed all that.

Likewise, Dr Bahis of *Love's the Best Doctor,* provides an excellent example of professional automatism when he advises that 'It's better [for a patient] to die through following the rules than to recover through violating them'. This argument of course helps us to explain the fun in much of Molière, and the comedy of snobbery in Lady Bracknell, and how in Fry's *The Lady's Not For Burning* Tyson's pomposity as mayor is belied by his having a frightful cold in the head. It explains all manner of caricature in character and action on the stage. It explains the prohibition of much emotionality from the comic theatre. It does not explain the force of its *presence,* and emotion is often present to great purpose in comedy. Bergson declares rigidly 'laughter is incompatible with emotion', when we know well enough from experience, if not from countless moments on the comic stage, that we *do* have the faculty of laughing and feeling at one and the same time. It must exclude Shakespeare once again, and, what is more, it cannot approach our true sense of Molière's greatest achievement, *The Misanthrope.* Bergson's laughter is a 'social corrective', as Meredith's was an 'agent of civilization', but it trades on the debased and degraded in human nature and cannot respond to the warmth of comic humanity which remains after the eccentricities have been skimmed off.

The argument was not quite over. Freud[5] arbitrarily narrowed his field to include only what he pleased to call 'wit', and satisfactorily explains to us, after much belabouring, that wit serves as an escape from authority just as nonsense serves as an escape from critical reason (with occasional help from alcohol). Having said this at great length, he has said little that we did not know already. Others have since taken up the challenge, and J. B. Priestley's essay on humour[6] was a hopeful advance on his predecessors. Where Freud started from mimimal instances, with little wish to move into the wider world of comedy, Priestley saw all the limitations and difficulties and perhaps would embrace too much. He would admit Shakespeare into the ranks, and goes some way to explaining his humour as the product of the close observation of human character and behaviour in its incongruities.

---

[5] Freud, *Wit and its Relation to the Unconscious,* trans. Brill (London, undated, ?1906).
[6] J. B. Priestley, *English Humour* (London, 1929).

Among all the hints offered by these writers, certain recurring elements in the comic stand out. A sense of incongruity, with a resulting release of tension, is felt within the mind. Whether by the laughter of success or of failure, whether arising from the recognition of a friend or a tune, or from Santayana's 'little triumph' of the mind when it receives an illumination, whether by the laughter that follows upon bathos or upon the loss of a lady's dignity when her hat is blown off by the wind, some bulwark of our natural resistance, little or big, is broken down, and a weapon of unquestionable power is in the hands of the one who can effect this artificially. The comedian is suddenly free to pour his shafts through the gap, rebuffing us with mockery or drawing us with tears. Whatever the technique he employs he has his audience captive.

On the other hand, that a comedy *should* make you laugh is not admissible as an argument: incongruity is not necessarily laughable. There are too many plays, patently not tragedies, which clearly evoke no laughter, or little that is perceived as laughter; too many fine plays end in questions and by sobering us, from *Troilus and Cressida* and *The Misanthrope* to the comedies of Pirandello. The interested reader should look into that excellent discussion initiated by L. J. Potts in a more recent essay on our subject.[7] Where it does arise laughter can be a means to a greater end than itself, creating the conditions for the dramatic achievement of other things. The values of the comic attitude appear only when we measure the *uses* to which it is put. Nor should we deceive ourselves into thinking that its uses are not infinitely variable. The evidence suggests that the conventions of the comic stage readily admit an admixture of seemingly extraneous elements like the tragic and the pathetic, whereas tragedy has its fabric dangerously stretched to admit the comic or the farcical. What then are the traditional uses of comedy?

Broad comedy had contrived the release of laughter for partly satirical purposes by a relatively uncomplicated incongruity. Just as we laugh at the clown who sacrifices his self-respect by wearing trousers that are excessively too big for him, or at Charlie Chaplin for his exaggerated delight in a 'house' whose wall afterwards collapses when he leans on it, so we laugh at Harpagon, grotesque in his avarice, faced with the costly processes of being in love; or we laugh at the newly honoured Lord Foppington's airs and graces as he incongruously rehearses his part for the evening's *levée* while still in his nightgown: 'Well, 'tis an unspeakable pleasure to be a man of quality—Strike me dumb—My Lord—Your lordship—My Lord Foppington. . . .' Of course, it is the situation which the dramatist may complicate, and the wink at the audience can be very much more subtle when, say, Lady Bracknell finally succumbs to hard cash in lieu of the desirable attributes of an elegant lineage, or when Volpone the fox out-foxes himself. The bookworm is funnier and more like a bookworm on a dance-floor than in a library, the flirt funnier and more of a flirt in a library than on a dance-floor.

Even at the level of the near-farcical, where the merely physical sensationalism of the laugh is uppermost in the playwright's mind, such drama can sometimes justify itself morally by being acutely pointed in its object of derision. The contrivance of derisive laughter by the exaggeration of some affectation of human behaviour is a time-honoured method used since the days of Aristophanes.

---

[7] L. J. Potts, *Comedy* (London, 1948), esp. pp. 18–22.

Thus the learned Meton of *The Birds* arrives in Cloudcuckooland to 'subdivide the air into square acres':

METON Observe:
    The conformation of the air, considered as
    a total entity, is that of a conical damper.
    Very well. At the apex of this cone we apply
    the ruler, bracketing in the dividers to allow
    for the congruent curve. Q.E.D. . . .

But his notions are not received as gratefully as he expected:

PISTHETAIROS . . . we've passed a law
    that charlatans shall be whipped in the public square.
METON Oh. Then I'd better be going.
PISTHETAIROS   You're almost too late.
    Here's a sample, God help you!   (*Knocks him down.*)
METON   My head! My head![8]

One would not of course think that there were a majority of learned mathematicians in the Greek audience to make the satirical and corrective point of this very far-reaching. Nor would Molière have expected to find too many hypochondriacs like Argan in the court of Louis XIV. These comedies can nevertheless give us, perhaps incidentally, many tiny and momentary insights into human nature through the agency of puppets like Meton and Argan. We all share a little of Meton's desire to make order of fantasy, to stiffen what should be flexible. Even if we would not confess to being, each of us, a little of the hypochondriac with a natural fear for our health, we must feel just a touch of fellow-feeling for Argan when M. Purgon the doctor wreaks his rage like this.

M. PURGON I foretell that within four days you'll be in an incurable condition.
ARGAN Oh mercy!
M. PURGON You'll fall into a state of bradypepsia.
ARGAN M. Purgon!
M. PURGON From dyspepsia into apepsia.
ARGAN M. Purgon!
M. PURGON From bradypepsia into dyspepsia.
ARGAN M. Purgon!
M. PURGON From apepsia into diarrhoea and lientery.
ARGAN M. Purgon!
M. PURGON From lientery into dysentery.
ARGAN M. Purgon!
M. PURGON From dysentery into dropsy.
ARGAN M. Purgon!
M. PURGON And from dropsy to autopsy that your own folly will have brought you
    to.
ARGAN Oh my God! I'm dying.[9]

---

[8] Aristophanes, *The Birds*, version by D. Fitts (London, 1958).
[9] Molière, *The Imaginary Invalid*, in *The Misanthrope and Other Plays*, trans. J. Wood (London, 1959).

Here character, situation and dialogue are 'artificial' and the playing demands a special degree of stylized speech and movement, all apparently earnest in manner. The characters' behaviour tends to puppetry, and the situations, though still recognizable, may be outrageous: the ways of the actors are deliberately shown at some 'distance' from normal behaviour in order that the spectator can freely laugh across the gap at what he believes different from his own. The classical methods of comedy, whether broad and low, romantic and pastoral, or high and mannered, have always been anti-naturalistic. A stage extravagant in word and deed permitted those excesses which still compel us to deride certain characters and their attitude to life. To talk of 'stylization' equally to cover *As You Like It, Volpone, The Way of the World, The School for Scandal, The Importance of Being Earnest* and *Man and Superman* is perhaps an impertinence, but in each of these plays the dramatist invented a world to different degrees fantastic the better to compare our own. Artificial characters in an artificial situation gained him more freedom and more force for his dramatic effects. It is only after we have laughed spontaneously that we perhaps perceive that the laugh has rebounded upon us, and that the artificiality was all a snare. In the same way a simple verbal witticism can leave some permanent mark upon us—if it includes some quality of illuminating humour too.

Thus the best comedy teases and troubles an audience; it *can* be painful. Comic method can serve to create an imaginative but dispassionate attitude; to create the conditions for thinking; to free the dramatist in his attempt to tap certain rational resources of mind in his audience. Derisory laughter may be used for this and it may arise from this; it may not. Clearly it must do so in mannered comedy like Shaw's *Arms and the Man* or *Heartbreak House*, where we are encouraged for the most part to keep our critical distance from the central characters Raina and Ellie the better to recognize their whole significance. It may do so in surrealistic comedy like Samuel Beckett's *Waiting for Godot*, where the slapstick convention of the play deceives us most of the time into thinking that we are not looking at ourselves. It probably will not do so in *King Lear*, where an ironic joke from the Fool, laughable out of its context, is the more caustic in context because we feel our sympathies are too directly its butt. The urgent fact remains that, whether we laugh or not, the 'comic' attitude may be present in any genre of play. The best jokes are not only compatible with the most solemn intention, but are likely to be the best jokes for that reason.

As the gap narrows so that what remains incongruous is still funny, but too close to the bone to laugh at, then we move swiftly across the frontier into the realms of the tragic. We have seen that plays with large measures of sympathy felt through the laughter, like Shakespeare's romantic comedies, were inconvenient to the theorists. Similarly, plays which came near to closing the gap between the normality of the audience and the abnormality of the stage, plays like *Measure for Measure* or *The Misanthrope*, have been regarded as on the suspect fringe of the comic tradition, unwelcome exceptions to the rule. The presence of the comic eye in the midst of tragedy, as in *King Lear* or *Hamlet*, was put down to the licence of genius. Now, in the work of Chekhov, Pirandello and Anouilh, and many others, it is the rule and not the exception to mingle the laughter and the tears; large numbers of plays today merely *use* the mechanism of laughter without granting its expected release of tension.

For our overall understanding of the comic in drama today, we should turn, not to Hazlitt and Meredith, nor to Bergson and Freud, but to Pirandello, whose essay *L'Umorismo* offers the key to the comedy of our own times. In this he suggests a brilliant example, which demonstrates among other things how flexible and serviceable for serious purposes is the comic attitude once the dramatist can evoke it. Imagine, he says, an elderly lady: we are immediately predisposed to be sympathetic. But she is overdressed, her face painted, her hair dyed like a girl's: we find this comic and we are ready to laugh. Yet suppose she is aware of the figure she is cutting, and is behaving in this way in order to hold the affections of her husband: we are sobered. The old lady seems pathetic again, and the laugh is 'on us'. The comic may be no laughing matter.[10]

Pirandello in 1908 was feeling for those qualities demanded by the modern stage in acknowledging with some finality the flexible nature of the theatre as a medium. Through it an audience could, and should, be drawn, repelled and drawn again, the 'gap' closed, opened and closed again. Since the comic view has always been instinctively felt to be an indispensable, if not quite respectable, prophylactic in drama as in life, so the methods of broad and artificial comedy were devised to make the comic view presentable. Now Pirandello insists that the comic view is a powerful and essential element in the effective control of an audience and an immensely serviceable corrective for its image of the play in the process of its formation. The fidelity of the drama to truth of feeling, and its accuracy of understanding in its handling of life on the stage, may depend upon the command the author has of the comic view and the keenness of his comic eye. How the comic may make of the drama a world living and flexible, and yet one unnaturally confined within the strict bounds of the stage, is also our concern in this study.

A simple short example for analysis is chosen to demonstrate the way impressions flow from actor to spectator with the kind of ironies most typical of the drama of recent times. In *The Rose Tattoo*, Tennessee Williams is catching at the incongruities of life by overtly setting them on the stage in their barefaced opposition. The scene is the home of Serafina delle Rose, who lives in a Sicilian colony on the coast between New Orleans and Mobile. The cottage is presented as a sectional 'frame', set in the semi-tropical vegetation of the place and in 'extremely romantic' lighting; this method of stage-setting is one that Williams has practised carefully both in order that we should retain a sense of environment throughout the play by actually seeing it, and that we should feel some initial detachment from the persons of the play. The characters are to be both typical and particular: we are to spy on them without joining them, and Serafina is to be 'a strange beast in a cage.'

Against the romantic setting and lighting we see the odd details of the living-room, introducing both Serafina and the incongruities of feeling that are to ensue. Serafina takes in sewing, and in a room cluttered with 'at least seven' dressmaker's dummies 'in various shapes and attitudes,' as the author's production notes tell us, we see

> an interior that is as colourful *as a booth at a carnival*. There are many religious articles and pictures *of ruby and gilt*, the *brass* cage of a *gaudy* parrot, a large bowl of *goldfish*, cutglass decanters and vases, *rose-patterned* wallpaper and a *rose-coloured* carpet. . . . There is a small shrine against the wall between the rooms, consisting of a prie-dieu and a little statue of the Madonna in a *starry blue* robe and a *gold*

[10] Pirandello, *L'Umorismo*, 2nd ed. (Florence, 1920), p. 179.

crown. Before this burns always a vigil light in its *ruby* glass cup. [The italics are mine.]

This is the passionate but limited world of the heroine of the play, bold in its contradictions. Williams significantly adds the comment, 'Our purpose is to show these gaudy, childlike mysteries with sentiment and humour in equal measure, without ridicule.'

Serafina, fiercely in love with her truck-driver husband, learns in the course of the play that not only has he been killed, but that he was, in spite of her love, unfaithful to her. She has regarded her marriage with the same kind of reverence that she reserved for the Madonna, and now her worship of her dead Rosario is turned to bitter grief, in its expression a kind of blasphemy. This little tragedy is presented to us against the incongruous details of her ordinary life, which includes the chase of a symbolic goat around the house by Serafina dressed in high-heeled slippers and a tight silk skirt, frequent screaming matches with the neighbours and their children, and the grotesque intrusion of the two prostitutes, Flora, 'tall and angular,' and Bessie, 'rather stubby.' It is these who reveal the husband's infidelity against a background noise of a Sousa march indifferently played by the band of her daughter's high school. Every ironic impression is a signal to the audience to revalue its estimate of Serafina's importance. Curiously she grows more weighty the more her simple dignity is undermined, and the strength of the ironic method Williams uses carries the play through many of the crudities of the theme's heated overstatement.

In the second act, the man who is to replace the magnificent Rosario arrives: 'He is short in stature, has a massively sculptural torso and bluish-black curls. His face and manner are clownish; he has a charming awkwardness.' Serafina's first comment upon him when she is alone sums up the whirling mixture of our own image: 'Madonna Santa!—*My husband's body*, with the head of a clown! (*She crosses to the Madonna.*) O Lady, O Lady! (*She makes an imploring gesture.*) Speak to me!' But Alvaro Mangiacavallo, for that is indeed his name, is, we learn, hardly sincere in his feelings for Serafina in the way that she wants him to be.

The following, finally, is the kind of sequence with which the play impresses itself upon its audience. The last act begins with both the widow and the wooer prepared ludicrously for their assignation. Serafina has put on an intolerably tight girdle, which she has only just managed 'with much grunting' to strip off again before the arrival of her lover. Alvaro has soaked rose oil in his hair and has had a rose tattooed upon his chest, reminder of the dead Rosario, and the better to appeal, as he thinks, to Serafina's sensibilities. Now—horror!—a contraceptive drops from his trousers' pocket—their ludicrous passions thus merging into the repulsive.

SERAFINA   . . . You think you got a good thing, a thing that is cheap!

ALVARO   You made a mistake, Baronessa! (*He comes in and drops to his knees beside her, pressing his cheek to her flank. He speaks rhapsodically.*) So soft is a lady! So, so, so, so, so *soft*—is a lady!

SERAFINA   Andate via, sporcaccione, andate a casa! Lasciatemi! Lasciatemi stare! (*She springs up and runs into the parlour. He pursues. The chase is grotesquely violent and comic. A floor lamp is overturned. She seizes the chocolate box and threatens to slam it into his face if he continues towards her. He drops to his knees, crouched way over, and pounds the floor with his fists, sobbing.*)

ALVARO   Everything in my life turns out like this!

SERAFINA   Git up, git up, git up!—you village idiot's grandson! There is people
watching you through that window, the—strega next door. . . .

So Alvaro is humiliated, though not as much as Serafina herself.

If we examine the impressions passed to us by the actors within this short
space of time, we may begin to feel something of the way modern dark comedy
operates. First, any sympathy we felt for Serafina in her grief is taken up and
strengthened by her new agony, much as she had brought it upon herself. Her
implication that she is not a 'thing' to be bought so cheaply, spoken with all the
ferocious dignity of her Sicilian birth, is entirely as we would have her speak. To
this extent we are self-composed, a relaxed audience, and Alvaro's abasement in
his half-drunken state, with Serafina's spitting and lashing abuse of him, com-
forts us in our need to raise the widow as someone worthy of our commiseration.
She has been outraged enough already.

But at this point in the play, Serafina's own baser instincts begin to emerge,
though she cannot this time begin to elevate her new relationship to the holy level of her intimacy with her late husband. In all her self-righteous fury, she is already unbending a little, and in her 'Lasciatemi stare', 'let me be', we hear the
old note re-enter her voice. We feel some of her willing pity for this fool who
presumes to take the place of Rosario. And in her one ironic gesture of *running*
from him, inviting his pursuit, our composure is shattered by a contradictory impression, and our image of the play once again turns turtle. Instead of growing to
a nobility, Serafina, with the incongruous rose in her hair, shrinks to be another
clown with Alvaro: 'The chase is grotesquely violent and comic.' She fights with
the box of chocolates he had brought her, he drops to the floor sobbing like a
frustrated child: 'Everything in my life turns out like this!' We might say that
here an incipient tragic convention has become a comic one by inversion.

This is the way that Serafina's romantic obsession is punctured. We know
her humiliation more than she knows it herself, since we have the complete situation in view and the whole counterpoint of the action violently registered in our
minds. And it seems even Serafina has some sense of objective appearances, feeling her indignity, when she draws attention to the 'witch' next door: 'There is
people watching you.' As she says this she knows the eyes are on herself.

This is a play about human illusions, about a simple woman who believes
too much in herself; it is about her sin of pride. It is not about the man Mangiacavallo, who has few illusions and no pride. He is introduced into the action, this
man with the head of a clown, simply as an agent of destruction, not so much to
destroy Serafina as to destroy our image of human worth. But, oddly, the heroine in her simplicity and in spite of her littleness and nakedness, is given by this
author an ineluctable stature by her very weaknesses, warmly comprehensive
and curiously close to us. The summation of the individual ironies of the play's
action is the huge particular irony of the total image the play leaves with us. We
do not now deal in tragedies, nor in comedies, nor indeed in the nondescript 'tragicomedy'. There flourish—what?—dramas of 'mood'. These are not necessarily
plays calling up a peculiar atmosphere, but plays which attempt to control the
exceptionally disparate audiences of modern times by teasing the mind and the
emotion this way and that, making the one deceive, encourage and contradict
the other. . . .

Whatever Happened to Comedy?*

Richard Duprey

When your world becomes black and blue and you retreat into the corners of your life, feeling for all the world like the monkey in the schoolyard rhyme who chased his tail around the flagpole, there is nothing like a little comedy to prove to you that things might be considerably worse. As you roar at the lady who sat on the coconut-cream pie or at the discomfiture of Sganerelle or at Malvolio's humiliation at the hands of Sir Toby, there is a certain release of your own torrent of troubles onto the heads of these hapless ones. Just as the tragic figure assumes our burden in the rhythm of the tragedy with its sacrificial inevitability, the comic butt takes another human burden upon himself as he executes the comic pratfall.

For all the jollity of the comic form, however, comedy is one of the most truly serious things in this world and in its surgical "pessimism" lies most of its value and much of its appeal. While noble tragedy with its so-called cathartic action on the emotions cleanses one, so they tell us, of fear and pity, comedy, with an appeal to the mind rather than to the heart, shows us the stupidity of our earthly ways. In the failings of the common man we see more than a faint glimmer of our own imperfection. Dealing as it does with the folly of mankind, the comedy lays bare man's foolishness, ferocity, frivolousness, and the phoniness of so many of his human institutions. As a social corrective it helps us to see our own faults, both as individuals and in groups, and it provides us with a sort of "misery loves company" refreshment as we see other men struck down with the slapstick. We sit smiling from the relative safety of our theatre seat.

There is a need for laughter in this macabre age, but in the words of G. K. Chesterton, ". . . in a world where everything is ridiculous, nothing can be ridiculed. You cannot unmask a mask; when it is admittedly hollow as a mask. You cannot turn a thing upside down, if there is no theory about its being right side up. If life is really so formless that you cannot make head nor tail of it, you cannot pull its tail; and you certainly cannot make it stand on its head." (*Eight Great Comedies*, Mentor Books.)

Perhaps this is the problem of our theatre that is vastly more critical than our contemporary failure to write Aristotelian tragedy. We haven't been able to write comedy—something vastly more necessary to society's well-being. There have been an increasing number of theories heard lately concerning the demise of great comedy in our theatre. Since the last George S. Kaufman comedy left

* Richard Duprey, "Whatever Happened to Comedy?" in *Just off the Aisle* (Newman Press, 1962), pp. 149–156.

the boards a few years back, American stage humor has been restricted to the sex farces of George Axelrod, the specialized humor of Thurber, the work of an occasional European wit (usually too ironical for sentimental Americans), or the grand, but again specialized work of those who create revues for the Yiddish stage.

Now and then we find flashes of comic brilliance in plays that are not essentially comic, as for example, in Paddy Chayefsky's *The Tenth Man*, but for the most part, great comedy has disappeared from our stage and no one seems to know why.

Great comedy is the result of keen observation of the world. The comic writer, a sharp and perceptive man who stands on the sidelines and views the staggering gyrations of mankind, records in his detached and facile manner the errors of humanity. He sees all the silly, preposterous, utterly absurd things that his fellow man does. He takes note of the countless deviations from the norm in the lives of his colleagues in flesh. Not, in truth, feeling anything for them but a careful objectivity, he dispassionately compares them with what they ought to be. The writer who pictures a fat-bottomed friar solemnly peddling an English bicycle, who depicts an irate political leader paddling a baby's behind rather than kissing its cherubic face, or who visualizes for his readers the glorious absurdity of a garbage man in white tie and tails, is observing the violation of a standard—the shattering of an expected pattern of human action.

Today, our human society is a fragmented thing. Dwelling in an age of self-centeredness, our eyes are turned inward and every man has attempted to make of himself a social and ideological island. Though we conform blindly to hollow mores and obsolete social usages, we cry out for individual interpretation of nearly everything else, and even those of us who follow a faith, who subscribe to a-set philosophy, or who vote consistently with one political party, hear ourselves—our own voices—speaking out from time to time in terms of relative truth. Rather than right reason we are guided by sentiment and often our religious orientation, our philosophy of life, our political affiliations, become a matter of "team spirit" or mass psychology rather than a matter of earnest conviction. With the playwright Luigi Pirandello, father of a whole school of artistic relativists, we say "Right you are, if you think you are!"

Our forefathers in theocratic Greece, in medieval Europe, in Elizabethan England, knew how to laugh, for they had before them in the ideals and attitudes of their societies a requisite for true comedy. With a sense of order, a knowledge of the nature of things—a knowledge that all society shared—they could see clearly the incongruity of man's deviations from the norms and natural laws of a sensible universe. Human nature was a known thing, subject to the laws of God and the "ground rules" of his creation.

Today, every man sets himself up as a prophet, subject to his own rules of behavior. Fortunately there is some semblance of respect for law and order persisting, though there are indications that the evident breakdown of the family and the softening of paternal authority in our society, even this regard is beginning to fade. If there are no generally held social norms, then there can be no great comedy. The break *from* the norm has no meaning unless there is a commonly held norm from which to break. This is the axiom of both human culture and the historical patterns of art. It is also common sense.

Another factor that holds our theatre back from the heights of comic fulfillment is the element of fear. Man is too frightened today with all the world's unrest really to laugh with heartiness. One must remain rather unemotional about something to enjoy real laughter at its expense. When a loved one, your father, let's say, falls flat on his face in a mud puddle after having meticulously prepared himself for a fancy dress ball, our laughter fades when we realize who it is and that he may have hurt himself. Even the comedian, like Chaplin, or more recently, Jackie Gleason, who sees fit to flirt with pathos, must hide his real humanity behind certain stereotyped symbols like the strange walk, the Hitlerian moustache, and the trademark bowler, in order to keep us from experiencing an excess of emotional identification which would immediately banish mirth from the scene.

With the ever present fear of contemporary life gnawing at us, it is difficult to become detached enough even for the initial guffaw. The great problems of the century are too grim for our laughter. With the absurdity of these cruel times, the chortle of amusement sounds too much like "the death rattle," and so our prophets of the absurd, Camus, Sartre, Duerrenmatt and all the rest, see absurdity from the position of "engagement" rather than that of comic detachment. Thus comedy dies as we allow our small fears to mushroom into great ones.

For example, no one is writing quality comedy about the spectre of atomic war, the race problem, the withering of the family, and the threat of economic and ideological takeover by the Soviet Union. We are far too worried about these things and we have allowed too many of them—these troubles we exist with from day to day—to progress to the brink of disaster. The Romans, in the decadent autumnal days of their Empire, did not write comedy about the threat of barbarian invasion and how ill-equipped they were to face so frightening an eventuality. Instead they chatted about sex and social usages in their theatres. They did not direct the comic barrage to point up their weaknesses in the hope of transmuting them into strengths. They were a people who had fallen in love with their own infirmities. And so Rome fell!

Like the Romans, we follow suit: We produce our tedious sex jokes; our joshings of earnestness and sincerity wherever and whenever we find them, and now and then, on the threshold of panic, we write grim sociological tracts about the dangers of mass "genocide-by-the-bomb" or other things equally cheery— serious warnings which do little to relieve the tension of the times or to rectify its problems.

The laughter of comedy is a social corrective. Many a grievous problem has been laughed away, for evil, based as it is on pride, cannot bear the stings of society's laughter. The comedies of Aristophanes and Molière, to cite but two of the greatest, lashed out at the evils of their day. Aristophanes tried with some measure of success (though who can measure the results of this sort of thing) to discredit the Sophists and some of the political demagogues of Athens. Molière sought to expose the charlatans of the then fraudulent medical profession, the hypocrisy of some of the churchmen at court, the *poseurs* and *dilettanti* of his society. They were not thanked for making these exposures, and they give evidence to the fact that the comic artist—one who would satirize the foibles of the world—must be made of heroic stuff. His targets are not only moving ones but they often fire back and usually their ammunition is physical or social punishment rather than a mere barrage of wit. Most of the great comic artists in the theatre—Gogol, Synge, Cervantes, Gay and others—were slandered and villified, if not subjected to worse treatment. Who is there now with the solid, generally accepted ideology *and* the courage to strike down the frauds and cheats of today?

With stringent libel laws and the extreme sensitivity of the great medias of publishing and the electronic media, it is all but impossible to stand up and expose the evils of society in anything but the most general way, for fear of treading on the toes of some influential fool. Only noted public bogeys like Señor Castro and Tovarich Khrushchev are legitimate goats. If we start striking too close to home with our comic brickbats, someone screams "foul" and the world starts battening down the hatches against us.

Our theatre today does laugh, but its laughter could better be characterized as a snicker than an honest roar of delight. It ridicules the staunchly honest, the intellectual, the chaste, and the peaceful. In the professional playscript, a girl who wants to stay chaste, the man who wishes to stay faithful to his wife, one who seeks knowledge for its own sweet sake, and one who bids for peace, are the butts and gulls of audience laughter. Of course we know that humor always had a talent for iconoclastic attack. The rich, the learned, the powerful, those who appear virtuous, have always provided targets for laughter down through the centuries. The Romans managed to attack the gods and the medieval Christian had many a good laugh at one saint or another. However, there is a *malaise* in our contemporary theatre in which good becomes the butt and evil the heroic quality *almost always*, as they are exposed to a shifting and, in a sense, ghostly standard of morality.

It's a sorry state of affairs with no immediate solution in view. It makes one think upon certain ominous historical parallels and precedents. The person who loses the ability to laugh at himself and the society which loses sight of its own foibles and failings are both riding for a fall. "Pride goeth before the fall," we are told. May we someday find our way back to a theatre that can laugh and say, "What fools we mortals be!"

Though we have lost the real comic sense—that of Aristophanes and Molière—the ability to detect absurdity has not been totally lost today. Though it has clearly passed out of the comic realm where it can inspire true laughter, there is a force somehow comic that can precipitate action from absurdity—from the serious comtemplation of human irrationality.

Writers like the late Albert Camus and the remarkable Swiss novelist-playwright Friedrich Duerrenmatt have manifested that they possess a clear vision of the world's absurdity—its deviation from its very own standards of humanity. Camus, rendering loathsome portraits of man's behavior toward his fellow man, shows a clear vision and a perceptive analysis of the horror that a lack of love or, at bottom, respect, can wreak. Duerrenmatt with crystal-clear conception sees through a crawling mass of rationalization to the selfishness of what we humans too often call justice—self-interest. There is no question that these men perceive a standard and write with that standard in mind.

Their problem, like that of many other sincerely engaged writers of our times who revile the world in their writing, is the very vehemence with which they write. They become so enmeshed—so passionately involved—in the emotion of disgust that they often lead their audiences to the brink of hopelessness and despair. Does the work of Camus make us want to go out and rectify things or does it force us back to the lonely barricade of desperation? In the play *Caligula,* are the issues clear enough for us to know what to fight or are we so choked with his catalogue of moral horrors that our intellect refuses to act? We could wish that Camus had aimed his works deliberately at the comic effect rather than attempting tragedy, for the tradition of tragedy precludes action. Who walks away from Oedipus wanting to cure anything? Rather, one walks off saying, "Oedipus, despite his sin—despite the fact that he is but corrupt flesh—has won, through his pain, a moral victory and has saved his people. All is well with the world." By the passion of his *agon* he has saved us and we have been cleansed by his victory.

In comedy, the problem is quite different. We seek to cure the sores and boils that have formed on the susceptible flesh of history. This can be accomplished only by a *controlled* and *reasoned* disgust: a disgust that doesn't release the intellect from the problem of witnessing man and his actions in the theatre; a disgust that *involves* and yet does not excuse one from responsibility; a disgust of such a nature that it leaves room for hope and engenders a feeling within us that the wrongs can be and ultimately must be righted.

Bertolt Brecht, the strange genius of East Germany's *Berliner Ensemble*, found the recipe for this therapeutic drama, this dark-masked comedy where absurdity is shown, where we are prompted to make corrections in the direction of our lives and our ideals. We see in his plays a world where man must sell himself in order to live—where he must not hesitate to drain his fellow man in order to sustain life. In the case of Brecht, the comic dynamism is put to use in the service of Marx—in the pursuit of the revolutionary paradise of economic, social, and political "pie in the sky." Brecht would essay to point out inconsistencies in our moral code based on our failure to conform and then send us from the theatre to revolt against our ideals, fashioning new ones more conformable to present expectations. For instance, in the concluding passages of *The Good Woman of Setzuan* the prescription is "bigger, better gods or none." To be sure, Brecht is stacking the cards against us, but he has at least found a way to use humor significantly. He gives us the technical plan for a theatre to serve as a social scourge.

Perhaps today there is something to be called "the black mask of comedy." It may be that in our times we can find a certain new dramatic dimension which can serve as a social corrective—a leaven to bring forth this reasoned disgust of which we speak so as to precipitate meaningful and effective action.

It is indeed no accident that the ancient mask of "Arlecchino" is one of comedy's traditional symbols. It is a black, ugly thing, patched with grotesque hair, and staring out at life with an exacting, bestial intelligence. Comedy itself is a basically pessimistic thing which shows us man, not as he ought to be, but as he is—calced over with the lewd scales of vice and wrapped in the hypocrisy of his fallen nature. In the work of Boccaccio, in that of Rabelais, that of Chaucer, Swift, Gogol, and Cervantes we see an image of the same poor foolish man that was driven naked from Paradise, his flaccid haunches lashed raw by the angel with the flaming sword.

V
THE PSYCHOLOGY
OF COMEDY

Jokes and the Comic*

Sigmund Freud

It is only with misgivings that I venture to approach the problem of the comic itself. It would be presumptuous to expect that my efforts would be able to make any decisive contribution to its solution when the works of a great number of eminent thinkers have failed to produce a wholly satisfactory explanation. My intention is in fact no more than to pursue the lines of thought that have proved valuable with jokes a short distance further into the sphere of the comic.

The comic arises in the first instance as an unintended discovery derived from human social relations. It is found in people—in their movements, forms, actions and traits of character, originally in all probability only in their physical characteristics but later in their mental ones as well or, as the case may be, in the expression of those characteristics. By means of a very common sort of personification, animals become comic too, and inanimate objects. At the same time, the comic is capable of being detached from people, in so far as we recognize the conditions under which a person seems comic. In this way the comic of situation comes about, and this recognition affords the possibility of making a person comic at one's will by putting him in situations in which his actions are subject to these comic conditions. The discovery that one has it in one's power to make someone else comic opens the way to an undreamt-of yield of comic pleasure and is the origin of a highly developed technique. One can make *oneself* comic, too, as easily as other people. The methods that serve to make people comic are: putting them in a comic situation, mimicry, disguise, unmasking, caricature, parody, travesty, and so on. It is obvious that these techniques can be used to serve hostile and aggressive purposes. One can make a person comic in order to make him become contemptible, to deprive him of his claim to dignity and authority. But even if such an intention habitually underlies making people comic, this need not be the meaning of what is comic spontaneously.

This irregular survey of the occurrences of the comic will already show us that a very extensive field of origin is to be ascribed to it and that such specialized conditions as we found, for instance, in the naïve are not to be expected in it. In order to get on the track of the determining condition that is valid for the comic, the most important thing is the choice of an introductory case. We shall choose the comic of movement, because we recollect that the most primitive kind of stage performance—the pantomime—uses that method for making us laugh. The answer to the question of why we laugh at the clown's movements is

* Sigmund Freud, "Jokes and the Comic," in *Jokes and Their Relation to the Unconscious*, James Strachery, ed. and tr. (W. W. Norton and Routledge & Kegan Paul Ltd, 1960), pp. 188–221. [Footnotes have been renumbered; editor's minor footnotes were deleted.]

that they seem to us extravagant and inexpedient. We are laughing at an expenditure that is too large. Let us look now for the determining condition outside the comic that is artificially constructed—where it can be found unintended. A child's movements do not seem to us comic, although he kicks and jumps about. On the other hand, it *is* comic when a child who is learning to write follows the movements of his pen with his tongue stuck out; in these associated motions we see an unnecessary expenditure of movement which we should spare ourselves if we were carrying out the same activity. Similarly, other such associated motions, or merely exaggerated expressive movements, seem to us comic in adults too. Pure examples of this species of the comic are to be seen, for instance, in the movements of someone playing skittles who, after he has released the ball, follows its course as though he could still continue to direct it. Thus, too, all grimaces are comic which exaggerate the normal expression of the emotions, even if they are produced involuntarily as in sufferers from St. Vitus's dance (chorea). And in the same way, the passionate movements of a modern conductor seem comic to any unmusical person who cannot understand their necessity. Indeed, it is from this comic of movement that the comic of bodily shapes and facial features branches off; for these are regarded as though they were the outcome of an exaggerated or pointless movement. Staring eyes, a hooked nose hanging down to the mouth, ears sticking out, a hump-back—all such things probably only produce a comic effect in so far as movements are imagined which would be necessary to bring about these features; and here the nose, the ears and other parts of the body are imagined as more movable than they are in reality. There is no doubt that it is comic if someone can "waggle his ears," and it would certainly be still more comic if he could move his nose up and down. A good deal of the comic effect produced on us by animals comes from our perceiving in them movements such as these which we cannot imitate ourselves.

But how is it that we laugh when we have recognized that some other person's movements are exaggerated and inexpedient? By making a comparison, I believe, between the movement I observe in the other person and the one that I should have carried out myself in his place. The two things compared must of course be judged by the same standard, and this standard is my expenditure of innervation, which is linked to my idea of the movement in both of the two cases. . . .

Thus a uniform explanation is provided of the fact that a person appears comic to us if, in comparison with ourselves, he makes too great an expenditure on his bodily functions and too little on his mental ones; and it cannot be denied that in both these cases our laughter expresses a pleasurable sense of the superiority which we feel in relation to him. If the relation in the two cases is reversed— if the other person's physical expenditure is found to be less than ours or his mental expenditure greater—then we no longer laugh, we are filled with astonishment and admiration. . . .[1]

Mankind have not been content to enjoy the comic where they have come upon it in their experience; they have also sought to bring it about intentionally, and we can learn more about the nature of the comic if we study the means which serve to *make* things comic. First and foremost, it is possible to produce

---

[1] The contradictoriness with which the determining conditions of the comic are pervaded—the fact that sometimes an excess and sometimes an insufficiency seems to be the source of comic pleasure— has contributed no little to the confusion of the problem. Cf. Lipps (1898, 47).

the comic in relation to oneself in order to amuse other people—for instance, by making oneself out clumsy or stupid. In that way one produces a comic effect exactly as though one really were these things, by fulfilling the condition of the comparison which leads to the difference in expenditure. But one does not in this way make oneself ridiculous or contemptible, but may in some circumstances even achieve admiration. The feeling of superiority does not arise in the other person if he knows that one has only been pretending; and this affords fresh evidence of the fundamental independence of the comic from the feeling of superiority.

As regards making *other people* comic, the principal means is to put them in situations in which a person becomes comic as a result of human dependence on external events, particularly on social factors, without regard to the personal characteristics of the individual concerned—that is to say, by employing the comic of situation. This putting of someone in a comic situation may be a *real* one (a practical joke)—by sticking out a leg so that someone trips over it as though he were clumsy, by making him seem stupid by exploiting his credulity, or trying to convince him of something nonsensical, and so on—or it may be simulated by speech or play. The aggressiveness, to which making a person comic usually ministers, is much assisted by the fact that the comic pleasure is independent of the reality of the comic situation, so that everyone is in fact exposed, without any defence, to being made comic.

But there are yet other means of making things comic which deserve special consideration and also indicate in part fresh sources of comic pleasure. Among these, for instance, is *mimicry,* which gives quite extraordinary pleasure to the hearer and makes its object comic even if it is still far from the exaggeration of a caricature. It is much easier to find a reason for the comic effect of *caricature* than for that of more mimicry. Caricature, parody and travesty (as well as their practical counterpart, unmasking) are directed against people and objects which lay claim to authority and respect, which are in some sense '*sublime*.'[2] They are procedures for *Herabsetzung,* as the apt German expression has it. What is sublime is something large in the figurative, psychical sense; and I should like to suggest, or rather to repeat my suggestion, that, like what is somatically large, it is represented by an increased expenditure. It requires little observation to establish that when I speak of something sublime I innervate my speech in a different way, I make different facial expressions, and I try to bring the whole way in which I hold myself into harmony with the dignity of what I am having an idea of. I impose a solemn restraint upon myself—not very different from what I should adopt if I were to enter the presence of an exalted personality, a monarch, or a prince of science. I shall hardly be wrong in assuming that this different innervation in my ideational mimetics corresponds to an increased expenditure. The third instance of an increased expenditure of this kind is no doubt to be found when I proceed in abstract trains of thought instead of in the habitual concrete and plastic ones. When, therefore, the procedures that I have discussed for the degradation of the sublime allow me to have an idea of it as though it were something commonplace, in whose presence I need not pull myself togeth-

---

[2] 'Degradation' [in English in the original]. Bain (1865, 248) writes: 'The occasion of the Ludicrous is the Degradation of some person or interest, possessing dignity, in circumstances that excite no other strong emotion.' [The English word 'degradation' has accordingly been used in all that follows as a translation of '*Herabsetzung.*']

er but may, to use the military formula, 'stand easy,' I am being spared the in-creased expenditure of the solemn restraint; and the comparison between this new ideational method (instigated by empathy) and the previously habitual one, which is simultaneously trying to establish itself—this comparison once again creates the difference in expenditure which can be discharged by laughter.

Caricature, as is well known, brings about degradation by emphasizing in the general impression given by the exalted object a single trait which is comic in itself but was bound to be overlooked so long as it was only perceivable in the general picture. By isolating this, a comic effect can be attained which extends in our memory over the whole object. This is subject to the condition that the ac-tual presence of the exalted object himself does not keep us in a reverential atti-tude. If a comic trait of this kind that has been overlooked is lacking in reality, a caricature will unhesitatingly create it by exaggerating one that is not comic in itself; and the fact that the effect of the caricature is not essentially diminished by this falsification of reality is once again an indication of the origin of comic pleasure.

Parody and *travesty* achieve the degradation of something exalted in an-other way: by destroying the unity that exists between people's characters as we know them and their utterances by inferior ones. They are distinguished from caricature in this, but not in the mechanism of their production of comic plea-sure. The same mechanism is also used for *unmasking,* which only applied where someone has seized dignity and authority by a deception and these have to be taken from him in reality. We have already met with a few examples of the comic effect of unmasking in jokes—for instance, in the story of the aristo-cratic lady who, at the first onset of her labour-pains, exclaimed 'Ah! mon Dieu!' but who the doctor would not assist till she cried out 'Aa-ee, aa-ee!' Having come to know the characteristics of the comic, we can no longer dispute that this anec-dote is in fact an example of comic unmasking and has no justifiable claim to be called a joke. It only recalls jokes by its setting and by the technical method of 'representation by something very small' [loc. cit.]—in this case the patient's cry, which is found sufficient to establish the indication for treatment. It nevertheless remains true that our linguistic sense, if we call on it for a decision, raises no ob-jection to our calling a story like this a joke. We may explain this by reflecting that linguistic usage is not based on the scientific insight into the nature of jokes that we have arrived at in this laborious investigation. Since one of the functions of jokes is to make hidden sources of comic pleasure accessible once more, any device that brings to light something that is not manifestly comic may, by a loose analogy, be termed a joke. This applies preferably, however, to unmasking as well as to other methods of making people comic.[3]

Under the heading of 'unmasking' we may also include a procedure for making things comic with which we are already acquainted—the method of de-grading the dignity of individuals by directing attention to the frailties which they share with all humanity, but in particular the dependence of their mental functions on bodily needs. The unmasking is equivalent here to an admonition: such and such a person, who is admired as a demigod, is after all only human like you and me. Here, too, are to be placed the efforts at laying bare the monot-

---

[3] 'Thus every conscious and ingenious evocation of the comic (whether the comic of contemplation or of situation) is in general described as a joke. We, of course, cannot here make use of this concept of the joke either.' (Lipps, 1898, 78.)

onous psychical automatism that lies behind the wealth and apparent freedom of psychical functions. We came across examples of 'unmasking' of this kind in the marriage-broker jokes, and felt a doubt at the time whether these anecdotes have a right to be counted as jokes. We are now able to decide with greater certainty that the anecdote of the echo who reinforced all the assertions of the marriage-broker and finally confirmed his admission that the bride had a hump with the exclamation 'And *what* a hump!'—that this anecdote is essentially a *comic* story, an example of the unmasking of a psychical automatism. Here, however, the comic story is only serving as a façade. For anyone who will attend to the hidden meaning of the marriage-broker anecdotes, the whole thing remains an admirably staged joke; anyone who does not penetrate so far is left with a comic story. The same thing applies to the other joke, about the marriage-broker who, in order to answer an objection, ended by confessing the truth with a cry of "But I ask you, who would lend such people anything?" Here again we have a comic unmasking as the façade for a joke, though in this instance the characteristic of a joke is much more unmistakable, since the marriage-broker's remark is at the same time a representation by the opposite. In trying to prove that the people are rich he at the same time proves that they are *not* rich, but very poor. Here a joke and the comic are combined, and teach us that the same remark can be both things at once. . . .

Every theory of the comic is objected to by its critics on the score that its definition overlooks what is essential to the comic: 'The comic is based on a contrast between ideas.' 'Yes, in so far as the contrast has a comic and not some other effect.' 'The feeling of the comic arises from the disappointment of an expectation.' 'Yes, unless the disappointment is in fact a distressing one.' No doubt the objections are justified; but we shall be over-estimating them if we conclude from them that the essential feature of the comic has hitherto escaped detection. What impairs the universal validity of these definitions are conditions which are indispensable for the generating of comic pleasure; but we do not need to look for the essence of the comic in them. In any case, it will only become easy for us to dismiss the objections and throw light on the contradictions to the definitions of the comic if we suppose that the origin of comic pleasure lies in a comparison of the difference between two expenditures. Comic pleasure and the effect by which it is known—laughter—can only come about if this difference is unutilizable and capable of discharge. We obtain no pleasurable effect but at most a transient sense of pleasure in which the characteristic of being comic does not emerge, if the difference is put to another use as soon as it is recognized. Just as special contrivances have to be adopted in the case of jokes in order to prevent the use elsewhere of the expenditure that is recognized as superfluous, so, too, comic pleasure can only appear in circumstances that guarantee this same condition. For this reason occasions on which these differences in expenditure occur in our ideational life are uncommonly numerous, but the occasions on which the comic emerges from those differences are relatively quite rare.

Two observations force themselves on anyone who studies even cursorily the conditions for the generation of the comic from difference in expenditure. First, there are cases in which the comic appears habitually and as though by force of necessity, and on the contrary others in which it seems entirely dependent on the circumstances and on the standpoint of the observer. But secondly, unusually large differences very often break through unfavourable conditions, so that the comic feeling emerges in spite of them. In connection with the first of these points it would be possible to set up two classes—the inevitably comic and the occasionally comic—though one must be prepared from the first to renounce the notion of finding the inevitability of the comic in the first class free from exceptions. It would be tempting to enquire into the determining conditions for the two classes.

The conditions, some of which have been brought together as the 'isolation' of the comic situation, apply essentially to the second class. A closer analysis elicits the following facts:

(*a*) The most favourable condition for the production of comic pleasure is a generally cheerful mood in which one is 'inclined to laugh.' In a toxic mood of cheerfulness almost everything seems comic, probably by comparison with the expenditure in a normal state. Indeed, jokes, the comic and all similar methods of getting pleasure from mental activity, are no more than ways of regaining this cheerful mood—this euphoria—from a single point of approach, when it is not present as a general disposition of the psyche.

(*b*) A similarly favourable effect is produced by an *expectation* of the comic, by being attuned to comic pleasure. For this reason, if an intention to make something comic is communicated to one by someone else, differences of such a low degree are sufficient that they would probably be overlooked if they occurred in one's experience unintentionally. Anyone who starts out to read a comic book or goes to the theatre to see a farce owes to this intention his abililty to laugh at things which would scarcely have provided him with a case of the comic in his ordinary life. In the last resort it is in the recollection of having laughed and in the expectation of laughing that he laughs when he sees the comic actor come on to the stage, before the latter can have made any attempt at making him laugh. For that reason, too, one admits feeling ashamed afterwards over what one has been able to laugh at the play.

(*c*) Unfavourable conditions for the comic arise from the kind of mental activity with which a particular person is occupied at the moment. Imaginative or intellectual work that pursues serious aims interferes with the capacity of the cathexes for discharge—cathexes which the work requires for its displacements—so that only unexpectedly large differences in expenditure are able to break through to comic pleasure. What are quite specially unfavourable for the comic are all kinds of intellectual processes which are sufficiently remote from what is perceptual to bring ideational mimetics to a stop. There is no place whatever left for the comic in abstract reflection except when that mode of thought is suddenly interrupted.

(*d*) The opportunity for the release of comic pleasure disappears, too, if the attention is focused precisely on the comparison from which the comic may emerge. In such circumstances what would otherwise have the most certain comic effect loses its comic force. A movement or a function cannot be comic for a person whose interest is directed to comparing it with a standard which he has clearly before his mind. Thus the examiner does not find the nonsense comic which the candidate produces in his ignorance; he is annoyed by it, while the candidate's fellow students, who are far more interested in what luck he will have than in how much he knows, laugh heartily at the same nonsense. A gymnastic or dancing instructor seldom has an eye for the comic in his pupils' movements; and a clergyman entirely overlooks the comic in the human weaknesses which the writer of comedies can bring to light so effectively. The comic process will not bear being hypercathected by attention; it must be able to take its course quite unobserved—in this respect, incidentally, just like jokes. It would, how- ever, contradict the nomenclature of the 'processes of consciousness' of which I made use, with good reason, in my *Interpretation of Dreams* if one sought to speak of the comic process as a necessarily unconscious one. It forms part, rather, of the preconscious; and such processes, which run their course in the precon- scious but lack the cathexis of attention with which consciousness is linked, may aptly be given the name of 'automatic.' The process of comparing expenditures must remain automatic if it is to produce comic pleasure.

(*e*) The comic is greatly interfered with if the situation from which it ought to develop gives rise at the same time to a release of strong affect. A discharge of the operative difference is as a rule out of the question in such a case. The af- fects, disposition and attitude of the individual in each particular case make it understandable that the comic emerges and vanishes according to the standpoint of each particular person, and that an absolute comic exists only in exceptional instances. The contingency or relativity of the comic is therefore far greater than that of a joke, which never happens of its own accord but is invariably *made*, and in which the conditions under which it can find acceptance can be observed at the time at which it is constructed. The generation of affect is the most intense of all the conditions that interfere with the comic and its importance in this re- spect has been nowhere overlooked.[4] For this reason it has been said that the comic feeling comes easiest in more or less indifferent cases where the feelings and interests are not strongly involved. Yet precisely in cases where there is a re- lease of affect one can observe a particularly strong difference in expenditure bring about the automatism of release. When Colonel Butler[5] answers Octavio's warnings by exclaiming 'with a bitter laugh': '*Thanks* from the House of Aus- tria!' his embitterment does not prevent his laughing. The laugh applies to his memory of the disappointment he believes he has suffered; and on the other hand the magnitude of the disappointment cannot be portrayed more impres- sively by the dramatist than by his showing it capable of forcing a laugh in the midst of the storm of feelings that have been released. I am inclined to think that this explanation would apply to every case in which laughter occurs in circum- stances other than pleasurable ones and accompanied by intensely distressing or strained emotions.

(*f*) If we add to this that the generating of comic pleasure can be encour- aged by any other pleasurable accompanying circumstance as though by some sort of contagious effect (working in the same kind of way as the fore-pleasure principle with tendentious jokes), we shall have mentioned enough of the condi- tions governing comic pleasure for our purposes, though certainly not all of them. We can then see that these conditions, as well as the inconstancy and con- tingency of the comic effect, cannot be explained so easily by any other hypoth- esis than that of the derivation of comic pleasure from the discharge of a differ- ence which, under the most varying circumstances, is liable to be used in ways other than discharge.

---

[4] 'It is easy for you to laugh; it means nothing more to you.'
[5] [In Schiller's tragedy *Wallensteins Tod* (II.6). Colonel Butler, a veteran Irish soldier in the Imperial army during the Thirty Years War, believes that he has been snubbed by the Emperor and is prepar- ing to desert to his enemies. Octavio Piccolomini, his superior officer, begs him to reconsider the po- sition and reminds him of the thanks which Austria owes him for his forty years' loyalty, and to this Butler replies in the words quoted above.]

On the Psychology of Comedy*

Ludwig Jekels

We are indebted to psycho-analysis for much valuable insight into the psychology of tragedy. Not only has psycho-analysis made us recognise that the "tragic guilt" of the hero, postulated by aesthetics, actually stems from the repressed Oedipus-wishes of the dramatist but it has also drawn our attention to the inter-relation of dramatist and audience; that is, to the fact of a common guilt as the decisive psychological factor which, on the one hand, enables the dramatist to create his work and, on the other, produces the Aristotelian catharsis, or "purging of the passions." Freud,[1] in particular, established the psychological traces of the primal crime in classical tragedy and following in his tracks, Winterstein[2] has recently subjected the origins of tragedy to intensive study and radically clarified them.

By contrast, how little has psycho-analysis bothered about comedy! So far it has hardly attracted any interest worth mentioning: at most it was granted a modest domicile in that basement of research, the footnote, there to be dealt with in a cursory manner.

And yet it seems to me that comedy well deserves serious and detailed investigation, and not only because it contains the problem of the comic, which is admittedly one of the most difficult and complicated in psychology; a problem, in fact, which even Freud[3] approached "not without some trepidation," although he was able later to clarify it greatly. As this rough outline will help to show, the psycho-analytical investigation of comedy can bring to light much that may claim our fullest interest.

My analysis of several classical comedies led to the surprising result that I found them characterized by a mechanism of inversion: *the feeling of guilt which, in tragedy, rests upon the son, appears in comedy displaced on the father; it is the father who is guilty.*

This fact was probably already noticed by Diderot; at the same time it seems to have elicited an effective disagreement on his part, for in his *Discours sur la poésie dramatique* he writes: "It seems to me that Terence succumbed, on one occasion, to this fault. His 'Heautontimorumenos' (The Self-Tormentor'), is a father who grieves over the violent decision to which he has driven his son by excessive strictness; he therefore punishes himself by miserably depriving himself

* Ludwig Jekels, "On the Psychology of Comedy," in *Selected Papers of Ludwig Jekels*, I. Jarosy, tr. (International Universities Press, 1952).

[1] Freud, *Totem and Taboo.*
[2] Alfred Winterstein, *Der Ursprung der Tragödie.*
[3] Freud, *Jokes and Their Relation to the Unconscious.*

of food and clothing, shunning all company, dismissing his servants and tilling the soil with his own hands. One may justly remark that such a father does not exist. The largest town would hardly be able to furnish an example of such strange sorrow in a hundred years."

We shall attempt to substantiate our thesis, though only in outline, with the help of other examples. The jumbling together of works belonging to very different cultures, and to epochs which are frequently millennia apart, may be explained by the fact that we are guided by, and seek to establish, one particular point of view and so, for the time being, consciously neglect all others.

The *Merchant of Venice*, until fairly recently, was regarded by Shakespearean scholars as one of the most debatable works of the poet—not only as concerns its basic theme, but as regards its dramatic genre. On the basis of our theory, which postulates that, in comedy, the father-figure must be represented as weighed down by guilt, we must regard this work as comedy, for the father's guilt is almost expressly indicated. Antonio, who is so dangerously threatened by Shylock, is certainly a father-figure. That this psycho-analytical assumption is well-founded, is shown by the fact that he derives from the Messer Ansaldo of the text which Shakespeare used as his source (Fiorentino's *Pecorone*); that Messer Ansaldo who appears as a "fatherly friend" in the story is a man full of love, of infinite patience and ready to make great sacrifices for his adopted son. The poet, however, allows Antonio to become "guilty" in the first act of the play:

> Therefore go forth;
> Try what my credit can in Venice do:
> That shall be rack'd, even to the uttermost,

and to give Shylock his bond.

It need hardly occasion surprise if we here regard a money debt as a mere substitute for moral guilt. The extremely close connection between the two, which, so far as I know, Müller-Braunschweig[4] first demonstrated among psycho-analysts, Nietzsche had already emphasized in his *Genealogy of Morals*.[5] The intimate connection between these two groups of ideas, as well as their substitutive relation, is unquestionable. The very ancient provision of monetary fines in criminal law, and the fact that not only German, but also many other languages (among them French and Polish) use the same word to denote both a material debt and moral guilt, provides eloquent testimony to the truth of this view. And, last but not least, the substitution of the idea of a money debt for that of moral guilt is hardly surprising to the psycho-analyst, who frequently observes this substitutive relation in the dreams and resistances of his patients.

The same expression of this motif is also found in that finest of German comedies, Lessing's *Minna von Barnhelm*.

The complications of the plot, it will be recalled, are based on events which occur before the play opens: Major van Tellheim, entrusted to collect a levy from a hostile Diet, in order to avoid resorting to harsh measures, himself advances the money to the King against a note of credit issued by the said Diet. But when he requires its repayment once peace is concluded, his demand is rejected

---

[4] Dr. Karl Müller-Braunschweig: *Psychoanalytische Geischtspunkte zur Psychogenese der Moral, insbesondere des moralischen Aktes.* Imago VII (1921).
[5] Chapter 4: ". . . that the cardinal moral idea of 'guilt' originates from the very material idea of 'debt.'"

and, suspected of accepting enemy bribes, he is compelled to submit to a judicial enquiry. This he regards not only as a heavy blow to his honour, but as an insurmountable obstacle to his marriage with Minna, who loves him and whom he loves.

Again we can only reduce this coherent and richly elaborated story to the bald formula that it is the father (the King) who is guilty. This is confirmed not only by the fact that the ensuing entanglements are resolved by the King's personal intervention and payment of his debt, but even the minor scenes of the comedy, as those in which the valet Just and Werner appear, are permeated with Tellheim's resistance: "I will not be your debtor." In spite of excellent rationalisations, one can hardly regard this constant resistance as indicating anything but the son's complete rejection of all guilt, the more completely and demonstratively to stress the father's.

With this interpretation we have, however, penetrated straight to the root of that guilt which is levelled against the father: the King stands in the way of Tellheim's love and marriage!

That this, in fact, is the play's latent basic trend is shown by the following circumstance, as I have already pointed out in my study of *Macbeth*;[6] namely, that in dramatic works the basic motif is presented twice; in a way that is nearer consciousness, and then in a remoter manner; i.e. in a fairly direct as well as a veiled form. This phenomenon can be observed with such regularity that even the converse—every motif that occurs twice in a drama is its basic theme—now seems to me, after considerable re-examination, entirely valid.

Now *Minna von Barnhelm* does actually contain such a second, considerably less veiled hint of the father as obstacle between the lovers. It is the passage where, somewhat mysteriously, Minna informs the obdurate Tellheim that she is persecuted by her uncle and guardian Count Bruchsall, who has disinherited her for not wishing to accept a husband of his choosing. Hardly has the Count made Tellheim's acquaintance, however, when the latter addresses him as "my father" and the Count, in turn calls him "son."

The reproach "Father—disturber of love," which establishes the father's guilt, is the latent content of most comedies of the kind discussed.

This motif is brought out extremely clearly in Molière's *L'Avare*, where neither the father-son relationship nor their sexual rivalry is in any way masked. Here Harpagon steps between his son and the latter's bride, because he himself desires to marry her.

But the same motif also appears in *Tartuffe*, if one regards the hypocrite as a mere derivative of the father Orgon who, thereby, becomes the son's rival for the mother's affections.

In Terence's *Phormio*—one of the finest of classical comedies—the father, who is opposed to the love-choice of his son (Phaedria), is similarly made amenable to the son's will by the unmasking of his sexual misbehaviour. The play significantly closes with the father's words: "But where is Phaedria, who must be our judge?"[7]

The following comedies betray, in their manifest content, nothing of those "family" relationships which, in the plays just discussed, stood out so clearly; their basic psychological situation is, nevertheless, the same.

[6] Cf.: "The Riddle of Shakespeare's *Macbeth*" and "The Problem of the Duplicated Expression of Psychic Themes."
[7] *The Plays of Terence*, trans. William Ritchie (London, 1927).

In Plautus's justly famed *Miles Gloriosus* for instance, the bombastic, vain fool, Pyrgopolinikes, is placed in a double relationship: as father towards the young Athenian Pleusikles, whose sweetheart he carries off, and so as son towards the jovial Ephesian Periplekomenos, whose supposed wife, in the intrigues of the plot, he attempts to seduce away from him.

In conclusion we may cite Kleist's *Der zerbrochene Krug,* which is no less illustrative of our thesis. Its theme is an investigation into whether the father (Judge Adam) or the son (Ruprecht) is responsible for a nocturnal burglary, and the "breaking of Eve's pitcher!"

In complete accordance with our thesis, the verdict "guilty" is passed on the father.

The significance of these conclusions will be elucidated by a passage from Bergson's *Laughter.*[8] He believes that the essence of the comic consists in the mechanisation of life, an effect which can be obtained by the process of *inversion* as well as by two other processes, *repetition* and *reciprocal interference of series.* He states:

> Picture to yourself certain characters in a certain situation; if you reverse the situation and invert the rôles, you obtain a comic scene . . . There is no necessity, however, for both the identical scenes to be played before us. We may be shown only one, provided the other is really in our minds . . . The plot of the villain who is the victim of his own villainy, or the cheat cheated, forms the stock-in-trade of a good many plays. We find this even in primitive farce . . . In modern literature we meet with hundreds of variations on the theme of the robber robbed. In every case the root idea involves an inversion of rôles, and a situation which recoils on the head of its author.

"Here we apparently find the confirmation of a law, some illustrations of which we have already pointed out. When a comic scene has been reproduced a number of times, it reaches the stage of being a classical type of model. It becomes amusing. Henceforth, new scenes, which are not comic *de jure,* may become amusing *de facto,* on account of their partial resemblance to this model. They call up in our mind a more or less confused image which we know to be comical. They range themselves in a category representing an officially recognized type of comic. The scene of the 'robber robbed' belongs to this class. It casts over a host of other scenes a reflection of the comic element it contains. In the end it renders comic any mishap that befalls one through one's own fault, no matter what the fault or mishap may be—nay, an allusion to this mishap, a single word that recalls it, is sufficient."

It is probably unnecessary to stress that we claim this central significance of the "model scene" for the element we have singled out.

In this passage a penetrating philosopher has approached remarkably near our own position and has even increased the area within which we assumed the factor we discovered in comedy, and its allied manifestations, to hold valid. As regards the riddle which comedy presents, little however has been gained towards solving it.

[8] Henri Bergson, *Laughter. An Essay on the Meaning of the Comic,* trans. C. Brereton and F. Rothwell (London, 1911), pp. 94–96.

It can be taken for granted that the writer of comedies possesses the same creative impulses, and is subject to the same psychological laws, as those long known to be valid—especially through the excellent work of Sachs[9] for the writer of tragedies; this applies especially to the imperative urge to effect the discharge of his repressed complexes, which the dramatist is able to satisfy by, as it were, distributing his feeling of guilt among the many.

On the other hands, the analyses of the comedies cited, summary though these be, leaves little doubt that the material employed is identical with that employed by the writer of tragedies: in both cases the Oedipus situation is involved.

It may be due to this identity that, in so many plays, their nature remains unclear long after the action begins to unfold, so that for a time the final result may equally be comedy as tragedy: it is only a delayed swift turning-point which finally decides us as to its genre.

But how does it happen that from such identical psychological pre-suppositions, such completely, even diametrically opposite effects, result; that from a similar foundation, tragic guilt and expiation arise in one case, and effervescent high spirits in the other?

We believe that we possess the key to this riddle in the factor we have isolated in our analyses: namely, displaced guilt.

In the last resort, this infantile phantasy of the father as the disturber of love is nothing but a projection of the son's own guilty wish to disturb the love of the parents. *By displacing this phantasy on the father, by endowing him with this specifically filial attitude, it becomes clear that the father is divested of his paternal attributes, and thus is removed as a father and degraded into a son.*

This displacement proceeds from the same psychological motives as the "unmasking" generally employed in so many comedies, of which we cited *Tartuffe, Der zerbrochene Krug,* and *Phormio;* which motives are summed up by Freud in the formula "You, too, are only a human being like myself." Like the unmasking, this phantasy is employed in comedy in order to degrade the father, to degrade him to a son, or to the level ordinarily appropriate to the son. This turning-the-father-into-a-son, this inverted world, *"le monde renversé,"* as Bergson puts it, represents the very core of his *"inversion,"* the innermost purpose of the displacement of guilt.

Only the fact that the father is given the status of a mere son explains why, in comedy (from classical comedy to the contemporary bedroom farce), it is generally the father who is beaten in the trial of strength. For the same reason, returning to our examples, Harpagon must lose the game and, thereby, the love-object, and the King in *Minna von Barnhelm* must not only clear obstacles away, but even far exceed the necessary need of reparation.

Only this reduction of the father to a son can explain how writers of comedies can unleash so wide a range of aggression (scorn, derision, etc.) against the father, and allow, for instance, Antonio in the *Merchant of Venice,* and even more obviously Bramabras, taken by surprise in his love-suit, to stand in such open danger of being castrated. Only by such a reduction can we understand the call to the pardoned man: " 'Twill soon be finished with your fatherhood!"

This doing away with the father and his dissolution in the son, the withdrawal of the superego and its merging in the ego, are all in complete psychological conformity with the phenomena of mania.

---

[9] Hanns Sachs, *Gemeinsame Tagträume.*

In each case we find the ego, which has liberated itself from the tyrant, un-inhibitedly venting its humour, wit, and every sort of comic manifestation in a very ecstasy of freedom.

We shall resist the temptation to discuss the psychological relation, now very apparent, between tragedy and melancholic depression—a connection al-ready hinted at in the words of the Byzantine Suidas: "*ê chrê tragôdein pantas ê melagcholan,*"[10] and shall limit ourselves to the statement that comedy repre-sents an aesthetic correlate of mania.

[10] I am indebted to Winterstein for drawing my attention to this passage.

Beyond Laughter:
A Summing Up*

Martin Grotjahn

A happy life is not necessarily all fun and laughter or amusing or entertaining. The happiness of a person, of a period of time, or of a culture cannot be measured by the length and strength of laughter. Happiness is a function of creativity. The analytic study of laughter is a study of creative communication between the unconscious and the conscious, leading to the experience of happiness in fulfilling one's potentialities. This is man's challenge, his destiny, and the meaning of human life.

We started our task historically in these pages. When Sigmund Freud discovered the unconscious meaning of dreams and when he told his friends about it, they laughed. Freud became interested in the unconscious reason for this merriment of his students and started to investigate the similarities between dreams and jokes. Five years after the publication of his history-making book, "The Interpretation of Dreams," he published his work on jokes and their relation to the unconscious (1905).

Freud's thesis is simple and straightforward: Laughter occurs when repressing energy is freed from its static function of keeping something forbidden under repression and away from consciousness. A witticism starts with an aggressive tendency or intent—an insultlike, shocking thought. This has to be repressed and disappears into the unconscious like a train into a mountain tunnel. The wit work begins there in the darkness of the unconscious, like the dream work; it disguises the latent aggressive thought skillfully. It combines the disguised aggression with playful pleasure, repressed since childhood and waiting for a chance to be satisfied. After this wit work is accomplished, the witticism reappears at the other end of the tunnel and sees the daylight of consciousness and conscience again. By now it has become acceptable, and the energy originally activated to keep the hostility under repression is freed into laughter. The repressed energy is no longer needed; the shock of freedom of thought and freedom from repression is enjoyed and leads to laughter.

Because of the double-edged character of wit, its disguise must be tested by telling the joke. The reaction of the third person (the teller and the victim of the joke are the first two) shows the success or failure of the wit work. The disguise must go far enough to avoid guilt; it must not go so far that the thrill of aggression is lost. The quality of the witticism is judged only according to the skill of the disguise, not according to the content. If the disguise is unsuccessful, pleasure will change to displeasure, embarrassment, shame, and guilt about aggressive

* Martin Grotjahn. "Beyond Laughter: A Summing Up," in *Beyond Laughter* (McGraw-Hill, 1957), pp. 255–264. Copyright © 1957 by McGraw-Hill Book Company. Used by permission.

and infantile indulgence in a childhood pleasure.

While wit saves energy by releasing repression of an aggressive thought, the enjoyment of the comic liberates energy from an intended motor outlet, according to Freud. In humor, especially in Freud's favorite "gallows" humor, energy is saved from the repressing emotion: I do not need to pity the condemned criminal because he is strong, he can take it, he does not need my pity. He is stronger than his fate and possibly stronger than reality.

We then considered the humorist as a personality type. We found him to be related to the masochist and to the melancholic. He behaves as if he knows the misery of this world but resolutely proceeds to disregard it. He remains aware of this valley of tears but behaves as if it is still the Garden of Eden. He proceeds not by denying the existence of misery but by pretending to be victorious over it. He illustrates for us the hope for the victory of infantile narcissism over all experience. His victory is only partial and temporary; what he may gain in inner strength and kindness, he will lose in the world of reality and adjustment. He may be free but not necessarily happy or well adjusted to his environment.

The wit as a person is closely related to the sadist. Under the disguise of brilliance, charm, and entertainment the wit—and we do not mean only the practical joker—is a sadist at heart. He is sharp, quick, alert, cold, aggressive, and hostile. He is inclined to murder his victims in thought; if he inhibits himself and if he does not succeed in transforming his brain child into a joke, he may develop a migraine attack instead.

The sense of humor develops in stages and gradually during a lifetime. Every step is connected with mastery of a new anxiety, and each conflict mastered at the different developmental stages is marked by a growth of the sense of humor. So people are inordinately proud of it—often even those who have no sense of humor at all. It is the mark of distinction, of having achieved strength and maturity.

The smile is older than laughter and appears when the human infant is only a few days old. It characterizes the baby as genuinely human. It signifies the intimate contact between human mother and human infant. The human mother is more a mother than any animal mother, and the human infant is more and longer an infant than any animal baby. (Regretfully, we pointed out that the human male is not necessarily more masculine than his opposite number from the animal kingdom. This is a sad fact, and the consequences are not yet settled.) With the mother smiling at the child in her arms and the child looking up into the mother's face and smiling back, human communication was born and facial expression originated.

In the development of mankind a similar chain reaction was started when man assumed the upright posture; this freed the hand for reaching and holding, and the human mouth was free to talk, to smile, and to laugh, no longer being needed to hold things, like the mouth of a dog. When man developed intelligence, he progressed from the sign to the symbol and the word, leading to the great human triumph of verbal speech over the language of the body. The human brain is the most fetal and infantile brain of all animals, looking, with its grotesquely enlarged forebrain, like a prematurely born fetus of one of the lower animals. To be youthful, to be unfinished, means to be human. Being the oldest of all animals, man is simultaneously the youngest of them all. Only he understands the symbol in word and thought and may react with laughter.

Physical, instinctual, and biologic development was replaced in man's evolution by his greatest achievement: culture. The start of cultural development is symbolized in the Sphinx, the union of man and beast, combining animal spirits and human intelligence. The Sphinx, who is so significantly placed by Sophocles at the beginning of the Oedipus trilogy, seems to ask in her riddle: Who loves the one he is not allowed to love? In this way the Sphinx declares that at the beginning of cultural development stands the incest taboo and the repression of man's love for his mother. This repression separates man's instinctual life from that of the animal, where any cub growing sexually mature is just another competitor, free to woo his mother. In contrast to all other animals, only the human animal must not approach his mother for purposes of procreation.

The child does not begin to laugh until it has mastered or almost mastered the movements of the body. Flatus is the forerunner of the belly laugh. The child's understanding of jokes and witticisms begins when the language of the body is replaced by the mastery of speech. The Little Moron jokes are a horrible example of this period, as the pun is a later residue of it. In the third phase—not always reached by everybody—the enjoyment of humor occurs as a sign of emotional maturity and mastery. The humorist finally recreates in himself the good, kind, tolerant mother who has to smile at the misery of her unruly and guilty child whom she more or less willingly forgives.

When Freud discovered the unconscious during his great creative period, he found also in the Oedipus situation the genuine meaning of all great human tragedy: the infatuation with the mother, the taboo of incest, the rebellion of the son against the tyrannical father, the guilt and the punishment by castration for the crime in thought or action, conscious or unconscious. The Oedipus situation is the gravestone on the lost paradise of our childhood and at the same time the cornerstone of all culture as we know it. After the repression of the sexual longing for the mother, cultural development took the place of physical and instinctual or biologic process.

The psychodynamics of the comedy can be understood as a kind of reversed Oedipus situation in which the son does not rebel against the father but the son's typical attitudes of childhood longing are projected upon the father. The son plays the role of the victorious father with sexual freedom and achievement, while the father is cast in the role of the frustrated onlooker. The reversed Oedipus situation is repeated in every man's life when the younger generation grows up and slowly infiltrates and replaces the older generation in work and in life. The clown is the comic figure representing the impotent and ridiculed father. He also represents the sadness of things and finally comes to stand for death in the person of the tragic truly great clown. This is the point where tragedy and comedy finally meet and symbolize human life.

As the spirit of irreverence is necessary for laughter, it is not easy to use the symbol of the mother for the purpose of ridicule There are no female clowns; the Red-hot Mama, the burlesque queen, and the comedienne have to be specially censored in order to conceal the return of the repressed longing for the mother in new disguise. The symbol of the mother who understands the desires of her son is greatly treasured by the Oedipus in all of us who try courageously to grow up as long as we live. The mother figure may show with the smile of Mona Lisa that she understands the desires of her son and secretly accepts them. She gives hope to Oedipus. To seduce is a mother's destiny. When the son finally reaches her embrace it is the embrace of death, for the grave is, symbolically speaking, similar to the cradle.

The Oedipus drama, the essence of tragedy and comedy, helps the audience to work through their difficulties in the mastery of cultural discontent and collective repression. Problems as the child experiences them before he feels the full impact of the Oedipus situation do not belong on the stage of the legitimate theater but in the circus arena. While we, at least within ourselves, participate in the performance on the stage, we are only onlookers at the "Greatest Show on Earth." Physical mastery, terror and nightmares, problems of bisexuality and of ambivalence, of time, space, and balance, of animal instincts and beauty are illustrated in the show, but no real conflicts are worked out. In the circus the child is participating only with his eyes, while on the stage of the theater the adult is actually working-through his residual Oedipus conflict. The strange institution of amusement parks and fun fairs with their mechanized fairylands illustrates similar dynamics.

Dreams at night and in the light of day, fantasies and fairy tales—all art leads us to islands of true freedom where we do not need to submit to cruel reality, to renunciation and repression. Following the creative artist into the artistic experience, we work on our unconscious conflicts. This makes us stronger, more mature, and better able to live in the world of reality and civilization after our experience in the realm of esthetics. Mere entertainment does not offer this kind of analytic working-through. Psychoanalysis aims at a similar working-through, but on a different level and with different methods. Where the artist works in the esthetic dimension, the psychoanalyst tries to reach the level of scientific interpretation, integration, and insight.

A peculiarly distorted childhood curiosity explains our interest in the mystery story. There was a time when we were all mystery fans, when we were all Peeping Toms and would almost risk our lives to see and hear and learn what happened on the hidden stage of the parental bedroom. The primal scene appears to the child like a bloody, cruel, wild, and lustful performance, with the mother as the victim, the father as the rapist or murderer, the child as the clever little detective who connects the clues and explains it all to the stupid Dr. Watson. The police, of course, protect the vested interests of the parental authorities and do not help in discovering the mystery of crime and sex. Actually the facts of life are obvious. In the mystery story, the facts of the crime can be deduced from obvious clues by anyone who wants to see. Clues are all around us, and so is murder and crime and lust—if we only are allowed or allow ourselves to see. The mystery fan is a Peeping Tom who looks desperately and persistently through the wrong keyhole.

The contemporary Oedipus may appear in cowboy boots and enliven our movie and television screen. The difference between art creation and the trashy sentimentality of so much shallow entertainment is related to the lifting and working-through of repressions in art and analysis.

Laughter is taken as a sign of strength, freedom, health, beauty, youth, and happiness. It may appear in dreams and even in psychoanalysis. A patient may bring a favorite joke, which can then be used like a dream or a recollection or a stream of free associations to gain insight. Uncontrollable laughter, however, can be a sign of hysteria as well as a sign of intoxication or encephalitis or brain tumor. Inappropriate laughter is a significant sign of deterioration. It may herald the danger of an approaching psychosis.

The importance and meaning of Ferdinand the Bull and Mickey Mouse, together with Alice in Wonderland, illustrated our need for free and episodic regression—or communication with our unconscious, as in sleep and dream—in order to gain strength for this reality we live in. We need such anxiety-free communication with our unconscious to keep our imagination and intuition alive; to create freely; to form our life. With such rebirth, experienced without guilt, fear, or anxiety, performed with grace and with ease, with a smile and with laughter, we become essentially—and incurably—human.

The Comic Actor*

Jean-Paul Sartre

Farcical comedy has just as much of a cathartic function as tragedy in that it preserves laughter as dissociative behavior and permanently provides the social individual with an opportunity to dissociate himself from the absurdities or flaws he discovers in his neighbor which implicate him because he does not always have time or is not always able to hold them up to ridicule. A cuckold is of course absolutely ludicrous; but if he is my brother and I know that he is suffering, I am very liable to display a suspect compassion for him. The theater is there to get me out of the difficulty, for the theater is where people laugh at cuckolds, and there I can implicitly mock at my brother because he is lumped in with the rest; the monarch of nature strides majestically to the performance to affirm with a hale and virile gayety his *racial* supremacy over the submen who are impertinent enough to imitate him. A helot will dedicate himself there to exciting a collective laughter of self-satisfaction by wallowing in subhumanity in order to smear his own self with the stains that might tarnish the "human personage" and to display them as the taints of an inferior race vainly trying to approximate to ours. In the darkened halls the "human person," relaxed and unnumbered, guffaws on every seat, asserting its domination by the violence of its mirth. Unlike the magistrate who has the mischance to fall down and *become laughable* by a sudden and spontaneous serialization[1] of the bystanders and suffers, vainly rejecting the status of externality imposed upon him, the professional comic actor knowingly tries to provoke his audience's serialization by demonstrating to it the manifest contradiction between his being-external-to-himself and his subjective illusion. He takes himself seriously[2] so that this seriousness

* Jean-Paul Sartre, "The Comic Actor," *Sartre on Theater*, translated by Frank Jellinek. (Pantheon Books, 1976). Copyright © 1976 by Random House, Inc. Reprinted by permission of Pantheon Books, a Division of Random House, Inc.
[1] A concept introduced and explained by Sartre in the *Critique de la raison dialectique* (see especially pp. 308 ff.).

In his Preface to Michèle Marceaux's *Les Maos en France* (Paris: Gallimard, 1971; pp. 10–11), he gives the following definition of "seriality": "An aggregate is called serial when each of its components, although neighbor to all the others, remains alone and is defined by its neighbor's thinking, insofar as this neighbor thinks *like the others;* that is to say, each is other than itself and behaves like another which itself is other than itself."

[2] In the passage preceding this extract Sartre discusses a theory of laughter in which he borrows from Bergson (*Laughter: An Essay on the Meaning of the Comic*, 1899) the well-known example of the man tripping in the street, falling down, and arousing the passers' mirth. The following definition is worth noting: "Laughter is the property of man because man is the only animal that takes itself seriously; mirth denounces false seriousness in the name of true seriousness" (*L'Idiot de la famille*, vol. 1, p. 821).

may be instantly denied by a remorseless mechanism—both outside him and within his false internality—which can reduce him to pure appearance; he commits himself to acting only with the intention that his act, baffled, deflected, negated, or retorted against himself by the force of circumstance, shall proclaim itself a ridiculous dream of sovereignty at once revealing that praxis, the privilege of the human race, is forbidden to submen. The cathartic function begins where that of the uncontrolled laughter ends; the laughter starts the derealization of the guilty, and the comic actor completes it: he unrealizes himself into *another,* a fixation abscess of this or that absurdity of ours or of all of them at once; and the public is solemnly forewarned by posters that he never existed. He is as it were an admonition to the public: the object of your uncontrolled laughter will never implicate you, for it does not exist; the drunkard does not exist nor the bewigged justice of the high court who fell flat on his face, for these are the dreams of submen and promptly exposed. Nothing is real which is not serious and nothing is serious which is not real. The comic actor therefore appears as a clown who releases man from himself by an ignominious sacrifice for which no one thanks him. Let him not expect any sympathy from those who laugh at him, for is he not instigating a whole theater to dissociate itself from him and to treat him as *external?* But in the first place, is it conceivable that the serious persons watching his contortions will not view his proclaimed intention to arouse their mirth as suspect and fundamentally *ridiculous?* Laughter safeguards the serious; but how can anyone be serious if his job is to make himself a ridiculous object? How can he help being placed on the same footing as the submen whom the uncontrolled laughter *institutes* as ridiculous, since he is, after all, simply embodying them? And if he is a man like the spectators, how strange his intention to present himself night after night as a subman. Their subhumanity must fascinate him. If so, he is more disquieting and guiltier than a drunkard or a cuckold, for they do not know what they are doing. But he quite knowingly presents himself for punishment by laughter, and so is a traitor to his kind, a "human person" who has sided with the enemies of man. The comic performance is healthy, of course, it reassures and releases and ought to be approved of—though cautiously—as an *institution;* but the social individuals who *present* it must be vile or flawed, for what a man worthy of the name *ipso facto* rejects—actually does not even need to reject—is being exiled by the laughter of the company of his kind; how could he do other than despise wretches who do their utmost to get themselves expelled from it every night? Better still, how could he help dissociating himself from them by laughing *at them,* since they are, after all, those most likely to implicate him?

It is no use arguing that people do not laugh at them, but at the characters they are playing. The public hardly knows the difference. It is not entirely wrong in this, because anyone who harbors the project of presenting a comic character to others must be predestined to it, that is to say must already be ridiculous, which we know means already derealized by the mirth of others. In this sense, the alter ego which the laughers assign to the ridiculous object and the persona displayed to them by the comic actor have this much in common, that both of them are imaginary. Odette Laure, the comic singer, let the cat out of the bag when she said one day in an interview, "If you want to be a comic singer, *you must not like yourself much.*" That is the root of the matter: if the comic actor is to throw himself to the wild beasts every night, knowingly excite their cruelty, refuse all recourse to internality, and publicly reduce himself to external appearance, then he must have been constituted in externality to himself at some decisive period of his life. We laugh at very young children, and they know it and delight to make us laugh at them. But this laughter is kindly; the adult is amused at these submen imitating the man he is; and he laughs at the sight of his own gestures decomposed by these clumsy little bodies as they try to learn them; it is kindly because he knows quite well that these submen are men in embryo. The children exaggerate their clumsiness and seriousness to ingratiate themselves. The stage of putting on an act does not last long, however; it disappears as soon as the child acquires the inner certainty of his singularity and is able to set what he makes of himself within his self-awareness against what he is to and through others. *The future comic actor is one who fixes himself at the age of the ridiculous.* Some accident or the family structure must have constituted him in externality; they must have kept him at a distance, must have refused to consider the inner motivation of his acts and to share in his pleasures and pains, and they must have appraised his behavior by the degree in which it conformed to the imperatives of a pre-established model rather than by its singular meaning. The child will first discover that he is someone in whose place no one ever puts himself; he will find that the sovereign authority of the grown-ups insists on making his externality the truth of his life and regarding his awareness as mere chatter; he will observe, without grasping the reason for it, that the kindly laughter which he delighted to excite is turning sour. What has happened is that for some reason or other, his parents and kin hold that his development has been arrested, that his clumsiness—which they found so charming only a year before—now shows that he will never internalize the "human person" which society proposes to him, and that consequently this reveals the impossibility of his ever being a man—which is the specific definition of subhumanity. The family laughter at once becomes as it were a dissociation, for the parents vow that they cannot recognize themselves in their offspring and do not believe that he is *of their blood*. A good debut for a future comic actor. If the small boy is docile enough to find a growing difficulty in *putting himself in his own place*, still experiencing his feelings but no longer entering into them, and if, anguished by his estrangement, he lives in the clandestinity of the unreflecting and then dissociates himself in the full light of reflection and is willing to see it only as a means of arousing mirth in others out of an agonized desire to be the first to laugh at himself in order to rejoin the adults in their seriality, then a vocation as comic actor has come into being, together with a *ridiculous image*, a furious enslavement of the internal to the flat appearance of the external. Thus you have a monster, unrealized by the uncontrolled laughter of others; a traitor to his own self, he will henceforth do his utmost to feed the image which others have of him. If he later becomes an actor in earnest and acts Sganarelle or Pourceaugnac, what has changed? These are, it is true, *roles*. But what inner certainty does he have to set against them? Far from being able to stand aloof from these characters, he must have been *constituted* a character himself if he is to be capable of embodying them. Within him there is a permanent persona, which is quite simply *the ridiculous*, and other temporary personas, which are images for a night or a season. But we should not go further and believe that he unrealizes himself in the one rather than in the others, for, clearly, the basic unrealization has been constituted and the unfortunate actor has long been doomed to exploit his body and his internality as the *analogon* of the basic *imago*, that of the subman taking himself seriously. It is true that the permanent persona professes to be his own person and passes over its unreality in silence rather than that the characters are imper-sonations and the public is informed by poster that it will be laughing that eve-ning at Hirsch in *Arturo Ui.* But the role is in fact merely a singular piece of in-formation about the basic persona, namely that it will be worked up, chased, toned down in some places and accentuated at others, but no more. *With what* is the actor to excite laughter but with the only *analogon* available to him, and by what means other than by methodically exploiting his personal experience is he to produce the ridiculous? Tonight Pourceaugnac is on the program; he may have a hundred different faces, but the face he has tonight, on these boards, in the blaze of these footlights, is Fernandel's; it is Fernandel's body and no one else's that lends itself to the squireen from Périgord, it is his buttocks and no one else's that are threatened by the enemas leveled at them by the apothecaries. And if the player is to express the poor provincial's bewilderment, let us not as-sume that he will be drawing his inspiration from traits of behavior he has stud-ied in others. Observation is useful, of course; he will use it to supervise himself. But he does not reproduce; he invents. And in this specific case we can agree with Wilde that nature imitates art, for there are no perfect idiots except on the stage. In short, he nourishes his character from his own substance. To say that he *acts like an idiot* or that in unreality he becomes the idiot he would be if he were stricken with idiocy *is still not going far enough;* for in order to produce the *an-alogon* of the persona he displays he makes himself the fool that he *is.* The actor awakes in himself the cloudy mass of panic, terrorized incomprehension, fear, obstinacy, slyness, and ignorance which is everybody's sign of alienation passing under the name of stupidity, and he churns it up to unrealize himself through it into a magnificent idiot. What, in brief, is he doing except what he has always done, ever since some contact that went amiss constituted him ridiculous? A dia-lectic is most certainly initiated between the character and the player of the role; the former transforms the latter to exactly the same degree as the latter trans-forms the former. But these relations are between images. The role, moreover, serves as an alibi, for the actor seeks release from his persona and believes that he can escape into the character. In vain: for within the gay and intoxicating exhila-ration of being no more than an alien image, there persist a disquiet and a pro-found hostility which drives him to debase himself so that others may triumph, because he is in fact conscious that he is choosing this or that disguise to *make people laugh at him,* as he always has.

The public is not fooled, for when rubberneckers recognize a famous comic in the solitary and grave passerby wrapped in meditation, they burst out laugh-ing. Many actors have complained of this: one of them says that he cannot take a train journey without seeing smirking faces flattened against the windows of his compartment at every stop; another is irritated at being unable to enter a restau-rant without arousing the diners' mirth; a third has had to give up bathing ex-cept in lonely coves because there was a tempest of laughter along the beach whenever he appeared in a bathing suit. We *make people laugh,* all of them say, at certain times, for that is our job; but outside working hours we are no less seri-ous than you are. From one point of view this is perfectly true, for what would we see if we did not know "what they do for a living"? A man just like all men and, more particularly, a bourgeois just like all bourgeois; comfortably and ele-gantly dressed, they have indecipherable and vacuous faces just like everyone else, an easy courtesy, an engaging manner, reassuring in every respect; special peculiarities—none. And their normal preoccupations are precisely those of all bourgeois—money, the family, the job, an affair perhaps, most certainly the car. There is nothing noticeable about them. But do what they will, the crowd unmasks them; something is bound to happen; the elastic, tranquil stride and the air of relaxation are bound to be shattered, the gent is bound to fall down and his face will mirror the dismay and idiocy that have made him famous; a bird will shit on his head; the universal clumsiness or his own brand of it is sure to disclose his secret ridiculousness—that is to say, what the public takes to be his truth. The only mistake made by these fairly malevolent witnesses is that they confuse ridicule with truth. Strictly speaking, the comic actor has no truth, since he sacrifices concrete existence to the abstract being of appearance; and the seriousness he displays off the stage, though just as "authentic" as that of those who laugh at him, has one feature that distinguishes it from all others: that it is constituted *against* the basically ridiculous; in this sense, it does not much differ from the seriousness he displays on the stage, the function of which is to assert itself against the comic and ultimately to be defeated by the implacable concatenation of disasters and to be proclaimed as a false seriousness. There is only one difference: on the stage the disasters are *certain*, the character is bound to lose his human dignity, whereas off the stage they may be said to be improbable; or in other words, this respectable and slightly intimidating gentleman will cross the street without mishap and soon be out of sight; nothing will befall him. Nevertheless, the passers take his dignity as an invitation to laughter, for it offers itself to *destruction* amidst mirth; and if heaven or hell does not take it at its word, that is their affair, not his, for the actor has done all he should. They are quite right; the worthy character is a role which the actor assumes in his private life; arising as it does from an attempt to mask the ridiculous, it is neither more nor less true than the ridiculous: let us say that it is convenient in certain circumstances and the actor could not live if he were not able to assume respectability at the proper moment. Yet it is true that he scarcely believes in it and that it is a composite role, or rather one which he borrows from his characters—and where else would he get it from if not from them?—and is, so to speak, thesis without antithesis, the moment of sovereignty established for its own sake, severed from self and negative, when the force of circumstances unmasks the imposture of it and reveals that the sovereign is merely a disconnected mechanism running free. In this sense, clearly he himself is summoning the witnesses who recognize the actor by the hilarious expectation of a denial. Or rather, the moment of the contradiction incorporated in the paroxysm of laughter is the moment of recognition: here's a respectable man—but no, it's not, it's Rigadin. The serious is proposed, is decomposed and recomposed, only to be disintegrated once more: being dissolving into appearance. In this case the laughter is aggressive, because it comes from indignation: you tried to dupe us, to get us to take you for a man, but we're not that stupid, we know you are a clown.

(*L'Idiot de la famille*, vol. 1, pp. 825–31)

VI
FARCE, SATIRE, AND TRAGICOMEDY

Farce*

Eric Bentley

Violence

I have been speaking about the violence in, and of, melodrama. Farce is perhaps even more notorious for its love of violent images. And since the violence of farce and melodrama is not excluded from comedy and tragedy, it will be well to ask the question: What about violence in art? What does it signify? What does it do to us? Here is the classic statement on the subject:

> When we listen to some hero [in Homer or] on the tragic stage moaning over his sorrows in a long tirade, or to a chorus beating their breasts as they chant a lament, you know how the best of us enjoy giving ourselves up to follow the performance with eager sympathy... Few I believe are capable of reflecting that to enter into another's feelings must have an effect on our own: the emotions of pity our sympathy has strengthened will not be easy to restrain when we are suffering ourselves... Does not the same principle apply to humor as well as to pathos? You are doing the same thing if, in listening at a comic performance or in ordinary life to buffooneries which you would be ashamed to indulge in yourself, you thoroughly enjoy them instead of being disgusted with their ribaldry. There is in you an impulse to play the clown, which you have held in restraint from a reasonable fear of being set down a buffoon; but now you have given it rein, and by encouraging its impudence at the theatre you may be unconsciously carried away into playing the comedian in your private life. Similar effects are produced by poetic representation of love and anger and all those desires and feelings of pleasure and pain which accompany our every action. It waters the growth of passions which should be allowed to wither away and sets them up in control, although the goodness and happiness of our lives depend on their being held in subjection.

Thus Plato in the tenth book of *The Republic*. The question has come up again and again down the centuries, not least in our own age, the age of the most extensive, as well as the most atrocious, violence that the world has ever known. In such an age, it is naturally a matter of concern to the humane that the reading matter of the mass of men (and one should now include the "viewing" matter) has no tendency to wean them from violence but, on the contrary, tends to inure them to it. And one of the glaring moral contradictions of our cultural scene is that protests are made against the presentation of healthy sensuality in good art by people who quietly accept outrageous cruelty in bad art. All this being so, it is not surprising to find a warm-hearted physician like Dr. Fredric Wertham com-

* Eric Bentley, "Farce," in *The Life of the Drama* (Atheneum, 1964), pp. 219–256. Copyright © by Eric Bertley. Reprinted by permission of Atheneum Publishers.

ing out, in his book *Seduction of the Innocent,* against the violence in our so-called "comic books." And I for one had not realized how ugly and nasty-minded these books are until I read Dr. Wertham's text and examined the illustrations. Comic books are bad art, and bad humanity, and therefore meager and possibly noxious food for the minds of the young—or old.

This much could probably be accepted by any humane person, but Dr. Wertham will not rest his case there. On at least one page he indicates that artistic merit is, as it were, no excuse: the cruelties of Grimm's fairy tales are to be condemned along with those of the "comic books." Here surely we have caught the good doctor regretting that art is serious, for if art did not treat violence, it could not go to the heart of things. Without violence, there would be nothing in the world but goodness, and literature is not mainly about goodness: it is mainly about badness. When, on another page, Dr. Wertham complains of sympathy being thrown to bad characters, we realize that he is placing himself squarely in that Puritan tradition which is hostile to art as such, and whose father is Plato—or part of Plato: the part that would have thrown the poets out of his ideal republic.

The Platonists in this argument disregard the distinction between fact and fantasy. Suppose you saw one man force the head of another through the glass of a street lamp so that the latter will be gassed by the fumes. It sounds like some Nazi atrocity, and Plato would no doubt be indignant at the notion of re-enacting the incident in a work of art. Nonetheless it *was* re-enacted in Charlie Chaplin's film *Easy Street,* and in all the years no one has protested. We have all very much enjoyed seeing Mack Swain gassed and Charlie triumphant. And in general—though what we consciously remember from the Chaplin films may be Chaplin's incomparable delicacy, they are for the most part taken up with violent pursuit and violent combat. Here fantasy multiplies movements and blows by a thousand. The villain is a giant whose strength passes the limits of nature. He can bend lamp posts with his bare hands. Since the "little man's" revenges have to be more than proportionate to the provocation (as with Brecht's Pirate Jenny), he can drop a cast-iron stove on the villain's head and ram that head inside a street lamp with the gas turned on.

Another symptom of cruelty is the abstractness of the violence. Prongs of a rake in the backside are received as pin pricks. Bullets seem to pass right through people, sledge-hammer blows to produce only momentary irritation. The speeding up of movement contributes to the abstract effect. So, even more, does the silence proper to the screen of those days, many of the effects being lost when a sound track is superimposed. The cops shoot, but there is no noise. Heavy objects fall, but there is no crash. Gruesome infighting has the air of shadowboxing. All of which signifies that, in farce, as in drama, one is permitted the outrage but spared the consequence. Chaplin's delicacy of style is actually part of the pattern: he parades an air of nonchalance when acting in a manner that, in real life, would land him in Bellevue or Sing Sing.

Though Plato has shown us the importance of thought, and modern psychology has exhibited the power of fantasy, we cannot allow ourselves to be jockeyed into regarding the distinction between thought and act, fantasy and fact, as a sort of minor detail. The person who confuses the two sets of categories is not eccentric, he is insane. Conversely, it is possible for a thinker and fantasist to bank heavily on the sanity of his audience; and this is what Charlie Chaplin or any other farceur emphatically does.

Certainly, teachers and parents have to cope with the fact that in some situations children do not make a clear distinction between fantasy and reality. But they must understand that these situations do not include all the violence in drama and other fiction. Think of the tremendous violence in fairy tales, and ask yourself how many small children have actually tried to duplicate it in real life. Grimm's fairy tales do not seem to justify Dr. Wertham's fears.

For people who can distinguish between fantasy and reality certain indulgences are possible in fantasy which should not be permitted in "real life." Most notably: they can indulge in reckless violence. That extraordinary passage in *The Republic* was answered by Aristotle, though perhaps not intentionally and certainly not at length. His answer is to be found in the famous phrase about tragedy in *The Poetics:* "through pity and fear effecting the proper catharsis of these emotions." True, there is a permanent debate about the meaning of the word "catharsis," but all the debaters could agree, I think, on that solid part of the meaning that is relevant here, namely: Aristotle is rejecting the notion that tragedy might reduce us to a quivering jelly of pity and fear, and is formulating an exactly contrary conclusion: tragedy is not only an excitement but a release from excitement. It will not burst the boiler with its steam because it is precisely the safety valve. It is the exactly contrary character of Aristotle's view to Plato's that most powerfully suggests that it might be a deliberate reply. And it is this character that makes it perhaps somewhat polemical, and hard to go all the way with. One feels that the cathartic theory exaggerates. Surely not all this happens to one's emotional system during a performance of *Hamlet?* But the theory can hardly be rejected in substance unless one wishes to side with Plato, Bishop Bossuet, Dr. Wertham, and the Motion Picture Production Code.

Gilbert Murray has suggested that the idea of catharsis is easier to apply to comedy than to tragedy—easier in the sense that we agree to it more easily. There is already a certain consensus of opinion that some of our psychic violence—what our grandparents called excess animal spirits—can be worked off in laughter. It is generally agreed that a good laugh does us good, and that it does us good as a sort of emotional "work-out."

Impropriety is of the essence. As Murray put it: "Comedy . . . must . . . not be spoilt by any tiresome temperance or prudential considerations of the morrow." And again: "The anarchist and the polygamist, close-prisoned and chained in ordinary life, enjoy their release in comedy." Murray thought of comedy as continuous with orgies and fertility rites. Perhaps his doctrine implies the same error as that of the Platonists: a disregard of the difference between doing and imagining. The image of an orgy that we may get in a work of art should not be equated with the acting out of an orgy in real life; and comedy gives only a faded image of an orgy at that. Still, since the rise of Christianity, even the image of an orgy is a little more than many people bargain for. And there has been war between comedy and established religion down through the ages. The Motion Picture Production Code is but its latest embodiment. We mustn't laugh at a priest, it implies, or religion is in danger.

Scoffing at Marriage

Above all we must not laugh at the family and its source, the institution of marriage. If crime comics are rampant among the underprivileged young, equally rampant among the overprivileged middle-aged is a literature whose patron saint is Tartuffe. In one of those family magazines that are so moralistic as to be morally nauseating, I came across an article entitled "Don't Let Them Scoff at Marriage" in which the moral crisis of our times was confidently attributed to jokes against marriage. "The gross libel on marriage is the notion," the author wrote, "that the chase, the allure, is the goal. Marriage is seen as a dull aftermath." As a psychologist the writer should have known that even gross libels aren't made without provocation. Or if they are, they don't last for centuries and appeal to the whole human race. Obviously the human race finds more interesting what this man calls a gross libel than what he presents as the truth.

It is true, however, that the joke against marriage could be abolished if the family were the unmixed blessing that many of our contemporaries take it for. The chief of the division of Social Medicine at an important American hospital writes as follows:

> The family is central to the development of humanity not only for the perpetuation of the race but because the proper psychological development of an individual can only occur within the warm circle of the nuclear family. Social and psychological studies indicate quite clearly that a strong family structure helps to develop and maintain a personality free of dangerous (to self and society) characteristics.

And the author draws the conclusion that sexual deviation and juvenile delinquency can be prevented by closer, warmer family relations. "The family that prays together stays together." "Where family life stops delinquency starts."

No doubt there is some truth in all this. Unhappily there is truth in a precisely opposite proposition. The close, warm family is also the seedbed of neurosis, vice, and crime. About the same time as this article appeared, a newspaper picture caught my eye. It showed a beaming public-relations executive with his good-looking wife and three attractive children. They seemed a model American family in a model American home and one could imagine the picture passing in triumph around the public-relations office. The caption underneath, however, reported that the mildest and most candid-looking of the boys had just killed the mother and sister and told the police that he had planned to kill the rest of the family as well. It would be comforting to think that such a shocking event could be declared irrelevant to the experience of normal folk. But it isn't, because normal folk share his wishes though they do not carry them out. An art like farce embodies such wishes: wishes to damage the family, to desecrate the household gods.

And tragedy is no different in this respect. The Greeks, who invented it, did not do so before they had created the patriarchal family and an ideology to fit it. They seem to have found the supreme virtue in the pious and loyal relation of husband to wife, of child to parent, of sibling to sibling. The subject of tragedy, over and over again, was the violation of such piety. Now what would be the worst conceivable violation of both the marital and filial pieties? Why, the double crime of Oedipus.

An entry in *The Oxford Companion to the Theatre* reads:

> The word *farce* is applied to a full-length play dealing with some absurd situation hingeing generally on extra-marital relations—hence the term *bedroom farce*. . . .

The phrase "some absurd situation hingeing . . . on extra-marital relations" suggests various tragic plots, that of *Othello*, for example. But what "situation hingeing . . . on extra-marital relations" is not full of absurdities and therefore potentially melodramatic or farcical, tragic or comic, according to the temperament, state of mind, and view of life of the witness? Outrage to family piety is certainly at the heart of farce as we know it—"hence," as our companionable book says, "the term *bedroom farce.*"

It is, of course, Freud who has taught us to find such impieties in tragedy. And one of his early followers, Ludwig Jekels, applied the idea of the Oedipus complex to comedy. If tragedy, he says, shows the son paying for his rebellion against the father, comedy shows the son victorious, the father discomfited. Father and son compete for the possession of the mother, and the son wins. The element of disguise by which this naked fantasy is clothed consists very often in the son's being presented as just some young man who happens along. But many of the disguises for the theme are more elaborate. It seems to me that the modern "triangle" drama might be regarded as one of them: husband, wife, and lover being the disguise for father, mother, and son. If this were so, then the answer to the question why modern playwrights have been obsessed with adultery is that they have *not* been obsessed with adultery: they have been obsessed with incest. In Bernard Shaw's *Candida*, Morell, Candida, and Marchbanks would be the mask of a father, mother, and son. (I do not cite the evidence from Bernard Shaw's life that the three characters were indeed father [or foster-father], mother, and son [himself] to the author. That is a matter of origin. More relevant here is the possibility that Morell, Candida, and Marchbanks would still be *a* father, mother, and son for the unconscious of spectators even if we knew nothing of Shaw's life.) Such is the conversion to late nineteenth-century problem drama of the Oedipus story. In another early Shaw play, *Mrs. Warren's Profession*, the incest theme shows through, as it already had in two of the most famous plays of Shaw's playwright-father, Henrik Ibsen: namely, *Ghosts* and *Rosmersholm*. Yet for contemporaries all three of these plays seemed to be about current social problems exclusively (white slavery, hereditary syphilis, advanced ideas, etc.). For them, the incest theme remained under a veil, and when one notes what that veil was, one may begin to see social realism in a different light. By which I do not mean that the "social" content is always mere camouflage for psychological motifs but only that it can serve as such camouflage vis à vis a given public. The plays I have named are better understood today when audiences recognize the Oedipal theme at once and so take the plays to be what they are: "social" and "psychological" at the same time.

Comic Catharsis

Gilbert Murray has spoken of the "close similarity between Aristotle and Freud," and actually Freud carried the idea of Catharsis further than any Aristotelian commentator had ever dreamt of. In the eighteen-nineties the new therapy escaped being named cathartic instead of psycho-analtyic only by a hair's breadth. For Freud, jokes are fundamentally cathartic: a release, not a stimulant. This is why Freud, unlike our magazine moralists, would "let them scoff at marriage." (He would also know he could never stop them.) It is a sort of open secret, Freud says in his book on jokes, that "marriage is hardly an arrangement to satisfy the sexual demands of the husband," also that this secret is half-kept, half-told, in a million male jokes against marriage. I would add that the supreme form of the marriage joke takes a couple of hours to tell and has a cast of three characters known as *le mari, la femme, et l'amant*—"hence the term *bedroom farce.*" Just as Restoration Comedy was provoked by the Puritans and is forever dedicated to their memory, the farce of adultery throughout our Protestant-bourgeois epoch has been provoked by faithful husbands and will only end when they become unfaithful on principle.

Farce in general offers a special opportunity: shielded by delicious darkness and seated in warm security, we enjoy the privilege of being totally passive while on stage our most treasured unmentionable wishes are fulfilled before our eyes by the most violently active human beings that ever sprang from the human imagination. In that application of the formula which is bedroom farce, we savor the adventure of adultery, ingeniously exaggerated in the highest degree, and all without taking the responsibility or suffering the guilt. Our wives may be with us leading the laughter.

Why do we laugh at jokes? The point of a joke can be explained, but the explanation is not funny. The intellectual content is not the essence. What counts is the experience which we call "getting" the joke or "seeing the point." This experience is a kind of shock, but, whereas shocks in general are unpleasant, this one opens a sluicegate somewhere and brings a sudden spurt or gush of pleasure. Nor is the pleasure of the laugh continuous with the mild amusement that precedes it. A joke is a purling stream most of the way, then suddenly from one of its pools rises up a veritable geyser.

The phenomenon seems less mysterious if we see it as limited to grown human beings, and grown human beings as full of anxiety and guilt. Neither supermen nor babies have a sense of humor. They don't need one. Men and women do because they have inhibited many of their strongest wishes.

How does the sense of humor go to work? Its aim is to gratify some of the forbidden wishes. But what is repressed is repressed. We cannot get at it. Our anxiety and guilt are taking care of that. Only, there are tricks for eluding anxiety and guilt, and the commonest, the least artificial, is the sense of humor. The mildly amusing preliminaries of a joke allay our fears, lower our resistance. The gratification of the forbidden wish is then slipped upon us as a surprise. Before our guilt and anxiety have time to go into action, the forbidden pleasure has been had. A source of pleasure far deeper than those directly available has been tapped. Inhibitions are momentarily lifted, repressed thoughts are admitted into consciousness, and we experience that feeling of power and pleasure, generally called elation. Here is one of the few forms of joy that are readily available. Hence the immense contribution of humor to the survival of the species.

Hence also a paradox. Through the funny, we tap infantile sources of pleasure, we become infants again, finding the intensest satisfaction in the smallest things, the highest ecstasy in the lowest thoughts. And yet infants themselves are without humor. But the paradox is no contradiction, for at bottom no experiences could be further apart than is the momentary return to childhood from the experience of being a child. The actual innocence of infancy is never regained but as far as pleasure is concerned there is an increment in sheer nostalgia. No little girl can love little-girlhood as Lewis Carroll did. No infant shares the grown-up's enjoyment in returning, or seeming to return, to infancy. Humor has a great deal to do with the distance between the infancy returned to and the point from which the return journey is undertaken. In fact the premise that children have no sense of humor, useful at the outset, needs qualification at a later stage of the investigation. Children *develop* a sense of humor as they move away from primal innocence. They have only to hear a few of the "songs of experience," which are songs of setback, disappointment, and disillusion, and the wholehearted cheerfulness of a baby's smile can give place on the face of a three-year-old to the aggressive smirk or the twisted half-smile of defeat. "Innocence" is whole and single. With "experience" come division and duality—without which there is no humor, no wit, no farce, and no comedy.

Jokes and the Theatre

One of the key insights of both Bergson and Freud is that to make jokes is to create a theatre. Bergson says that any witticism, if articulated at all, articulates itself in scenes—which are an inchoate comedy. Freud points out that it takes, not one or two, but three to make a joke. These are the jokester, the butt of the joke, and the listener. The trio is familiar in the form of comedian, straight man, and audience. This trio of vaudeville suggests in turn the ironist, the impostor, and the audience of the traditional comic theatre.

To say that the jokester needs a butt is only to say that he needs a joke. Does he need even a joke as much as he needs a listener? Let each of us ask himself why, at a given moment, he wishes to tell a joke. It cannot be because one wishes to be amused by it, since jokes are not amusing the second time around, and one cannot tell a joke one has not already heard. (I exclude from consideration any superman who can invent his jokes as he goes along. He is irrelevant here because the subject I am now approaching is the comedian, who certainly does not write his lines as he goes along.) Anyhow, if one's need was to *hear* the joke one could tell it to oneself. It is inescapable that the need is not for the joke at all: it is for the audience.

Anyone who has known comedians off stage can testify, I think, that they are often men with a need of applause and appreciation that goes beyond even that of other actors. And there is a reason why men with this need—whether they are gifted humorists or not—should seek out the comedian's profession. Only the joke gets from its audience a reaction whose tenor is unmistakable and enthusiastic: laughter. The tragic actor gets no such indication, at the end of his "To be or not to be" speech, that it went over well. He will be pleased if there was silence in the house; even so he may wonder if everyone had gone to sleep. He may wonder whether his feeling that it went well is an illusion. But there is no such thing, as Ramon Fernandez puts it, as an illusion that an audience is laughing. So their laughter is peculiarly attractive to a person who needs an audience reaction every minute or two and needs to be sure that it is highly favorable. On the night when the audience does not laugh, the clown goes out and shoots himself. At least he might as well, since the only thing he has lived for is not forthcoming.

I have suggested that the comedian is the man whose need of applause is the most insistent and mistrustful. An alternative interpretation is that the comedian is the most gifted of compulsive talkers. Every cocktail party entertains many people who will not stop talking so long as they have an audience. The jokester is such a compulsive talker, it could be, who gets away with it because his talk is amusing. The burst of laughter that greets each story is a diploma stating that he has succeeded in not boring his audience. He may now be tempted to tell his stories to larger and larger groups. If he ends up on a stage talking to people he has never met, he is a professional comedian.

That what purport to be studies of comedy often turn out to be only studies of laughter is to be regretted, yet the circumstance faithfully reflects the mentality of the comedian. His wish is to capture and hold captive his audience, and he knows his wish fulfilled only when the audience laughs. Hence, though laughter may be no proper emblem for comedy, it does set the seal on jokes. For this reason entertainment merchants may be forgiven a certain hysteria on the subject, and we should receive more in sorrow than in anger the news that the television people are measuring the duration and volume of laughs with laugh meters.

If philosophers can reduce comic art to laughter, then surely the entrepreneurs can reduce laughter to the noise it makes. But in both cases, the real topic is narrowed down too much. The student of laughter should study the whole curve of which the burst of noise is but the final inch. Before people will burst out laughing they have to be prepared to burst out laughing. The only sure preparation is a particular state of expectation and sensitivity that amounts to a kind of euphoria. It can be more important than the joke itself. A stage of excitement can be reached at which people will laugh at anything. The performer may have to ask himself what they will *not* laugh at if he is to forestall chaos. He has to watch that the girls don't get the giggles and the ladies the hysterics.

In all this, the theatre stands with the art of telling jokes, not with the art of writing books. We read in solitude; and we think it remarkable if once in a while we laugh out loud. At that it is a single burst of laughter, a self-conscious, if loud, single bark. The rest of the family is sure one did it to attract attention, and asks what's so funny. And very likely one did. But when Cousin Seamus tells us his Irish jokes, we can really let go, and in ten minutes we are as "high" as any whiskey could make us. Such is the psychology of the comedian in the theatre.

In this respect, as in others, the art of farce is but joking turned theatrical—joking fully articulated as theatrical characters and scenes. It is correct to say that its aim is laughter, but this is to say no simple thing. Laughter may signify this or that, and in any case has to be most carefully prepared. Also modulated. Future students of the subject would do well to drop the individual joke and the reasons why it is funny and turn to the question: just how funny is it in particular contexts? It will be found that sometimes it is hardly funny at all, and that other times it is very funny indeed. It is a matter of how the audience was led to the point where the laugh should break out and the fun be proved.

I have been speaking of one burst of laughter with one preparation, and even in so small an event there is plenty to observe. But any farce that lasts more than a minute or two has to make the audience laugh out loud a considerable number of times. This cannot be done by just stringing along the jokes one after the other. The general elation is so much more potent than any particular punch line that one may begin to wonder: what *is* a joke? As I have said, if one succeeds very well with a first joke, the audience may get into a state of mind where anything seems funny. All one needs is a new turn of events, and a new shriek of laughter will greet it. But this state of mind will not last very long unaided. And it may not be wise to try to sustain it indefinitely lest the result be sheer exhaustion. He who organizes a whole evening of "merriment" must indeed be an organizer. Nothing could be more fatal than to stake all on making a good beginning and then to let events take their course. Which is something any good vaudeville producer always knew; and it is something every author of a farce must have in mind—or, better, in his bones.

A sidelight is provided by something Sir John Gielgud once said about producing *The Importance of Being Earnest*. It was to the effect that the director must learn to prevent the audience from laughing in too many places. Those who saw Sir John's production of the play will know what he meant. The comic temperature was raised so high, the elation of the audience was so intense, that the performance at many points could hardly continue. Wilde had written dialogue so witty that any line whatever could be the signal for renewed shrieks and whoops. The breakup of the performance—even in shrieks of merriment—is no desirable aim. What the actors had to do was the opposite of "milking" every line for the fun in it. It was to throw away a lot of the fun of individual lines for the sake of more important fun. The aim of Sir John's strategy was not merely the avoidance of riot. It was the fullest enjoyment of the occasion. Spectators are babies, and have no idea what they will like. If one lets them, they will laugh so hard that later on they can only have the hysterics or the sulks. They have to be prevented from doing violence to their own nervous systems. Laughter cannot be regular and sustained. It cannot begin *pianissimo* and then get gradually louder *ad infinitum*. Nor can it maintain the same intensity steadily like a factory siren. It is tied to our very limited respiratory and vocal system, not to mention our psychology.

If a laugh meter could measure the merit of a show, then the ideal show would be one that elicited a single uninterrupted peal of laughter which lasted from eight thirty till eleven o'clock. It would therefore consist of a play which not only could not proceed but could not begin. Actually, there is no ratio between enjoyment and the duration of audible laughter. But too little laughter is better than too much. If no comedy, however great, could make people laugh all the time, there could be a great comedy that never made them laugh at all.

How often, incidentally, does one really listen to laughter? It is quite an ugly sound. How often has one looked at people while they do it? It is not a pretty sight. And how little laughter there is on stage in a good theatre! The place for laughter is the auditorium. Perhaps one reason is that in the auditorium one does not have to see it. One sees the actors. They laugh seldom, and chiefly for negative effects. Only the other day I opened a magazine and came upon a most expressive laugh on the face of an actor. The caption told me that is was Gustav Gruendgens—as Mephistopheles.

Sweet and Bitter Springs

Freud distinguishes two kinds of jokes, one which is innocent and harmless, and one which has a purpose, a tendency, an end in view. He distinguishes in turn two kinds of purpose: to destroy and to expose—to smash and to strip. Destructive jokes fall under such headings as sarcasm, scandal, and satire, denuding jokes under such headings as obscenity, bawdry, ribaldry.

I think the only startling thing about this classification is that it places obscenity side by side with satire. If we agree, we may take another step by observing that there is destructive force also in the joke that exposes. It is hostile either to the thing exposed or to the audience watching the exposure or both. Modifying Freud's formulation, I conclude that both the satiric and the obscene come under the heading of aggression.

We have, then, aggressive jokes and nonaggressive jokes. Everyone, in fact, assumes no less, and quite widespread in our middle-class culture is a preference for the nonaggressive joke. Are we not a Christian civilization? I myself was brought up on a little hymn that went:

> Teach us delight in simple things
> And mirth that has no bitter springs.

It seemed a reasonable enough demand to make, especially since, at the time, I was not aware that mirth *ever* had bitter springs. I certainly did not know that the author of that very hymn was a man of inordinate pugnacity. (It is by Kipling.)

Some people want their jokes pleasant and harmless, and some people want their farces pleasant and harmless. Indeed it is common to interpret farce as precisely the pleasant treatment of what would otherwise have been an unpleasant subject. Here is the great theatre critic of nineteenth-century France—Sarcey—discussing the greatest farceur of nineteenth-century France:

> I had often complained that they bored us constantly with this question of adultery, which nowadays is the subject of three quarters of the plays. Why, I asked, take pleasure in painting its dark and sad sides, enlarging on the dreadful consequences which it brings with it in reality? Our fathers took the thing more lightheartedly in the theatre and even called adultery by a name which awoke in the mind only ideas of the ridiculous and a sprightly lightheartedness. . . . Chance brought it about that I met Labiche. "I was very struck," he said to me, "with your observations on adultery and on what could derive from it . . . for farce . . . I agree . . ." I had almost forgotten this conversation when I saw the title posted outside the Palais Royal . . . It was my play: it was adultery treated lightheartedly . . .

Anglo-Saxon opinion has been against admitting such subjects as adultery into the nonserious drama at all, and yet there is one English critic who, before Sarcey, had carried Sarcey's argument yet further. This is Charles Lamb in his once-famous essay on Restoration Comedy. In substance, though this is not his vocabulary, he argues that the subject matter of Restoration comedy becomes palatable if we regard the finished product as farce rather than satire. For this is to judge leniently as in play, not harshly as one would in real life.

> I could never connect those sports of a witty fancy in any shape with any result to be drawn from them to imitation in real life. They are a world of themselves almost as much as fairy land. . . . The Fainalls and the Mirabells, the Dormants and the Lady Touchwoods, in their own sphere, do not offend my moral sense. . . . They break through no laws, or conscientious restraints. They know of none. They have got out of Christendom into the land—what shall I call it?—of cuckoldry—the Utopia of gallantry, where pleasure is duty, and the manners perfect freedom. It is altogether a speculative scene of things, which has no reference whatever to the world that is.

Now both Sarcey and Lamb are saying things that are undeniably true. If adultery in the drama is becoming a solemn bore, then certainly it would be fun to try the farceur's approach. If parents are becoming solemn bores in suggesting that a Restoration comedy might have an inordinate and immoral influence on their daughters, then certainly it is good to remind them of the distinction between art and life, fiction and fact. But the real question is the significance of the gaiety Sarcey speaks of, and of what Lamb calls the sports of a witty fancy, his Utopia of gallantry, his land of cuckoldry. Both critics assume that they have closed the discussion once they have invoked the twin spirits of gaiety and fantasy. Yet that is where the real discussion begins, and that is where Freud takes it up in his monograph on jokes. Granting that jokes exist which are "innocent,"

Freud goes on to say that it is only the tendentious ones, the jokes with a purpose, which can make people burst out laughing. The innocent jokes don't pack that much of a punch. We do not feel them so keenly. Our need for them is not so great. We crave stronger meat. We want satire. We want ribaldry. Our receiving apparatus is not so sensitive to them. We want to attack and to expose.

To say that only the joke with a purpose can actually arouse laughter is tantamount to saying that only this type of joking is of much use in the theatre of Farce. And it seems to me that if farces are examined they will be found to contain very little "harmless" joking and very much that is "tendentious." Without aggression farce cannot function. The effects we call "farcical" dissolve and disappear.

What happens in farces? In one of Noel Coward's, a man slaps his mother-in-law's face and she falls in a swoon. Farce is the only form of art in which such an incident could normally occur.

No one ever denied that W. C. Fields' films were aggressive. Audiences became so conscious of the aggressions that they started staying away from Fields' pictures. In Charlie Chaplin's case, they said they liked him because he was less violent. He *seemed* less violent because he put the violence in the other characters. The violence was done *to* him, not *by* him, and masochistic farce always seems more gentlemanlike than sadistic. But the Tramp of Chaplin is not exclusively masochistic. He is also a sadist. One remembers what happens in *The Kid* when Charlie finds himself literally holding the baby. By all means, he is going to become a charming and sentimental foster-father, but as he sits there with his feet in the gutter he notices an open drain, and he has almost thrown the baby down it before sentiment comes again into its own. It is by touches like that—and never by sentiment alone—that Chaplin has shown himself a great comic.

> Teach us delight in complex things:
> Mirth has both sweet and bitter springs.

The Dialectic of Farce

To the simple all things are simple. Yet farce *can* seem a simple thing, not only to the simple-minded but even to those who recognize its depth. Farce is simple, on this view, because it goes right "at" things. You knock your mother-in-law down, and no beating about the bush. One can wonder, certainly, if this is not the absolutely direct, unmediated vision, without that duality of mask and face, symbol and object, which characterizes the rest of dramatic literature.

A second way in which farce may seem simple is in its acceptance of the everyday appearances and of everyday interpretations of those appearances. It does not present the empurpled and enlarged images of melodrama. No, farce can use the ordinary unenlarged environment and ordinary down-at-heel men of the street. The trouble is that farce is simple in both these ways at once, thereby failing to be simple at all. Farce brings together the direct and wild fantasies and the everyday and drab realities. The interplay between the two is the very essence of this art—the farcical dialectic.

If behind the gaiety of farce lurks a certain gravity, it is equally true that behind the gravity lurks a great deal of gaiety. Farce can certainly present a grave appearance. Those unsmiling actors again!—or rather the unsmiling down-at-heel roles which farce offers them. Here is a point of decisive importance in performance. The amateur actor misses it, and tries to act the gaiety. The professional knows he must act the gravity and trust that the author has injected gaiety into his plot and dialogue.

Actually, to press the analysis a step further, the surface of farce is grave and gay at the same time. The gay antics of Harlequin are conducted with poker-faced gravity. Both the gaiety and the gravity are visible and are part of the style. If we go on to speak of a contrast in farce between mask and face, symbol and thing symbolized, appearance and reality, this will not be a contrast in styles but a contrast between either the gravity or the gaiety on the surface and whatever lies beneath. What do the gravity and gaiety have in common? Orderliness and mildness. What lies beneath the surface, on the other hand, is disorderly and violent. It is a double dialectic. On the surface, the contrast of gay and grave, then, secondly, the contrast of surface and beneath-the-surface. The second is a larger and even more dynamic contrast.

What farce does with this larger contrast is best seen by comparison with what comedy does. Comedy makes much of appearances: it specializes, indeed, in the *keeping up* of appearances. Unmasking in comedy will characteristically be the unmasking of a single character in a climactic scene—like that of Tartuffe. In farce, unmasking occurs all along. The favorite action of the farceur is to shatter the appearances, his favorite effect being the shock to the audience of his doing so. Bring on stage a farcical comic like Harpo Marx, and all appearances are in jeopardy. For him, all coverings exist to be stripped off, all breakables to be broken. It would be a mistake to bring him into a drawing-room comedy: he would dismantle the drawing room.

If what farce offers is the interaction of violence and something else, it follows that violence by itself is not the essence of farce. The violence of Chaplin is dramatized by a context of great gentleness. The violence of Harpo Marx is offset by something equally important to his roles: his perfectly serious performances on that most delicate of instruments, the harp.

A common mistake is to think that Charlie's and Harpo's effects are softened by the gentleness and delicacy, as if the aim were to reach a compromise between violence and sobriety. But compromises are for life, not art. The purpose of this gentleness and delicacy is to heighten, not lower, the effect of the violence, and vice versa. Dramatic art in general is an art of extremes, and farce is, as it were, an extreme case of the extreme. Farce characteristically promotes and exploits the widest possible contrasts between tone and content, surface and substance, and the minute one of the two elements in the dialectic is not present in its extreme or pure form, there is likely to be a weakening of the drama. This could be exemplified by Noel Coward's little play in which, while an extreme lightness of tone is achieved, punches are pulled (more or less literally) where a straight left to the jaw was just what was needed. In farce, we say: "I'll murder you with my bare hands," playfully, or with that mixture of the grave and gay which defines the tone as farcical, but in a degree we also have to mean it: by some flicker, at least, in word or act, it must become evident that murderous wishes exist in this world—and at this moment. If they exist in Noel Coward, he was too genteel to let his public know it. In our theatre, talents such as his drift away from farce without encountering real comedy, landing in that worst of both worlds, the sentimental "light comedy" of the West End and Broadway.

If it is dangerous to attempt a compromise between the two conflicting opposites of a dialectic, it is disastrous to accept one and forget the other. Sheer aggression is just oppressive, as many motion picture cartoons illustrate. Sheer flippancy is just boring, as most "light comedy" illustrates. The dialectical relation is one of active conflict and development. A dialogue has to be established between the aggression and the flippancy, between hostility and lightness of heart.

Mischief as Fate

Every form of drama has its rendezvous with madness. If drama shows extreme situations, *the* extreme situation for human beings—short of death—is the point where our sanity gives out. In a very famous scene Ibsen has shown this point reached on stage; and Racine's *Andromache* had ended in much the same way as Ibsen's *Ghosts*.

Our colloquial use and abuse of words is always full of meaning, and what we mean when we say of some non-theatrical phenomenon, "It's a farce," or "It's absolutely farcical," throws light back on the theatrical phenomenon. We mean: farce is absurd; but not only that, farce is a veritable structure of absurdities. Here the operative word is *structure*, for normally we think of absurdities as amorphous. It is only in such a syndrome as paranoia that we find reason in the madness: the absurdities which we would be inclined to call stupid are connected in a way we cannot but consider the reverse of stupid. There is an ingenious and complex set of interrelationships.

I was speaking in the previous chapter of the long arm of coincidence in melodrama. It is an arm that does not get any shorter in farce. In both cases there is an acknowledgment of absurdity—and in both cases, a counterclaim to a kind of sense. A paranoiac finds a structure in coincidences, which is to say that to him they are not coincidences. The playwright incorporates coincidences in a structure, which is to say that they will not be coincidences to his audience. The melodramatist creates a sense of fatality, and, in the light of that sense, apparent coincidence reveals itself as part of a baleful pattern. And do not imagine, as William Archer did, that the tragic writer is any different. Think, rather, how the Oedipus of Sophocles has spent a lifetime just happening to be at the wrong place at the wrong time and meeting the wrong person there. Farce differs from the other genres in that its use of coincidence is accepted. People have such a low opinion of farce that they don't mind admitting it uses such a low device.

What do the coincidences of farce amount to? Not surely to a sense of fate, and yet certainly to a sense of something that *might* be called fate if only the word had less melancholy associations. In farce chance ceases to seem chance, and mischief has method in its madness. One final effect of farce is that mischief, fun, misrule seem an equivalent of fate, a force not ourselves making, neither for righteousness nor for catastrophe, but for aggression without risk.

Perhaps every type of dramatic action has to have its inevitability, including the types, such as the comic types, that seem dedicated to the opposite. The heaping up of crazy coincidences in farce creates a world in which the happily fortuitous is inevitable. And so, in a Feydeau play, the careful plan for the husband to be absent when the lover arrives is a gilt-edged guarantee that he will turn up.

What is usually said about surprises in farcical plots has to be qualified. On the surface of our minds we are surprised; but somewhere deeper down we knew all along. The convention itself creates certain expectations without which we would not have paid the price of admission. The expectation may go back before the first scene of the play to the rubric "A Farce" in the program or before that to the name "Feydeau" in the advertisements.

I have suggested that the characteristic melodramatic situations and plots derive directly from more or less paranoid fantasies—generally the fantasy of innocence surrounded by malevolence. Pity and fear are certainly aroused and possibly "abreacted"—worked through and worked off. If there is an equivalent in farce and comedy for pity and fear in melodrama and tragedy, it is sympathy and contempt. As pity is the weaker side of melodrama, sympathy is the weaker side of farce. It usually amounts to a little more than mild fellow feeling with the hero and heroine. Charlie Chaplin, as an exception, was able to make more of it because he was not a juvenile lead but a character man. The character he chose—that of the Tramp—was such as to make the audience's sympathy play a very large part in the proceedings.

Innocence is probably as important to farce as to melodrama. We are as firmly identified with it. The difference is that whereas in melodrama we recoil from the enemy in fear, in farce we retaliate. If melodrama generally depends for its power on the degree of fear it can arouse, farce depends on the degree of aggression. "The comedian," says Sidney Tarachow, "is a hostile sharpshooter loudly proclaiming his own innocence." In this respect, the writer of farces is a comedian. The hostility, like the terror of melodramas, is so unqualified by any sense of justice or truth, that it creates forms that resemble sick fantasies. The closed structure of the Well Made Play as used by Georges Feydeau suggests a closed mental system, a world of its own lit by its own lurid and unnatural sun. If we were not laughing so hard, we would find such worlds terrifying. Their workings are as perilous as acrobatics. One touch, we feel, and the whole thing might go spinning into space. A Feydeau play has points in common with a highly elaborated and crazy delusion.

The masters of French farce in the nineteenth century used incredibly elaborate plots, and it is often said of their plays that they are "all plot." Here we have another aspect of the madness of farce. Human life in this art form is horribly attenuated. Life is a kind of universal milling around, a rushing from bedroom to bedroom driven by demons more dreadful than sensuality. The kind of farce which is said to be "all plot" is often much more than ingenious, it is maniacal. When one saw the actors of the Montreal *Théâtre du nouveau monde* giving positively spastic movements to Molière's farce characters, one said to oneself: after all there is something spastic about farce generally. Dryden says: "The persons and actions of a farce are all unnatural and their manners false."

Much more is involved in the movement of the story than we commonly realize. Why, for example, do directors of farce always call for tempo, tempo, tempo? It is not just because they admire business efficiency, nor is there anything to the common belief of theatre people that *fast* is always better than *slow*. It is a question of the speeding up of human behavior so that it becomes less than human. Bergson might say this was one of the ways in which human behavior becomes funny by resembling the working of high-speed machines. The speeding up of movement in the typical silent-movie farces had a definite psychological and moral effect, namely, of making actions seem abstract and automatic when in life they would be concrete and subject to free will. It is a conception that bristles with menace.

Conversely, to think of a good farcical pattern of action is to think of a good pretext for rapid movement. The chase was the pride and glory of the Keystone

Cops. The plot of *An Italian Straw Hat* is one long pretext for flight and pursuit. So is the plot of that homely English imitation of French farce, *Charley's Aunt*.

In the Image of the Ape

The farceur is a heretic: he does not believe that man was made in God's image. What are the principal images of men in farce and what do they amount to?

If one tells the story of some farces, one will start talking of young lovers, but if instead of telling the story, one looks at what has remained in one's memory from a farce, one will not find young lovers there but two other characters: the knave and the fool. One will then find that the plot itself hinges less on what the young lovers do than on what the knave does. The knave in farce is the equivalent of the villain in melodrama. "Passions spin the plot." If the passion that spins the melodramatic plot is sheer wickedness, the passion that spins the farcical plot is that younger brother of wickedness, the spirit of mischief. Shakespeare's Puck could be the knave of a farce. He is not deep or purposive enough to be a villain. He is a trouble-maker by accident and even by nature but not always by design and never with intent to do serious damage. He is a prankster—like Harlequin.

If mischief becomes a sort of comic equivalent of fate, it is usually through the Puck, the Harlequin, the Brighella, the Scapin, the Figaro that it does so. In its simpler forms, the idea of a prankster is desperately primitive, and even in Shakespeare the pranks hover on the brink of the abysmally unfunny. (What, for example, is so fascinating about the gulling of Malvolio in *Twelfth Night?* If we didn't know the name of the author, we would dismiss it as tiresome.) On the other hand, modern names and interesting ideas should not hide from us the fact that, for example, Signor Laudisi in Pirandello's *Right You Are* is the same old prankster in sophisticated disguise.

If knaves are more influential, fools are more numerous. How many fools are there to each knave of one's acquaintance? The Romans seem to have thought the normal ratio is three to one. Their Atellan Farces had four type characters: the Blockhead, the Braggart, the Silly Old Man, and the Trickster. Only the last is a knave. The others are three different kinds of fool: the moron, defeated before he starts; the braggart, defeating himself as he goes along; and the man who has recently become a fool through senility and can remember the gay days when he was a knave and heard the chimes at midnight.

It is perhaps wrong to speak of knaves and fools separately, for what has most value to farce and comedy is their interrelationship. F. M. Cornford has shown that one of the oldest relationships in the comic drama is that between the ironical man and the impostor. These are the comedian and the straight man, one a knave, the other a fool, the fun resulting from the interaction between the two. If we say that the farcical image of man is the image of a human couple, that couple will not be the *jeune premier* and the *ingénue* but the knave and the fool, the ironist and the impostor, Sir Toby Belch and Sir Andrew Aguecheek, Jack Tanner and Octavius Robinson.

To this polarity, add a paradox. In the last analysis the knave, too, is a fool. Farce and comedy are forever demonstrating that the knave's ingenuities get him nowhere. The cleverness which seems to be capability proves in the end a rhetorical or gymnastic flourish.

The farceur does not show man as a little lower than the angels but as hardly higher than the apes. He shows us man in the mass, in the rough, in the raw, in anything but fine individual flower. If Mr. Auden is right in saying that "art can have but one subject; man as a conscious unique person," then farce is not an art. The *Oxford Companion* seems to regret that the characters of farce are stupid. But they are deliberate monuments to stupidity, disturbing reminders that God has lavished stupidity on the human race with His own unrivaled prodigality.

I have mentioned some points, and they are many, where farce and tragedy meet, but here we find them at the poles. Pascal called man a thinking reed. The metaphor embraces two characteristics: intellect and weakness. If farce shows man to be deficient in intellect, it does not show him deficient in strength or reluctant to use it. Man, says farce, may or may not be one of the more intelligent animals, he is certainly an animal, and not one of the least violent either. He may dedicate what little intelligence he possesses precisely to violence, to plotting violence, or to dreaming violence. (Mona Lisa's smile might mean that she was plotting murder, but is more likely to signify that she was dreaming murders she would never plot.)

"A Mad World, My Masters!" A play with a cast of fools tells us that it is a world of fools we live in. If that is not a tragic image, it is not, on the other hand, an image which the tragic poets would find beneath them. I take from what is perhaps the greatest of tragedies these words:

> When we are born we cry that we are come
> To this great stage of fools.

What wisdom can there be without a poignant sense of wisdom's opposite, which is folly?

The Quintessence of Theatre

When we talk of Charlie Chaplin are we talking of acting or the thing acted? Nearly all discussions of him pass imperceptibly from the one topic to the other, and this is as it should be. Meyerhold said: "The idea of the actor's art, based on the worship of the mask, gesture, and movement, is inseparably linked with the idea of farce."

If melodrama is the quintessence of drama, farce is the quintessence of theatre. Melodrama is written. A moving image of the world is provided by a writer. Farce is acted. The writer's contribution seems not only absorbed but translated. Melodrama belongs to the words and to the spectacle; the actor must be able to speak and make a handsome or monstrous part of the tableau. Farce concentrates itself in the actor's body, and dialogue in farce is, so to speak, the activity of the vocal cords and the cerebral cortex. Consider the figures in Jacques Callot's engravings, *Dances of Naples (Balli di Sfessania).* One cannot imagine them performing melodramas. They have always been considered the very incarnation of *commedia dell'arte;* and obviously they are the incarnation of farce. One cannot imagine melodrama being improvised. The improvised drama was pre-eminently farce. In its pride it would call itself *commedia.* But we do not hear of *tragedia dell'arte.* And so I am reversing Meyerhold's dictum and saying: the idea of farce is inseparably linked with the idea of the actor's art, the *arte of commedia dell'arte.*[1] The theatre of farce is the theatre of the human body but of that body in a state as far from the natural as the voice of Chaliapin is from my voice or yours. It is a theatre in which, though the marionettes are men, the men are supermarionettes. It is the theatre of the surrealist body.

The entertainments of the *commedia dell'arte* were Atellan Farces raised to a higher power. The fools are no longer limited to three kinds, nor the knaves to one. There is a complete human menagerie.

The celebrated types of the *commedia* have deeper roots than social manners or even society itself. In Callot's *Dances* the animal origin of the characters is clear. It has been suggested that Callot may not be giving an accurate portrait of the *commedia,* but it is likely that any deviation came from knowledge and intuition as to what the *commedia* in essence was. Aristophanes' birds represent a sophisticated use of animal fable, which could not have been sophisticated from the beginning. The characters of comedy come in time to stand for the human in the most restricted sense, the human cut off from Nature. But originally they represented human nature as part of Nature-in-general, human life as part of all life. Conversely, external nature was not external: the general forces of life were to be found in the human figures. If on the tragic side, gods merge with heroes, on the comic side the knaves and fools merge with the lower orders of spirits, as they are still doing in Shakespeare's *Midsummer Night's Dream* and *The Tempest.*

The *commedia dell'arte* petered out in the eighteenth century. The nearest thing we can see to it today is a type of theatre that is not influenced by it: the so-called Peking Opera. But there is a vestige of the *commedia* in the theatre of Eduardo de Filippo in Naples, and there have been convincing attempts to reconstruct entertainments in *commedia* style by the Piccolo Teatro di Milano.

Charlie Chaplin's silent comedies are not merely vehicles for the greatest comedian of the twentieth century, they are masterpieces of farce. And there are dozens of them. No one at the time realized what they were worth, and only, I believe, the Cinemathèque in Paris has made a systematic attempt to preserve them. Even now, if these works are spoken of as art, it is the art of film that is meant. The idea of a masterpiece *of farce* seems an unacceptable proposition, perhaps even to Mr. Chaplin himself, who in later life has aimed at forms with higher standing—not with uniformly happy results.

That the era of great farce in the motion picture runs from about 1912 to about 1927 seems to many a result of mechanical accident. The motion picture camera had just been invented, the sound track had not yet been combined with it: farce was happily suited to the silent screen. It is true that certain aspects of farce could be developed on the screen far beyond the possibilities of the stage. The screen could obviously do much more with the traditional chase and pursuit. Trick photography opened up new territory for zany behavior. Even pantomime changed. The old mimes delighted to work with imaginary props. Part of their art was to do without the actual objects. On the screen, objects—from the automobile to the alarm clock—became a vast new subject matter for farce and gave us what was in many ways a new kind of farce.

But the flowering of an art form could never be mainly the result of a mechanical invention. It happened that the invention was made toward the end of an era of great farce, one of the few. "In our day," said Nietzsche in 1870, "only

---

[1] Following Allardyce Nicoll (in his *The World of Harlequin,* Cambridge University Press, 1963, p. 26), I am assuming that the traditional interpretation of the word "arte" as "the acting profession" is incorrect. But that interpretation presents no threat to my thesis about farce.

the farce and the ballet may be said to thrive." He was right, but no one seems to know it. To the extent that the history of Victorian theatre and drama is taught at all in the schools, the word has been that before Shaw and Wilde there were only some shadowy and austere figures like Bulwer Lytton and Tom Robertson. That is misleading because the real glory of the Victorian stage lay in the farce, the extravaganza, and the comic opera. The great names are Gilbert and Sullivan, and the young Pinero.

As for France, there is the same contrast between what one is told and the actual situation. One is told of the serious thesis drama of the younger Dumas and Augier, drama that has seemed dated since around 1900. But there is French theatre of 1860 that is still fresh today, notably the operettas of Offenbach and the farces of Labiche. In the wake of these two geniuses of light theatre came Georges Feydeau, possibly the greatest writer of farce of any country at any time. He has not had worthy successors. The era of modern farce ended with his death in 1921—which was almost exactly the time when Chaplin began to give farce up.

Chaplin's farces, then, mark not the beginning of an era, but the end of one. The movie-makers did not follow in his footsteps. And though the farcical bits were the best parts of the later Chaplin pictures, they were only parts—of satire, of tragicomedy, of drama of ideas.

There is a special niche for the pictures that the Marx Brothers made in the thirties and for those of W. C. Fields in the same period and a little later. But whereas the early Chaplin films had been a pure triumph, both the Marx Brothers and Fields had an uphill battle to fight with the times. The age of phony seriousness was upon us. There was too much aggression in Chaplin, in Fields, in the Marx Brothers for the age of Rodgers and Hammerstein, Norman Vincent Peale, and Dwight D. Eisenhower.

"The Breath of Imaginary Freedom"

While defining melodrama as savage and infantile, I have sought also to defend it as an amusing and thrilling emanation of a natural self which we do well not to disown. And I follow Aristotle, rather than Plato, on the question of violence in art, concluding that melodrama, far from tending to make Hitlers of us, affords us, insofar as it has any effect at all, a healthy release, a modest catharsis. Much the same can be said of farce, except that the principal motor of farce is not the impulse to flee (or Fear), but the impulse to attack (or Hostility). In music, says Nietzsche, the passions enjoy themselves. If in melodrama fear enjoys itself, in farce hostility enjoys itself.

A generation ago people used to talk against the idea of art as escape—they had in mind escape from social problems. Melodrama and farce are both arts of escape and what they are running away from is not only social problems but all other forms of moral responsibility. They are running away from the conscience and all its creations, as at the orgies that the classical scholars have sometimes talked about. Charles Lamb called Restoration Comedies "those Saturnalia of two or three brief hours," and again we can apply Lamb's words to farce:

> I am glad for a season to take an airing beyond the diocese of the strict conscience—
> not to live always in the precincts of the law-courts—but now and then, for a dream-
> while or so, to imagine a world with no meddling restrictions. . . . I wear my shackles
> more contentedly for having respired the breath of imaginary freedom.

"Not to live always in the precincts of the law-courts." To escape the law courts, to escape the tyranny of society and public opinion, to escape also the law courts of the mind and the tyranny of the judge within each breast, the inner conscience—this sounds like an admirable prescription for the pursuit of pleasure. Then why and how do these law courts and these tyrannies get into dramatic literature? Is plain pleasure not the aim of literature? Or is there another and higher pleasure to be found "in the precincts of the law-courts," both kinds of law courts?

A Note on Farce[*]

John Dennis Hurrell

Farce is one of the oldest theatrical forms, and the audience for it is almost world-wide. But criticism—and dramatic criticism is no exception—dearly loves a hierarchy, and farce, having once been relegated to the lowest level of the series headed by tragedy, has been continually taken for granted as something if not actually beneath criticism, at least beneath the need for critical discussion. Everybody knows what happens in farce: a dozen definitions in standard reference books testify to the fact that it is a "low" form of theatrical presentation, the sole object of which is to excite laughter. It is inferior in every way to "true" drama: it makes use of excessively complicated plots, improbable situations, and type characterization. It is highly unrealistic, purely ephemeral in interest, and no fit subject for serious consideration as dramatic literature.

Yet farce has enjoyed great popularity during several long periods of dramatic history; it has occupied the attention of Aristophanes, Shakespeare, Molière, and Wilde, to name but four major dramatists. It is easy to say that farce caters to a poorly educated, artistically degenerate public, but the facts do not bear this out. The farces of the Roman comedians were performed in Renaissance England by and for the university population; there is evidence to suggest that at least one early farce of Shakespeare, *The Comedy of Errors*, was designed for and appreciated by an audience of lawyers; Molière's audience was certainly not composed solely of the uneducated; and the taste for Wilde has never been a vulgar one. The taste for farce has been continuous, too, not limited to any one historical period. There has probably not been a season in London, Paris, or New York without a successful farce on the boards, new or revived, and it has been a staple of the cinema since that medium's earliest days.

Clearly there is something in the nature of farce that seems to defy its dismissal by academic critics. We all enjoy it in the theatre, yet we concur in accepting "farce" as a term of abuse. We have been made to laugh, but we feel that the laughter has not been legitimately directed. On this point there seem to exist two schools of thought. One, which gives tacit recognition to the didactic purpose of art, is fairly represented by the *Encyclopedia Britannica's* definition of farce: "Farce is a form of the comic in dramatic art, the object of which is to excite laughter by ridiculous situations and incidents rather than by imitation with intent to ridicule, which is the province of burlesque, or by the delineation of the play of character upon character, which is that of comedy."

This attack (and almost every available definition of farce constitutes a

[*] John Dennis Hurrell, "A Note on Farce," *Quarterly Journal of Speech*, Vol. XLV, No. 4 (December, 1959).

form of attack) is double-edged. Farce is a lower form than burlesque because it has no satiric purpose, and a lower form than comedy because it relies on situation rather than character for its theatrical effects. We are left laughing, apparently, like lunatics, without cause, and after our indulgence we experience a sense of shame at our behavior. We have seen the serious business of the world (usually love, honor, and marriage) treated as though moral laws did not exist, and when the lights go up in the auditorium we are aware that for a brief spell we have not been seeking the highest. The world is a well-ordered place, thanks to our hard-won sense of morality, and we have allowed ourselves temporarily to forget this. According to his theory and its implications, then, farce exists and is enjoyed because of the dual nature of man, and for this very reason can never be openly accepted as having any relationship to that image of our morally directed lives which we keep constantly before us, especially in our art.

This leads us to the second school of thought about the legitimacy of our laughter at farce, whose views have been expressed most recently in an admirable essay by Mr. Eric Bentley.[1] His view is the Freudian one: farce permits us to look on while our repressed desires are acted out before us. The relation of farce to life is almost equivalent to that between the dream world and the waking world. The improbabilities of plot do not matter, for the action of farce is purely symbolic. At the center of our society is the institution of marriage and the family, and farce is an outlet for our repressed desire to desecrate these holy places. Farce must, therefore, rest on a basis of moral society. Man is not naturally, however, a moral creature (here the two views seem to coincide) and would like to break the laws which he has created to preserve the structure of his society, and in farce this dream of freedom is fulfilled: "in farce, as in dreams, one is permitted the outrage but is spared the consequences."[2] Farce is, to use Mr. Bentley's term, a "safety valve." Neither is it an unrealistic form of art, except for distortion of "the external facts." We all have the desire to outrage our society: this is the Freudian truth, and farce adheres to it, so "to the inner experience, the farceur tries to be utterly faithful."[3]

This is perhaps the most penetrating comment on farce that has yet appeared; but while it explains the relation of farce to the inner life of man, it does little to explain its relationship to the other dramatic forms, or to drama as a reflection of man's waking life. Mr. Bentley skillfully illustrates the illegitimate nature of our laughter at farce, but he is committed, by the logic of his argument, to the precept that it *is* illegitimate. He glosses over the improbabilities of plot in farce by his theory of adherence to the truth of "inner experience." While accepting almost all of his remarks as justified comment on the *psychology* of farce, I think it is possible to suggest a theory that goes beyond this to its *philosophy*, enabling us to formulate a definition of farce that has no pejorative undertones.

Briefly, my argument is that farce, like other dramatic forms, is a comment on the human situation, and that it represents a tenable theory, expressed through its artistic form, concerning our relationships with our fellow men in the society we have created. Tragedy functions in the area of moral solutions to the

---

[1] Eric Bentley, "The Psychology of Farce" (introduction to *Let's Get a Divorce and other plays*, ed. Eric Bentley, 1958).
[2] Eric Bentley, p. xiii.
[3] Ibid., p. xv.

problems which constantly suggest themselves to creatures conscious of a higher purpose than day to day existence: tragedy is thus highly selective, dealing with those men who are capable of, or capable of being driven to, purely moral choices. Comedy takes as its province a wider area of man's activities, concerning itself with the laws, written or unwritten, which govern men in their communities rather than those which link man with a higher force outside himself. Farce ignores both the moral and the social laws, not because it denies their existence, but because it sees an alternative to this constant reference to laws, moral or social, an alternative followed by the majority of mankind. The common denominator of farce characters is *ingenuity*, and it is on this level that in farce as in life most problems are solved. In the classic and typical situation, common to all forms of drama, of adulterous relationships, the question to be asked is not as in tragedy, "Having sinned against moral laws, how can I redeem my soul?", or as in comedy, "Having sinned against the sanctity of a social institution, how can I preserve my reputation?" (tragedy being concerned with *character*, comedy with *reputation*, as Shakespeare well knew), but "Being caught in this predicament, how can I *contrive* escape or concealment, so that our world can continue smoothly and safely as it did before human weakness asserted itself?" Farce recognizes that there are alternatives to the solutions provided by tragedy and comedy, and that it is these alternatives that shape the majority of our decisions. The character in farce is barely conscious that he is a moral creature; he is always conscious that he is a thinking and devising creature.

It is in this connection that the term "lower" can be aptly applied to farce without any pejorative connotations; we are concerned with a hierarchy still, but it is a hierarchy of human abilities, moral and mental, not of dramatic types. It is, in fact, possible to speak of a "good" farce and mean considerably more than that the play in question was amusing. Farce has a particular aspect of human existence to present, and its form, far from being accidental or uneconomical, is designed specifically to present that aspect. One might argue that farce, with its temporary reversal of the well-ordered and morally-directed world, is a kind of assertion of man's continual capacity for setting his house in order through the ingenious use of his capacity to make practical, rather than ethical decisions. One sentence might sum up the action of any successful farce: a situation or a relationship gets out of hand and somehow, inefficiently perhaps but eventually successfully, it is put right.

In this respect, then, farce concerns itself with a wider area of human activity than either comedy or tragedy. It may be an accurate representation of man's suppressed inner life, as Mr. Bentley suggests, but it is also, and more obviously and intentionally, an allegory of man's outer life. I use the term "allegory" advisedly, since the relationship between the typical situation in farce and its counterpart in life is not one of imitation but of symbolization. This symbolization is not only that of the inner life, but also of the form and pattern of our outer life. The common term for what I have called symbolization is, of course, "improbable situation," but this is unsatisfactory, for it does not suggest where the nature of the improbability lies. Mr. Bentley's answer to this question is prompted by his "safety valve" theory of farce "While, certainly, the external facts are distorted, the inner experience is so wild and preposterous that it would probably be impossible to exaggerate it. To the inner experience, the farceur tries to be utterly faithful. This fact raises the question whether farce is as indirect a form of literature as it is commonly supposed to be."[4]

This statement surely avoids the question that must be asked if farce is to be regarded as a responsible form of drama: in what way are the external acts distorted? Farce is rarely completely fantastic (*i.e.*, impossible) but only improbable, and the improbability seems to me to reside, in most cases, not in the farce-situations themselves but in the fact that these situations are carried to their logical conclusions. Taken this far they are, in terms of everyday life, absurd. The actions of most farce characters are, for the duration of the play, the actions of monomaniacs. Indeed, this is one of the chief sources of dramatic unity in farce, although it is popularly assumed to lack any unity at all. For example, the practical solution to Fadinard's problem in *An Italian Straw Hat!* is the finding of a hat; this is a situation which has, at the beginning, only a touch of the improbable about it. But when, as the action progresses, Fadinard is committed to this single solution, his behavior becomes absurd, simply because it constitutes reason followed beyond any possibility of compromise. This carrying of a situation to its ultimate conclusion provides the unity for the play; but it also places Fadinard, and the characters with whom he comes into contact, in other situations from which they must extricate themselves, and again the practical, or what seems to be practical, method is chosen, disaster being averted time after time until a point is reached where this kind of solution is no longer efficacious and the dramatist has only two ways open to him—morality or coincidence. Taken to this extreme the situation is, in terms of real life, absurd, distorted. But a human situation carried to such an extreme that it stands out recognizably *as* a situation, with a form and shape of its own, and not merely as a part of the irresolute, untidy, compromising flux of daily life, becomes in a sense not so much unreal as *abstract*, and so the term "allegory" seems to apply.

Another element in farce, noted by most critics, is one form or another of the "chase." The common view is summed up neatly by Leo Hughes.

> The chase has the advantage of providing suspense without at the same time distracting our attention too much from the discrete episodes. At the same time it allows the dramatist to maintain a pace too fast for the leisurely examination which the wildest flights of fancy do not readily survive. The suspense-packed movies of Mr. Hitchcock, to cite a parallel case, have exploited the advantages of fast pacing to forestall a too close scrutiny of motivation. Professor Greig has even suggested a similar benefit from the same device on a somewhat higher literary plane: our acceptance of evil in a Falstaff or a Gargantua, he believes, is earned so easily simply because the vigorousness or the furious pace does not permit us to examine the darker side of our ambivalent attitude too closely.[5]

Here again, then, the question of ambivalence, of the duality of human nature, is brought to bear on the subject of farce. But is this really necessary? The "chase," too, can be regarded as allegorical, the abstract representation of the constant forward movement of life, the tendency to solve problems not by contemplation of their moral significance but by ingenuity and action. Yet the example of Falstaff certainly is relevant. Falstaff's views on honor are, as most

---

[4] *Loc. cit.*
[5] Leo Hughes, *A Century of English Farces* (1956), p. 25. Hughes quotes from J. Y. T. Greig, *The Psychology of Laughter and Comedy* (1923), pp. 147–149.

Shakespearian scholars have recognized, a corrective to Hotspur's and to Hal's. If these "nobler" characters are reminders to us that man can direct his life according to principles beyond mere survival, Falstaff is always there to show us that survival is, after all, a prerequisite without which the principles would have no point. Those who accept the view that farce has as its purpose nothing but the excitement of laughter might well ponder the essential sanity of a Falstaff in a world where the honor of nations is placed before the survival of the race. There is surely something to be said for *l'homme moyen sensuel*, the perennial hero of farce, who frequently knows that he can get along very well with his ingenuity, without recourse to morality, for he is aware that the average man must pit his wits against a world that seems always ready to collapse about his ears, and that he must do a great deal of running to stay in the same place. If farce ignores morality it is because, to be an artistically effective reflection of the life of the average man, it must do this. The writer of farce knows that morality is what we turn to when all else fails, but he is a man who has not been made cynical by this knowledge.

Our definitions of farce need not, then, be in any way pejorative or apologetic. It is not necessarily a lower form of drama simply because it portrays what, for want of a better term, we must continue to call a "lower" human faculty. It does not deny morality: it simply isolates it and leaves it for treatment in a different form. It is not comedy which has failed to come off, since it does not undertake to criticize life in any way, and constantly refuses to generalize. Where, then, does it stand in the hierarchy in relation to tragedy? The answer is simple. It stands to one side and makes the very positive and valuable statement that tragedy might not even be necessary and might, even, be a little ridiculous.

"It's Hideously True"*

Al Capp

You may, unless you had something better to do, have been reading my comic strip *Li'l Abner* this week. If so, you are probably startled to see that my hero is apparently being married to one Daisy Mae Scragg. This time it's the real thing. Yes, after 18 years the poor lout is finally, hopelessly married, and in one of Marryin' Sam's cheapest, most humiliating weddings.

I never intended to do this. My comic-strip characters are not the kind who grow through boyhood and adolescence, get married and raise their own kids. The Yokums of Dogpatch are the same sweet and brainless characters they always were. And the fact that Abner always managed somehow to escape Daisy Mae's warm, eager arms provided me with a story that I could tell whenever I couldn't think of anything better. Frankly I intended to go through life happily and heartlessly betraying you decent, hopeful people who want to see things come out right. I never intended to have Li'l Abner marry Daisy Mae because your pathetic hope that I would was one of the main reasons you 50 million romance lovers read my strip.

For the first few years it was easy to fool you; you didn't know me well then. You followed developments eagerly, trustfully. When I met any of you, I was asked, "When will Li'l Abner marry Daisy Mae?" in a friendly, hopeful tone. Later, as I betrayed your hopes in more and more outrageous ways, your tone became a little bitter. One year I had Daisy Mae marry a tree trunk, thinking that Abner was hiding inside it. Next day, naturally, it turned out that the contents were an old pair of socks, but that Daisy's marriage to them was irrevocably legal. That was a pretty problem. Your tone became threatening. Later on I poisoned her, and Abner consented to marry her because it was her dying wish (Why not? She would be safely dead in a minute anyway.); but just as you thought the wedding had finally taken place, I let her drink some of Dogpatch's sizzling superfluid, "Kickapoo Joy Juice," which instantly restored her to life, so Abner was no longer bound by his promise. You still asked me when they would *really* marry, but your tone was a little more threatening. Then I let Daisy ecstatically marry a boy who not only turned out to be merely Abner's double but a bigamist too, so even that marriage didn't count. Now your tone was downright mutinous, and your question went something like: "For God's sake, will Abner EVER marry Daisy Mae?" Just the same, I knew you would still keep watching and waiting. This was the kind of suspense I needed to keep you reading my comic strip, so, no matter how impatient or indignant you got, I never intended to let your foolish, romantic dreams come true.

*Al Capp, "It's Hideously True," *Life*, Vol. 32, No. 13 (March 13, 1952), pp. 100–108.

So why did I do it this week? Why, after all these years of tricking you, did I finally trick myself? Well, the real reason isn't as simple as Abner, Daisy or even suspense. To understand why I have done this awful thing you will have to bear with me while I explain how and why I created them in the first place.

When I was in my early 20s and about to start a comic strip, I found myself in a terrible dilemma. The funny comic strip, the kind I wanted to do, was vanishing from the funny page. A frightening new thing had been discovered: namely, that you could sell more papers by worrying people than by amusing them. Comic strips which had no value except that they were comic were beginning to vanish from the funny papers. Rube Goldberg's dazed *Mike and Ike*, Fred Opper's *Happy Hooligan*, who wore a tomato can on his head, Milt Gross's *Count Screwloose*, who regularly escaped from the booby hatch only to return to it because things were more normal there—this beloved procession of clowns, innocents and cheerful imbeciles—slowly faded. In their place came a sobbing, screaming, shooting parade of the new "comic"-strip characters: an orphan who talked like the Republican platform of 1920; a prizefighter who advised children that brains were better than brawn while beating the brains out of his physically inferior opponents; detectives who explored and explained every sordid and sickening byway of crime and then made it all okay by concluding that these attractively blueprinted crimes didn't really pay; and girl reporters who were daily threatened with rape and mutilation.

Don't get me wrong. I was terrified by the emergence of this new kind of comic strip 18 years ago only because I didn't have the special qualities they required—not because they didn't have quality. *Dick Tracy* is a magnificently drawn, exquisitely written shocker comparable, in its own terms, with Poe. But "suspense" strips, though enormously effective, disdain fun and fantasy. Suspense was what editors wanted when I was ready to create my own comic strip—but all I could do was fun and fantasy.

Good'uns and Bad'uns

So I tried to draw straight-faced suspense comic strips. I tried to create smart and superior heroes, and submerged them in bloodcurdling tragedies, increasing in complexity, hopelessness and horror and thereby creating reader anxiety, nausea and terror—i.e., suspense. But I couldn't do it. I just couldn't believe in them. The suspense strips require one-dimensional good guys and bad guys—as I drew them. I discovered good things in the bad guys, and vice versa. So my hero turned out to be big and strong like the suspense-strip heroes, but he also turned out to be stupid, as big, strong heroes sometimes are. His mammy, like mine, and possibly yours, turned out to be a miracle of goodness, but at the same time she was kind of bossy, quite self-righteous and sweetly ridiculous. His girl, although wildly beautiful, is vaguely sloppy and, although infinitely virtuous, pursues him like the most unprincipled seductress.

The good people in my hero's town, possibly like those in your town, often are a pain in the neck. And the bad 'uns, like some bad 'uns in real life, are often more attractive than the good 'uns. The Scragg Boys, Lem and Luke, are fiendish when they are snatching milk from whimpering babies or burning down orphan asylums to get some light to read comic books by (only to realize that they can't read, anyway); but even the most horrified reader can't help being touched by their respectfully asking their pappy's permission to commit all this manslaughter and mayhem. Monsters they certainly are, but they are dutiful children too.

The society people in *Li'l Abner* always have impressive names, but there is always something a little wrong with them too—like Henry Cabbage Cod, Daphne Degradingham, Sir Cecil Cesspool (he's deep), Peabody Fleabody and Basil Bassoon. Dumpington Van Lump seemed a harmless, hospitable kid until it developed that his favorite book was *How to Make Lampshades Out of Your Friends.* Colossal McGenius was so brilliant in giving business advice that he seemed to be justified in charging $1,000 a word for talking to worried tycoons; but it turned out that his weakness was telling long, involved jokes (at $1,000 a word) about three Bulgarians, whereupon he remembered, much too late, that they were actually three *Persians,* and so he had to start the story all over again. When he finally got to the advice it was great, but by that time the tycoon had gone bankrupt.

When I introduced a mythical country, Lower Slobbovia, I was as technical as the straightest suspense-strip creator, and gave readers a map. The map was perfectly reasonable except that the names of its parts created some distrust and disrespect for the country. The oceans were the Hotlantic and Pitziffic, and there was another body of water called the Gulf of Pincus. The capital, Ceaser Siddy, home of Good King Nogoodnik, was flanked by the twin cities of Tsk-Tsk and Tch-Tch. Its leading citizens had familiar and famous, but somehow embarrassing names like Douglas Snowbanks Jr., Harry S. Rasputintruman and Clark Bagle. Everything in *Li'l Abner* was my effort to be as straight as the straight strips, but colored, however, with my conviction that nothing is ever entirely straight, entirely good, entirely bad, and that everything is a little ridiculous. As in the straight suspense strips, I dutifully created the standard, popular suspense situations, but something forced me to carry them so far that terror became absurdity.

For instance, when the Yokums make gigantic sacrifices for what they are convinced is a noble and beneficial cause, the reader knows they are swindling themselves; even victory will benefit only the enemy. When the Yokums are being heroes they are being not only heroes—they are being damned fools at the same time. When their adversaries are being villainous, they are not only vile, they are also confused and frightened.

Li'l Abner had to come out that way, because that's the way things seem to me. Well, it happened to make a big hit. It was a success because it was something I hadn't thought much about as such. It was a satire. Nobody had done one quite in these terms before. I was delighted that I had. I was exhilarated by the privilege this gave me to kid hell out of everything.

Good Old Jack S.

It was wonderful while it lasted; and I had no reason for marrying Abner off to Daisy Mae. But then something happened that threatens to shackle me and my kind of comic strip. It is what I call the gradual loss of our fifth freedom. Without it, the other four freedoms aren't much fun, because the fifth is the freedom to laugh at each other.

My kind of comic strip finds its fun wherever there is lunacy, and American life is rich in lunacy everywhere you look. I created labor-hating labor leaders, money-foolish financiers, and Senator Jack S. ("Good old Jack S.") Phogbound.

When highway billboard advertising threatened to create a coast-to-coast iron curtain between the American motorist and the beautiful American countryside, I got some humorous situations out of that too. Race-hate peddlers gave me some of my juiciest comedy characters, and I had the Yokums tell them what I know is true, that all races are God's children, equally beloved by their Father. For the first 14 years I reveled in the freedom to laugh at America. But now America has changed. The humorist feels the change more, perhaps, than anyone. Now there are things about America we can't kid.

I realized it first when four years ago I created the Shmoo. You remember the Shmoo? It was a totally boneless and wildly affectionate little animal which, when broiled, came out steak and, when fried, tasted like chicken. It also laid neatly packaged and bottled eggs and milk, all carefully labeled "Grade A." It multiplied without the slightest effort. It loved to be eaten, and would drop dead, out of sheer joy, when you looked at it hungrily. Having created the animal, I let it run wild in the world of my cartoon strip. It was simply a fairy tale and all I had to say was wouldn't it be wonderful it there were such an animal and, if there were, how idiotically some people might behave. Mainly, the response to the Shmoo was delight. But there were also some disturbing letters. Some writers wanted to know what was the idea of kidding big business, by creating the Shmoo (which had *become* big business). Other writers wanted to know what was the idea of criticising labor, by creating the Shmoo, which made labor unnecessary.

It was disturbing, but I didn't let it bother me too much. Then a year later, I created the Kigmy, an animal that loved to be kicked around, thus making it unnecessary for people to kick each other around. This time a lot more letters came. Their tone was angrier, more suspicious. They asked the craziest questions, like: Was I, in creating the Kigmy, trying to create pacifism and thus, secretly, nonresistance to Communism? Were the Kigmy kickers secretly the big bosses kicking the workers around? Were the Kigmy kickers secretly the labor unions kicking capital around? And finally, what in hell was the idea of creating the Kigmy anyhow, because it implied some criticism of some kinds of Americans and any criticism on anything American was (now) un-American? I was astounded to find it had become unpopular to laugh at any fellow Americans. In fact, when I looked around, I realized that a new kind of humorist had taken over, the humorist who kidded nothing but himself. That was the only thing left. Hollywood had stopped making ain't-America-wonderful-and-ridiculous movies, and was making ain't-America-wonderful-but-anyone-who-says-it's-ridiculous-too-deserves-to-be-picketed movies. Radio, the most instantly obedient to pressure of all media, had sensed the atmosphere, an atmosphere in which Jack Benny is magnificent but in which Will Rogers would have suffocated.

So that was when I decided to go back to fairy tales until the atmosphere is gone. That is the real reason why Li'l Abner married Daisy Mae. At least for the time being, I can't create any more Shmoos, any more Kigmies; and when Senator Phogbound turns up now, I have to explain carefully that, heavens-to-Betsy, goodness-no, he's not typical; nobody like THAT ever holds public office. After a decade and a half of using my characters as merely reasons to swing my searchlight on America, I began all over again to examine them, as people. Frankly, I was delighted with them. (Frankly, I'm delighted with nearly everything I do. The one in the room who laughs loudest at my own jokes or my own comic strip is me.) I became reacquainted with Li'l Abner as a human being, with Daisy Mae as an agonizingly frustrated girl. I began to wonder myself what it would be like if they were ever married. The more I thought about it, the more complicated and disastrous and, therefore, irresistible, the idea became.

Will They Live Happily Ever After?

For instance, Li'l Abner has never willingly kissed any female except his mother and a pig. Well—if he got married, he'd *have* to. Even he couldn't avoid it for more than a month or so. What would happen? Would he approve of kissing? Would he say anything good about it? (And thus make it popular with millions of red-blooded young Americans whose "ideel" he is.) Would he do it again? As a bachelor he is frankly a bum. He just sleeps, eats and goes catfishing. As a married man he would have to support his own household. How would he do it? Is there anybody stupid enough to hire someone as stupid as he is? Is there *any* profession that requires as little intelligence as he has? And how about Mammy Yokum? She has always ruled Abner with an iron fist. Would she continue to after he has his own home? And how would Daisy Mae take this? Sure, she's been sweet and docile with Mammy Yokum all these years, but that might only have been because she needed her help in trapping Abner. Now that he's her'n, will she show her true colors and tangle with Mammy for the lightweight championship of the new Yokum home? How about babies? Married people frequently have babies. Would *they* have a baby? Will he really be born on the Fourth of July? Is it possible that they'd name him Yankee Doodle Yokum? Babies have uncles. Could I freeze the blood of the entire nation by having Mammy Yokum (who can accomplish anything, even singlehanded) produce a baby of her own, five minutes after Li'l Yankee Doodle Yokum was born? Would this child be known as Oncle Yokum?

And how about Sadie Hawkins Day? It has become a national holiday. It's my responsibility. It doesn't happen on any set day in November; it happens on the day I say it happens. I get tens of thousands of letters from colleges, communities and church groups, starting around July, asking me *what* day, so they can make plans. Well, Sadie Hawkins Day has always revolved around Li'l Abner fearing marriage to Daisy Mae. Now that his worst fears have come hideously true, what will he and Daisy Mae do on Sadie Hawkins Day? Will Lower Slobbovia inaugurate its own "Sadie Huckins Day" and import Li'l Abner and Daisy Mae as technical advisers? In short, once Abner and Daisy Mae are married, do they live happily ever after like other people or is this just the beginning of even more complicated disasters, more unbearable miseries? They are married, all right. But if you think the future is serene for them, you're ("Haw! Haw!") living in a fool's paradise.

Tragicomedy*

Robert W. Corrigan

> It all comes to the same thing anyway; comic and tragic are merely
> two aspects of the same situation, and I have now reached the stage
> where I find it hard to distinguish one from the other.
>
> EUGENE IONESCO

So far we have discussed four major forms of drama. We have discovered that at
the heart of each of them is the experience of some kind of pain or discord within a context of conflict. Yet each of the forms is markedly different and we have
no trouble distinguishing among them.

The final form we will consider is tragicomedy. As the term suggests, it
combines some of the qualities of tragedy and some of those of comedy. In tragicomedy, the serious merges with the ridiculous; helplessness is cast in a humorous vein; pain and despair are transcended or are miraculously overcome; joy
and sadness become indistinguishable from one another. It is an interesting hybrid form that has dominated American and European drama since the second
half of the last century.

At certain times in history, the more or less clear distinctions between the
forms of drama seem to break down or to become blurred. Tragicomedy flour-
ishes at these times. This breakdown is not due to anything that happens in the
theatre but is caused by shifts in values that take place in the larger society of
which the theatre is a part. In fact, we can generalize that whenever social values are in a state of radical change, distinctions between the forms of drama tend
to become blurred.[1] The most striking example of this phenomenon has been in
Europe and America in the past 125 years. Tragicomedy seems to thrive in a society in a state of flux.

* Robert W. Corrigan, "Tragicomedy," *The World of the Theatre*, Scott, Foresman and Company,
Glenview, Il., 1979. Copyright © 1979 by Scott, Foresman and Company. Reprinted by permission.
[1] This was certainly the case in the second half of the fifth century B.C. in Greece and is reflected in
the plays of Euripides. (*Alcestis* is a good example.) The last plays of Shakespeare (*Measure for Measure, Cymbeline, The Winter's Tale,* and *The Tempest*) and several of those by the Jacobean dramatists reveal that something similar happened early in the seventeenth century in England after the
death of Queen Elizabeth I. The theatre in the seventeenth-century France after Louis XIV is another instance.

Tragicomedy and Changing Values

The meaning and significance of the traditional forms of drama in any period of history depend on the existence of generally accepted standards of value within a society. Such norms make it possible to get wide agreement on what is serious and what is funny. All the forms of drama we have discussed thus far are based on this agreement. This publicly shared view of what is true provides the artist with a basis for communication. It enables the playwright to communicate emotion and attitude by simply describing incidents; it provides a storehouse of symbols with guaranteed responses; above all, it enables the playwright to construct a plot by selecting and organizing events that, because of this community of belief, are significant to the audience. The dramatist is bound more by plot than other writers are (novelists, for instance) because a play's action is first perceived by the audience through the events of the plot. The very existence of plot depends on agreement between writer and audience on what is significant in experience. All drama, if it is to communicate to an audience, depends on a shared view of what is significant in experience. Issues must really matter before we can consider any outcome tragic or comic.

Once this shared public truth is shattered and replaced with our individual private truths, all experience tends to be equally serious or equally ludicrous. This is what has happened in the last century. There is no publicly shared view of what is significant. This is the meaning of the contemporary French playwright Eugene Ionesco's statement with which we opened this discussion of tragicomedy.

Let us look at an example that illustrates what this means. The subject is the sexual seduction of a young woman. In the English theatre of the Restoration (the late seventeenth and eighteenth centuries), seduction was comic in both theme and situation. Its use as subject matter in the theatre—which was very common—reflected the commitment to dalliance, infidelity, and sexual conquest which characterized the lives of the court nobility who made up the audience of that theatre. A playwright like William Congreve (1670-1729) or William Wycherley (1640-1715) could introduce a seduction scene into one of his plays and know exactly how his audience would respond to it. They would laugh and enjoy it. His only task (no small one, to be sure) would be to do it with wit. To achieve any response other than laughter would require an elaborate manipulation of the plot and characters, since the audience's attitude toward seduction was so firmly fixed. But by the end of the eighteenth century and all through the nineteenth century, the public attitude toward seduction changed radically. The seduction of the innocent during that period was seen as a horrible catastrophe ("Poor Nell!") and as the source of personal tragedy, family dishonor, abandonment, and any number of other soul-wracking, handwringing results. Once again the public attitude, although completely different, was clearly defined and known, and a playwright could use a seduction scene (or plot) with the certainty that it would evoke a guaranteed response—shock and disapproval.

Now, what about our own times? What is the commonly shared public attitude toward seduction? Although each of us might have his or her own view on the subject—including seduction of whom by whom and what sex by what sex— we would all probably have to admit that if there is any widespread public view on the subject at all, it is "Who cares?" A playwright using this theme today has to build into the play not only the event but the ways the audience is supposed to respond to it. Even this will at best create only ambiguity, for since there is no commonly held public attitude, neither the playwright nor the members of the audience can know for certain how they will respond. We know that seduction can be harmless and even joyful. We also know that it can be the occasion of sadness, pain, outrage, and a deep sense of loss. Which one is it? Both? Neither? We can never be sure, and a world of ambiguous values is the miasma from whence tragicomedy emerges.

Tragicomedy and the Modern Theatre

Tragicomedy has thrived at various times throughout the history of the Western theatre, but without question the most significant period has been the past hundred years. Indeed, it is becoming increasingly difficult to use the terms *tragedy* and *comedy* with any precision at all. A striking characteristic of the modern drama is the way the old distinctions between the tragic and the comic (the serious and the ludicrous, the painful and the painless) have been erased. Ours has been a time of mongrel moods, and there are a number of reasons for this.

The drama's general pattern of development during this time can best be described as a gradual but steady shift away from publicly shared philosophical and social concerns toward the cries and conflicts of an individual's inner and private life. This very major change in the concerns of the theatre grew out of and reflected profound social changes in the period.

One of the dominant ideas of the modern period is the conviction that it is impossible to know what the world is really like. Before Martin Luther (1483–1546), society generally believed that there is a direct and recognizable relationship between our external actions and our innermost motivations and feelings. In rejecting a direct relationship between the outer and inner worlds, Luther began a revolution in thought that gradually made it impossible for humanity to attach any objective value to the world of experience. This insistence on such a clear-cut division between the physical and the spiritual aspects of reality had a profound effect on modern dramatists, who grew increasingly distrustful of sensory responses to the "outside" world. At the same time they tended to lose whatever belief they might have had in the truth of their own feelings and sensations. Playwrights could no longer hold a mirror up to nature, at least not with any confidence. They could only reflect their own feelings and responses to the world, knowing that these feelings and responses are inconsistent, often contradictory, and deeply personal.

One force in the nineteenth century that did much to destroy belief in an established norm of human nature and to begin this process of internalization in the theatre was the development of psychology as a field of study. Psychology has demonstrated that the distinction between rational and irrational behavior is not clear-cut, and that labelling any behavior as abnormal or inappropriate is a tremendously complicated task. Psychology has made it difficult, if not impossible, for the dramatist to present characters in a direct way. In earlier times, when it was believed there was a sharp distinction between the sane and the insane, irrational behavior was dramatically significant because it could be defined in terms of a commonly accepted standard of sane conduct. It seems clear, for instance, that in Shakespeare's presentation of them, Lear on the heath is insane while Macbeth at the witches' cauldron is not. But for the modern dramatist, deeds do not necessarily mean what they appear to mean, and in themselves they are not directly related to the characters. For example, we can never be sure why Hedda Gabler or Miss Julie acts as she does. Once a playwright believes that the meaning of every human action is relative, the dramatic events of the plot cease to have meaning in themselves. The playwright cannot count on a commonly shared view of truth to give meaning to events in a play. They take on significance only as the individual motivations of the characters are revealed. (The technique of earlier drama was just the reverse: the motivations of the characters were revealed by the events of the plot.)

While the development of psychology was a very powerful force in shaping the modern theatre, there were other factors at work as well. The industrial revolution and developing industrial technology brought incredible change to working and family life, and the speed of change made the future increasingly unpredictable. People were forced to live with uncertainty and growing isolation.

At the same time, discoveries made by nineteenth-century archeologists and the resulting interest in anthropology tended to break down existing attitudes toward human nature. Early anthropologists made it clear that human nature is not something fixed and unchanging but only a kind of behavior learned in each culture. Furthermore, by the middle of the century, democracy was finally beginning to be established both as a way of life and as a form of government. Today we tend to forget what a revolutionary idea democracy is and the shattering effects it had on the values of eighteenth- and nineteenth-century Europe. In 1835 Alexis de Tocqueville had observed in *Democracy in America:*

> Not only does democracy make every man forget his ancestors, but it hides his descendants and separates his contemporaries from him, it throws him back forever upon himself and threatens in the end to confine him entirely within the solitude of his own heart.

By the second half of the nineteenth century, every established view of God, human nature, social organization, and the physical universe was beginning to be seriously challenged, if not rejected outright.

These profound changes in values and attitudes had a tremendous influence on the nature of dramatic form. As belief and values crumbled and changed, the clear-cut distinctions between the established forms of drama became fuzzy. This was particularly true of the forms of tragedy and comedy. When you can't be sure what actions really mean, and when the relationship between actions and results is unclear, the serious tends to be inseparable from the ludicrous. Or you can turn this idea around, and it still comes out much the same way: the trivial can become the most effective way of communicating the serious. Either way, it is the best way to describe the vision dominant in the theatre during the past one hundred years. It is certainly the controlling vision of most of the plays of Ibsen, Strindberg, Chekhov, Pirandello, Giraudoux, Brecht, Duerrenmatt, Beckett, Ionesco, Pinter, and Albee. Even Eugene O'Neill—who had a tragic sense of life, if anyone ever did—remarked as far back as 1939 that:

> It's struck me as time goes on, how something funny, even farcical can suddenly without apparent reason, break up into something gloomy and tragic. . . . A sort of unfair *non sequitur,* as though events, as though life, were to be manipulated just to

confuse us. I think I'm aware of comedy more than I ever was before—a big kind of comedy that doesn't stay funny very long.[2]

In the modern theatre the lines of the comic mask have become indistinguishable from those of the tragic. This is the realm of tragicomedy. Probably no one embodies the spirit of this realm more fully than Gogo and Didi, the central characters of Samuel Beckett's *Waiting for Godot*. We don't know who Godot is, or why Gogo and Didi are waiting for him. By the end of the play Godot has still not come and they decide to go.

VLADIMIR   Well? Shall we go?
ESTRAGON   Yes, let's go.

But the last line of the play is a stage direction: *"They do not move."*[3] Gogo and Didi are two irreducible specimens of a humanity whose only capacity is to remain comically, tragically, ambiguously alive with the courage of their hallucinations as they wait for a Godot who may or may not ever come.

"Hope Springs Eternal . . ."

The vision of tragicomedy is one of almost unrelieved despair. It lacks the heroism, the sense of accomplishment, and the spirit of fulfillment we discovered in tragedy. Tragedy may be painful and at times even sad, but there is something glorious and affirming in the hero's capacity to become one with his or her own fate. Tragicomedy also lacks the life-enhancing energy and the sense of triumph we associate with comedy. All the qualities of the comic world—reconciliation, change, the restoration of social order, and the celebration of new possibility— are either absent or not working.

If the version of tragicomedy is despairing to the point of horror, why would playwrights feel compelled to choose this form? More important, why would audiences want to experience it? What healthy need could this kind of theatre fulfill? Clearly, we do not go to the theatre to witness representations of our own happiness and despair. We do not need theatre for that. Actually, the explanation is quite the reverse. Of the dramatic forms, tragicomedy is most like life itself as we live it day by day. Think about it: How often do we achieve a clear resolution to anything? We fall in love, but how often does true love last? How often is suffering ennobling or the source of wisdon? Why does success so often prove to be hollow and empty? How capable are we of really changing things? Our experience tells us that all we can do is to "grin and bear it." That is the perfect motto for tragicomedy. It expresses the way life really is with an unsparing honesty.

That brings us back to the original question: Why do we pay our hard-earned cash to spend two or three hours of our leisure time watching unhappiness and frustration when we have our fill of that in our everyday lives outside the theatre? The answer is—and this is one of the mysteries of human life—most of us never give up hope. "Hope springs eternal in the human breast!" Going to the heart of tragicomedy—beyond the despair—we find hope. Why do Beckett's Gogo and Didi keep on waiting for Godot rather than hang themselves? Why do

---

[2] Eugene O'Neill. Cited by Croswell Bowen. *The Curse of the Misbegotten: A Tale of the House of O'Neill.* New York: McGraw-Hill Book Co., 1959, p. 259.
[3] Samuel Beckett. *Waiting for Godot.* New York: Grove Press, 1954, p. 61.

Chekhov's three sisters go on living even as their dream of Moscow is shattered? Why does Brecht's Mother Courage, all her children dead, go trudging on? Because though their lives may be meaningless and empty, broken and sad, they never give up the hope that maybe tomorrow things will change for the better. For most of us, hope is the miracle of existence, and tragicomedy insists that we need never give up hoping. Tragicomedy may bring us pictures of despair about the meaning of existence, but does not stop there. It celebrates the fact that despair can be transcended because of our undying capacity for hope.

> Real hope can be found only through real depair. . . . The appeal of that comedy which is infused with gloom and ends badly, that tragedy which is shot through with a comedy that only makes the outlook still bleaker, is that it holds out to us the only kind of hope we are in a position to accept. And if this is not the hope of a Heaven in which we would live forever, it is not the less precious, perhaps, being the hope without which we cannot live from day to day.
>
> ERIC BENTLEY, *The Life of the Drama*

VII
THE CRITICISM
OF COMEDY

Aristophanes:
Discourse of Fantasy[*]

Cedric H. Whitman

Although the art of Aristophanes is generally recognized as a compound of the fantastic and the realistic, interpreters have on the whole based their views on the realistic and satiric element, and dismissed, or better subsumed, the fantastic aspect as simply the mode appropriate to comedy, the vehicle by which the satirical message is conveyed. By this approach the poet's point becomes an essentially critical one, with reformative overtones, and the plays turn into explicit commentaries on the daily social and political life of Athens. Such commentary is, of course, present, but if the whole play exists to serve this part, then poetry is being put to a practical use from which its nature recoils. Indeed, the degree of recoil is measured by the difficulty, as we have seen, of discovering any consistency of practical intention in any play among the true Old Comedies of Aristophanes. Poetry, one feels, never exists for such a purpose, even when it claims to. It was the convention of Roman satire to avow a reformative end, but the result of all Juvenal's *saeva indignatio* is a picture of the Roman underworld which exists for its own lurid sake, an enticingly evil image which the true reformer could have better done without. Bertolt Brecht has often asserted the didacticism of his plays, and even called them parables; yet his poetic force and his use of legends and paradigmatic characters have given these plays a relevance beyond the evils which they criticize. It is the business of a poet, says Aristotle, to make myths; and it is the mythopoeic factor in Aristophanes which is the controlling one.[1] The comic fantasy, which becomes a myth of its own times, is at once the source and the final end of Aristophanean art, and by its powerful impulse all the satire, all the sharp realistic images, all the wit and slapstick, are carried along as the spokes of a wheel are carried by the rotation of the rim. To interpret thus is not to deprive Aristophanes of his relevance or "seriousness" as an artist, but to insist that his relevance is of the larger, rather than the smaller, variety.

Fantasy may be regarded as a kind of harmless, and perhaps aimless, free-wheeling of the mind, by which it entertains an assortment of mirages, signifying nothing save perhaps the vague desires of a pipe dream. Viewed so, fantasy is as amorphous and insubstantial as smoke, and where there is smoke of this kind, one suspects, there may not be very much fire. But nothing so vapid is the case with Aristophanes. An Aristophanean fantasy is a structure, an elaborate

---

[*] Cedric H. Whitman, *Aristophanes and the Comic Hero*. Harvard University Press, Cambridge, Mass., 1964. Reprinted by permission of the publishers. © 1964 by the Board of Trustees of Oberlin College.
[1] *Poetics* 1451627 f.

and powerful one; as such, it evokes response from the mind's most basic function, which is to transform the chaotic spate of sense experience into an order of intelligible classes. To say that the classes are intelligible only because they are created by the mind for that purpose is, of course, simple nominalism; but after what has been seen of the power of words to affect reality in the *Birds,* and elsewhere, one may be confident that nominalism and Old Comedy have their points in common. When things become what they are called, rather than being called what they are, one has—though the *Frogs* may be something of an exception—the Aristophanean view; the true nominalist also believes that the thingness of a thing is in its name, not in its essence. Hence the demiurgic property of the Aristophanean pun: the *polos* literally becomes a *polis; nomos,* "law," and *nomos,* "melody," merge into each other, to form a symbol of the new dispensation of Nephelococcygia. The mind at first forms classes and gives them names; the names then further aid and abet the process through their own propensity for connotation, combination, and ambiguity. By this process, which might be called "treading on air," the intelligible world is extended to astonishing imaginative heights which could never be meaningful were it not for the fact that the verbal, poetic extension of reality is parallel to, and part of, the mind's formation of reality for itself. We may leave aside the extreme relativistic possibility that every mind forms only its own reality, which is therefore incommunicable—though this may have been the view of Gorgias—and assume that poetic structures are, by whatever way, communicative.

A fantasy, then, is a structure, an imaginatively erected reality akin in a way to the mind's erection of intelligible order. The medium is not always so highly verbal as it is in the *Birds,* though words always are important. There are numerous kinds of fantasy, and Aristophanes, in the extant plays at least, indulges in very little repetition. Each of the three "peace" plays has its distinctive fantasy: in the *Acharnians,* of an individual peace treaty in the form of a sack of wine, which is efficacious though the rest of the world is at war; in the *Peace,* of a flight to Olympus to recover the lost goddess; in the *Lysistrata,* of a *coup d'état* more fanciful in the fifth century B.C. than in the days of lady senators. But whatever the madness may be, a city in the sky or the trial of a dog, it is regularly the product of what is called, in Existential terms, a "boundary situation," where an individual's engagement in an action has brought him to the point where he must decide between a yea or a nay of grave import. Hitherto, some evasion of consequences or implications may have been possible; now there is only the absolute choice whereby one is to decide whether or not he is the man his actions have shown him to be. If he chooses yea, he accepts his responsibility, or "guilt," as it is sometimes called; if nay, he denies his responsibility and therewith his authenticity as a person.

In the opening chapter it was stated that the structure of this moral crux was the same for both tragedy and comedy; and indeed, the purest example is Oedipus, who, confronted by the choice of pursuing his quest or renouncing it, as Jocasta begs him to, unhesitatingly chooses yea, and becomes his true self. In tragedy the choice is ineluctable, though it is not always presented with such clarity as in *Oedipus;* there is never a third alternative. But herein comedy differs, and its difference responds to the helpless wish of the spirit writhing before an ineluctable choice; comedy invents a third alternative, and rides happily off on it. It is the release from ineluctable choice which gives Aristophanean comedy its initial free impulse, its heroic altitude, and its ability, noted earlier, to dissociate from moral or any other consistency. As Robert Frost once wrote, "Me for the hills where I don't have to choose." The comic alternative also involves the affirmation of *poneria*, the device, shift, or gimmick that will win, transform the world, and cure it of its intractability. Above all, it is the evasion of limit, and as such, it necessitates the creation of a new reality.

These statements are true, in varying degrees, of all the plays, though certainly not all comic alternatives are worked out in the same way; neither are all equally successful, for much depends on whether the protagonist is a real hero of *poneria*, like Peithetaerus, or a bungler, like Euripides in the *Thesmophoriazusae*. Sometimes, even, as in the *Clouds* and *Wasps*, we have a success balanced by a failure. The terms of these boundary situations vary considerably, some being more real than others. The debts of Strepsiades, the threat to Euripides' life, and Philocleon's love of jury duty cannot be regarded in quite the same light as the issue of the war, or the real "to be or not to be" question which confronted Athens in 405. But the content does not matter greatly; what matters is that the hero comes to the point where he feels called upon to act or be lost in the face of what seems like a hopeless situation. And act he does. The individual's rejection of society, such as is implied in the *Birds*, could be dramatized tragically into a play like the *Philoctetes;* or one could imagine Dicaeopolis' rejection of war developed tragically into a conscientious-objector play. In the tragic view these dilemmas could not be solved. Comedy goes between the horns.

Put so, it sounds again as if comedy were mere escapism. Yet like all poetry comedy reframes experience and orders reality as it sees it. In a way the sense of nothingness and absurdity so prevalent in the *Birds* is a major premise in all the plays. It becomes the function of poetry, therefore, to impose upon absurdity an order accommodated to the situation's need, and the process of doing so becomes the discourse of the fantasy. One may see the basic figure of this discourse as a kind of syllogism, or pseudosyllogism, of which the two premises state the boundary situation, and the conclusion, the comic alternative. Thus in the *Acharnians* we have: (a) disgust with war, (b) inability to stop the war; conclusion, make a private peace. In what we call real life this is impossible, but we are invited not to be bigoted about reality. In the *Birds* the syllogism would run: (a) Athens is bad; (b) no place is better; conclusion, build No-place and live there. Such licensed toying with reality is most clearly marked in the *Birds*, as the negative phrase "no place" is capitalized into the positive and satisfying "No-place," whose nothingness is constantly echoed in the contradictions of word play and wind egg. Again, in the *Wasps:* (a) constant litigation ruins home life; (b) you cannot keep an Athenian out of a courtroom; conclusion, bring the courtroom home. Here, the results are rather different from what is expected, for a variety of reasons, but chiefly because, as pointed out earlier, the fantasy is not the original creation of the hero, Philocleon, but of his son. The great scheme of salvation, therefore, is not in this play simply activated and brought to success by the hero; rather it is foisted upon him, up to the point where, under its influence, he bursts out of all limits in the drunken last scene, and, so to speak, runs away with the ball. The first perversion of reality has yielded to a second one, this time Philocleon's own.

As observed in earlier chapters, the fantasies which involve an unexpected turn carry a more ironical meaning than those in which the hero triumphs in unilinear course. These plots more or less invert the heroic idea, and show the hero either totally reduced, as in the *Thesmophoriazusae;* repentant and distracted, as in the *Clouds;* or asserting himself at best in a fugitive and momentary victory, as in the *Wasps.* The *Frogs* is a special case, of course; the heroic aspect, centered in Dionysus, follows the classical pattern of the death journey, but the return of Aeschylus reverses the original tenor of the quest and turns the whole into a funeral oration. In these plays the mingling of fantasy and realism is a different one; in varying degrees the hard facts crumble the fantastic effort. And yet even here, it is fantasy which gives the play its character, the hard facts serving, despite themselves, to limn the brilliance of the imaginative flight; the language is still the language of heroic absurdity.

The other comedies follow a more direct course, with the hero plunging between the dilemma's horns straight on toward the fabrication of a new reality. And it *is* a new reality, because the conclusion of the pseudosyllogism adds another dimension to the usual ones of experience. One may logically divide all things that exist into the class A and the class *Not-A*, and truthfully assert that there is nothing outside these two classes. But with equal logic, though of a different kind, one may posit a certain class which is neither A nor *Not-A*, but something else, and this must exist in another dimension. If asked what dimension, one may only answer, the dimension of realizable metaphor, which is, in simple fact, the dimension in which all true drama takes place. What is on the stage before us is never a mirror of life, but a metaphor of life, realized through the media of impersonation, dialogue, scene, or whatever. It is the metaphor which constitutes the reality of the play; it is a metaphor which disturbs the sense of ordinary reality and erects a new one. This function of metaphor may, of course, be exploited as a singularly self-conscious form of theatricalism, as it was by Pirandello. But all drama, tragic or comic, depends essentially on representing the world under an altered guise, in relation to which the limits of actual experience may be felt in a variety of ways, and sometimes scarcely at all. Aristophanic comedy plays a particularly bold and free hand, realizing metaphors which are so extreme as to be surrealistic. To say, "This man soars above us," is to use a metaphor. To dramatize men turning birds is to realize a metaphor of supremacy by means of the "other-dimensional" logic of fantasy. To say, "Athenian poetry will never die," is simple metaphor; to bring back Aeschylus from the dead is to dramatize the full poignancy of a wishful, retrospective dream.

Now to call this kind of thing surrealistic may seem to be presuming on terms, or even juggling them inexcusably. But the juggling and presumption, if such they be, may prove suggestive if one compares certain practices of the surrealists with what happens in Aristophanes, bearing in mind that the extralogical dimension of fantasy is the mainspring of Aristophanes' poetic power. Such fantasies look, quite of themselves, to something of deep human relevance, and are neither irresponsible childishness, nor mere sugar designed to coat and make palatable an allegoric or satiric pill.

Giuseppe Verdi once wrote, "It may be a good thing to imitate reality; it is better to invent it." By this remark he surely meant to call attention to the integrity of a dramatic work of art as determined by its own inner rules, apart from the content, historical or whatever, which it uses. The reality of any work of art lies in its form, in the artist's ability to discern and fulfill the emotional logic proposed by his original conception. Hence all art commits distortion, even when it least seems to. The apparently flawless body of the Velázquez Venus is attributable to the fact that she is conceived in terms of her elongated reclining posture. If she got up and tried to walk, we would discover that the disparity in the size of her hips had made her quite lame. It is the invented reality which works. Perhaps for this reason, that most inventive, though controversial painter, Dali, has long since eschewed the term surrealism, and called his work simply realism.[2] One may at first wonder by what right he does so, in view of his double heads, his deserts adorned with limp watches, and his marsupial centaurs with gaping, open bellies. Is it realistic to support eyelids on crutches, to protract the human head into a long lump of dough, to raise the epidermis of a grand piano, or to make three young women imitate the gestures of a schooner? The answer is obviously yes, if we are willing to create our own reality. Few of us have peered under the epidermis of a grand piano, or observed three women imitating the gestures of a schooner; above all, when we need to know what time it is, we rejoice that our watches do not go suddenly limp. But in the painting called the "Persistence of Memory" the three limp watches against the background of an utterly glassy and luminous sea add no little to the magic, as suggestive symbols of the stoppage of time in the moment of ineradicable memory.[3] And the "Family of Marsupial Centaurs" is a tender and exalted bacchanal of domesticity and fecundity, austerely structured in four triangles with a common apex. These, together with others far too numerous to mention, are inventions, inventions which indicate, if they do not actually embody, a different kind of reality, a reality born of imagination and brought to intelligible form through inner, otherdimensional logic. For the most part, they are quite serious extensions of experience, seldom satiric, and very often based on dream states and free association, which are among the deepest, and most inscrutable, sources of the poetic impulse.

Above all, perhaps, they illustrate the mind's subconscious transforming power. In one haunting work called "Nostalgic Echo" the outline of a keyhole in a wooden chest becomes successively, as it recedes through the planes of the picture, a girl skipping rope, a bell ringing in a tower, and a dim figure in the far background. Though there is nothing humorous about this painting, it differs formally very little from the successive changes of the imagery of coals or feathers in the *Acharnians*, or from Peithetaerus' smooth and logical transitions from a fugitive, to a bird, to a god. These developments are not particularly surrealistic; but other formally comparable ones distinctly are. For instance, in the treatment of scene: a Dalinian landscape is often a most ambiguous affair, as witness the "Impression of Africa," where faces fade in and out of nowhere, and distinctions of sea, sky, and earth are by no means clear. With this we might compare the middle scene of the *Peace*: Trygaeus has flown to heaven to find Peace; he finds, however, that she is buried in a deep pit, apparently in the ground. A chorus of farmers from all the cities in Greece now help to pull her out. We are bound to ask, where are we? If we are still up in heaven, whence the earthy pit and whence the farmers, who did not accompany Trygaeus on his flight; if we are now back on earth, why does Trygaeus have to descend to earth again later, this time, naturally enough, walking through air? It will not make sense except by its own logic, which in this case is governed by the regular nonsensical Aristo-

---

[2] For a concise account of Dali's development, see J. T. Soby, *Salvador Dali* (Museum of Modern Art, New York, 1946). See also S. Dali, *The Secret Life of Salvador Dali*, trans. H. M. Chevalier (New York, 1942), and *Fifty Secrets of Magic Craftsmanship* (New York, 1948); R. Descharnes, *The World of Salvador Dali* (New York, 1962).

[3] Dali has himself given different accounts at different times of the limp watches (see below, n. 12); one may be permitted yet another.

phanean associations with "up in the air" imagery.[4] The scene is a special landscape in the absolute elsewhere, especially designed to accommodate the
achievement of Trygaeus, and it works perfectly.

Now it might be claimed that some, at least, of the inventions of Dali are
monstrosities; indeed, one painting is entitled "The Invention of Monsters." But
these monstosities, though sometimes focusing some of the darker states of the
psyche, are no more monstrous than the hair-raising and side-splitting image of
Cleon in the *Wasps*, the Megarian girls transformed into pigs, the Socrates of the
Clouds, or Dicaeopolis in the rags of Telephus with his head on a chopping block
explaining that the Peloponnesian War was caused by the abduction of a couple
of loose ladies. Monstrosity is precisely the point: monstrosity and lyric have in
common a self-enclosed stancture, whereby both communicate as organism and
entity, rather than through discourse and comment; and both have much in
common with the grotesque, not only in its usual usage, but also in the specifically classical sense adopted above.

In his brilliant essay on the source of laughter Baudelaire distinguished between the significantly comic and the absolutely comic. The significantly comic
is the mode of satire and caricature, parody and wit, and all forms of humor
which arise from direct relevance to practical experience. They make fun of
something, or signify that something is laughable. In contrast, the absolutely
comic is an invention, a creation, which bears no direct relevance to anything
else, does not comment on anything, but merely is. The classical Aristophanic
grotesque, such as Trygaeus on the dung beetle, Peithetaerus with wings, or the
demiurgic Sausage Seller, are forms of the absolutely comic, and so are the inventions such as the town of Katagela. Where the significantly comic is reduc-
tive, and its laughter is that of deprecation, the absolutely comic is creative, and
its laughter is that of joy. It provides the inclusive vision which dwarfs all else to
its own greater glory.

Baudelaire's distinction is similar to that of Aristotle between lampoon and
true comedy, but he has carried it further, and his insight is of great importance
in understanding Aristophanes. For though Aristophanes abounds in the significantly comic, it is his creations of the absolutely comic which give his art its
main impetus and distinction. The hybrid grotesquerie of his heroes, and of numerous other images, is the stuff of the absolutely comic, and it is perhaps, this
aspect of his genius which prompted the ancient critics to find such grace,
charis, in his work. The bird-men, the market place of Dicaeopolis, the block
and tackle that hauls up Peace, all the basic fantasies in fact, are expressions of
joy, whatever else they may be, things comic in themselves to which the other
elements in the plays are subordinated. Even the most directly satiric elements,
like the ubiquitous Cleonymus, though significantly comic to begin with, tend in
the direction of the absolute and its chief touchstone, the grotesque; after many
transformations Cleonymus becomes a wonderful mythic tree of fat and fraud,
deciduously shedding its shields in the winter months.

Such poetry is in the mode of nonsense, and the structure of nonsense does
not point out the absurdity of something; it presents an image of absurdity itself.
In Dali's phrase, it systematizes confusion, and discredits the world of reality. Its
rules are its own, and though its content comes, as it must, from our everyday ex-

---

[4] See Wilam., "Wespen," p. 481, on comedy's mad disregard of place and time. Mazon's attempt, *Es-
sai*, p. 18, n. 1, to rationalize a comic *mise en scène* (*Acharnians*) seems to miss the point.

perience, the poem follows its own structural rules and achieves a new reality as the monstrous, lyrical, absolutely comic. The whole process is identical with Huizinga's view of play, as a magic circle within which a different reality exists by virtue of strict adherence to the given rules.[5] Within the circle seriously upheld assumptions, like the names which children give themselves in a game or the impersonations in a ritual, transform experience and enact a different, but more fully knowable world. The assumptions may be nonsense, but they create order. For nonsense is a kind of specially designed order. Thus, one may suggest a scale of comic techniques, all basic to Aristophanes: satire, wit, humor, nonsense. Satire denounces the world, wit penetrates it, humor accepts it, but nonsense transforms it. And it is the transforming function which distinguishes an art from a skill.

Nonsense is, therefore, the language of the absolutely comic, of monstrosity, and of the grotesque. The structural comparison made earlier between monstrosity and lyric suggests that nonsense might also be the language of lyric as well. It appears that what we call lyric differs from grotesquerie essentially only in possessing a content which we do not find laughable. Yet even that distinction can break down on occasion, in the poetry of Gertrude Stein, for example, and certainly in Aristophanes—witness, again, the Cleonymus tree, which has the charm of a tree for all its Cleonymosity, or the song of the frogs:

> Sing we on, if ever on sunny
> Days we hopped through the galingale
> And river weed, with melodious ploppings,
> Happy in song, or fleeing the rain,
> Sang our chorus, wet and wavering,
> Down in the depths, with bubbles a-popping,
> *Brekekekex, koax, koax.*[6]

Such delicate doggerel does not invite classification; it can be fairly called both lyrical and grotesque, and grotesque in strictest sense, if it be remembered that these are frogs who have died and are immortal, "swan-frogs" sacred to Apollo, the Muses, and Dionysus, and, as seen in the last chapter, somehow symbolic of Athenian salvation. For an inquiry into the nature of comic poetry, such a passage has the importance of a paradigm. The fullness of Aristophanes' genius seems concentrated in it.

But to return to the matter of fantasy and transformation: what the fantasy transforms is necessarily the familiar, for no mythical monster, however far-fetched, can be made except by imaginative recombination of known elements. This fact leads to a constant interplay of juxtaposed incongruities as the fantasy proceeds, picking up well-known bits of everyday experience and sweeping them into the general vortex; as each enters, one feels the jar of realism, as if one had suddenly run into a post. Sometimes these firm realities are completely transformed, like the Laurian owls in the *Birds*, where the distinction between a live owl and a silver coin is felicitously demolished by a metaphor.[7] At other times the realistic elements are left raw, so to speak, to produce a bumpiness in the texture, comic by virtue of incongruity, no doubt, but also poetic by virtue of

[5] Huizinga, *Homo Ludens, passim,* esp. chap. I.
[6] *Frogs* 242 f.
[7] *Birds* 1105 f.

juxtaposing two kinds of reality indispensable to the third reality, the poetic whole. Of this kind are the coarse and earthy interruptions of Euelpides as Peithetaerus develops his plan, or his notice of the fact that the nightingale's attractions are not exclusively musical. Here also belong the stolid replies of the Scythian policeman as Euripides tries to persuade him that Mnesilochus is really Andromeda; here belong the informers, oracle mongers, and other impostors who enter the heroic fantasy direct from the streets of Athens; here belong the bedbugs which nearly devour Strepsiades, together with certain unmentionable evidences of fear, outbursts of irrelevant abuse, Philocleon's chick-peas and chamber pot, and the blister which develops on Dionysus' posterior as he rows to the lilting rhythm of the frogs. Herein lies much of the delight, and perhaps one reason why the obscenities of Aristophanes, however broad, are so seldom offensive: they are an integral part of the "play with reality," the enormous, limitless game which the comic hero is playing. Once in a while, as with the old men in court in the *Acharnians,* these realisms strike a grim note, but for the most part their effect is pure hilarity, as when, in singing the joys of spring, the poet includes, along with the delight of swallows' song, the fact that two unlucky tragic poets have had their plays rejected, and invites the divine Muse to spit upon them generously, and come celebrate with him.[8]

Such juxtapositions, serious or comic, have a kind of analogue in the juxtapositions of fanciful and photographic in some of Dali's works. One painting is entitled, "Portrait of the Back of My Wife Contemplating Architectural Form." In the foreground Mrs. Dali sits, nude, and painted with the most direct representationalism: in the distance the outline of her form has become a fantastic palace of finely articulated arches, domes, and staircases. Beside her an uprooted dandelion puff comments on the transitoriness of all flesh, while a classic marble head follows her gaze toward the formal, architectural apotheosis of loving fancy. In another, rather haunting work attractively entitled "The Weaning of Furniture Nutrition," some perfectly recognizable boats are drawn up on a beach beside a woman with a large window in her back and some very oddly behaved pieces of furniture becoming other things. These are serious, even rather sombre works. But Dali can also be wonderfully humorous; one example is "Average Atmospherocephalic Bureaucrat in the Act of Milking a Cranial Harp." The title betrays the satire. The bureaucrat's head is produced in all directions in a cloudy, amorphous mass, from which a harplike shape depends with udderlike strings more liable to milking than to music. Below, the bureaucrat's left leg appears, almost photographically painted, and adorned by a dull garter upholding an unimaginative man's sock. Though Aristophanes' Demos is a more engaging figure, one feels that he has similar atmospherocephalic qualities, and is equally gartered to the earth. But in point of pure method, Peithetaerus' wings and the "wings" of the double Corcyrean whip are a fully comparable confrontation of the imaginative with the impact of familiarity.

One further example from Dali exhibits a truly Aristophanean delicacy and absurdity. This is the portrait of Harpo Marx. Harpo is represented quite in his own person, seated at his harp in a desert, and around him, listening, stand three giraffes, their necks wildly aflame. It is impossible not to feel the appropriateness of these fiery giraffes, more of whom are marching away on the horizon.[9] It

---

[8] *Peace* 796 f.
[9] Harpo is, presumably, "sympathetic" to giraffes; see Dali's discussion of "sympathy" and "antipathy" in objects, *Fifty Secrets,* pp. 48 f; for a reproduction, see Soby, *Salvador Dali,* p. 86.

is less easy to analyze them, but the effect of mingled tenderness and hilarity, of real and more than real, is entirely in the spirit of Aristophanes, and approaches some of his lyrical and grotesque visions of human creatures framed and magnified by subhuman and superhuman attributes. The transformation is before us, along with the thing transformed, and reality shimmers off into a new structure.

Another transforming mode is the double image. Even a common pun is a double image, and so in a way is parody. Aristophanes builds so much on puns and parodies that it would be impossible, not to say unnecessary, to analyze these aspects of the comic art; they have been extensively studied since antiquity, when the scholiasts devoted themselves to the dreary labor of explaining puns and parodies which, without their efforts, we would never have understood. Be it said here only that whereas a pun nearly always involves some kind of double imagery, some are very simple, while others have something akin to the lyrical, in possessing an added element which gives them a different structure and function. To use an illustration from the *Wasps*, described earlier: there is a simple double image pun in the slave's dream of Theorus: he dreamt that Theorus, a famous sycophant, had the head of a crow (*kórax*); *this word is then mispronounced to mean "flatterer"* (*kólax*), and the implication is little more than that the flatterer Theorus may go to the crows, Greek for going to the dogs.[10] Such a simple, perhaps feeble, drollery is indeed a double image, but it differs in kind from the city of Katagela, which is not only a double image of a Sicilian city and a verb of derisive mockery, but, as said earlier, a sort of invention, a birth, a new poetic reality. One might illustrate the difference in another way. In the matter of exaggeration, for instance, one may exaggerate simply, or one may compound the felony with elements from spheres outside the immediate thing exaggerated. Paul Bunyan's hot-cake griddle was so big that it had to be greased by a number of men skating over it with sides of bacon strapped to their shoes. A large griddle indeed! But what can we say to that great tree in the forest, which was so tall it took five men a week to see the top? This is more than exaggeration: it is a disturbing speculation on the nature of time and space.

Double imagery is a tour de force, a kind of trick; but it is a trick which hints at hidden, inner realities not always expressible otherwise. Its kinship with some of the methods of surrealism is clear from such a painting as Dali's *Spain*. Spain is represented as an apparently headless woman leaning on a chest of drawers in an autumnal landscape. As one looks at it, various elements in the landscape—furrows, people, a pair of knights tilting—slowly reform themselves into the woman's head and shoulders, and the head is deeply tragic in poise and expression. One would not wish to paraphrase the meaning, but clearly the same meaning could scarcely have been gained without the trick. Double imagery is a singularly delicate and light-touch method—though in the case of Aristophanes what it touches may not always be delicate. Again, it would be difficult to state exactly why, in his training years, Dali persisted in seeing a Gothic Madonna as a pair of scales; or why for a time he saw telephones as lobsters and lobsters as telephones; or precisely what aesthetic significance he found in poising a pair of raw pork chops on his wife's bare shoulders. Yet such insights are akin to some of Aristophanes' most basic impulses as a poet, involving, as they do, the juxtapositions and implied identities of disparate things in the light of ulterior, if inexpressible, realities.

---

[10] *Wasps* 42 f.

All this is, of course, the realization of metaphor, and Dali has called his own method of achieving it "paranoiac." He is using the term in a somewhat special sense, to indicate the mind's ability to fabricate reality out of images. He once wrote: "The double image may be extended, continuing the paranoiac advance, and then the presence of another dominant idea is enough to make a third image appear, and so on, until there is a number of images, limited only by the mind's degree of paranoiac capacity."[11] This statement aptly summarizes the way in which an Aristophanean fantasy proceeds—between the horns of a logical dilemma, along a new coordinate, and into the fecund irrealism of an invented world, where images breed images to the mind's capacity. If "paranoiac" seems an extreme word for it, still it is clearly a form of madness, and like paranoia it involves the hero's magnificent delusion of a triumphant self. Limitless in its intention, it can make use of everything with which it comes into contact. Such was the almost infinite sensuous and intellectual responsiveness of Aristophanes that the fantasy's ravenous hunger is fed to overflowing with constant images of all that the world contains, sometimes in clearly limned singleness, like the whispering elm, the shrewd Athenian corpse, the thieving slave girl; sometimes in great heaps and piles, like the bustle in the wartime shipyards, the rollicking lists of foods, the occupations of birdmad Athenians, or the iridescent images of countryside and sea. "I hate simplicity in all its forms," said Dali. There is certainly nothing simple about the art of Aristophanes.

If this whole view of the poet has any validity, we are bound to ask, finally, what its significance may be. Is Aristophanes merely leading us all into a paranoiac state by dramatizing the dreams of lunacy? Or does this elaborate effort have a higher purpose? We have repeatedly dismissed the idea that these extravaganzas conceal allegories implying political or moral reform. We must now confront the possibility that they are wish-fulfilling, purgative indulgences of the spirit's desire to defy law and transgress taboo. This is a popular theory today which owes its existence partly to the Aristotelian theory of catharsis, and partly to the Freudian doctrine of inhibition and sublimation. By this approach Aristophanean comedy would turn out to be, both in actual effect and subconscious purpose, a release, a discharge of certain drives of the libido, or ego, not otherwise to be satisfied amid the repressing society which surrounds it. Like the Roman Saturnalia, or the Medieval Season of Misrule, it would give the dog his day, and permit the safe renewal, for another year, of moral sanctions and custom-law.

There is something to be said for this view, but it does not provide a wholly satisfactory interpretation of Aristophanes. In the first place, like moral interpretations, it implies practicality of purpose and effect in the form of a psychotherapeutic purge, and there is no evidence for supposing comedy to have reduced the incidence of adultery, violence, or whatever by vicarious satisfaction. The taboo-smashing seems to have been enjoyable, but the cathartic function may be overestimated, especially for a society so open as that of late-fifth-century Athens, though it may have been efficacious for one reared under the ecclesiastical constraints of the Middle Ages. But more important, the cathartic view explains at most some of the content and not the form of Aristophanic comedy. There is an obvious relish in seeing a creditor get flogged instead of paid; we sympathize with illicit liaisons on the stage which might offend us in real life; violence, im-

[11] See Soby, *Salvador Dali*, p. 20.

proper language, and naked girls abound in Aristophanes. But mere vicarious satisfaction can be effected by a peep show, pornography, or the least artful of cartoons as well as, if not better than, by a developed work of art. The purgation theory misses the wholeness of Aristophanes, and therefore, in its partiality, misinterprets to a degree even the part upon which it is based.

There is, for instance, the matter of slapstick; in a way slapstick is one of the simplest and most basic ways of discharging suppressed desires. We do not know how much unwritten roughhousing took place in the actual performances of Aristophanes, but there are some scenes, usually beating scenes, which are quite clearly slapstick and little else: Strepsiades' creditors, the sycophant in the *Birds*, the burning of the Thinkery. These are ordinary, simple slapstick, and convey the usual sort of satisfaction. But there is also what one might call the "higher slapstick," which satisfies not just a suppressed desire, but something more like an intuition for the true nature of things. To illustrate: it is funny when anybody gets hit by a custard pie, though it is funnier if an alderman gets hit with a custard pie; but it is funniest of all when everybody gets hit with custard pie, from the offending wretch who caused the trouble, to the most innocent bystander, and especially the policeman who is trying to restore order. There is a superb example of this by Laurel and Hardy from the great period of slapstick movies. The timing and development are flawless, and not a pie, of the several thousand that are thrown, misses its mark, or some mark. By the end—though the scene does not seem to end, but to continue toward a glorious eternity—the total *mise en scène*, an everyday street corner, is draped, inundated, and festooned with the squashy viscosity of custard and cream; men, women, buildings, dogs, and automobiles are transfigured in a perfect apocalypse of pie. The feeling which overtakes the spectator of this rapturous scene is more than a vicarious satisfaction of individual desire; it is a feeling of sublime peace, of an access of knowledge which is true, of a revelation of the essence of things. Custard pie has become a way of life, and the world has been transformed by it. As always with a fully drawn monstrosity, that which is imaged is Absurdity itself. One well-thrown custard pie is a happy impiety; but if there are enough pies, the boundless swings into view, and the yearning which is satisfied is too deep and humane ever to be purged from the human psyche. It is the heroic longing, fulfilling its own metaphor of order, its own order, sprouting wings and deposing Zeus.

Now it is precisely this higher slapstick which Aristophanes is up to. There are no pies, to be sure, but there are other equally effective ways of achieving the purpose. For one of the secrets of good slapstick is its elaboration; sometimes this can be done by mere quantity, at other times a fiendishly careful and scientific preparation of the event brings off a sense of great accomplishment. Harpo Marx, for instance, on going to bed, punctiliously sets his alarm clock, puts a sledge hammer on the floor beside his bed, and goes to sleep. Eight hours later the alarm rings, Harpo takes the hammer, smashes the clock, and goes back to sleep. The delight here is in the elaboration of the act of smashing the clock. One might compare the scene in the *Acharnians* where, instead of simply driving off the informer with a whip, Dicaeopolis has him carefully packed up in a crate, upside down, and shipped off to Boeotia. An added pleasure lies in the fact that the informer who has come to denounce contraband has himself turned into an illegal commodity, quite properly sold in the free market of the hero. This scene is the higher slapstick, in that it effects a transformation.

Another fine scene comes in the *Frogs*, where the weighing of lines of poet-

ry in a scale involves a contrived, not to say labored, transformation of verses
into Aeschylean logs and Euripidean twigs. The scene itself, as a burlesque of the
Homeric *psychostasis*, somehow epitomizes the play's weighing of the meaning
of life and death, as Athens herself teeters in the fateful balances. If the scene is
not strictly slapstick in our sense, it is a physical rendering of the absurd for its
own sake, and looks to a meaning more poetic than purgative. Of the same kind
is the hoisting of Peace with the block and tackle. And yet, no individual scene
illustrates the point so well as any of the total conceptions. Each of Aristophanes'
invented worlds is a kind of higher slapstick, a gigantically elaborated violation
of the apparent way things are, in favor of the malleable absurdity of the comic
hero's remolding of them—or, as Dali would put it, "the tender, extravagant and
solitary paranoiac-critical camembert of time and space," the word camembert
here being Dali's private symbol for the ductile quality of reality.[12]

But in dealing with so individual an artist as Aristophanes, words like slapstick, or surrealism, do not absolutely fit; they can at best suggest the object and
methods of his art, and perhaps liberate criticism from subsuming its motives under some partial rubric, such as political satire, moral reform, or psychic purgation. Comic poetry is too large for that. There is only one answer to the question
of what end this comic poetry serves: it serves the same end as all poetry, as Dr.
Johnson said, "to expand the sensibilities." But that is an evasive answer, and one
might well counter with, "which sensibilities?" With his infinite range of awareness and expressiveness, there are few sensibilities that Aristophanes does not
reach, but peculiarly fundamental seems to be his transforming power, his ability to shift reality, unmake it and remake it before our eyes. Such tamperings are
always the business of poets, who serve our quest for reality by offering metaphors of it, extensions of knowability, constructs of the spirit in its wholeness.

The pleasure of tragedy, according to Aristotle, consists in its ability to present us with an action as a structured whole, like Robert Frost's "shapes against
chaos," for this gratifies the spirit's wish for wholeness, symmetry, and form.
Aristophanic comedy does likewise, and if the whole seems to be a different one,
it is nonetheless a product of the characteristically Greek conception of a hero,
the human individual who aspires to a godlike supremacy without losing his humanity. Since we have here the comic version of a hero, his structural essence
lies, as said, in that combination of animal, human, and divine attributes which
seem to have been the classical origins of the grotesque, a hybrid magic, providing a certain range of spirit, with some special keys to nature and a degree of
power over it. In addition, the comic hero's determining genius lies in *poneria*,
the craft and unrestrained, self-admiring pursuit of boundless life and power, a
quality which he exercises in the erection of a fantastic structure of the impossible and the absurd. Absurdity and structure, being mutually contradictory, of
course, meet not only in the mode of what we call nonsense; but once the structure is built, it becomes a bastion against the chaos of unknowable nature, and at
the same time, a natural and humane triumph. For human nature is both order
and chaos at once, and the comic hero embodies both its logic and its passionate
illogic. The comic hero fulfills his quest for wholeness by developing his nature
into a grotesque capable of matching and including the corresponding shapes of
absurdity, from Persian ambassadors and dung beetles to wings and Zeus. Only

---

[12] See Soby, *Salvador Dali*, p. 14. The quotation, describing limp watches, is from Dali's *The Conquest of the Irrational*; elsewhere Dali calls the limp watches masochistic symbols.

thus can he defeat confusion and assert life. To return to the modern Greek shadow plays, the lowly Karaghiozes and his counterego Alexander the Great are really one and the same on the deepest level of the hero's self. He is Aristotle's low character who masters all, and he does it by a wishful, even better, a willful tampering with reality.

Yet the hero's action is no common or small wish or will-fulfillment. The sense of human dignity runs high in Aristophanes, and he does not just invent substitute worlds where any petty psyche can revel in irrealism. Like the imagery in *Oedipus Rex*, of outer sight which is blindness and inner sight which is true, the upsetting of visible reality in Aristophanes implies another reality, a truth beyond the truth, so to speak, which is, in fact, the spirit's formulation of the way things are. This is a transfiguring function, and a metaphysical one. In the service of such a vision, it is right and truthful to pervert what meets the eye, to lavish every metaphorical resource on the effort to meet absurdity on its own terms, and to outdo it. Such poetry captures a psychic state not to purge it, but to exalt it; for the perception of absurdity, and the heroic realization that it must be manipulated to the greater clarity of the spirit, are among the truest actions which the spirit can perform. If the manipulations—the private peace treaties, the cities in the sky, the revivals from the dead—seem like nothing more than helpless dreams, we should recall that dreams are perfectly real experiences, and to dramatize them in poetry is to produce a structure of self-knowledge. This is not to say that any dreamer of a poet can truthfully create a dream world. But a poet of Aristophanes' sensitive and detailed knowledge of this life has a right, in his realism about this world, to create the reality of others.

To conclude, Aristophanes' comedy is the last ancient hymn to the spirit's victory over absurdity in its own terms; it presents no less of a triumph over external and apparent reality than does the revealing exaltation which follows upon the tragic hero's moment of final knowledge. All heroism discredits reality in favor of a vision involving divinity and the self. This vision is a counterimage of the things which are, and it is always the ardent self which contrives it. Heroes often seem self-centered, even selfish. But be it by the complicity of tragic self-sacrifice or the complexities of comic "selfmanship," the search is to find a truth which is viable. Truth of this kind is a "made" commodity, and cannot tolerate what is merely found or given; it needs heroism. The heroic nonsense of Aristophanes, whether by a delicate metaphor, a lame and obvious pun, or a resounding obscenity, strives to catch a counterimage, which then becomes the real. The Socrates, Cleon, and Euripides of Aristophanes are very much his own magnificent monsters and bugbears. But for him they are, like Nephelococcygia, the truth beyond the truth, not because they possess any factual being, but because they are the way they have to be in the created world of comic knowability. They are stuff of the absolutely comic, self-existent lyrics of broad laughter, absurdities designed to appall Absurdity's ownself. This could be done only by the poet whose loving concern for, and penetration of, the world could make a myth of it, the myth of the individual's smallness and greatness, hilarious but heroic; the poet who, with highhearted and shameless innocence, could commend his poetry to posterity:

> Keep my verses in your closet with the apples,
> So that all year long your clothes may smell of—wit.

The Saturnalian Pattern
in Shakespeare's Comedy[*]

C. L. Barber

MESSENGER *Your honour's players, hearing your amendment,*
   Are come to play a pleasant comedy....
BEGGAR   *... Is not a comonty a Christmas gambold or a tumbling trick?*
LADY   *No, my good lord; it is more pleasing stuff.*
BEGGAR   *What, household stuff?*
LADY   *It is a kind of history.*
BEGGAR   *Well, we'll see it. Come, madam wife, sit by my side and*
   let the world slip. We shall ne'er be younger.

   —Introduction to *The Taming of the Shrew*

Recent literature has accustomed us to the conscious use of mythical and ritual prototypes as a means of organizing the life of our time in the absence of a self-imposing tradition. *Ulysses* and *The Waste Land* expressed life in a modern city by representing it as recapitulating basic myths and rituals. Such creative ordering of experience by earlier archetypes has involved, in our time, a kind of explicit awareness of analogies not necessary in earlier periods, when traditional symbolic values came to the writer as a matter of course with his themes and materials. Psychology and ethnology have developed a corresponding set of generic names—"the Oedipus complex," "the fertility spirit," "the rebirth archetype." In earlier cultures such patterns were implicit in particular observances and did not need to be named. We have to name them, because for our cosmopolitan and relativistic mentality no particular symbolism is any longer self-evident. Our literary criticism is recognizing and describing in the writing of the past underlying configurations which earlier readers did not need to discriminate consciously. After the Nineteenth Century's preoccupation with the individual in society, with characters in drama, we are recovering, about art at least, an awareness of the creative function of form. To explore patterns which drama has in common with ritual is one way to develop this awareness, to see how the

[*] C. L. Barber, "The Saturnalian Pattern in Shakespeare's Comedy," *The Sewanee Review*, Vol. LIX, No. 4 (Autumn, 1951), pp. 593–611. The interpretation outlined in this essay is more fully developed in C. L. Barber's *Shakespeare's Festive Comedy: a Study of Dramatic Form and its Relation to Social Custom*, Princeton, 1959 (Meridian Paperback, 1962). [Footnotes in this selection have been renumbered.]

role precedes the character, how the larger rhythm of the whole action shapes and indeed creates the parts:

> O body swayed to music, O brightening glance,
> How can we know the dancer from the dance?

This essay will attempt to describe a major pattern in Shakespeare's gay comedy—the comedy before *Hamlet* and the problem plays. Proof by citation will not be feasible within the limits of an article; and I shall not be able to indicate in detail where my generalities do and do not apply to particular plays. But Shakespeare is so familiar that if I can express a notion of the dominant mode of organization of the comedy, the reader will be able to try it on the plays for himself. Shakespeare's gay comedy is fundamentally saturnalian rather than satiric. It dramatizes pleasure as release from normal limitations, and the judgments implicit in its humor primarily concern the relation between man and nature, not relations between social classes or types. The plays give form to feeling and knowledge by a movement which can be summarized in the formula: *through release to clarification.*

This pattern for organizing experience came to Shakespeare from many sources, both in social and artistic tradition. It appeared, for example, in the theatrical institution of clowning: the clown or Vice, when Shakespeare started to write, was a recognized anarchist who made aberration obvious by carrying release to absurd extremes. The cult of fools and folly, half social and half literary, embodied a similar polarization of experience. One could formulate the saturnalian pattern effectively by referring first to these traditions: indeed, Shakespeare's first completely masterful comic scenes were written for the clowns. I have chosen, however, first to approach the pattern of the gay plays by looking at them in relation to the social rituals of Elizabethan holidays. The festival occasion provides a paradigm for the organization of impulse and awareness not only of those comedies where Shakespeare drew largely and directly on holiday motifs, like *Love's Labour's Lost, A Midsummer Night's Dream,* and *Twelfth Night,* but also in plays where there is relatively little direct use of holiday, notably *As You Like It,* and *Henry IV.* The language that described festive occasions, or was used in them, provides a more adequate vocabulary than that of any other tradition for making explicit the "form in mirth" of the plays about pleasure. The attitudes adopted on holiday were archetypes in English Renaissance culture for the attitudes adopted about pleasure whenever people set out to have a good time.

We can get hold of the spirit of Elizabethan holidays because they had form. "Merry England" was merry chiefly by virtue of its community observances of periodic sports and feast days. Mirth took form in morris-dances, sword-dances, wassailings, mock ceremonies of summer kings and queens and of lords of misrule, mummings, disguisings, masques—and a bewildering variety of sports, games, shows and pageants improvised on traditional models. Such pastimes were a regular part of the celebration of a marriage, of the village wake, of Candlemas, Shrove Tuesday, Hocktide, Mayday, Whitsuntide, Midsummer-eve, Harvest-home, Hallow-e'en, and the twelve days of the Christmas season ending with Twelfth Night. Custom prescribed, more or less definitely, some ways of making merry at each occasion. The seasonal feasts were not, as now, rare curiosities to be observed by folklorists in remote villages, but landmarks framing the

cycle of the year. Shakespeare's casual references to the holidays always presume
that his audience is familiar with them:

> As fit as ten groats is for the hand of an attorney . . .
> as a pancake for Shrove Tuesday, a morris
> for May Day, as the nail to his hole. . . .

The whole society observed the holidays. Elizabeth's court, on occasion, went a-
maying; it always had a Midsummer bonfire, and kept the Christmas season
with high revels. So did the noble households. In the entertainments tendered
Elizabeth during her summer progresses, traditional festive observances were
developed in masque, pageant or play.[1]

Study of the historical process by which holiday came to be translated into
conscious art leads through the occasional literature produced for aristocratic entertainments. But my concern here is to describe the saturnalian pattern as it was
finally worked out in dramatic materials. For this purpose, connections of details
are less important than the correspondence between the whole comedy and the
whole festive occasion. The holiday archetypes provide a way of talking about
an underlying movement of feeling and awareness which is not adequately expressed by any one thing in the play, but is the play. At this level, one cannot say
just how far the analogies between ritual and art show an influence, and how far
they reflect the fact that a holiday occasion and a comedy are parallel manifestations of the same pattern in our culture, of a basic way that we can polarize our
human nature, moving through release to clarification.

I. Release and Clarification in the Idyllic Comedies

Release, in the idyllic comedies, is expressed by making the experience of the
whole play like that of a revel.

> Come, woo me, woo me; for now I am in a holiday humour, and like enough to con-
> sent.

Such holiday humour is often abetted by directly staging pastimes: dances,
songs, masques, plays extempore, etc. But the fundamental method is to shape
the loose narrative so that "events" put its persons in the position of festive celebrants: if they do not seek holiday it happens to them. A tyrant duke forces Rosalind into disguise: but her mock wooing with Orlando amounts to a Disguising,
with carnival freedom from the decorum of her identity and her sex. The misrule of Sir Toby is represented as personal idiosyncracy, but it follows the pattern of the Twelfth Night occasion; the flyting match of Benedict and Beatrice,
while appropriate to their special characters, suggests the customs of Easter
Smacks and Hocktide abuse between the sexes. Much of the poetry and wit,
however they may be occasioned by events, is controlled in the economy of the
whole play to promote the effect of a merry occasion where Nature reigns.

F. M. Cornford, in *The Origins of Attic Comedy*, points to invocation and

---

[1] The most authoritative and complete summary of court festivities is E. K. Chambers, *The Elizabethan Stage*, Oxford, 1923. Folk festivities of the Elizabethan period are treated with equal authority
in *The Medieval Stage*, Oxford, 1903. These two books, and especially the latter, contribute more
than any other work by recent scholars to enable one who is not a folklorist to look at Shakespeare's
drama from that point of view. Chambers himself, when he finally came to write about Shakespeare,
did little or nothing with this part of his immense knowledge.

abuse as the basic gestures of a nature worship behind Aristophanes' union of poetry and railing. The two gestures were still practiced in the "folly" of Elizabethan Maygame, harvest-home, or winter revel: invocation, for example, in the manifold spring garlanding customs, "gathering for Robin Hood"; abuse, in the customary license to flout and fleer at what on other days commanded respect. The same double way of achieving release appears in Shakespeare's festive plays. There the poetry about the pleasures of nature and the naturalness of pleasure serves to evoke beneficent natural impulses; and much of the wit, mocking the good housewife Fortune from her wheel, acts to free the spirit as does the ritual abuse of hostile spirits. A saturnalian attitude, assumed by a clear-cut gesture toward liberty, brings with it an accession of "wanton" vitality. In the terms of Freud's analysis of wit, the energy normally occupied in maintaining inhibition is freed for celebration. The holidays in actual observance were built around the enjoyment of vital pleasures: in the summer, love in out-of-door idleness; in the winter, within-doors warmth and food and drink. But the celebrants also got something for nothing from festive liberty—the vitality normally locked up in awe and respect. E. K. Chambers found among the visitation articles of Archbishop Grindal for the year 1576 instructions that the bishops determine

> whether the ministers and churchwardens have suffered any lord of misrule or summer lords and ladies, or any disguised persons, or others, in Christmas or at Maygames, or any morris dancers, or at any other times, to come unreverently into the church or churchyard, and there to dance, or play any unseemly parts, with scoffs, jests, wanton gestures, or ribald talk. . . .[2]

Shakespeare's gay comedy is closer to Aristophanes' than to any other great comic art because the matrix for its awareness of life is the form of feeling of such saturnalian occasions as these. Dicaeopolis, worsting pompous Lamachus in *The Acharnians* by invoking the tangible benefits of Bacchus and Aphrodite, acts the same festive part as Sir Toby baffling Malvolio's visitation by an appeal to cakes and ale.

The *clarification* achieved by the festive comedies is concomitant to the release they dramatize: a heightened awareness of the relation between man and "nature"—the nature celebrated on holiday. The process of translating festive experience into drama involved extending the sort of awareness traditionally associated with holiday, and also becoming conscious of holiday itself in a new way. The plays present a mockery of what is unnatural which gives scope and point to the sort of scoffs and jests shouted by dancers in the churchyard or in "the quaint mazes of the wanton green." And they include another, complementary mockery of what is merely natural, a humor which puts holiday in perspective with life as a whole.

The butts in the festive plays consistently exhibit their unnaturalness by being kill-joys. On an occasion "full of warm blood, of mirth," they are too preoccupied with perverse satisfactions like pride or greed to "let the world slip" and join the dance. Figures like Malvolio and Shylock embody the sort of kill-joy qualities which the disguised persons would project on any of Grindal's curates who would not suffer them to enter the churchyard. Craven or inadequate people appear, by virtue of the festive orientation, as would-be-revellers, comically inadequate to hear the chimes at midnight. Pleasure thus becomes the touch-

---

[2] *The Medieval Stage*, Vol. I, p. 181, note 2.

stone for judgment of what bars it or is incapable of it. And though in Shakespeare the judgment is usually responsible—valid we feel for everyday as well as
holiday—it is the whirligig of impulse that tries the characters. Behind the
laughter at the butts there is always a sense of solidarity about pleasure, a communion embracing the merrymakers in the play, and the audience, who have
gone on holiday in going to a comedy.

While perverse hostility to pleasure is a subject for aggressive festive abuse,
highflown idealism is critized too, by a benevolent ridicule which sees it is a not
unnatural attempt to be more than natural. It is unfortunate that Shakespeare's
gay plays have come to be known as "the romantic comedies," for they almost
always establish a humorous perspective about the vein of hyperbole they borrow from Renaissance romances. Wishful absolutes about love's finality, cultivated without reserve in conventional Arcadia, are made fun of by suggesting that
love is not a matter of life and death, but of springtime, the only pretty ring
time. The lover's conviction that he will love "for ever and a day" is seen as an
illusion born of heady feeling, a symptom of the festive moment:

> Say "a day" without the "ever". No, no, Orlando! Men are April when they woo,
> December when they wed. Maids are May when they are maids, but the sky
> changes when they are wives.

This sort of clarification about love, a recognition of the seasons, of nature's part
in man, need not qualify the intensity of feeling in the festive comedies: Rosalind when she says these lines is riding the full tide of her passionate gayety.
Where the conventional romances tried to express intensity by elaborating hyperbole according to a "pretty," pseudo-theological system, the comedies express
the power of love as a compelling rhythm in man and nature. So the term "romantic comedies" is misleading; "festive comedies" would be a better name.
Shakespeare, to be sure, does not always transform his romantic plot materials.
In the Claudio-Hero business in *Much Ado*, for example, the borrowed plot involved negative behavior on the basis of romantic absolutes. The caskets story in
The Merchant of Venice, again, is romantic narrative which, though handled
gayly and opulently, has not been given a festive orientation: Fortune, not Nature, is the reigning goddess. Normally, however, as in *Twelfth Night*, he radically alters the emphasis when he employs romantic materials. Events which in
his source control the mood, and are drawn out to exhibit extremity of devotion,
producing now pathos, now anxiety, now sentiment, are felt on the stage, in the
rhythm of stage time, as incidents controlled by a prevailing mood of revel.
What was sentimental extremity becomes impulsive extravagance. And judgment, not committed to systematic wishful distortion, can observe with Touchstone how

> We that are true lovers run into strange capers; but as all is mortal in nature, so is all
> nature in love mortal in folly.

To turn on passionate experience and identify it with the holiday moment,
as Rosalind does in insisting that the sky will change, puts the moment in perspective with life as a whole. Holiday, for the Elizabethan sensibility, implied a
contrast with "everyday," when brightness falls from the air. Occasions like
May-day and the Winter Revels, with their cult of natural vitality, were maintained within a civilization whose sad-brow view of life focused on the mortality
implicit in vitality. The tolerant disillusion of Anglican or Catholic culture al-

lowed nature to have its day, all the more headlong because it was only one day. But the release of that one day was understood to be a temporary license, a "misrule" which implied rule, so that the acceptance of nature was qualified. Holiday affirmations in praise of folly were limited by the underlying assumption that the natural in man is only one part of him, the part that will fade.

"How that a life was but a flower" was a two-sided theme: it was usually a gambit preceding "And therefore take the present time"; but it could also lead to the recognition that

> so from hour to hour, we ripe and ripe,
> And then, from hour to hour, we rot and rot . . .

The second emphasis was implicit in the first; which attitude toward nature predominated depended, not on alternative "philosophies," but on where you were within a rhythm. And because the rhythm is recognized in the comedies, sentimental falsification is not necessary in expressing the ripening moment. It is indeed the present mirth and laughter of the festive plays—the immediate experience they give of nature's beneficence—which reconciles feeling, without recourse to sentimentality or cynicism, to the knowledge they convey of nature's limitations.

In drawing the parallel between holiday and Shakespeare's comedy, it has been hard to avoid talking as though Shakespeare were a primitive who began with nothing but festival custom and invented a comedy to express it. Actually, of course, he started work with theatrical and literary resources already highly developed. This tradition was complex, and included folk themes and conventions along with the practice of classically trained innovators like Lyly, Kyd, and Marlowe. Shakespeare, though perfectly aware of unsophisticated forms like the morality and the jig, from the outset wrote plays which presented a narrative more or less in the round. In comedy, he began with cultivated models—Plautus for *The Comedy of Errors*, and literary romance for the *Two Gentlemen of Verona;* he worked out a consistently festive pattern for his comedy only after these preliminary experiments.

In his third early comedy, *Love's Labour's Lost*, instead of dramatizing a borrowed plot, he built his slight story around an elegant aristocratic entertainment. In doing so he sketched, in thin and overfanciful lines, the holiday sequence of release and clarification which comes into its own in *A Midsummer Night's Dream*. This much more serious play, his first comic masterpiece, has a crucial place in his development. To make a dramatic epithalamium, he expresses with full imaginative resonance the experience of the traditional summer holidays. He thus finds his way back to a native festival tradition remarkably similar to that behind Aristophanes at the start of the literary tradition of comedy. And in expressing the native holiday, he is in a position to use all the resources of a sophisticated dramatic art.

A combination of participation and detachment was necessary to express holiday pastimes as three-dimensional drama. In *A Midsummer Night's Dream*, the expressive significance of popular cult is kept, while its literal, magical significance is mocked. The lovers, like folk celebrants on the eve of May-day, "run gadding to the wood overnight." In the woods they take leave of judgment, immersed in irrational impulse under the influence of a Summer Lord and Lady who preside over the cleanly wantonness of nature. Oberon and Titania enter the great chamber to bring the blessings of fertility to the bridal couples, as country gods, half English and half Ovid, would bring their powers in tribute when Elizabeth was entertained, and as the group of folk celebrants making their quête would "bring in summer" to the village and manor house. Instead of garlands of flowers, Shakespeare uses poetry about "the rose distill'd" and "field-dew consecrate." The game is translated into dramatic and poetic action, the personifications of pageantry into dramatic personalities. But the magical events of holiday, when they are understood as human experience, are humorously recognized as mental, not actual happenings. The whole action in the magic wood is presented as a release of shaping fantasy which leads to clarification about the tricks of strong imagination. We watch a dream; but we are awake, thanks to a pervasive humor about the delusive tendency to take fancy literally, whether exhibited in love, or in superstition, or in Bottom's mechanical dramatics. It is part of the aristocratic urbanity of Titania, Oberon and their jester Puck to intimate in their own lines that they do not exist. So perfect an expression and understanding of folk cult was only possible in the moment when it was still in the blood but no longer in the brain.

Shakespeare never made another play from pastimes in the same direct fashion. But the pattern for feeling and awareness which he derived from the holiday occasion in *A Midsummer Night's Dream* becomes the dominant mode of organization in subsequent comedies until the period of the problem plays. The relation between his festive comedy and naïve folk games is amusingly reflected in the passage from *The Taming of the Shrew* which I have used as an epigraph. When the bemused tinker Sly is asked with mock ceremony whether he will hear a comedy to "frame your mind to mirth and merriment," his response reflects his ignorant notion that a comedy is some sort of holiday game— "a Christmas gambold or a tumbling trick." He is corrected with: "it is more pleasing stuff . . . a kind of history." Shakespeare is neither primitive nor primitivist; he enjoys making game of the inadequacy of Sly's folk notions of entertainment. But folk attitudes and motifs are still present, as a matter of course, in the dramatist's cultivated work; so that even Sly is not entirely off the mark about comedy. Though it is a kind of history, it is the kind that frames the mind to mirth. So it functions like a Christmas gambol. It often includes gambols, and even, in the case of *As You Like It*, a tumbling trick. Though Sly has never seen a comedy, his holiday mottoes show that he knows in what spirit to take it: "let the world slip;" "we shall ne're be younger." Prince Hal, in his festive youth, "Daff'd the world aside and bid it pass." Feste sings that "Youth's a stuff will not endure."

II. Release and Clarification in the Clowning and in *Henry IV*

The part of Shakespeare's earliest work where his mature patterns of comedy first appear clearly is, as I have suggested, the clowning. Although he did not find a satisfactory comic form for the whole play until *A Midsummer Night's Dream*, the clown's part is satisfactory from the outset. Here the theatrical conventions with which he started writing already provided a congenial saturnalian organization of experience, and Shakespeare at once began working out its larger implications. It was of course a practice, going back as far as the *Second Shepherd's Play*, for the clowns to present a burlesque version of actions performed seriously by their betters. Wagner's conjuring in *Dr. Faustus* is an obvious example. In the drama just before Shakespeare began writing, there are a great many parallels of this sort between the low comedy and the main action.[3] One suspects that they often resulted from the initiative of the clown performer; he was, as Sidney said, thrust in "by head and shoulders to play a part in majestical matters"—and the handiest part to play was a low take-off of what the high people were doing. Though Sidney objected that the procedure was "without deceny or decorum," such burlesque, when properly controlled, had an artistic logic which Shakespeare was quick to develop.

At the simplest level, the clowns were foils, as one of the aristocrats remarks in *Love's Labour's Lost:*

> 'Tis some policy
> To have one show worse than the King's and his company.

But burlesque could also have a positive effect, as a vehicle for expressing aberrant impulse and thought. When the aberration was made relevant to the main action, clowning could provide both release for impulses which run counter to decency and decorum, and the clarification about limits which comes from going beyond the limit. Shakespeare used this movement from release to clarification with masterful control in clown episodes, as early as *Henry VI, Part II*. The scenes of the Jack Cade rebellion in that history are an astonishingly consistent expression of anarchy by clowning: the popular rising is presented throughout as a saturnalia, ignorantly undertaken in earnest; Cade's motto is: "then are we in order when we are most out of order." In the early plays, the clown is usually represented as oblivious of what his burlesque implies. When he becomes the court fool, however, he can use his folly as a stalking horse, and his wit can express directly the function of his role as a dramatized commentary on the rest of the action.[4]

In creating Falstaff, Shakespeare fused the clown's part with that of a festive celebrant, a Lord of Misrule, and worked out the saturnalian implications of both traditions more drastically and more complexly than anywhere else. If in the idyllic plays the humor of perspective can be described as a looking outward from a reigning festive moment to the work-a-day world beyond, in the two parts of *Henry IV* the relation of comic and serious action can be described by saying that holiday is balanced against everyday and doomsday. The comedy expresses impulses and awareness excluded by the urgency and decorum of political life, so that the comic and serious strains are contrapuntal, each conveying the ironies limiting the other.

The issue, so far as it concerns Prince Hal, can be summarized quite adequately in our key terms. As the non-historical material came to Shakespeare in *The Famous Victories of Henry the Fifth,* the prince was cast in the traditional role of the prodigal son, while his disreputable companions functioned as tempters in the same general fashion as the Vice of the morality plays. At one level, Shakespeare keeps this pattern; but he shifts the emphasis away from simple moral terms. The issue, in his hands, is not whether Hal will be good or bad, but whether his holiday will become his everyday, whether the interregnum of a Lord of Misrule, delightful in its moment, will develop into the anarchic reign of

---

[3] William Empson discusses some of the effects achieved by such double plots in *English Pastoral,* New York, 1938.

[4] See C. L. Barber, "The Use of Comedy in *As You Like It*," *Philological Quarterly,* Vol. XXI, No. 4 (October, 1942).

a favorite dominating a dissolute king. Hal's secret, which he confides early to the audience, is that for him Falstaff is merely a pastime, to be dismissed in due course:

> If all the year were playing holidays
> To sport would be as tedious as to work.

The prince's sports, accordingly, express not dissoluteness but a fine excess of vitality—"as full of spirit as the month of May"—together with a capacity for looking at the world as though it were upside down. His energy is controlled by an inclusive awareness of the rhythm in which he is living: despite appearances, he will not make the mistake which undid Richard II, who lived saturnalia until it caught up with him in earnest and he became

> a mockery king of snow
> Standing before the sun of Bolingbroke. . . .

During the battle of Shrewsbury, when in Hotspur's phrase "Doomsday is near," Hal dismisses Falstaff with "What, is it a *time* to jest and dally now?"

But of course Falstaff is not so easily dismissed. Hal's prodigal's role can be summarized fairly adequately in terms of the holiday-everyday antithesis. But no formula derived from words current in Shakespeare's work is adequate for the whole effect produced by the dynamic interplay of serious statement and comic counter-statement in the drama as a whole. The more one reads the two *Henry IV* plays, the more one feels that Shakespeare was doing something with Falstaff which he could not summarize, which only the whole resources of his art could convey. His power of dramatic statement, in developing saturnalian comedy, had reached to primitive and fundamental modes of organizing experience for which general terms were not available in his culture.

It is here that our modern command of analogies between cultures can help—by providing a vocabulary to describe the pattern given dramatically by Shakespeare. We can read in Frazer how such figures as the Mardi Gras or Carnival first presided over a revel, then were tried, convicted of sins notorious in the village during the last year, and burned or buried to signify a new start. In other ceremonies described in *The Golden Bough*, mockery kings appear as recognizable substitutes for real kings, stand trial in their stead, and carry away the evils of their realms into exile or death. One such scapegoat figure, as remote as could be in space and time from Shakespeare, is the Tibetan King of the Years, who enjoyed, until very recently at least (if not even now), ten days' misrule during the annual holiday of Buddhist monks at Lhasa. At the climax of his ceremony, after doing what he liked while collecting bad luck by shaking a black yak's tail over the people, he mounted the temple steps and ridiculed the representative of the Grand Lama, proclaiming heresies like "What we perceive through the five senses is no illusion. All you teach is untrue." A few moments later, discredited by a cast of loaded dice, he was chased off to exile and possible death in the mountains.[5] One cannot help thinking of Falstaff's catechism on honor, spoken just before another valuation of honor is expressed in the elevated blank verse of a hero meeting death: "Can honor take away the grief of a wound? no . . . What is honor? a word. What is that word honor? What is that honor? air." And Hal's final expulsion of Falstaff, which so offended humanitarian nine-

---

[5] See James G. Frazer, *The Scapegoat*, London, 1914, pp. 218–223.

teenth-century critics, appears in the light of these analogies to carry out an impersonal pattern, not merely political but ritual in character. After the guilty reign of Bolingbroke, the prince is making a fresh start as the new king. At a level beneath the moral notions of a personal reform, we can see a non-logical process of purification by sacrifice—the sacrifice of Falstaff. The career of the old king, a successful usurper whose conduct of affairs has been skeptical and opportunistic, has cast doubt on the validity of the whole conception of a divinely ordained and chivalrous kingship to which Shakespeare and his society were committed. But the skeptical and opportunistic attitude has been projected also in Falstaff, who carries it to comically delightful and degraded extremes. In turning on Falstaff as a scapegoat, in the same way that the villagers turned on their Mardi Gras, the Prince can free himself of the sins, "the bad luck," of his father's reign, to become a king in whom chivalry and the sense of divine ordination are restored.[6]

The use of analogies like the scapegoat rituals can be misleading, or merely amusing, if the pattern is not rigorously related to the imaginative process in the play. Janet Spens, a student of Gilbert Murray's, wrote in 1916 a brief study which attempted to establish the presence of ritual patterns in Shakespeare's work.[7] Although she throws out some brilliant suggestions, her method for the most part consists of leaping intuitively from folklore to the plots of the plays, via the hypothesis of lost intermediary folk plays. But the plots, abstracted from the concrete emphasis of their dramatic realization, can be adjusted to square with an almost unlimited range of analogies. Miss Spens argues, for example, that because Antonio in *The Merchant of Venice* is enigmatically detached from personal concerns, and because in accepting the prospect of death at Shylock's hands he says "I am the tainted wether of the flock," he "is" the Scapegoat. To be sure, at a very general level there is a partial analogy to scapegoat rituals, since Antonio is undertaking to bear the consequence of Bassanio's ex-

---

[6] The old king, about to die, says

> all the soil of the achievement goes
> With me into the earth.

The new kings says

> My father hath gone wild into his grave;
> For in his tomb lie my affections. . . .

The image in these two passages of getting rid of sin or appetite by burying it appears again in Hal's final, menacing joke about Falstaff's belly, symbol of the misrule to which he has subscribed:

> Know the grave doth gape
> For thee thrice wider than for other men.

But an extended treatment is necessary to show how the scapegoat pattern is concretely symbolized. Shakespeare's culture did not afford general terms of the sacrificial part of it, so that there are no summary passages for quotation. L. C. Knights, in discussing *Henry IV, Part I* in *Determinations* (ed. F. R. Leavis, London, 1934), acutely explored a number of imaginative connections between Falstaff's counterfeiting and the king's. He concludes that Falstaff, himself corrupt, completely undercuts irrational honor in Hotspur and hollow majesty in Bolingbroke, so that the play is a drastic satire on the institutions of war and government. "Thus ever did rebellion find rebuke" is to be taken with ironic scorn by the audience. This is an anachronistic, philosophical-anarchist interpretation which Shakespeare's heroic lines simply cannot admit. But the only way to avoid it, once one has faced the fact that Falstaff's role acts on the historical part, is to recognize that in the irrational rhythm of the whole action, misrule works to consolidate rule.

[7] *An Essay on Shakespeare's Relation to Tradition*. Oxford, 1916.

travagance; and perhaps the pound of flesh motif goes back ultimately, through the tangle of legend and story tradition, to some such ceremonial. But there is no controlling such analogies if we go after them by catching at fragments of narrative; and one can understand, on that basis, the impulse to give up the whole approach as hopelessly capricious.

The case is altered, however, if attention is focused, not on this or that group of people in this or that story, but on the roles the persons are given in the play. When we are concerned to describe dramatic form—the rhythm of feeling and awareness in the audience which is focused through complementary roles in the fable and implemented by concrete patterns of language and gesture—then the form of rituals is relevant to the form of the plays as a parallel expression of the same kind of organization of experience. Shakespeare arrived at Falstaff's speech on honor, which has a function so extra-ordinarily similar to the heretical speech of the King of the Years, by working out the implications of the clown's established role—in the directions suggested by the saturnalian customs and sensibility of his time. The pattern of all clowning involves, moment by moment, the same movement from participation to rejection that appears at large in scapegoat ritual: the clown expresses our aberrant impulses for us; but he undercuts himself, or is undercut from outside, so that we can divert sympathy to laughter. In *Henry IV* Shakespeare developed a scapegoat's role for Falstaff which writes this movement large. In other words, Falstaff's part in the story is a manifestation of the meaning of the saturnalian form itself.

The sort of interpretation I have proposed in outline here does not focus on the way the comedies imitate characteristics of actual men and manners; but this neglect of the social observation in the plays does not imply that the way they handle social materials is unimportant. Comedy is not, obviously enough, the same thing as ritual; if it were, it would not perform its function. To express the underlying rhythm his comedy had in common with holiday, Shakespeare did not simply stage mummings; he found in the social life of his time the stuff for "a kind of history." We can see in the Saint George plays how cryptic and arbitrary action derived from ritual becomes when it is merely a fossil remnant. In a self-conscious culture, the heritage of cult is kept alive by art which makes it relevant as a mode of perception and expression. The artist gives the ritual pattern aesthetic actuality by discovering expressions of it in the fragmentary and incomplete gestures of daily life.[8] He fulfills these gestures by making them moments in the complete action which is the art form. The form gives life meaning.

---

[8] One can watch this process, carried out with a modern consciousness of psychological and historical implications of artistic form, in the Circe episode of *Ulysses*. Joyce uses a version of the saturnalian pattern, though what is released is often so shameful by everyday standards that amusement converts to shock or pathos. He casts Bloom as a clown and dramatizes the aberrant motives latent in his responses during the past day by having him act out a series of scapegoat roles. Exemplars of the pattern taken from contemporary life are syncretized with archetypes as diverse as the hunting of the wren on St. Stephen's Day and the sacrifice of the Messiah. See in particular pages 469 to 499 (Modern Library edition), where Joyce merges an astonishing variety of temporary king ceremonials with modern equivalents, to provide a social correlative for an upsurge in Bloom of libidinal egotism followed by anxiety and counterwishes for punishment.

Molière and Farce[*]

Gustave Lanson

We are so used to speaking piously of Molière, we pay such respectful attention to his maddest pranks as though they were serious and full of deep meaning, that when one of his contemporaries tells us that he is "the first jester of France,"[1] or that he is the heir of Scaramouche, this inadequate praise seems to us to be an insult. We grow angry, we shrug our shoulders with pity, when we read in some obscure satire that our great Molière studied the role of a quack and pleaded for the part, or that his plays drew upon manuscripts that he bought from Prosper, the mountebank Braquette's fool, or from Guillot-Gorju's widow.

We prefer to ascribe these remarks to pure malice and mad envy. It is true that critics quickly set aside the stories of buying manuscripts—an easy way to deny the talent of an author whose success cannot be denied; and it would be imprudent to accept as historical truth the account of the relationship between Molière and the quack-doctor.

But there is some truth in every legend. And if these malicious stories were complete lies, they would be too idiotic to be dangerous. Can Molière be a jester, an author of farce, a monkey at play, a plagiarist in his plays? These malicious rumors would have no effect if the public did not feel an affinity between Molière's character and that of farce; and this affinity is the basis for slander and calumny.

But what do we do, we who scorn the Somaizes and the *Hypochondriac Elomire (Elomire hypocondre)* and all such miserable gossip? Tuesdays at the Comédie-Française there is ice in the air when slaps, blows, and kicks are distributed on the face, back, and other parts of the anatomies of the Sganarelles and Gérontes, when squirts of liquid pursue a frightened clown, when grotesque and outrageous figures deliver themselves of smutty stories that seem "to be picked up in the gutters of les Halles." We show frozen faces, frowns of disdain; it would take very little to make our fashionable audience say, "This Molière is fit for the fair!"

Our critics do their utmost to separate these low and coarse aspects from the delicate and refined parts. They manufacture divisions and definitions— comedy of character, comedy of manners, farce—in order to isolate the profound masterpieces, and to prevent the trivial antics, "through the contagiousness of

---

[*] Gustave Lanson, "Molière and Farce," Ruby Cohn, tr., *Tulane Drama Review*, Vol. 8, No. 2 (Winter, 1963), pp. 133–154. Reprinted by the permission of the translator and *Tulane Drama Review*.
[1] The phrase in French is "le premier farceur de France." It is difficult to translate, meaning at once "the greatest creator of farce in France" and "the greatest farce actor in France."—*Translator's note.*

their image," from soiling the noble and pure conception of comic genius given to us by *The Misanthrope* and *Tartuffe*. They explain to us that blows, pranks, and slapstick are an easily detachable trimming, that Molière descended so low to attract a large audience, to make a living for his company, and to enable himself to write and perform the lofty works that did not make money. We can, of course, prefer to believe that it was in spite of himself, forcing himself, that he created all these little scenes and plays, low and trivial if you like, but spontaneous and bursting with verve.

Have we, who believe ourselves so free in our taste, made much progress since Boileau wrote:

> Molière might have won the prize for his writing if he had been less popular in his instructive plays, if he had not made his characters grimace, abandoning the pleasant and refined for the slapstick, combining Tabarin and Terence; I do not recognize the author of *The Misanthrope* in the ridiculous sack enveloping Scapin.

Actually, the poet's friend saw less clearly than his enemies. Molière would not be Molière if he were not "a good jester."

I do not want to enumerate all the farcical effects that fill Molière's comedies, nor to persuade people to take pleasure or delight in them; one does not laugh when one wishes, or take delight through demonstrable proof. Nor do I wish to pause to discover whether it is easy to separate farce from high comedy in Molière, or whether the effects, words, and techniques of farce lie in such scenes as the Miser catching his own arm to stop himself, or pretending to be dead, or obstinately blowing out a candle as obstinately relit by Maître Jacques. In *Learned Ladies (Femmes Savants)* Philaminte is played by a man, by that same Hubert who played Mme. Jourdain; there is that lout of a viscount, in the pure and noble *Misanthrope*, spitting in a well to make circles in the water, and the frightened valet seeking a letter in all his pockets; in the serious and tragic *Tartuffe*, the husband under the table while the hypocrite courts his wife. One can scarcely deny that farce is everywhere in Molière, and a little analysis discovers it even in works where it would seem absurd to look for it.

I do not say this to denigrate Molière's genius, but to understand it. The trouble with the disgust of refined people and the distinctions of critics, is that they cut Molière off from reality, leaving him in the void, separated from his ancestors and from the popular ground in which his comedy is rooted.

This comedy is very rich and complex: like all great geniuses, Molière was a big profiteer, for even in literature, nothing is produced from nothing. He made use of Latin, French, Italian, and Spanish comedy, Italian and French farce, Italian and French fiction, and just about everything in existence in the domain of comic, satiric, and moral literature, whether in dramatic form or not. But these materials, which he took from everywhere, slipped into a form and were assimilated into a pattern; where did this form and this pattern come from? They could come from only two sources, the only kinds of comic drama that then existed: literary comedy derived from Latin through Italian Renaissance comedy, and popular comedy or farce.

And between these two, one cannot possibly hesitate. Farce is at the root of all Molière's comedy, even in its highest forms, the comedy of manners and comedy of character. That is Molière's springboard: upon the trunk of farce was grafted everything his superior genius invented through an original vision of life, every seriousness and profundity his robust and free mind introduced into these hilarious images of the ridiculous. And it is by the cultivation, by the transformation—extraordinary, if you like—of farce that Molière came to those masterpieces that seem furthest from farce.

Let us imagine the dramatic education that Molière might have received in Paris under Louis XIII, where he was born and brought up. Literary historians scarcely see anything but the literary comedy of the intellectuals, of the coteries and the Academy—the comedy we still read. They scarcely mention farce, of which a very few rare and coarse examples survive. But in the first half of the seventeenth century farce delighted both the masses and the middle classes. It was everywhere: on makeshift stages on the Pont-Neuf, starring Tabarin, Descomes (who went under the title "Baron of Scratchfat") and their successors; it was at the Fair of St. Germain; it was at the Hotel de Bourgogne following the main play, a tragedy, tragi-comedy, or comedy. It was farce that guaranteed box-office receipts, attracting to the theatre merchants from Rue St-Denis, clerks, scholars, and lackeys.[2] It was farce that made actors famous; until about 1630, until the time of Bellerose and Mondory, we have no specific information about the talent of any actor, except in farce.

The farces played in Paris under Louis XIII were no longer those of the French tradition that flourished in the fifteenth and sixteenth centuries, although those little plays in a few scenes, with rudimentary or no action, in octosyllabic couplets, had not disappeared. A certain number of them were published in Paris, Lyons, and Troyes between 1610 and 1635; certainly they were published only because they were played. In the provinces this was still a living form, and in 1659 La Fontaine wrote and played in a farce: the circumstances of composition and performance, subject, tone, length, octosyllabic couplets all show that *The Mockers of Handsome Richard (Rieurs De Beau Richard)* is a farce, although it was called a ballet.

But in Paris Italian farce had replaced French farce. The success of the *commedia dell'arte* during the reign of Charles IX is well known; the dialogue was governed by a supple, loose plot and by rigid comic types or *masks*,[3] Pantaloon, the Doctor, the Captain, Brighella, Harlequin, etc., whose moods, characteristics, and poses the actors kept in all plays, in every situation. From the time of the success of *Gelosi* (in the reigns of Henri III, Henri IV, and Louis XIII), Italian actors had frequently returned to France, and were always appreciated for their vivacity and inventiveness, and for the expressive originality of their *masks*, which were enriched with new traits from one company to the next, one actor to the next. The valets above all developed into various charming types: Scapin and Trivelin were added to Brighelle and Harlequin, and, finally, the famous Scaramouche. During his lifetime, each actor had exclusive use of the *mask* that he had modified or created.

French players of farce worked on this popular model. This was evident among the performers on the Pont-Neuf about 1620. If the one extant farce of Descombes, *The Hunchbacks (les Bossus)* is based on an old French *fabliau*, it nevertheless follows Italian custom in that prose replaces verse in the dialogue of

---

[2] "If comedy were not seasoned with this accessory (farce), it would be a meat without sauce, and a bread without flour." (Guillot-Gorju, *Apology*, 1634).

[3] For convenience, I shall designate as masks stock types of the *commedia dell'arte* and their French counterparts. In italics, *mask* will have this meaning, in Roman type, mask will have its usual meaning of face-covering.

Patelin and Cornette. In the four extant farces of Tabarin, we also find prose and Italian plots; lovers with designs on the wife or daughter of a neighbor, tricks and misunderstandings serving or crossing these designs, letters inadvertently delivered to husbands, disguises—not to mention the famous sack in which the old man or captain is beaten. In these plots stock characters figure: old Piphagne and old Lucas, both married and both libertine, Captain Rodomont, an Isabelle who is a malicious young wife or maiden, and finally Tabarin, the tricky valet, and his wife Francisquine.[4] Antoine Girard, brother of the charlatan Mondor, picked up this Italian stock character of Tabarin, and marked it with originality. The Tabarin-Francisquine couple is a marriage of the theatre; they are married by farce. In life, Antoine Girard married Vittoria Bianca in Rome, and a certain Anne Begot played the *mask* of Francisquine.

Towards 1630 and 1632, we find similar shows at the Hotel de Bourgogne, prose farces with sketchy plots: the valet who is supposed to watch his master's daughter, but delivers her lover's messages while he makes off with his gifts, or the valet helping his amorous master seduce the wife of an old bourgeois.[5] Their Italian origin is betrayed by the way in which the valet directs the action.

But what appears most clearly is the way the acting company was formed to play farce, in the Italian manner: each actor had his *mask*, his stock type, the same name every time he played. And that is why the actors of the Hotel de Bourgogne had three names: a real name, a name for the theatre, and a name for farce: Robert Guérin, also la Fleur, also *Gros-Guillaume;* Henri Le Grand, also Belleville, also *Turlupin;* Hughes Guéru, also Fléchelles, also *Gaultier-Garguille*. The last name, the name from farce, is the *mask*. The actors use this name in their roles, it is the name that designates the type.

There are two valets. Gros-Guillaume, "covered with flour, like a miller," red cap, white blouse, and trousers with broad red stripes, a huge stomach circled with a hoop and emphasized by two belts that support it from above and below, underneath the blouse: this is the drunken, good-natured valet; he has a "visible naïveté," "a way of talking grandiloquent nonsense," and "a funny face." In contrast is Turlupin, masked, in about the same costume as Brighella, a clever valet, a rogue and wit.

Then there are the old men, husbands or fathers, and ridiculous lovers: Gaultier-Garguille, tall and thin, masked, white-haired with round glasses, black doublet with red sleeves, skull-cap, black shoes and stockings, inkstand,[6] game-pouch and belt, stick in his hand. This is the Italian doctor, Frenchified into a lawyer. He is jealous, greedy and lascivious. His successor was Guillot-Gorju, summoned from a company in the country. This *mask* was the creation of an actor who had studied medicine, and introduced into his role a much-appreciated imitation of the jargon and ridiculous ways of doctors; his specialty was to exaggerate these. Boniface, another old man, was a merchant, sometimes a Doctor or Pedant. Lady Perrine (certainly a man) played the wife of Gaultier-Garguille, who fought with him and was seduced by Horace (*mask* of Bellerose) with the help of Turlupin.

---

[4] In one farce Francisquine is Lucas' wife. She is a vigorous gossip of the people, but honest.

[5] The Italian provenance is evident in the fact that the old *Parisian* does business with India, and intends to leave on one of his ships: here we can recognize the Venetian Pantaloon.

[6] In *The Testament* that humorous author makes him write, Gaultier-Garguille wills his dagger with his game-pouch: in the drawing of Guillaumot, it is impossible to see in this "dagger" anything but a writer's inkstand.

Terrible Captain Fracasse, mixing the rodomontades of the Spaniard from Naples (recalling the country from which he came), with the braggadocio of the Gascon (which was the living model in France); Alison, *mask* of an old nurse or gossip, played by a man; and Florentine, the lady in love, completed the company. About this same time, other less famous types appeared: a Doctor Fabrice, a lady Gigogne, a Gringalet (which seems to be a *mask* played by various actors in the first half of the century), Goguelu, a kind of scrounger, whom a contemporary print shows going to a picnic, carrying in one hand his plate, and behind his back in a basket his whole family, wife, children, dog and cat who will devour much more than he contributes—it has been claimed that he replaced Gros-Guillaume.

As we know it, this company of the Hotel de Bourgogne was the counterpart of Italian companies. But the French tradition did not completely disappear; it was blended with the foreign inspiration. Side by side with the actors masked in the Italian fashion we find the white-face of the French tradition: Turlupin has a mask, but Gros-Guillaume is in white-face.[7] Side by side with Italian plots, we see simple dialogues, without a shadow of plot, such as in the two-character farces of Turlupin and Gros-Guillaume—Turlupin the husband arguing with Gros-Guillaume, his wife. In spite of the prose and improvisation, nothing could be more firmly in the French tradition.

Mondory, who founded a rival company in Paris, scorned farce and did not produce any; he wished to dedicate his talent and his theatre to regular and literary plays which the middle classes and ladies could enjoy. Nevertheless, in order to live, he had to introduce farce into his theatre. We know several characters of Marais' farce: Tibaut Garray "with his puffed up mask and pygmy size," trying to compete with Gaultier-Garguille, the valet Filipin, but above all Captain Matamore, the Bellemore's creation who eclipsed Captain Fracasse of the rival company, and Jodelet, "the naïve one in white-face," long, thin, speaking through his nose. For fifty years, in many theatres, without tiring his public, Julien de L'Espy presented this *mask* of a valet who was a foolish and insolent milksop.

This is what the ten- or twelve-year-old Poquelin might have seen if, as tradition has it, his grandfather took him to the theatre.

The vogue of farce, and above all of its *masks*, was such that more than one author introduced the best-known actors of farce into his plays, keeping their names and stock types. Du Ryer put Gros-Guillaume into his *Harvest of Surène;* Alison was the main character in a five-act comedy; Corneille and others put Captain Matamore's swashbuckling into high style; and the *mask* of Jodelet gave its name to several comedies by Scarron and his contemporaries.

Nevertheless, farce tended to disappear by the middle of the century. Literary comedy absorbed it and smothered it. In the long run it probably was the victim of the middle class and the ladies. Mme. de Rambouillet, says Tallemant, who blamed her for it, could not listen to an obscene word; and farce put precious ears to a cruel test. Corneille, Rotrou, and other polite writers introduced, instead of farce, a witty and respectable comedy which, even in the daring plays of Scarron, did not disgust the refined and fashionable world.

Although abolished in Paris (except for Jodelet, who played at the Marais)

---

[7] Clémont Marot, *Epitaph for Jean de Serres, excellent actor in farce:* ". . . When he came on stage, with a dirty shirt, and his forehead, cheek, and nostril covered with flour . . . "

farce lasted in the provinces, in country companies, and above all in the Béjart company of Molière. When they arrived in Paris in 1658, they resembled the actors who played twenty-five years earlier in farce at the Hotel de Bourgogne. Each actor of the company had his fixed *mask*, name, and character. For old men, there were the Doctor and Gorgibus. For valets, there was first of all Gros-René or the Painted One, meaning the "floured one," with his white face, his big belly, his naïveté (for he is a "big round man in every way"), his drunkenness which resurrected Gros-Guillaume, his philosophical nonsense, his double-talk of doctrine. Besides Gros-René, there were Mascarille and Sganarelle, two masks composed and played successively by the chief of the company.

After playing *Nicomede* before the king at the Louvre on October 24, 1658, Molière requested his Majesty's permission to play "one of these little entertainments which had made his reputation and which amused the provinces"; and he gave *The Amorous Doctor (le Docteur amoureux).* This is a *farce*, but since farce was no longer fashionable, Molière dared not use the word, and he employed the more elegant word *entertainment.* "Since for a long time these little comedies were not mentioned, the invention seemed new."[8]

Thus, as author and actor, it is in farce that Molière was first revealed to Louis XIV and the Parisian public. Between the Hotel and the Marais, the originality of his company lay in the resurrection of this genre. He revived the tradition of Gros-Guillaume, Gaultier-Garguille, and Turlupin; isn't this the grain of truth in the absurd accusation that he bought the manuscripts of Guillot-Gorju?

Moreover, when he offered his own inimitable novelty to Paris, it was not high comedy in the manner of *The Fool (l'Étourdie)* or *The Liar (le Menteur),* but farce. For how else can we designate *The High-Browed Ladies (Les Précieuses Ridicules)*? In publishing it, the author called it a comedy, and we reject the word *farce* through respect to him. But never mind the label; let us look at the play. First of all, there are three *masks*, characters straight from the *commedia dell'arte,* already presented to the public with their names and comic faces: Gorgibus, Mascarille, Jodelet. The other characters are nameless; they keep the names of the actors who play them, La Grange, Du Croisy, and also Madelon, Cathos, Marotte; for it is probable that "Madelon" is Madeleine Béjart, "Cathos," Catherine du Rosé (Mlle. de Brie), "Marotte," Marotte Beaupré. Is this the way of literary comedy? No more than prose, which was so rare in seventeenth-century comedy before Molière—and the few exceptions were closely linked to farce.

What is the fundamental comic idea upon which the satire is built, the characters of Mascarille Marquis and Jodelet Viscount? We have already seen Gros-Guillaume as the wife of Turlupin, and the improvised Italian comedy will show Scaramouche as a hermit, Harlequin as a wardrobe-keeper of the Palace, Colombine as a lawyer; can we not then see the quality of Molière's scenario?

Old Jodelet rushed to join this young company that was reviving the tradition he alone maintained, and Molière rushed to welcome him; is it mere deference to a friend that he allowed him to invent the slapstick climax of being stripped of many jackets? Is Mascarille of a different quality from Jodelet? Like Turlupin before Gros-Guillaume, a masked Mascarille stands before Jodelet with his floured face; and here are the entrance and costume of the character:

[8] La Grange, in his preface to the 1682 edition of Molière. But La Grange was mistaken; there was still Jodelet, but Jodelet alone.

Imagine, Madame, his wig was so big that it swept the floor every time he bowed, and his hat was so small, that one could easily see that the marquis carried it much more often in his hand than on his head; his lapel could be called a fair-sized dressing-gown, and his canions seemed to be made only to serve as hiding-places for children playing hide-the-haversack; in truth, Madame, I do not believe that the tents of the young Massagetes could be more spacious than these respectable canions. A torch of elegant sayings came from his pocket as from a horn of plenty, and his shoes were so covered with ribbons that I cannot tell you whether they were made of Russian, English, or Morroccan leather; what I do know is that they were at least six inches high, and I was most anxious to know how such high, fine heels could carry the marquis and his ribbons, his canions, and powder.[9]

Doesn't this quotation indicate the tone of the part? And isn't the character taken right from farce?

Everybody knows how close Molière's acting was to that of Italian farce, how he admired Scaramouche with whom he shared the applause of the Petit-Bourbon. Everybody knows how his enemies condemned his grimaces, contortions, and poses, and that this meant that Molière had adopted the expressive gestures, the vivid mimicry of the Italians. But does it follow that Molière the author had the same teachers as Molière the actor, that his written work had the same source as his acting style?

First of all, it must be said that a certain way of acting imposes a certain style when the author is an actor and is writing what he will play. Before Molière, literary comedy, like tragedy, neither saw nor displayed bodies; it expressed manners by abstract discourse, by fine analysis or lively, stylized images, and it underlined thought only by the accent of the voice, at most supported by an oratorical gesture; before Molière, a comic part was merely the voice of a witty or foolish spirit. In Molière, on the other hand, the inner feeling thrusting itself outward sets the entire man into motion, and his discourse is accompanied by a grimace, a pose, which interprets and complements it. There is no room for literary development, for words that do not include a revealing gesture of character. The impersonal naïveté of Molière's style is closely linked to his acting; because he clung to the greatest economy of words in order to give an animated picture of the original, he had neither the time nor the desire to show off his wit.

Let us look at Molière's development. In the provinces he began with farce: *Gros-René the Scholar (Gros-René Écolier), The Dowdy One (le Fagoteux), Gorgibus in the Sack (Gorgibus dans le Sac), The Amorous Doctor, The Jealousy of the Painted One (la Jalousie du Barbouillé)*: one act in prose, which was still the form in *The High-Browed Ladies*, not to mention the *masks* or stock types. After *The High-Browed Ladies* came *Sganarelle*, also a farce in both subject and tone, and again in one act, but this time in verse. Then Molière tried the unfortunate experiment of *Don Garcie*, a literary comedy in verse in five acts, with Italian plot and witty dialogue; then he went back to one act plays: then he moved on, in verse, to three acts, which was usual in the *commedia dell'arte: School for Husbands (l'École des Maris)* and *The Angry Ones (les Fâcheux)*. Again he tried the full form of five acts with *School for Wives (l'École des Femmes)*. After these attempts, he grew through his talent and craftsmanship, not by mechanical observation of conventions.

[9] Mlle. Desjardins, *Story of the Farce of the Precieuses*. Nor was she an enemy; on the contrary.

Molière followed two paths: that of literary comedy in *The Fool, The Chagrin (le Dépit), Don Garcie*, and that of farce in *The Dowdy One* and, analogously, *The High-Browed Ladies* and *Sganarelle*. In which will we finally find those superior manifestations of Molière's comic genius, comedy of manners and comedy of character? Does *The Fool* promise more than a Rotrou or a Regnard? But is not *The High-Browed Ladies* high comedy? Is it astonishing that the man who created the dialogue for Mascarille and Madelon created that used by the miser or the hypocrite? Is it astonishing that the man who revealed the imagination of Sganarelle created Arnolphe and his terror, or Chrysale and his wrath?

One might raise this objection: "But that is the point, *The High-Browed Ladies* and *Sganarelle* still preserve elements of farce but are already comedy. Molière's growth consists in a double effort, in which he progressively reduced, if he did not entirely eliminate, farce, while he developed the elements of true comedy which are still hidden under farce, even in *The High-Browed Ladies*. He produced his masterpieces when he just about got rid of farce."

But here we must distinguish between two things to avoid confusion: the scenic effects of farce and the esthetic principle of farce. The effects of farce are coarse, and that is explained by the public it seeks. It is certain that these effects are rare in Molière's masterpieces, for he evokes laughter by more subtle methods than blows of the stick and coarse caricature. But that is only the exterior, the envelope of farce. Although the words may seem pretentious, farce is a dramatic genre that has its own esthetic, its method of invention. And it is this esthetic of farce, this method of invention, a certain original fashion of dealing with the stuff of life, that I am claiming to find even in Molière's masterpieces.

If there was one part of his art that Molière neglected or scorned, it was putting together a plot, manipulating its threads to lead the spectator to the dénouement by every sort of detour and surprise. Molière's art was never one to entangle in order to disentangle, to give new impetus to an action whose momentum seems exhausted, to scramble it up the moment it seems clear, and to unscramble it suddenly by a facile trick just when it seems insoluble. He is just a little boy in this domain, compared to Beaumarchais, Scribe, Sardou, or even Corneille. Must we refer to *School for Wives*, clumsily built on an overlong quidproquo and disentagled by a badly prepared recognition; *The Learned Ladies (les Femmes Savantes)* and the naïve and convenient invention of false letters; *Tartuffe* and the miracle of the king's intervention—a deus ex machina whatever one says; *The Miser* and its cascade of recognitions that permits marriages needed by the comedy without sacrificing anything of Harpagon's character; *George Dandin* which has no dénouement, leaving things hanging after the play, as they ran ahead in the play? Even *The Misanthrope* with its minimal action cannot attain its dénouement without the unexpected artifice of letters suddenly discovered.

But that is enough to prove the point; it is not through plot that Molière's comedy rates high. Everybody admits it. But let us examine the implications of this admission. Plot is precisely that characteristic of literary comedy that the Italian Renaissance derived from classical comedy. It is plot that Italy gave to Spain and France for their modern comedy. Invention consists in scrambling and unscrambling a skein of deceptions and errors; the *inganno* is the inexhaustible source of interest and laughter. The principal theatrical agents are valets, messengers, fools of every kind and every costume; they take triumphant possession of the stage because in them are the springs of action.

Moreover, it is plot that characterizes most French comedy before Molière: *The Gallantries of the Duke of Ossone (les Galanteries du duc d'Ossone)* by Mairet and Corneille's *Liar (le Mentuer), The Sister (la Soeur)* by Rotrou and *The Invisible Beauty (la Belle invisible)* by Boisrobert, *The Foolish Spirit (l'Esprit follet)* of d'Ouville and *The Foolish Master (le Maître étourdi)* of Quinault. And when young Molière wishes to aspire to authorship, he first handled comedy in his own way; he wrote *The Fool*, a series of deceptions, and *The Chagrin of Love*, a web of error.

But by the time he wrote *The High-Browed Ladies*, and when he offered *The Misanthrope* or *The Forced Marriage (le Mariage forcé)*, *Tartuffe* or *Pourceangnac, The Learned Ladies* or *The Imaginary Invalid (le Malade imaginaire)*, then, as in the plays in which Trivelin and Scaramouche acted, the plot is only a thread to link comic situations, a framework for witty scenes. It is only a pretext to control the strings of human puppets whose expressive gestures make the comedy.

I do not even mention *The Angry Ones*: the insignificant plot serves to put on stage a hunter, a musician, a scholar, a gambler, etc. Is this not the resurrection of our ancient theatre's comic monologue? But rather than a single character like the marvelous "Archer of Bagnolet," the masterpiece of the genre, the plot permits a whole series of types to present themselves through their own words.

The Angry Ones is an exception, but all through Molière we find scenes that are scarcely attached to the plot, and yet do not compete with it. The scenes of *Chagrin of Love*, artificially divided into three different plots, can be detached from any of them, and isolated, as the Comédie-Française produces them, make a delightful little farce. Similarly, we find Sganarelle's discussions with his master, and Don Juan getting rid of a creditor in *Don Juan;* in *The Miser (l'Avare)*, the calculations of the miser who wants to give a dinner and the memorable scene of the flocks that the moneylender wants to lend instead of money; in *Learned Ladies*, the conference of wits and Chrysale's quarrels with his wife: in *The Misanthrope*, the scene of the sonnet, the conversation of the coquette and the prude. There are many more such scenes, whose resonance goes far beyond the plot, and whose effect does not reside in the help or hindrance that they give to the dénouement, to the marriage that is essential to literary comedy. Separated from the plot, they retain their essential value and their full flavor, which lie entirely in the naïve and witty interpretation of manners and character through dialogue. But plotless and expressive dialogue of manner and character is the domain of Italian farce, with its imaginative slapstick, and of French farce, with its coarse platitudes. Molière enlarges the boundaries, multiplies the stock types and the reactions of each type; he does not change the principle, which is always to seek the comic in some relationship with life, not in a relationship to a climax.

It may seem audacious to link farce to the great comedy of character of which Molière alone was capable. Nowhere else was he more truly creative. But where did he get the idea?

Certainly not from literary comedy, dominated by a plot upon which one generalized. From each actor the situation drew feelings adapted to his role in the play. Dialogue was assigned to the characters by a vague classification into humors or taste, based on age, sex, and profession, and this classification was supported by generalizations from Aristotle and Horace on the four seasons of life, and by the models of Terence. The same situations called for similar feelings in various people, and different situations evoked different feelings in the same person. Facial expressions that could scarcely be distinguished from one another, generally believable moods, but without specific and individual cohesion—that is what literary comedy offered Molière. There were no *characters*.

For Molière a character is a person who is powerfully unified by the domination of a passion or vice that destroys or subdues all other likes and dislikes of his soul, and this quality becomes the motivating force of all his thought and action. Love alone can sometimes resist this tyranny, and the comic springs forth from this resistance, from its partial defeat or its unforeseen compromises.

Nevertheless, there are several works of literary comedy that might have guided Molière in this way. Not *The Liar*, which no one today dreams of playing as a comedy of character, but *The Comic Illusion (l'Illusion Comique)* with the startling fantasy of the braggart; *The Pedant Fooled (le Pédant joué)*, with the caricatures of pedant, captain, and peasant; *The Parasite (le Parasite)* by Tristan, with another captain playing with the parasite; *Don Japhet* and *Jodelet* by Scarron, those monstrous caricatures; and above all Gillet de la Tessonnerie's *The Countryman (le Compagnard)*, in which the conventional character of the captain is almost completely transformed into a country gentleman through real observation. Aren't these works, whose plots contain a marked and burlesque figure, sketches and models for comedy of character? Molière might have started there.

He might have, since almost all these comedies take on a distinctive quality through introducing into the plot a stock type taken from French or foreign farce.[10] He might have, but he did not. Otherwise, why did he not continue Corneille's *Braggart (le Matamore)* or Gillet's *Countryman* in verse comedies? Why in his first effort at character did he turn to the limitations of prose, in the style of farce?

If the comedy of character is sketched in *The High-Browed Ladies* and *Sganarelle*, there is proof that Molière first conceived character in the form of the Italian *mask*, which the French actors of farce had made their own.

Masks of the *commedia dell'arte*, for that matter, are nothing but sketches of general characteristics. Originally, to be sure, the *masks* had local and professional traits that particularized them: Pantaloon was a Venetian merchant; the Doctor was from Bologna, and, as his name indicates, knew his law; Harlequin was a peasant from Bergamo; Scaramouche, a Neapolitan adventurer; and the Captain (also Neapolitan vaguely crossed with Spanish), although not the great lord he claimed to be, was a rich gentleman.

But in France these origins and professions were not noticed, and were transformed into general characteristics. The Captain is no more than vanity and cowardice: Scaramouche, roguery and impudence; Brighella, the insolent tricky valet; Harlequin, the naïve and awkward valet; the Doctor becomes a pedant of philosophy and letters; and Pantaloon is melancholy old age, miserly and foolish.

[10] Le Metamore and Jodelet are taken from contemporary French farce. Scarron, Thomas Corneille, and others draw upon the Spanish genre called *commedia de figuron*, and these *figurones* seem to be stock types transplanted from popular comedy to literary comedy. In the works of Tristan, his parasite, aside from being a personal satire, is merely a mold for tirades, a theme with variations in the manner of farce. I would say the same about Desmarets' *Visionaries;* its characters are mere labels tacked on to several kinds of literary amplification.

Italian authors in France modified the original types, varying them to bring out their general meaning and thus transforming Trivelin and Harlequin. In spite of dialects and costumes that still continued to reveal the local origin of more than one *mask*, the French spectator saw and could see only general expressions of foolishness and deceit, of lasciviousness and avarice—all humanity gracefully individualized by the imagination and personal observation of the actor.

And that is exactly the principle of *character* as Molière uses it. He knew it so well that he first molded his observation and invention into *masks*.

He began by creating Mascarille and Sganarelle,[11] two *masks* of valets that, in the Italian manner, he submitted to various conditions.

Mascarille, *fourbum imperator*, close relative of Scapin, completely Italian in features and costume, helped Molière ridicule *The High-Browed Ladies*. But his valet's mask is narrow. He is only a rascal, he can only *imitate* others by exaggerating their foibles. With him, there could be no true and exact portrayal of French manners; he would remain Mascarille carrying out his duties, Mascarille imitating the marquis, and not what the poet now envisaged, a true marquis lifted from life on to the stage.

Then Molière took up another valet, Sganarelle, from the pageants of his youth. Only his name is still Italian, and if he was masked at first, Molière unmasked him. Valet though he is, he seems to be the heir of Guillot-Gorju; he ridicules doctors. We find him rigged out in doctor's robes three times: in *The Flying Doctor (le Médecin Volant)*, in *The Doctor in Spite of Himself (le Médecin malgré lui)*, and in *Don Juan*. But Molière broadens the mask and transforms Sganarelle. In contrast with Mascarille, who is essentially a valet, Sganarelle is only occasionally a valet. In essence, he is of the people, ignorant, selfish, a drunkard and coward, rather simple except when fear or acquisitiveness sharpens his mind. His gift is for coarse common sense rather than brilliant grace and light verve. He may be mature or old, peasant or bourgeois, husband, teacher, or father, but as any of these, he is robbed, deceived, and beaten. Between 1660 and 1666, having rejected Mascarille, Molière gave us Sganarelle in six plays, but we can see the *mask* disintegrate in his hands. These Sganarelles share little more than their name; the permanence of Italian Harlequin and Pantaloon are gone, and under this one name we now find a whole family of spirits and temperaments.

However, Molière got rid of Sganarelle as well. The Italian *masks* helped him to simplify life, to delineate moral aspects in the physical; when he had acquired the method, he rejected the *mask*. The artificial identity created by a name hampered him. If Sganarelle remains in the drunken peasant whose wife's revenge converts him into a doctor, the old amorous bourgeois of *The Forced Marriage* is no longer Sganarelle. There are two men and two lives, no longer a single man in two roles. And Molière broke the last bond that attached him to the comedy of the *commedia dell'arte*. He even strove to wipe out of the public mind the identity of these Sganarelles; he dressed them differently (as the inventory of his wardrobe shows): here in crimson satin, there in "musk-colored" sat-

---

[11] Of these two *masks*, only Mascarille is masked. From *School for Husbands* on, Sganarelle is not masked. In various documents of the time, he has exaggerated, pencilled (or perhaps inked) eyebrows and moustache; Ronsard in *The Royal Grove* speaks of "A Janin whose face is marked with flour or ink." This actor without a mask, whose face is made up but not in white-face, belongs more than the masked actor to the French tradition.

in, elsewhere in "olive-colored breeches and coat" and "underbreeches of flower yellow."[12]

Before 1666, he often liberated himself from Mascarille and Sganarelle; after 1666, he no longer returned to these *masks*. How much Tartuffe would have lost in being called Mascarille the hypocrite, and Orgon, Sganarelle the pious! In giving each bourgeois or fool his own name, the author revealed no less of their basis in good common sense and fearful credulity, of ingenious wit and audacious mischief. But he did not allow the abstract, general type to dominate. He permitted himself to individualize that type, to give it characteristics that renewed it. Thus he came closer to life. Sganarelle shows progress over Mascarille; the disappearance of Sganarelle marks a new step in the true imitation of manners.

To arrive at this point, Molière had to go through half his Parisian career. But although he rejected its appearance, he kept the structure of the *mask*. Arnolphe, Harpagon, Tartuffe, Alceste, are made up no differently from the six Sganarelles, from Pantaloon or Scaramouche. They retain the invariable fixity of character in any situation of Italian *masks*. They are placed before the public, they are allowed to take any positions, to make all gestures relevant to their character. We see the Misanthrope with the flatterer, with the vain wit, the prude, the flirt; with everyone, he says the word, makes the grimace, that characterize him. The *mask*, emphasized by melancholy, contains and makes entertaining the dialogue of the jealous lover;[13] and Alceste, retaining certain speeches from *Don Garcie* and literary comedy, is unique. Everywhere else, the only purpose of the action is not to show a change of feeling, but to bring forth inexhaustibly, by different acts and under different light, that feeling which is the single mainspring of the character. As Harlequin, through all his contortions, invariably expresses his own sly naïvetè, so Harpagon is a miser in every syllable of his part—and Tartuffe a hypocrite.

The permanence of their types is dazzling and changeless; for this reason La Bruyère found them coarse and Fénlon forced. For this reason, too, their comedy has no dénouement, because they have to be as they are from start to finish; they cannot say *yes* after having said *no*, a *no* which resides in the necessity of their essence; for such characters, dénouements would be artificial. Lapses and repentances are as impossible for them as an act of bravery or decency for Scaramouche.

But in Molière's comedy, there is an important part that Italian farce does not contain, at least for the French spectator: the painting of social conditions and relationships.

Molière shows us all the classes and relationships that composed French society in his time: peasants, bourgeois, squires, wits, great lords, servants, middle-class women, young and older ladies. A large part of his gift lies in spreading vices and ridiculous qualities through these different classes.

Already, under the name of Sganarelle, he had created a figure that was

[12] Similarly, in his last years, Molière changed Mascarille from his Italian original; the frontispiece of the 1682 edition shows Mascarille of *The High-Browed Ladies*, recognizable in wig and costume, but without a mask; he no longer has one, but shows his face, that of Molière as Sganarelle.
[13] As everyone knows, *The Misanthrope* borrows its strongest scene and its finest lines from *Don Garcie*. But the development of the feeling of jealousy is subordinated to the comic caricature of the man who would speak openly.

well known in our comic tradition. Sganarelle, valet or master, widower or husband, lover or father, resembles the rascal of our farce more than he does Pantaloon or Harlequin of the *commedia dell'arte*. Like him, he is always beaten, robbed, and deceived. Saint-Beuve realized it—Sganarelle contains Arnolphe, Dandin, and Orgon; in spite of his Italian name, he is pure French.

And what was distinctive about our own farce, as opposed to the character sketches of the Italian *masks*, was the witty image of social relationships. Our farce shows not libertines or misers or scoundrels, but a gentleman, a priest, a lawyer, an old soldier, a rascal, a cobbler, a tailor, a hosier. It portrays not love but home life, and love as a disturbance in home life, and a worry for the husband. It displays the details of quarrels and mistakes in the home, but the eternal conflict between feminine ruse and masculine brutality results less from opposition of two moral natures than from a conflict between two social conditions. It is the state of marriage that is revealed to us in this conflict of the two sexes' maliciousness.

In that way Molière reflects old French farce. How did he come to know it? Could its spirit and trends still be seen under its Italianized form in the farces at the Pont-Neuf and the Hotel de Bourgogne? Did he see it in the provinces, where it was still being played? Could he envision it through the printed text? Did he come upon booklets like those of Oudot, Rousset, and Barnaby Chaussard that chance has preserved for us? He knew French farce—the fact is certain, since he borrowed from it; the path is uncertain. Although there is a marked difference, due to his poetic genius and the refinement of his classical art, the figures of Arnolphe, Jourdain, Dandin, Pourceaugnac recall the Naudet's, George le Veau's, Colin's of old farce, as well as the draper Guillaume, and the lawyer Patelin. These are the germs that Molière developed, the first use of the comic method of his masterpieces. Although his characters are infinitely richer in substance, far less spare in design, they are constructed by the same method. They have no other way of looking at life than these coarse creatures who so easily amused the subjects of Louis XI and Louis XII.

On the one hand are the great characters with conventional names, Alceste, Tartuffe, Harpagon, who are like *masks* of humanity, on the other hand are characters with real and probable names, Pourceaugnac, Dandin, Jourdain, Arnolphe (or Arnould), deriving from a more purely French tradition. The first are more abstract and moral, the second more localized and social.

What they share, and what unites them in the theatre, is their naïve expression in dialogue. Comedy is *active conversation;* dialogue is all, if we mean that expressive and mimed dialogue of which I have spoken, that copious dialogue spilling over the plot so that the internal originality of a vigorously characterized nature reveals itself without reservation or hesitation, with candid passion.

And finally old French farce, differing from the pure artistry of Italian farce, contains a social moral which is usually low and coarse. The farce evokes a judgment about the character and situation. *The Wash-Tub (le Cuvier)* or *The Bridge for Asses (le Pont aux ânes)* contains an implicit ideal of what relationships should exist between husband and wife; *Georges le Veau,* a statement about bad matches; *Master Minim the Student (Maitre Minim Étudiant)* or *Pernet Who Goes To School (Pernet qui va à l'ècole),* judgments on the practical usefulness of knowledge. *Naudet* applauds the vengeance of the thief over the gentleman; this is the morality of Figaro wishing to serve his master with what he fears to receive from him. Both "The Archer of Bagnolet" and Colin who "goes to Naples and brings back a Turkish prisoner" judge, the brutal, pillaging soldiers by portraying them. In other words, many farces are expressions of popular conscience, of its way of looking at domestic and social relationships. There is an infinite distance between this rudimentary morality and the profound philosophy of Molière's comedies, which contain a seriousness, force, and personal freedom of thought that are unique. Nevertheless, the conception of life of these comedies is also not that of Corneille's *Liar*, nor of Rotrou, nor Scarron, nor Machiavelli, nor Aretino, nor Rojas, nor Moreto; consciously or not, Molière followed in the path of French farce, where what is laughable is what shocks the moral judgment and social prejudice of the public.

No matter how much we pay homage to Molière's genius, to his creative powers, to the suggestions of classical, Italian, French, and Spanish comedy, it is here that we have his true roots. He began with farce, and there he formed his true and expressive style. There he found the principle of *pantomime,* of *active gestures* that freed him from seeking witty words and brilliant dialogue. There he found a tendency that he could develop, and a method that he could use, the principle of concentration on a general character or on the socially ridiculous, there above all he found the habit of situating the source of laughter outside of the plot and entirely in the relationship that his people bear to people in real life.

Let us therefore accept the title thrust upon him by his malicious contemporaries: Molière is "the first jester of France." This is truer than the criticism of his friend Boileau, who reproaches him with having been too close to the people. Boileau dreamed of an academic Molière, but the true Molière is seen in a picture of the Comédie-Française, where he stands amid other illustrious actors of farce, both Italian and French. In this picture of *farceurs,* Molière figures in the company of Harlequin and Gros-Guillaume, of Scaramouche and Guillot-Gorju. These are his masters, these are his origins. And he is great enough not to blush at them.

He is the best farceur, and for this reason he is the best creator of comedy. That is why he has not dated in two hundred and fifty years. Whereas Corneille and especially Racine are practically inaccessible except to the educated who are trained to appreciate their intelligence and beauty, mass audiences without instruction or training respond at once to Molière; Molière enters their minds and goes right to their hearts. He appeals to the people, because he springs from the people; because his works, having assimilated all the learned and witty inventions, take their main form and their essential flavor from popular Italian or French comedy; because popular comedy revealed to him that in the "strange enterprise of amusing decent people" and others as well, nothing is more effective than holding "the mirror up to nature."

Restoration Comedy: The Reality and the Myth*

L. C. Knights

I

Henry James—whose "social comedy" may be allowed to provide a standard of maturity—once remarked that he found Congreve "insufferable,"[1] and perhaps the first thing to say of Restoration drama—tragedy as well as comedy—is that the bulk of it is insufferably dull. There are long stretches of boredom to be found in the lower ranges of Elizabethan drama, but there is nothing comparable to the unimitigated fatigue that awaits the reader of *Love in a Tub, Sir Martin Mar-all, Mr. Limberham, The Relapse,* or *The Mourning Bride.* And who returns to Dryden's heroic plays with renewed zest? The superiority of the common run of plays in the first period to that of the second is, at all events, a commonplace. It should be equally commonplace that the strength of the Elizabethan drama lies partly in the kind and scope—the quality and variety—of the interests that the playwrights were able to enlist, partly in the idiom that they had at their command: the drama drew on a vigorous non-dramatic literature, and literature in general was in close relation with non-literary interests and a rich common language. That is not the whole story, but it is an important part of it, and it seems profitable in a discussion of Restoration comedy, to keep these facts in mind for comparison. Ever since Collier published *A Short View of the Profaneness and Immorality of the English Stage* opponents of Restoration comedy have conducted their case almost entirely in moral terms, and it has been easy for recent critics, rightly discarding Lamb's obvious subterfuge, to turn the moral argument upside down, to find freedom of manners where Macaulay found licentiousness. "Morals" are, in the long run, decidedly relevant— but only in the long run: literary criticism has prior claims. If, to start with, we try to see the comedy of manners in relation to its contemporary non-dramatic literature—to take its bearings in the general culture of the time—we may at least make possible a free and critical approach.

During the forty years that followed the Restoration, English literature, English culture, was "upper-class" to an extent that it had never been before, and was not, after Addison, to be again. "Now if they ask me," said Dryden, "whence it is that our conversation is so much refined? I must freely and without flattery, ascribe it to the court," and his insistence, as a writer, on "the benefit of converse" with his courtly patrons was not merely dedicatory fulsomeness; the

---

*L. C. Knights, "Restoration Comedy: The Reality and the Myth," in *Explorations* (London: Cambridge University Press, 1964). [Footnotes in this selection have been renumbered.]
[1] *Letters,* Vol. I, p. 140.

influence of the current conception of "the gentleman" is shown plainly enough by the urbane ease of his critical prefaces; and Dryden's nondramatice prose is fairly representative of the new age.[2]

It is this that explains why, if one comes to Restoration literature after some familiarity with the Elizabethans, the first impression made by the language is likely to be a sense of what has been lost; the disintegration of the old cultural unity has plainly resulted in impoverishment. The speech of the educated is now remote from the speech of the people (Bunyan's huge sales were, until the eighteenth century, outside "the circumference of wit"), and idiomatic vigour and evocative power seem to have gone out of the literary medium. But there was gain as well as loss. The common mode of Restoration prose—for there is now a common mode, a norm—was not evolved merely in the interests of good form and polite intercourse; it had behind it a more serious pressure. When, in 1667, Sprat attacked "this vicious abundance of phrase . . . this volubility of tongue, which makes so great a noise in the world," he had in mind the needs of scientific inquiry and rational discussion. "They have therefore," he said of the Royal Society, "been most rigorous in putting in execution the only remedy that can be found for this *extravagance*, and that has been a constant resolution to reject all amplifications, digressions, and swellings of style; to return back to the primitive purity and shortness, when men delivered so many *things* almost in an equal number of *words*. They have exacted from all their members a close, naked, natural way of speaking, positive expressions, clear senses, a native easiness, bringing all things as near the mathematical plainness as they can."[3] For the first time the English language was made—and to some extent made consciously—an instrument for rational dissection.

> When once the aversion to bear uneasiness taketh place in a man's mind, it doth so check all the passions, that they are dampt into a kind of indifference; they grow faint and languishing, and come to be subordinate to that fundamental maxim, of not purchasing any thing at the price of a difficulty. This made that he had as little eagerness to oblige, as he had to hurt men; the motive of his giving bounties was rather to make men less uneasy to him, than more easy to themselves; and yet no ill-nature all this while. He would slide from an asking face, and could guess very well. It was throwing a man off from his shoulders, that leaned upon them with his whole weight; so that the party was not gladder to receive, than he was to give.

This is from Halifax's *Character of Charles II*, and the even tone, the sinuous ease of movement and the clarity of the analysis mark the passage as unmistakably post-Restoration. Halifax, of course, is in some ways an unusually handsome representative of his age; he is racy (the apt adjective is supplied by his editor, H. C. Foxcraft) as well as polite. But the achievement represented by his style was far from being merely individual achievement. The shrewd and subtle portrait of Charles II is unlike anything that had appeared in English before his time, and it could only have appeared when it did.

Now an upper-class culture that produced *Absalom and Achitophel, The Character of a Trimmer*, Dryden's critical prefaces and Locke's *Second Trea-*

---

[2] On "the last and greatest advantage of our writing, which proceeds from *conversation*," see in particular the *Defense of the Epilogue*. And the dialogue form in which Dryden cast the *Essay of Dramatic Poesy* was not unrecognizably far from actuality.

[3] *The History of the Royal Society of London: Spingarn, Critical Essays of the Seventeenth Century*, Vol. II, pp. 112 ff.

tise of Government, may have been limited, but it was not altogether decadent. If the drama is inferior it is not because it represents—by Elizabethan standards—a limited culture, but because it represents contemporary culture so inadequately; it has no significant relation with the best thought of the time. Heroic tragedy is decadent because it is factitious; it substitutes violent emotionalism for emotion, the purple patch for poetry, and its rhetoric, unlike Elizabethan dramatic rhetoric, has no connexion with the congenial non-dramatic modes of the age; it is artificial in a completely damaging sense, *and by contemporary standards.* If we look for an early illustration of the bad mid-eighteenth-century conception of poetry as something applied from the outside[4] we find it in Dryden's verse plays, where he adopts canons of style that he would not have dreamed of applying—apart from his Odes—in his non-dramatic verse. Tragedy, he said, "is naturally pompous and magnificent." Nothing in English literature is more surprising—if we stop to consider—than the complete discrepancy between the sinewy ease of Dryden's satires and the stiff opaqueness of his dramatic verse; and "the lofty style," since it cannot modulate, is always coming down with a bump.

> I'm pleased and pained, since first her eyes I saw,
> As I were stung with some tarantula.
> Arms, and the dusty field, I less admire,
> And soften strangely in some new desire;
> Honor burns in me not so fiercely bright,
> But pales as fires when mastered by the light:
> Even while I speak and look, I change yet more,
> And now am nothing that I was before.
> I'm numbed, and fixed, and scarce my eyeballs move;
> I fear it is the lethargy of love![5]

It is only in the easy strength of occasional lines ("A good, luxurious palatable faith") that we hear his natural voice. In the plays as a whole—each made up of a succession of "great" moments and heroic postures—the "nature" that is "wrought up to a higher pitch"[6] bears little resemblance to the Nature that was to figure so largely in the Augustan code.

This, or a similar account, would probably be accepted by all critics of the Restoration heroic play. What is not commonly recognized (it is, at all events, not said) is that the comedy of manners exhibits a parallel attenuation and enfeeblement of what the age, taken as a whole, had to offer. I am not, for the moment, referring to the moral or social code expressed. The observation to start from is that the prose in which Restoration comedy is written—select which dramatist you like—is poor and inexpressive in comparison with the staple non-dramatic prose.

Congreve is usually accepted as the most brilliant stylist of the five or six comic dramatists who count. But place beside the extract quoted from Halifax a

---

[4] ". . . enriching every subject (otherwise dry and barren) with a pomp of diction and luxuriant harmony of numbers."—Gray's note to *The Progress of Poesy,* 1754.
[5] *The Conquest of Granada,* Part I, III, i.
[6] ". . . the nature of a serious play; this last is indeed the representation of nature, but 'tis nature wrought up to a higher pitch."—*Of Dramatic Poesy.* The final paragraph of the Preface to *Religio Laici* has some interesting remarks in this connexion; e.g. "The florid, elevated, and figurative way is for the passions."

passage or two from *Love for Love* or *The Way of the World* (it makes no difference whether the speaker is Scandal or Mirabell), and Congreve's style shows
as nerveless in the comparison:

> A mender of reputations! ay, just as he is a keeper of secrets, another virtue that
> he sets up for in the same manner. For the rogue will speak aloud in the posture
> of a whisper; and deny a woman's name, while he gives you the marks of her per-
> son: he will forswear receiving a letter from her, and at the same time show you
> her hand in the superscription; and yet perhaps he has counterfeited the hand
> too, and sworn to a truth; but he hopes not to be believed; and refuses the reputa-
> tion of a lady's favour, as a doctor says *No* to a bishopric, only that it may be
> granted him. In short, he is a public professor of secrecy, and makes proclamation
> that he holds private intelligence.
> A. To give t'other his due, he has something of good nature, and does not always
> want wit.
> B. Not always: but as often as his memory fails him, and his common-place of
> comparisons. He is a fool with a good memory, and some few scraps of other
> folks' wit. He is one whose conversation can never be approved, yet it is now and
> then to be endured. He had indeed one good quality, he is not exceptious; for he
> so passionately affects the reputation of understanding raillery, that he will con-
> strue an affront into a jest; and call down-right rudeness and ill language, satire
> and fire.

This reminds me of Arnold's definition of Macaulayese, "The external characteristic being a hard metallic movement with nothing of the soft play of life, and
the internal characteristic being a perpetual semblance of hitting the right nail
on the head without the reality." Both construction and movement are so far
from being expressive of anything in particular that the main function of some
words is, it seems, to complete an antithesis or to display a riddling wit.[7] The verbal pattern appears at times to be completely unrelated to a mode of perceiving.
The passages quoted have an air of preening themselves on their acute discriminations, but the antitheses are mechanical, and the pattern is monotonously repeated: "She has beauty enough to make any man think she has wit; and com-
plaisance enough not to contradict him who should tell her so" —the common
form soon loses the sting of surprise. Burnet can write in an antithetical style
which also penetrates:

> And tho' he desired to become absolute, and to overturn both our religion and
> our laws, yet he would neither run the risk, nor give himself the trouble, which so
> great a design required. He had an appearance of gentleness in his outward de-
> portment: but he seemed to have no bowels nor tenderness in his nature: and in
> the end of his life he became cruel.[8]

The nearest approach to subtlety that Congreve's style allows is represented by
such things as this:

> FAINALL You are a gallant man. Mirabell; and though you may have cruelty
> enough not to satisfy a lady's longing, you have too much generosity not to be

---

[7] *The Old Bachelor* shows the riddles in the process of manufacture. *Bellmour:* He is the drum to his
own praise—the only implement of a soldier he resembles; like that, being full of blustering noise
and emptiness. *Sharper:* And like that, of no use but to be beaten, etc.
[8] Quote from Professor Nichol Smith's excellent anthology, *Characters from the Histories* and *Mem-
oirs of the Seventeenth Century* (Clarendon Press).

> tender of her honour. Yet you speak with an indifference which seems to be af-
> fected, and confesses you are conscious of a negligence.
>
> MIRABELL   You pursue the argument with a distrust that seems to be unaffected,
> and confess you are conscious of a concern for which the lady is more indebted to
> you than is your wife.

It isn't really, very subtle. As for the "wit," when it isn't merely verbal and obvious ("Fruitful, the head fruitful;—that bodes horns; the fruit of the head is
horns," etc.) it is hopelessly dependent on convention.

> She that marries a fool, Sir Sampson, forfeits the reputation of her honesty or
> understanding: and she that marries a very witty man is a slave to the severity
> and insolent conduct of her husband. I should like a man of wit for a lover, be-
> cause I would have such a man in my power; but I would no more be his wife
> than his enemy. For his malice is not a more terrible consequence of his aversion
> than his jealousy is of his love.

An intelligent husband, you see, must be jealous; take away that entertaining assumption and the point is blunted. Halifax is a witty writer, but his wit springs
naturally from the situation he is concerned with and illuminates it. "A partner
in government is so unnatural a thing that it is a squint-eyed allegiance which
must be paid to such a double-bottomed monarchy."[9] Congreve's wit is entirely
self-regarding.

   If there were space to discuss the manner of Wycherley, Etherege and Vanbrugh, it is a similar account that would have to be given. I am not suggesting
that they write in a completely indistinguishable common mode (though they all
have passages that might come from any play); but in essentials—in the way in
which they use their similes and antitheses, in the conception of "style" and
"wit" that they exhibit—they all stand together. Not one of them has achieved a
genuinely sensitive and individual mode of expression; and in each the pattern
of the prose inhibits any but the narrowest—and the most devastatingly *expected*—response. That, I should claim, is the judgment to which an analysis of their
prose inevitably leads. The trouble is not that the Restoration comic writers deal
with a limited number of themes, but that they bring to bear a miserably limited
set of attitudes. And these, in turn, are factitious to exactly the same degree as
the prose is artificial and non-representative of the current nondramatic medium.

II

   Apart from the presentation of incidental and unrelated "wit" (which soon
becomes as tiring as the epigrams of the "good talker"), Restoration comedy has
two main interests—the behaviour of the polite and of pretenders to politeness,
and some aspects of sexual relationships. Critics have made out a case for finding
in one or other of these themes a unifying principle and a serious base for the
comedy of manners. According to Miss Lynch, the "thoroughly conventionalized
social mode" of the courtly circle "was discovered to have manifestly comic aspects, both when awkwardly misinterpreted, and when completely fulfilled

---

[9] Also from *The Character of a Trimmer:*—" . . . the indecent courtship of some silken divines, who,
one would think, did practise to bow at the altar, only to learn to make the better legs at Court."

through personalities to which, however, it could not give complete expression,"[10] and both these discrepancies were exploited by Etherege and his successors. Bonamy Dobrée, attributing to the comic dramatists "a deep curiosity, and a desire to try new ways of living," finds that "the distinguishing characteristic of Restoration comedy down to Congreve is that it is concerned with the attempt to rationalize sexual relationships. It is this that makes it different from any other comedy that has ever been written. . . . It said in effect, 'Here is life lived upon certain assumptions; see what it becomes.' It also dealt, as no other comedy has ever done, with a subject that arose directly out of this, namely sex-antagonism, a consequence of the experimental freedom allowed to women, which gave matter for some of its most brilliant scenes."[11]

These accounts, as developed, certainly look impressive, and if Restoration comedy really answered to them—if it had something fresh and penetrating to say on sex and social relations—there would be no need to complain, even if one found the "solutions" distasteful. But Miss Lynch's case, at all events, depends on a vigorous reading into the plays of values which are not there, values which could not possibly be expressed, in fact, in the prose of any of the dramatists. (The candid reader can turn up the passages selected by Miss Lynch in support of her argument, and see if they are not all in the factitious, superficial mode that I have described.)

We may consider, by way of illustration, Etherege's *The Man of Mode*. When the play opens, Dorimant ("the finest of all fine gentlemen in Restoration comedy") is trying to rid himself of an old mistress, Mrs. Loveit, before taking up with a new, Bellinda, whilst Young Bellair, in love with Emilia, is trying to find some way out of marrying Harriet, an heiress whom his father has brought to town for him. The entertainment is made up of these two sets of complications, together with an exhibition of the would-be modishness of Sir Fopling Flutter. Events move fast. After a night spent in various sociabilities Dorimant keeps an appointment with Bellinda at 5 A.M. Letting her out of his lodgings an hour or so later, and swearing to be discreet "By all the Joys I have had, and those you keep in store," he is surprised by his companions, and in the resulting confusion Bellinda finds herself paying an unwilling visit to Mrs. Loveit. Dorimant appears and is rated by the women before he "flings off." Meanwhile Young Bellair and Emilia have secretly married. Dorimant, his equanimity recovered, turns up for the exposé, followed by his mistresses. The lovers are forgiven, the mistresses are huddled off the stage, and it is decided that Dorimant, who, the previous day, had ingratiated himself with Harriet's mother, and whose "soul has quite given up her liberty," shall be allowed to pay court to the heiress.

It seems to me that what the play provides—apart from the briskly handled intrigue—is a demonstration of the physical stamina of Dorimant. But Miss Lynch sees further. For her, Dorimant is "the fine flowering of Restoration culture." Illustrating her theory of the double standard, she remarks: "We laugh at Sir Fopling Flutter because he so clumsily parodies social fashions which Dorimant interprets with unfailing grace and distinction. We laugh at Dorimant because his assumed affectation admits of so poor and incomplete an expression of an attractive and vigorous personality."[12] The "unfailing grace and distinction"

[10] K. M. Lynch, *The Social Mode of Restoration Comedy*, p. 216.
[11] Bonamy Dobrée, *Restoration Comedy* pp. 22–23.
[12] *The Social Mode of Restoration Comedy*, p. 181.

are perhaps not much in evidence in Dorimant's spiteful treatment of Mrs. Loveit;[13] but even if we ignore those brutish scenes we are forced to ask, How do we know that there is this "attractive and vigorous personality" beneath the conventional forms? Dorimant's intrigues are of no more human significance than those of a barn-yard cock, and as for what Miss Lynch calls "his really serious affair with Harriet" (I feel this deserves a *sic*), it is purely theatrical, and the "pangs of love" are expressed in nothing but the conventional formulae: "She's gone, but she has left a pleasing Image of herself behind that wanders in my Soul." The answer to the question posed is that Miss Lynch's account is a mere assumption. Nothing that Dorimant actually *says* will warrant it—and nothing in the whole of Restoration comedy—in the words actually spoken—allows us a glimpse of those other "personalities" to which the conventional social modes "could not give complete expression." The "real values"[14] simply are not there.

A minor point can be made in passing. It is just possible to claim that Restoration comedy contains "social criticism" in its handling of "the vulgar." "Come Mr. Sharper," says Congreve's Belinda, "you and I will take a turn, and laugh at the vulgar; both the great vulgar and the small," and Etherege's Lady Townley expresses the common attitude of the polite towards the social nuisances: "We should love wit, but for variety be able to divert ourselves with the extravagancies of those who want it." The butts, unfortunately, are only shown as fools by the discrepancy between their ambitions and their achievements, not because their ambitions are puerile. The subject is hardly worth discussing, since it is obviously nothing but an easily satisfied sense of superiority that is diverted by the "variety" of a constant succession of Dapperwits, Froths and Fopling Flutters. "When a humour takes in London," Tom Brown remarked, "they ride it to death ere they leave it. The primitive Christians were not persecuted with half that variety as the poor unthinking beaus are tormented with upon the theatre . . . A huge great muff, and a gaudy ribbon hanging at a bully's backside, is an excellent jest, and new-invented curses, as, Stap my vitals, damn my diaphragm, slit my wind pipe, sink me ten thousand fathom deep, rig up a new beau, though in the main 'tis but the same everlasting coxcomb."[15]

III

In the matter of sexual relations Restoration comedy is entirely dominated by a narrow set of conventions. The objection that it is only certain characters, not the dramatists themselves, who accept them can be more freely encountered when the assumptions that are expressed most frequently have been briefly illustrated.

---

[13] See II, ii, and V, i, where Dorimant, trying to force a quarrel with Mrs. Loveit, attributes to her a fondness for Sir Fopling. The first of these scenes was too much for Etherege, and he makes Bellinda say:

> He's given me the proof which I desired of his love,
> But 'tis a proof of his ill nature too.
> I wish I had not seen him use her so.

But this is soon forgotten, and we are not, of course, called on to register an unfavourable judgment of Dorimant.

[14] "The love affairs of Courtal and Ariana, Freeman and Gatty [in *She Wou'd if She Cou'd*] are similarly embarrassed by social convention. . . . The conduct of these polite lovers acquires comic vitality through the continually suggested opposition of artificial and real values."—*Op. cit.*, p. 152.

[15] Tom Brown, Works, Vol. III, *Amusements Comical and Serious*, "At the Playhouse," p. 39.

The first convention is, of course, that constancy in love, especially in marriage, is a bore. Vanbrugh, who was the most uneasy if not the most honest of the comic dramatists (I think that in *The Provok'd Wife* he shows as unusually honest), unambiguously attributes this attitude to Sir John Brute:

> What cloying meat is love—when matrimony's the sauce to it! Two years marriage has debauch'd my five senses. . . . No boy was ever so weary of his tutor, no girl of her bib, no nun of doing penance, or old maid of being chaste, as I am of being married. Sure there's a secret curse entail'd upon the very name of wife!
>
> The woman's well enough; she has no vice that I know of, but she's a wife, and—damn a wife![16]

What Vanbrugh saw as a fit sentiment for Sir John had by that time (1697) served the Restoration stage—without change—for thirty years. In *She Wou'd if She Cou'd* Etherege had exhibited Sir Oliver Cockwood in an identical vein: "A pox of this tying man and woman together, for better, for worse." "To have a mistress love thee entirely" is "a damn'd trouble." "There are sots that would think themselves happy in such a Lady; but to a true bred Gentleman all lawful solace is abomination."[17] If Sir Oliver is a fool it is only because he is a trifle gross in his expression. "If you did but know, Madam," says the polite Freeman, "what an odious thing it is to be thought to love a Wife in good Company."[18] And the convention is constantly turning up in Congreve. "There is no creature perfectly civil but a husband," explains Mrs. Frail, "for in a little time he grows only rude to his wife, and that is the highest good breeding, for it begets his civility to other people."[19] "Marry her! Marry her!" Fainall advises Mirabell, "Be half as well acquainted with her charms, as you are with her defects, and my life on't, you are your own man again."[20] And Witwoud: "A wit should not more be sincere than a woman constant; one argues a decay of parts, as t'other of beauty."[21] Appetite, it seems (and this is the second assumption), needs perpetually fresh stimulus. This is the faith of Rhodophil in *Marriage à la Mode* and of Constant in *The Provok'd Wife*, as well as of Wycherley's old procuress, Mrs. Joyner. "If our wives would suffer us but now and then to make excursions," Rhodophil explains to Palamede, "the benefit of our variety would be theirs; instead of one continued, lazy, tired love, they would, in their turns, have twenty vigorous, fresh, and active lovers."[22] "Would anything but a madman complain of uncertainty?" asks Congreve's Angelica, for "security is an insipid thing, and the overtaking and possessing of a wish, discovers the folly of the chase."[23] And Fainall, in *The Way of the World*, speaks for a large class when he hints at a liking for sauce—a little gentleman's relish—to his seductions: "I'd no more play with a man that slighted his ill fortune than I'd make love to a woman who under-valued the loss of her reputation."[24] Fainall, of course, is what he is, but the attitude

[16] *The Provok'd Wife*. I, i, II, i.
[17] *She Wou'd if She Cou'd*, I, i; III, iii.
[18] *Ibid.*, III, iii.
[19] *Love for Love*, I, ii.
[20] *The Way of the World*, I, ii.
[21] *Ibid.*
[22] *Marriage à la Mode*, II, i, Cf. *The Provok'd Wife*, III, i: Constant, "There's a poor sordid slavery in marriage, that turns the flowing tide of honour, and sinks us to the lowest ebb of infamy. 'Tis a corrupted soil: Ill-nature, sloth, cowardice, and dirt, are all its product."
[23] *Love for Love*, IV, iii.
[24] *The Way of the World*, I, i.

that makes sexual pleasure "the bliss," that makes woman "delicious"—something to be savoured—as well as "damned" and "destructive," demands, for its support, "the pleasure of a chase."[25]

> Would you long preserve your lover?
> Would you still his goddess reign?
> Never let him all discover,
> Never let him much obtain.[26]

Restoration comedy used to be considered outrageously outspoken, but such stuff as this, far from being "outspoken," hovers on the outskirts of sexual relations, and sees nothing but the titillation of appetite (" 'Tis not the success," Collier observed, "but the manner of gaining it which is all in all").[27] Sex is a hook baited with tempting morsels;[28] it is a thirst quencher;[29] it is a cordial;[30] it is a dish to feed on;[31] it is a bunch of grapes;[32] it is anything but sex. (This, of course, explains why some people can combine a delighted approval of Restoration comedy with an unbalanced repugnance for such modern literature as deals sincerely and realistically with sexual relationships.)

Now the objection referred to above was that sentiments such as these are not offered for straightforward acceptance. Many of them are attributed to characters plainly marked as Wicked (Maskwell, for example, is the black-à-vised villain of melodrama), or, more frequently, as trivial, and the dramatist can therefore dissociate himself. He may even be engaged in showing his audience the explicit, logical consequences of the half-conscious premises on which they base their own lives, saying, as Mr. Dobrée has it, "Here is life lived upon certain assumptions; see what it becomes." To this there are several answers. The first is that reflexions of the kind that I have quoted are indistinguishable in tone and style from the general epigrammatic stock-in-trade (the audience was not altogether to be blamed if, as Congreve complained, they could not at first "distinguish betwixt the character of a Witwoud and a Lovewit"); and they are largely "exhibited," just as all the self-conscious witticisms are exhibited, for the sake of their immediate "comic" effect. One has only to note the laughter of a contemporary audience at a revival, and the places where the splutters occur, to realize

[25] *The Old Bachelor*, I, i; III, ii ("O thou delicious, damned, dear destructive woman!"). IV, ii.

[26] *Ibid.*, II, ii.

[27] *A Short View of the Profaneness and Immorality of the English Stage*, Fifth Edition, 1738, p. 116.

[28] " 'Tis true you are so eager in pursuit of the temptation, that you save the devil the trouble of leading you into it: nor is it out of discretion that you don't swallow the very hook yourselves have baited, but . . . what you meant for a whet turns the edge of your puny stomachs."—*The Old Bachelor*, I, i. "Strike Heartwell home, before the bait's worn off the hook. Age will come. He nibbled fairly yesterday, and no doubt will be eager enough to-day to swallow the temptation."—*Ibid.*, III, i.

[29] "What was my pleasure is become my duty: and I have as little stomach to her now as if I were her husband. . . . Pox on't! that a man can't drink without quenching his thirst." —*The Double Dealer*, III, i.

[30] "You must get you a mistress. Rhodophil. That, indeed, is living upon cordials; but as fast as one fails, you must supply it with another."—*Marriage à la Mode*, I, i.

[31] "Because our husbands cannot feed on one dish, therefore we must be starved."—*Ibid.*, III, i.

[32] "The only way to keep us new to one another, is never to enjoy, as they keep grapes, by hanging them upon a line; they must touch nothing, if you would preserve them fresh."—*Ibid.*, V, i.

how much of the fun provides a rather gross example of tendency wit.[33] The same attitudes, moreover, are manipulated again and again, turning up with the stale monotony of jokes on postcards, and the play that is made with them demands only the easiest, the most superficial, response. But it is, after all, useless to argue about the degree of detachment, the angle at which these attitudes and assumptions are presented. As soon as one selects a particular comedy for that exercise one realizes that all is equally grist to the mill and that the dramatist (there is no need, here, to make distinctions) has no coherent attitude of his own. A consistent artistic purpose would not be content to express itself in a style that allows so limited, so local an effect.

But it is the triviality that one comes back to. In Dryden's *Marriage à la Mode* the characters accept the usual conventions: constancy is dull, and love only thrives on variety.

> PALAMEDE   O, now I have found it! you dislike her for no other reason but because she's your wife.
>
> RHODOPHIL   And is not that enough? All that I know of her perfections now, is only by memory . . . At last we arrived at that point, that there was nothing left in us to make us new to one another . . .
>
> PALAMEDE   The truth is, your disease is very desperate; but, though you cannot be cured, you may be patched up a little; you must get you a mistress, Rhodophil. That, indeed, is living upon cordials; but, as fast as one fails, you must supply it with another.

The mistress that Rhodophil selects is Melanthra, whom Palamede is to marry; Palamede falls in love with Doralice, Rhodophil's wife, and the ensuing complications provide sufficient entertainment (the grotto scene, III, ii, is really funny). Mr. Dobrée, however, regards the play as a witty exposure of the impossibility of rationalizing sex relations, as Palamede and Rhodophil attempt to rationalize them. Dryden "laughs morality back into its rightful place, as the scheme which ultimately makes life most comfortable."[34] But what Dryden actually does is to *use* the conventions for the amusement they afford, not to examine them. The level at which the play works is fairly indicated by the opening song:

> Why should a foolish marriage vow,
> 　　Which long ago was made,
> Oblige us to each other now,
> 　　When passion is decayed?
> We loved, and we loved, as long as we could,
> 　　'Till our love was loved out in us both;
> But our marriage is dead, when the pleasure is fled:
> 　　'Twas pleasure first made it an oath.

---

[33] The Freudian "censor" is at times projected in the form of the stage puritan. The plays written soon after the Commonwealth period appealed to Royalist prejudice by satirizing the "seemingly precise"; and even later, when "the bonfires of devotion," "the bellows of zeal," were forgotten, a good deal of the self-conscious swagger of indecency seems to have been directed against "our protestant husbands," city merchants, aldermen and the like; the "daring" effect was intensified by postulating a shockable audience somewhere—not necessarily in the theatre. Not that the really obscene jokes were merely bravado: Collier quite rightly remarked that "the modern poets seem to use smut as the old ones did Machines, to relieve a fainting situation."—*A Short View*, Fifth Edition, p. 4.
[34] *Restoration Comedy*, p. 133.

> If I have pleasures for a friend
>   And further love in store,
> What wrong has he, whose jobs did end,
>   And who could give no more?
> 'Tis a madness that he should be jealous of me,
>   Or that I should bar him of another:
> For all we can gain, is to give ourselves pain,
>   When neither can hinder the other.

The lovers make no attempt to "rationalize sex" for the simple reason that genuine sexual feelings no more enter into the play as a whole than feelings of any kind enter into the song. (The obviously faked emotions of the heroic plot are, after all, relevant—and betraying.) And according to Mr. Dobrée, "In one sense the whole idea of Restoration comedy is summed up in the opening scene of *Marriage à la Mode*."[35]

In a sense, too, Mr. Dobrée is right. Restoration comedy nowhere provides us with much more of the essential stuff of human experience than we have there. Even Congreve, by common account the best of the comic writers, is no exception. I have said that his verbal pattern often seems to be quite unrelated to an individual mode of perceiving. At best it registers a very limited mode. Restoration prose is all "social" in its tone, implications and general tenor, but Congreve's observation is *merely* of the public surface. And Congreve's, too, relies on the conventional assumptions. In *The Way of the World*, it is true, they are mainly given to the bad and the foolish to express: it is Fainall who discourses on the pleasures of disliking one's wife, and Witwoud who maintains that only old age and ugliness ensure constancy. And Mirabell, who is explicitly opposed to some aspects of contemporary manners, goes through the common forms in a tone of rather weary aloofness: "I wonder, Fainall, that you who are married, and of consequence should be discreet, will suffer your wife to be of such a party." But Congreve himself is not above raising a cheap snigger;[36] and, above all, the characters with some life in them have nothing to fall back on—nothing, that is, except the conventional, and conventionally limited, pleasures of sex. Millamant, who says she loathes the country and hates the town, expects to draw vitality from the excitement of incessant solicitation:

> I'll be solicited to the very last, nay, and afterwards . . . I should think I was poor and had nothing to bestow, if I were reduced to an inglorious ease, and freed from the agreeable fatigues of solicitation. . . . Oh, I hate a lover that can dare to think he draws a moment's air, independent of the bounty of his mistress. There is not so impudent a thing in nature, as the saucy look of an assured man, confident of success. The pedantic arrogance of a very husband has not so pragmatical an air.

Everyone seems to have found Millamant intelligent and attractive, but her attitude is not far removed from that expressed in

> Would you long preserve your lover?
> Would you still his goddess reign?

---

[35] *Ibid.*, p. 106.

[36]   Ay there's my grief; that's the sad change of life,
    To lose my title, and yet keep my wife.
        The Way of the World, II, ii

and she shares with characters who are decidedly not attractive a disproportionate belief in "the pleasure of a chase." Which is not surprising in view of her other occupations and resources; visiting, writing and receiving letters, tea-parties
and small talk make up a round that is never for a moment enlivened by the
play of genuine intelligence.[37] And although Congreve recognizes, at times, the
triviality of his characters,[38] it is to the world whose confines were the Court, the
drawing-room, the play-house and the park—a world completely lacking the
real sophistication and self-knowledge that might, in some measure, have redeemed it—that he limits his appeal.

It is, indeed, hard to resist the conclusion that "society"—the smart town society that sought entertainment at the theatres—was fundamentally bored.[39] In
The Man of Mode Emilia remarks of Medley, "I love to hear him talk o' the intrigues, let 'em be never so dull in themselves, he'll make 'em pleasant i' the relation," and the idiotic conversation that follows (ii, i), affording us a glimpse of
what Miss Lynch calls "the most brilliant society which Restoration comedy has
to offer."[40] suggests in more than one way how badly society *needed* to be entertained. It is the boredom—the constant need for titillation—that helps to explain
not only the heroic "heightening" of emotion, but the various scenic effects, the
devices of staging and costume that became popular at this period. (Charles II
"almost died of laughing" at Nell Gwynn's enormous hat.) The conventions—of
sexual pursuit, and so on—were an attempt to make life interesting—an impossible job for those who were aware of so limited a range of human potentialities.

The dominating mood of Restoration comedy is, by common account, a
cynical one. But one cannot even say that there is here, in contrast to naïve Romantic fervours, the tough strength of disillusion. If—recognizing that there is a
place in the educational process for, say, La Rochefoucauld—one finds the
"cynicism" of the plays distasteful, it is because it is easy and superficial; the attitudes that we are presented with are based on so meagre an amount of observation and experience. Thus, "Elle retrouvait dans l'adultère toutes les platitudes
du mariage"[41] has, superficially, much the same meaning as, "I find now, by sad
experience, that a mistress is much more changeable than a wife, and after a little time too, grows full as dull and insignificant." But whereas the first sentence
has behind it the whole of *Madame Bovary*, the second comes from *Sir Martin
Marall*, which (although Dryden shares the honours with the Duke of Newcas-
tle) is perhaps the stupidest play I have ever read, and the context is imbecility.

But the superficially is betrayed at every turn—by the obvious rhythms of
the interspersed songs, as well as by the artificial elegance of the prose. And the
cynicism is closely allied with—merges into—sentimentality. One thinks of the

---

[37] As Lady Brute remarks. "After all, a woman's life would be a dull business, if it were not for the
men . . . We shou'd never blame Fate for the shortness of our days; our time would hang wretchedly
upon our hands."—*The Provok'd Wife*, III, iii.
[38] *Mirabell:* You had the leisure to entertain a herd of fools; things who visit you from their excessive
idleness; bestowing on your easiness that time which is the encumbrance of their lives. How can you
find delight in such society?—*The Way of the World*, II, i.
[39] The constitution, habits and demands of the theatre audience are admirably illustrated by Alex-
andre Beljame in that neglected classic of scholarship, *Le Public et les Hommes de Lettres en Ang-
leterre au Dix-Huitième Siècle, 1660-1740.* See also C. V. Deane, *Dramatic Theory and the
Rhymed Heroic Play,* Chapter I, Section 6.
[40] *The Social Mode of Restoration Comedy,* p. 177.
[41] [She found in adultery all the platitudes of marriage. From Flaubert's *Madame Bovary.*]

sentimentally conceived Fidelia in the resolutely "tough" *Plain Dealer;* and
there is no doubt that the audience was meant to respond sympathetically when,
at the end of *Love for Love,* Angelica declared her love for Valentine: "Had I
the world to give you, it could not make me worthy of so generous a passion;
here's my hand, my heart was always yours, and struggled very hard to make
this utmost trial of your virtue." There is, of course, a good deal of loose emotion
in the heroic plays, written—it is useful to remember—for the same audience:

> I'm numbed, and fixed, and scarce my eyeballs move;
> I fear it is the lethargy of love!
> 'Tis he; I feel him now in every part:
> Like a new lord he vaunts about my heart;
> Surveys, in state, each corner of my breast,
> While poor fierce I, that was, am dispossessed.[42]

> A secret pleasure trickles through my veins:
> It works about the inlets of my soul,
> To feel thy touch, and pity tempts the pass:
> But the tough metal of my heart resists;
> 'Tis warmed with the soft fire, not melted down.[43]

"Feeling," in Dryden's serious plays, is fairly represented by such passages as
these, and Dryden, we know, was not alone in admiring the Fletcherian "pathos." But it is the lyric verse of the period that provides the strongest confirma-
tory evidence of the kind of bad taste that is in question. It is not merely that in
Etherege, Sedley and Dorset the feelings come from much nearer the surface
than in the Metaphysical and the Caroline poets, intellectual "wit" no longer
strengthens and controls the feeling. Conventional attitudes are rigged out in a
conventional vocabulary and conventional images. (The stock outfit—the "fair
eyes" that "wound," the "pleasing pains," the "sighs and tears," the "bleeding
hearts" and "flaming darts"—can be studied in any anthology.[44]) There is, in
consequence, a pervasive strain of sentimental vulgarity.

> Farewell, ungrateful traitor!
>   Farewell, my perjured swain
> Let never injured creature
>   Believe a man again.
> The pleasure of possessing
> Surpasses all expressing,
> But 'Tis too short a blessing,
>   And lover too long a pain.
>
>   .   .   .
>
> The passion you pretended,
>   Was only to obtain;
> But when the charm is ended,
>   The charmer you disdain.

[42] *The Conquest of Granada,* Part I, III, i.
[43] *Don Sebastian,* III, i.
[44] See, for example, Aphra Behn's "Love in fantastic triumph sate," Buckingham's *To His Mistress*
("Phyllis, though your all powerful charms"), *Dryden's* "Ask not the cause why sullen spring," and
"Ah, how sweet it is to love," and Sedley's *To Chloris*—all in *The Oxford Book of English Verse,* or
Ault's *Seventeenth Century Lyrics.*

> Your love by ours we measure
> Till we have lost our treasure,
> But dying is a pleasure
> When living is a pain.

This piece of music-hall sentiment comes from Dryden's *The Spanish Friar*, and it does not stand alone. The mode that was to produce, among other things of equal merit; "When lovely woman stoops to folly," had its origin in the lyrics of the Restoration period. Most of these were written by the group connected with the theatres, and they serve to underline the essential criticism of the plays. The criticism that defenders of Restoration comedy need to answer is not that the comedies are "immoral," but that they are trivial, gross and dull.

Georges Feydeau: The Geometry of Madness[*]

Leonard C. Pronko

To make a good *vaudeville*, you take the most tragic situation possible, a situation fit to make a mortician shudder, and you try to bring out its burlesque side. There is no human drama which does not offer at least several comic aspects. That is why authors you call comic are always sad: they think "sad" first.[1]

GEORGES FEYDEAU

The tragic side of great comedies has often been emphasized. One need only think of the behavior of any major character of Molière and its tragic consequences for others. Molière avoids tragedy by his much remarked *deus ex machina* endings, and of course by the general tone he adopts toward his maniacs. But given another tone, and without the help of artificial endings, *Tartuffe*, *L'Avare* and even *Le Bourgeois gentilhomme* could become at least middle-class drama if not full-blown tragedies.

Feydeau's "tragic" situations do not arise from character—at least they do not arise from specific characters within a given play. Rather they arise from the nature of things, or from the character of the human animal, given as he is to pleasure and particularly to animal pleasures. "Why don't you kill the animal in you?" asks a married woman of her too insistent lover. "I could never stand to hurt animals," he answers. Most of Feydeau's men, and a few of the women, are very kind to the animal in them, allowing it to lead them where it will. And in order to give it a longer leash, they lie time and again, and invent the most preposterous excuses for their guilty acts.

The fundamental situation in a Feydeau play is one of deception. A husband is deceiving his wife, who discovers or suspects his infidelity and vows revenge . . . .

Deception is not always voluntary. A staple of the *vaudeville* had for many years been the *quiproquo*, literally the taking of this for that. Two characters meet, each believing the other is someone else, or that he is pursuing a subject different from the one he is actually pursuing. Some of Feydeau's most hilarious scenes are based upon such situations. His earliest plays, in fact, often take such a misunderstanding as the foundation of their action. In *Les Fiancés de Loches* (1888; The Fiancés from Loches) three provincials come to a Paris employment

[*]Leonard C. Pronko, *Georges Feydeau*. (Ungar Inc., 1975.)
[1]Léon Treich, "Le roe anniversaire de la mort de Feydeau," quoted in Arlette Shenkan, *Georges Feydeau*, Paris, Seghers, 1972, p. 156.

agency for servants, thinking they are in a marriage bureau, because the defunct matrimonial service on the floor above has left a note directing its clients to the floor below. The employment agency hires them out to a doctor, his fiancée, and an old maid sister whom they believe to be their future spouses. The familiarity of the "servants" and their astonishment at the things they are asked to do by their fiancés account for much of the humor in the play. Feydeau's first play in collaboration with Maurice Desvallières, who was to co-sign several of his most famous works, *Les Fiancés de Loches* runs lickety-split from beginning to end, each scene more absurdly insane than the last. Without the almost violent incongruity and speed, which liken it to a Marx Brothers' film, the constant reverting to the same technique would wear thin.

The simpler *Chat en poche* (1888; A Bird in Hand) derives its comic effects from a misunderstanding on the part of Monsieur Pacarel, a wealthy bourgeois who had telegraphed a friend in Bordeaux to send him the tenor Dujeton, who has made such a hit in the provincial city. Pacarel hopes to become the singer's protector and then "sell" him to the Paris Opera on condition that they perform his own daughter's new version of *Faust*. A young man arrives, actually the son of the friend in Bordeaux who never received the telegram. The son is surprised that Pacarel wishes to offer him a huge allowance, and humors the wealthy man when he asks him to sing. Everyone is astounded at his lack of voice, but his true identity is only discovered at the end. The young man is also confused as to the identity of the woman he is pursuing, for he recognizes Pacarel's wife as a woman he had met on a bus the day before, and attempts to court her. But since he was introduced to the two-family ménage at once, he thinks she is Amandine— the wife of Pacarel's friend—rather than Pacarel's wife, Marthe.

Madness, absurdity and *quiproquos* galore keep the play light and generally fast-moving. Occasionally, however, it becomes repetitious and dull in the forced humor of the situations. Feydeau had not yet found the precise formula which was to make his name only four or five years later.

That formula includes a plot which is complicated by a number of subplots, shaken by surprises and *coups de théâtre,* suddenly reversed or at least threatened by unexpected (but well-prepared and therefore at least subconsciously expected) incidents and finally, after a mad romp usually taking place in the second act where the chaos reaches its summit, slowly, meticulously, clearly and cleverly untied in a lengthy denouement.

Discussing, in an interview, his recipe for a *vaudeville,* Feydeau compares himself to a pharmacist preparing a prescription: "I put into my pill a gram of imbroglio, a gram of libertinage, a gram of observation."[2]

Observation supplies themes and characters and gives them life, libertinage whets the appetites of the blasé theatergoer and lightens the tone, but it is the imbroglio or action which either melds the elements into a successful theater piece or condemns them to the bookshelf or the drawer. "Theater is above all the development of an action." Feydeau wrote in a letter to a friend, "and action is the very basis of *vaudeville* and melodrama."[3] Those two much-maligned forms of theater, if not so sublime as tragedy or so socially useful as comedy (although both claims might be contested) are at least equally close to the ground base of theater. Indeed, this may account for their "vulgarity," for they are theater rath-

[2] Adolphe Brisson, "Une Leçon de vaudeville," quoted in Arlette Shenkan, *ibid.*, p. 152.
[3] Arlette Shenkan, *Georges Feydeau*, Paris, Seghers, 1972, p. 153.

er than drama. Feydeau, a number of times, inveighed against theater as pulpit, and dialogue as literature. Both tendencies, he claimed, killed theater.

Today, when much theater has turned its back upon the literary and the explicitly ideological, Feydeau seems quite modern, despite his *belle époque* décor and costumes. He discovered, at a time when serious theater was thrashing out social problems and art theater was lost in poetic fantasy, that movement was the "essential condition of theater." By this he meant the actual physical movement of the actors on the stage, as well as the more "Aristotelian" development of action from beginning to middle to end.

> I am in possession of a play as a chess player is in possession of his chessboard [he claimed]. The successive positions my pawns (that is to say, my characters) have occupied onstage are constantly present in my mind.[4]

Both action and movement are of prime importance in a Feydeau play, and the author was constantly in command of both. Indeed, like the great dramatists of the past, Feydeau was the director of his own plays, and he insisted that the actors perform the play he had imagined and not some other. For this reason, the most intricate movements, stage tricks, or intonations are noted minutely. In *Occupe-toi d'Amélie* one section of speech is even given in musical notation, so that the actor will use the proper intonation. The texts of some of the plays run many pages longer than most scripts, because the movement is spelled out in great detail. To fail to follow the author's instructions is to court trouble, for suddenly an actor or an object may turn up in the wrong place. The physical movement, like the development of the action, is constructed with a mathematical precision which cannot be upset with impunity.

So wedded was Feydeau to this concept that he refused to allow cuts in his plays. On one occasion when the director finally summoned the courage to send someone to ask him to cut a bit from a play, Feydeau inquired coldly, "How many minutes must be cut?" "About ten." "And how many pages does that represent?" "Twenty pages," was the reply. "Very well," responded the dramatist. "Tell them to begin on page 21."

Following the model of the well-made play, Feydeau always begins his action near its climax. In the first act, which is almost entirely devoted to exposition, each scene is usually created with three ends in mind: to make clear the fundamental situation at the play's outset, i.e., the deception or misunderstanding and what led up to it; to prepare the complex situations which will arise in the following acts in such a way that they will seem logical, inevitable, yet surprising; and to amuse the audience with situations which are droll or preposterous, but which always have a ring of truth. In his greatest works, while doing all this, Feydeau also succeeds in giving us insights into character, and flashes of a nightmarish picture of the human predicament in which men are victims of a wildly irrational universe.

Toward the end of Act I, the main action begins, usually set in motion by some fault, mistake, misjudgment, or lie. In Act II the results of this mistake are witnessed, usually in a bachelor apartment or a hotel, occasionally in a salon or bedroom. But wherever the scene, it has the intimacy of a subway station at rush hour, as the major characters from Act I appear, disappear, and reappear with a rigorous logic, often coming and going at breakneck speed through the three,

[4] Adolphe Brisson, *ibid.*, p. 151.

four, five or six doors which the author usually provides. In several cases new, and incidental, comic characters are brought into this act, but their presence is always felt as likely or even necessary.

It is in Act II, if not before, that Feydeau brings into play most rigorously the rule he established for himself:

> When writing a play, I seek among my characters the ones who should not run into each other. And they are precisely the ones I bring into a confrontation as soon as possible . . .[5]

Such a rule is fundamental to all drama, and particularly to melodrama and the Romantic drama which is so close to it. Without the accidental or coincidental meetings—so much better avoided—the majority of Romantic dramas would not get far along, or at least would not come to a head. Feydeau, as so often, has taken a standard theatrical device and pushed it to the limits of verisimilitude— or beyond.

In the similar instances, of characters who have just been pronounced either at death's door, irretrievably ill, or in some impossibly distant place, and who are promptly announced, Feydeau is again indebted to a device of the *drame*. But in the Romantic play, instead of bringing about amusing complications, such an encounter may draw down upon the characters the most dire results, at which we are scarcely disposed to laugh—unless, of course, we see the artifice through a late twentieth-century eye rather than the pathos through an eye of the 1830s. In Hugo's finest poetic drama, *Ruy Blas* (1838) the poor lackey in love with the queen has decided to die, and laments, "I shall never see her again. Never!" She immediately enters by a hidden door—right into the trap prepared for her. One could scarcely imagine a situation more Feydeau-like in its outlines, but the tone is far from light.

Even classical tragedy, with its action bearing on the inner man and his perception of truth, is not immune from this rule. One wonders what would have happened had Oedipus not met the sphinx, or not happened to have learned the answer to the riddle, or even having accomplished all that, if he had not gone on to Thebes and met Jocasta. Cocteau, in his beautiful modern treatment of the tale, *La Machine infernale*, plays upon the irony of such chance meetings. But Oedipus does not fear these encounters as do the characters of comedy. Indeed, tragic characters are often unaware of the implications of the meetings even while they are taking place, for the tragic meeting is one whose true meaning is revealed at the end, and only in retrospect does the hero know that he might well have feared it. The comic meeting is anticipated with distaste or experienced with displeasure.

The worst meeting of all is that between the guilty husband and his suspicious wife, or the suspecting husband and his wife caught in compromising circumstances. Such a scene corresponds to the "obligatory scene" of the well-made play, in which the secret explodes and we, the spectators, witness the encounter which seemed inevitable from the beginning. Scribe customarily placed such a scene near the end of his play and followed it with a lightning-like denouement, and often one which contained a new surprise. Feydeau most often places this high point of discovery at the end of the second act, leaving all of act three for a lengthy, quick-paced and very complicated untying of the knots. . . .

[5] Leon Treich, *op. cit.*, p. 155.

As we might expect in a theater which depends upon plot and movement, Feydeau's comedy is largely one of situation. He uses comedy of character and language as well. The former is found chiefly in the later short plays. The latter is a minor form in his plays, except as it relates to situation or character.

Indeed, Feydeau, unlike more facile writers of comedy or farce, refused to use comic material simply to make his audience laugh. He required that it arise naturally from the situations of characters. René Peter, who co-authored with Feydeau the last full-length play he signed, *Je ne trompe pas mon mari* (1914), recounts his first reading of the manuscript to the master. Peter, hoping Feydeau could help him place the play, had brought it for him to see, and was overjoyed when the famous dramatist consented to rework the play and sign it with the young man. Peter himself recounts his reading of the play:

> I'll never forget how, in the middle of my reading, he suddenly interrupted me:
> "Ah! charming! That is truly charming... What a beautiful line—witty, original."
> Naturally I was in seventh heaven. He concluded:
> "You'll have to cut it."
> I was dazed.
> "Cut it? But why?"
> "Because it doesn't arise from the situation. It's theater wit... And that, never. It's a witticism. A thing to be avoided above all else."
> "Then, one should never be witty?"
> "Yes, when it comes about naturally, when the play demands it. Otherwise, it interrupts the movement."[6]

Comic language in Feydeau reflects an imperfect command of standard French, as in the case of the numerous foreign or provincial characters who massacre the language. Or else it arises from a distraction or an emotional tension of the characters, as in the case of Mathieu in *L'Hôtel du Libre-Exchange*. Unable to speak without stuttering when it is raining, Mathieu graciously explains his unexpected visit to the Pinglets:

> PINGLET Scarcely have you arrived and your first call is on us!
> MATHIEU Of course! You can understand, my dear that no... hum! my dear, that no... hum!
> PINGLET What's he saying?
> MATHIEU That no visit was closer to my heart.
>
> *(I, xiii)*

As Bergson observes, true comic language cannot be translated: in this scene, "that no," in French "qu'aucu..." sounds like Mathieu is calling Pinglet, "my dear cuckold."

But plays on words are usually reserved for the uneducated classes in these plays, the servants and maids who do not quite understand what their masters are referring to and interpret them freely. A valet in an early play, for example, hearing that his mistress is playing some Beethoven, deforms it to the nearest

[6] René Peter, *Le Théâtre et la vie sous la Troisième République*, Volume II, Paris, Editions Marchot, 1947, p. 240.

recognizable expression he can extract from the already deformed French pronunciation of a German name: *bête à veine* (lucky beast).

In his masterly study of *Laughter*, the French philosopher Bergson, who was Feydeau's contemporary, considers the situational comedy of *vaudeville* to be made up of three principal techniques: repetition, inversion and interference of series. These are, indeed, the methods which Feydeau learned from his predecessors in the *vaudeville* form, and which are used most frequently by him.

Repetition of words is a much used comic device in classical comedy. With *vaudeville*, it is rather the repetition of situations which strikes us. When a situation is repeated sufficiently, it becomes not only comic, but begins to put on the appearance of a universal plot, particularly if viewed through the eyes of the character at the center of the situation. Bois-d'Enghien might well feel himself the victim of a plot to reveal to his mistress the secrets of his engagement, for almost every time he turns around a new character has entered and produced a copy of the morning *Figaro*, which contains both a review of Lucette's latest concert, and news of Bois-d'Enghien's forthcoming marriage. One after another, he seizes the newspaper from the hands of the surprised bearer and stuffs it into his own coat. . . .

Situational comedy, such as that found in farce and *vaudeville*— the comedy at which Feydeau excelled—has not traditionally stood high in critical esteem. It is placed above the lowly pun, but well below the level of comedy of character. The reason for this is given by Bergson. The *purpose* of laughter (and hence of comedy), he declares, is to correct behavior that is dehumanized or antisocial. At the base of all comedy, in the Bergsonian view, lies some distraction which renders a character momentarily (or temperamentally) incapable of reacting in a living human way. He fails to adapt to changing circumstances, and like a robot or a machine, continues what he has always done, when he should have been adaptable. In simplest terms, he falls into a hole or slips on a banana peel. On a more sophisticated level, he betrays his mania (which has dehumanized him, made him a miser, a misanthrope, a dreamer, etc.) in more complex acts and words. In comedy of character, comic acts and words derive always from character.

Situation comedy, on the other hand, reveals a distraction in *things*, life is seen as a mechanism with interchangeable pieces and reversible effects. The mathematical piling up of objects or events, with their repetitions, inversions and interferences, underlines the mechanical aspect of life itself which is unaware and comic. Unlike the comic of character, says Bergson, situational comedy corrects nothing. It was simply invented to make us laugh, because we enjoy laughter. It is therefore somewhat divorced from life and reality and does not, like character comedy, plunge its roots deep in life:

> Thus we can understand *vaudeville* which is to real life what the puppet is to a man who can walk, a very artificial exaggeration of a certain natural stiffness of things. The string connecting it to real life is slender indeed. It is scarcely more than a game, subordinated like all games to a convention which must be first accepted.[7]

In the *belle époque*, Bergson's observations may have been acceptable, but in the last half of the twentieth century life *has* become so dehumanized that Feydeau's plays stand today almost as a revelation of the threatening universe in

---

[7] Henri Bergson, *Le Rire*, Paris, Presses Universitaires, 1947, p. 78.

which we live. Viewing a revival of *La Main passe*, Jean Cocteau exclaimed, "It's a real nightmare . . . like Kafka."[8]

Everything allows us to concur, for life seen through two World Wars, and through the perspectives established by the theater of the absurd, particularly that of Ionesco, suggests that there is indeed a natural stiffness of things, life itself *is* given to distractions, and man is all too often the victim of these bad jokes. Instead of relegating situation comedy to an inferior position, writers like Beckett and Ionesco have suggested that it has metaphysical implications. It is these that we now can see in Feydeau, and that his contemporaries were not sensitive to.

Not every *vaudeville* suggests a truth beyond itself. Not every clown is representative of man lost in a meaningless universe. It takes the genius of a Chaplin or a Beckett to create such a clown. In the *vaudeville* it takes a craftsman who is master enough of the form to send it reeling into the void at breakneck speed. But it takes more than that, for theatrical abstraction, no matter how perfect, could not speak meaningfully to us. Despite his scorn for the Naturalists, despite his brilliant form in which the loose strings of life are at last neatly tied up, and everything is arranged artistically, we cannot overlook Feydeau, the realist. For Feydeau's characters, the situations in which they find themselves, and the words they speak, derive from a keen, sometimes kindly, sometimes caustic, observation of life. It is this which gives its strength and dimension to his brilliant mechanisms.

[8] Henri Jeanson, "Notes sur Georges Feydeau," *Cahiers de la Compagnie Madeleine Renaud-Jean-Louis Barrault*, No. 32, Dec., 1960, p. 20.

Shaw and Comedy*

Lionel Trilling

Shaw called *The Doctor's Dilemma* a tragedy, but it is hard to believe that he meant the description seriously. In manner and tone the play is a comedy; this is scarcely contradicted by the fact that one of the persons in the play dies before our eyes, for Louis Dubedat's histrionic last moments make a scene that is affecting in no more than a sentimental way.

The oddity of the author's having called the play a tragedy has never engaged the kind of speculation that has long gone on about Chekhov's insistence that *Three Sisters* is a comedy. A few critics have attempted to affirm its seriousness by observing that Ridgeon undergoes a moral decline, to the point where he commits a quasi-murder; they identify this as the tragic element in the play. But although it is true that Ridgeon's moral nature deteriorates, this is hardly a tragic event; at most, it touches with a certain grimness the comedy in which it occurs. The likelihood is that Shaw had no other reason for applying the misnomer than the wish to be impudent, to amuse himself by confusing his audience.

And of course it is only if we take the play to be a comedy that we can accept the artificiality that is one of its salient features. Comedy has always claimed the right to treat probability with blithe indifference, and *The Doctor's Dilemma* takes full advantage of this ancient license. The events of the play are shameless contrivances, beginning with the terms of the "dilemma," the all too pat juxtaposition of the immoral genius and the virtuous mediocrity. Nowhere except in comedy could an eminent physician give a dinner party at which certain of the guests are co-opted to sit as a kind of investigating committee to help the host decide whether or not another of the guests deserves to receive the medical treatment that will rescue him from impending death. We are then asked to believe that the committee, once formed, cannot bring itself to disband, that three of the busiest doctors in London are so captivated by the moral situation that they find time to pursue their investigations at a meeting in Louis Dubedat's studio, and that all of them make a point of turning up at his deathbed.

But even more than by the unblushing high-handedness of its dealings with probability, the play is a comedy by its commitment to one of the oldest enterprises of the comic genre, the exhibition of the absurdity of doctors. How very old it is has been suggested by the English scholar F. M. Cornford, who traces the comic doctor through various examples of folk drama, such as the Punch and Judy shows and the medieval mummers' plays, back to the comedy of ancient

* From *Prefaces To the Experience of Literature* by Lionel Trilling. Copyright © 1967 by Lionel Trilling. Reprinted by permission of Harcourt Brace Jovanovich, Inc.

Greece.[1] According to Cornford, Greek comedy had its roots in the primitive rituals of the winter solstice; the figure of the comic doctor descends from the once awesome medicine man who presided over the ceremonial representation of the death of the old year and the birth of the new. In the comedy of the Renaissance the doctor is a stock figure, mocked for his pretentiousness and pomposity. The tradition of doctor-baiting reached its climax and its classic form in the several plays in which Molière ridiculed the physicians of his day. To the traditional mockery he added an intellectual dimension by concentrating on the elaborate jargon of scholasticism by which the profession masked its invincible ignorance.

By the nineteenth century the tradition was on the wane, and now, in the popular drama of our time, no profession is accorded so much respect as that of medicine. The cinema and television seldom show the doctor as anything but virtuous and responsible, in his youth sternly dedicated to his unimpeachable profession, in his latter years endowed with a wisdom to which no layman can aspire. This change in the "image" of the doctor is connected with the advances that medicine made in the course of the nineteenth century. From our present perspective these may seem small, but they are significant because they were the result of the development of biological knowledge—medicine began to school itself in the sciences as it never had before and seemed on the point of making good the claims of its effectiveness that for so long had been empty.

It was in this period of not unjustifiable optimism, when the common opinion of the medical profession moved toward becoming what it now is, that Shaw mounted the elaborate attack, which, beginning in his youth, was to continue through the greater part of his life. *The Doctor's Dilemma* is but one of his innumerable writings on medical subjects. They have been accused of error, extravagance and perversity, in part because of their polemic style, which is often intentionally outrageous. But they are remarkably well informed, and in the main they make excellent sense.

The essence of Shaw's indictment is that the medical profession turned every new idea it acquired into authoritative doctrine and then into dogma, with the result that even its most promising discoveries became barren and often dangerous. Other of its deficiencies also contributed to his viewing it as a "conspiracy against the public," but Shaw directed his most active antagonism toward that aspect of medicine which its practitioners had come to believe was its greatest strength, its reliance on scientific research. He held that exactly when medicine based itself most confidently on science it was most likely to prove unscientific, establishing orthodoxies which stood in the way of truth. If the charge has bearing even upon the medical situation in our day, when the acceleration of research condemns received ideas to a shorter expectancy of life than they once had, in Shaw's time its cogency was still greater. A case in point is the germ theory of disease as it was then formulated. This was of obvious value, yet it served as the ground for untenable conclusions (such as that virtually all diseases are caused by germs), mistaken beliefs (such as that vaccination provided permanent immunity from smallpox and was wholly without danger), and unsalutary practices (such as Lord Lister's use of surgical antisepsis, eventually abandoned because the antiseptic interfered with the healing process).

But the scientific inadequacy of its accepted theories was not the whole of the objection that Shaw made to the state of the medical profession. He was dis-

[1] *The Origin of Attic Comedy.*

mayed by what he took to be its philosophical or spiritual failure. Central to his thought was the doctrine of vitalism, which holds that the life of organisms is the manifestation of a vital principle distinct from all physical and chemical forces. It was a view that led him to deny categorically the first premise of the medical practice of his day, that the human body is a mechanism and that any malfunction it may show is to be dealt with in a mechanistic way. Shaw's belief in vitalism stood in close relation to his social views, for he held that disease is best understood as a result of adverse conditions in the environment, and that health depends on comfort and beauty, which society has the duty to provide.

Even this summary account of Shaw's dealings with medicine will suggest that he must have come to the writing of his comedy of doctors in a spirit quite different from that of his predecessors in the long tradition. It is not possible to attribute any propagandistic purpose to the earlier comic writers. They mocked doctors with no intention of exciting indignation, only laughter. Even Molière, whose satire so tellingly exposes the intellectual deficiencies of medicine, does not propose that anything in particular can or should be done about the bad state of affairs. As one critic puts it, comedy for Molière was not a means but an end. Shaw often said in the most explicit way that the opposite was true of him, that he intended his art not as an end in itself but as a means to an end, the betterment of human life. He proclaimed his pre-eminent concern with ideas, and with ideas that were "constructive" and practical, and his proudest boast was that he belonged to the company of what he called the "artist-philosophers," those men who, by means of their art, addressed themselves to bringing about a change in the condition of human life. He spoke scornfully of the "pure" artists, those who did not undertake to solve life's problems but were content to represent life as it is, for what merely pleasurable interest the representation might have. Among these he includes Shakespeare, whom he lovingly scolds because "he was utterly bewildered" by life and because his "pregnant observations and demonstrations of life are not co-ordinated into any philosophy or religion."

Yet if we take *The Doctor's Dilemma* quite by itself, without reference to its author's other writings about medicine,[2] and without regard to his characterization of himself as an "artist-philosopher," the effect of the play is really not different from that of a play of Molière's. Many of the specific ideas expounded in Shaw's polemical writings find expression in *The Doctor's Dilemma*, but we feel that they are there for the sake of the comedy rather than that the comedy was written to serve them. Such conclusions as we may draw from the play are not about medicine at all; they are, rather, about "life," and do not seem different in kind from the conclusions that Molière's plays frequently yield—that Nature and common sense are good and should guide our judgment; that committing oneself to a ruling idea goes against Nature and common sense and leads to error or defeat or ridicule, or all three; that a genial flexibility of mind is a virtue, and that intellectual pride is a vice; that thinking in the terms prescribed by one's profession leads to personal and intellectual deformation; that true morality transcends moralistic judgment; that affectionate and charitable emotions are to be cherished, self-seeking motives to be condemned. Comedy has traditionally permitted us to derive just such generalizations from its laughter. They have

---

[2] Notable among them is the lengthy preface which Shaw wrote for the play when it was published in 1911. The large canon of what Shaw wrote about medicine over his lifetime is fully reviewed in Roger Boxill's admirable *Shaw and the Doctors*, a Columbia University dissertation.

great charm, and no doubt they serve a good purpose in disposing us to virtue, but they cannot lay claim to great intellectual originality or force. They can scarcely be "co-ordinated into any philosophy or religion"; they are not what we expect of an "artist-philosopher."

In short, *The Doctor's Dilemma*, although it advertises Shaw's ideas about medicine, does not propound them with any great didactic power. On this occasion, the "pure" artist in Shaw seems to have overcome the "artist-philosopher," and the latter cannot have put up a very determined resistance. He would appear to have been quite content to surrender into the hands of undidactic comedy all the ideas he took so seriously in his polemical writings: his doctors are menaces to the public welfare only secondarily and in a way that does not seem to matter or in some aspect other than the one in which they stand before us; we see them as on the whole rather pleasant-natured men, who are to be laughed at for comedy's usual reasons, because they are fools, or monomaniacs, or self-deceivers. And the "artist-philosopher" goes so far in conspiring in his own defeat as to make a hopelessly "pure" artist the spokesman for his cherished vitalism.

Louis Dubedat is the embodiment of an idea that had considerable interest for people at the end of the nineteenth century, as it still does—that art is not required to serve morality, that it exists for its own sake and is thus a paradigm of life itself, which is also said to exist for its own sake, for no other reason than to delight in its own energy and beauty. A corollary is that the artist is not necessarily a virtuous person, that indeed he is typically *not* virtuous and that his indifference or hostility to moral considerations is a condition of his creative power. There is no more truth in this than there was in Ruskin's assertion that only a good man can produce good art, but the new notion of the amoral artist, like the more general idea which it paralleled, served to liberate people from certain rather glum notions about art that prevailed in the Victorian age. Shaw, it may be supposed, stood in an ambivalent relation to the new conception of art and the artist. His moral temper, which he was willing to call Puritan, rejected it; yet at the same time he could respond to it affirmatively because it spoke of the energy, freedom, and beauty that life ought properly to have, and also because it outraged the merely respectable morality of the middle class, which, depressing in itself, stood in the path of ameliorating change.

As an example of the artist who stands outside the considerations of morality, Dubedat is in some ways not an altogether satisfactory creation. His infractions of the moral code are all on a small scale. Almost everything he does is touched with slyness or meanness; petty deceit is his natural medium. He can outdo the doctors themselves in conventionality: there is reason to believe that he is perfectly sincere when he mocks them for supposing that Jennifer is not married to him, for not seeing that she is "a lady" who carries "her marriage certificate in her face and in her character." He is a snob and a prig who can say of the girl he married under false pretenses that he could not stay with her long because she was "quite out of art and literature and refined living." And his stature as an artist is only little greater than as an immoralist; nothing that is said of his work leads us to believe that he is anything more than a brilliant and engaging but quite minor talent.

Dubedat's minuscule quality is in part dictated by the exigencies of comedy. If his stature were larger, if he enlisted our sympathies to a greater extent, his fate would be more moving than would have suited Shaw's purpose. As it is, his utterance of his "creed" on his deathbed creates an effect that, in its ambiguity, is quite in accord with the comic mode. When he folds his hands and affirms his belief "in Michael Angelo [sic], Velasquez, and Rembrandt; in the might of design, the majesty of color, the redemption of all things by Beauty everlasting, and the message of Art that has made these hands blessed," the conscious pathetic eloquence of the speech is meant to mock itself, at least a little, and his subsequent question about the newspaper reporter is an obvious ironic comment on it. Yet for Shaw a creed is always momentous, especially one that speaks of redemption and a blessing, and Dubedat's death-bed avowal of faith makes the vitalistic affirmation of life that is meant to stand as the condemnation of Ridgeon and his mechanistic views.

The character of Ridgeon is puzzling almost to a fault. Upon first acquaintance we like him very much and from the description of him upon his entrance it is plain that Shaw meant that we should. The first check upon this approving opinion appears at the end of the second act, when, with the help of Sir Patrick Cullen, he is confronting his dilemma. Only for a short time is the dilemma allowed to be one of principle: whether to save the honest, decent, but not very useful doctor, Blenkinsop, or the "rotten blackguard" artist, Dubedat, "a genuine source of pretty and pleasant and good things." No sooner has the dilemma been stated in its interesting simplicity than Ridgeon introduces a complication that alters its nature: he discloses to Sir Patrick his desire to marry Dubedat's wife. This frankness we find admirable; by openly stating what he has to gain by allowing Dubedat to die, Ridgeon assures us that he is a man of wholly objective judgment. But our admiration cools when Sir Patrick says, "Perhaps she won't have you, you know," and Ridgeon answers, "I've a pretty good flair for that sort of thing. I know when a woman is interested in me. She is." There is of course no reason why Jennifer should *not* be "interested" in Ridgeon; a woman is likely to have some interested response to a man who is attractive, powerful, and drawn to her. And when, at the end of Act V, Jennifer, who is not exactly a girl, says that she had never been interested in him because he was too old—he is fifty—we may well feel that Shaw, in contriving this humiliation for Ridgeon, has made Jennifer trivial and undeveloped. Nonetheless, Ridgeon's answer to Sir Patrick, which is made "with a self-assured shake of the head," is vulgar and fatuous. The moral elevation that Ridgeon seemed about to gain by his frankness is no longer possible.

By the end of Act III, Ridgeon has become a sentimental self-deceiver, convincing himself that the motive for his decision to let Dubedat die is the noble desire to preserve Jennifer's illusions about her husband. In Act IV he speaks in a voice that Dubedat authoritatively describes as "devilish." But these manifestations of his moral decline do not carry conviction; they seem less the result of the character's inner life than of the author's manipulation.

A Comic Complex
and a Complex Comic*

Ruby Cohn

Something old, something new,
Something borrowed, something blue.

The old wedding jingle may be used to symbolize and summarize Beckett's work, much as he himself used the round song about the dog in *Godot*, or Schubert's "Death and the Maiden" in *All That Fall*, or the duet from *The Merry Widow* in *Happy Days*. At first glance, a marriage rhyme might seem singularly inappropriate for an author haunted by man's loneliness and alienation, and yet Beckett conveys man's essential solitude through various couples, from Belacqua and his sundry *amours* to Winnie-Willie of *Happy Days*, passing through several sets of master and servant, friend and friend, Molloy and his mother, Moran and his son, Krapp and his tape recorder.

Even the first line of the wedding rhyme, "Something old, something new," may be illustrated by a double view of a single characteristic. Thus, the illiberal jest so central to Beckett's work is at least as old as the *Iliad*, but Beckett plays it for a new metaphysical resonance. Similarly, man's fate is one of the oldest themes of literature, but Beckett composes in a minor key that is constantly enriched by fresh comic overtones. Beckett's heroes are old fools in the old fool tradition of the one who gets slapped, but Beckett inveigles us to laugh at the slap and the slapper, as well as the one who gets slapped.

The Beckett hero incorporates other features of the fool tradition—his appearance of physical freak, his inspired idiocy that borders on wisdom, his alienation from a society that is criticized through his comic gift. And again Beckett, with comic astringency, gives new depth to these old traditions. Often a dwarf or cripple, the traditional fool is as spendid as a Greek statue by comparison with Beckett's protagonists in their various stages of disintegration. The wisdom of Beckett's heroes, bolstered by his own considerable learning, is maintained by tenacious ignorance in the face of modern stockpiling of information. Beckett's fools are alienated not only from society but from all the modern world. Beckett's buffoon rejects a social role, and yet by his fierce obsession with himself in a hostile world, he stands for every individual in that world. A sacrificial victim, Beckett's fool no longer achieves anyone's catharsis, least of all his own.

One of the best-educated men of our time, Beckett has undoubtedly read

* Ruby Cohn, "A Comic Complex and a Complex Comic," in *Samuel Beckett: The Comic Gamut* (Rutgers University Press, 1962), pp. 283–299.

the major philosophers from Aristotle, "qui savait tout," to Sartre, possibly the "agregé de philosophie" of the French *Murphy*. He adheres to no school, denying Existentialist affiliations. Yet he has mingled and published with French Existentialists; his theater has been called a "theater of existence."[1] Like the Existentialists, Beckett is haunted by death, and his ghosts react raucously to this climactic event of human life.

Beckett's first hero, the poet Belacqua Shuah, dies quietly enough on the operating table. His second hero, Murphy, is in a rocking trance when he is burned to death in his garret retreat. Watt seems too busy to have time for death. But Beckett's French heroes long explosively for death while they endure the sentence of their lives. From Molloy, the first of the writing heroes, each of them has to earn his way to death through his works. The process of writing becomes an approach to death; composition takes place during decomposition. In living, we slowly kill ourselves; however agonizing, however farcical, life kills time. It is a cruelly comic Beckett paradox: While we live, we die; we must compose while we decompose. And faced with death, what attitude can we adopt?

Just before his fatal operation, Beckett's Belacqua ponders this question:

> At this crucial point the good God came to his assistance with a phrase from a paradox of Donne: *Now among our wise men, I doubt not but many would be found, who would laugh at Heraclitus weeping, none which would weep at Democritus laughing.* This was a godsend, and no error . . . Belacqua snatched eagerly at the issue. Was it to be laughter or tears? It came to the same thing in the end, but which was it to be *now?* . . . He [Belacqua] must efface himself altogether and do the little soldier. It was this paramount consideration that made him decide in favour of Bim and Bom, Grock, Democritus, whatever you are pleased to call it. ("Yellow," 235–237)°

Even though tragic and comic "came to the same thing in the end," both Beckett and Belacqua consciously choose laughter some few hours before the latter's death. They ride in the wake of Pim and Bom, who joke about the things that other people would be shot for saying; of Democritus, the laughing philosopher of antiquity; and of Grock, the clown who mimicked human failure—"Nicht möglich."

Later Beckett heroes are less able than Belacqua to make this clearcut choice between tears and laughter. In *Watt*, the hero's predecessor Arsene, and his successor, Arthur, are both practiced laughers, but Watt himself alternates between smiles and tears. Moran "at the thought of the punishments Youdi might inflict . . . was seized . . . with mighty silent laughter and [his] features composed in their wonted stillness and calm." Malone, fighting the gravity into which he was born, "plays the clown." The Unnamable wonders whether his constant flow of tears can be tears of mirth at this joke of a life; later, however, he admits to weeping to keep from laughing, and he invokes Democritus as the last proper name in a comedy of namelessness. In *Godot*, it hurts Vladimir to laugh; in *Endgame*, Hamm muses, "You weep, and weep, for nothing, so as not to laugh." In *Embers*, Henry can only laugh a "long horrible laugh." The crawling creature of *Comment c'est* at first wants to laugh all the time, then only

---

[1] Jacques Guicharnaud, *Modern French Theatre from Giraudoux to Beckett* (New Haven, 1961), p. 219. The analysis of Beckett's theater is remarkably fine in this book.

° [Page references are to "Yellow," in *More Pricks Than Kicks* (London: Chatto and Windus), 1934.]

sometimes, three times out of ten, four out of fifteen, but he finally settles for "trois quatre rires réussis de ceux qui secouent un instant ressuscitent un instant puis laissent pour plus mort qu'avant" ("three four successful laughs of those that shake one an instant revive one an instant then leave one more dead than before"). Winnie asks Willie after a laugh, "How can one better magnify the Almighty than by sniggering with him at his little jokes, particularly the poorer ones?" At no time is there a hint of catharsis to be achieved through laughter, either for Beckett's characters or for us.

Of all Beckett's characters, the specialist in laughing matters is Arsene, Watt's predecessor and mentor at Mr. Knott's house. Arsene's hierarchy of laughs, "the bitter, the hollow, and the mirthless," suggests the ironic complexity of Beckett's own comic:

> The bitter laugh laughs at that which is not good, it is the ethical laugh. The hollow laugh laughs at that which is not true, it is the intellectual laugh . . . But the mirthless laugh is the dianoetic laugh, down the snout—Haw!—so. It is the laugh of laughs, the *risus purus*, the laugh laughing at the laugh, the beholding, saluting of the highest joke, in a word the laugh that laughs—silence please, at that which is unhappy. (48)°

Practitioners of the *risus purus*, Beckett's heroes laugh at suffering. Like the Surrealists, they laugh helplessly at cosmically illiberal jests upon themselves or others, and like the Surrealists, too, they enter into the cruel cosmic spirit by perpetrating sadistic jokes of their own. Responding to cosmic cruelty with "black laughter," the Surrealist hero defied and transcended his fate, triumphantly expelling a laugh with his last lungful of breath. But Beckett's laughter—the laughter he expresses and the laughter he evokes—is a mask for, not a release from, despair. It may start with a bang, but it trails off in a whimper; it is "yellow laughter," often rasped out in spite of the laughter. It defies no one and transcends nothing. Such laughter is as automatic and anguished as a response to tickling.

From Beckett's earliest writing, callousness and cruelty evoke bitter ethical laughter. An execution amuses Belacqua Shuah; the sadistic routines of the Magdalen Mental Mercyseat are itemized for our amusement; and all the heroes of Beckett's French fiction invite our laughter at their savage drives—Moran's towards his son, Molloy's towards his mother, Malone's towards his creations, the Unnamable's towards his creators. Vladimir and Estragon turn their stichomythic humor to suicide and murder. Hamm and Clov engage in verbal torture, to their and our ironic appreciation. In *Comment c'est* all men are paradoxically and statistically revealed as both victim and executioner, and the more one suffers, the more wildly one laughs: "j'ai toute la souffrance de tous les temps je m'en soucie comme d'une guigne et c'est le fou rire dans chaque cellule" ("all suffering of all time is mine but it doesn't phase me and it's the wild laugh in every cell"). Winnie quotes: "laughing wild amid severest woe."

By Arsene's definition, the dianoetic laugh is the obverse of the ethical laugh. The latter is inspired by the executioner, the former by the victim. Beckett's heroes swing from one to the other, from sadism to suffering and back again. Midway between the ethical and dianoetic laughs, Arsene situates the hollow or intellectual laugh, and, in a somewhat broader definition than Arsene al-

---

° [Page references are to *Watt* (Grove Press), 1959.]

lows, the middle range of laughter undergoes the most significant modification through Beckett's successive works.

Intellectual laughter, aroused by deviation from truth, may be compared to Bergsonian laughter, aroused by mechanical rigidity imposed upon the authentic free flow of life, which is a kind of truth. Beckett's early works exhibit the twists of plot, distortion of character, and tricks of language, much as Bergson analyzed them. Thus, in *More Pricks Than Kicks*, Beckett twists plots for comic effect when Belacqua abandons a damsel in distress, urges his fiancée to take a lover, is himself the object of a lady's lust, and is finally supplanted in the arms of his third wife by his best friend. In *Murphy* the hero consents to take employment so that his prostitute-mistress need not continue hers. After Murphy's death, his ashes, instead of being flushed down the toilet of Dublin's Abbey Theater, are dispersed in a busy London bar—in crooked comic comment on Murphy's teetotaling, solipsistic life.

From *Watt* on, however, Beckett's plots are so unpredictable that they cannot be twisted, since there is no norm from which to twist. One seemingly senseless incident follows another without sequence or motivation. Place, time, and season are described at inappropriate intervals; day and night, land and sea, town and forest, light and dark, cathedral and slaughterhouse figure incongruously in the plots. From volume to volume, these excursions into "reality" are reduced until in *Comment c'est* the narrator's encounters with Pim and Bom and maddeningly and ridiculously rehearsed. Amorphous and non-concatenated, the volumes of the French trilogy mock the well-made novel. Pointed and repetitive, *Comment c'est* mocks the traditional novel by diminishing plot to human situation.

In Beckett's fiction there is an almost straight-line movement to a single human center. The debonair and detached elegance of *More Pricks Than Kicks* is soon perforated by the embryonic philosophical explorations of *Murphy*. In *Watt*, the hero painstakingly attempts to make sense of his world; both his efforts and his failure are conveyed in a comic mode, and yet traditional comic distance is shortened as Beckett moves us closer and closer to his hero's suffering, for his predicament is that of everyman, is our own.

In the French fiction, with increased control and concentration in each successive work, Beckett channels man's absurd fate into anguish at that fate. As fiction follows fiction, Beckett reduces his plots, diminishes his characters, and compresses his language. It is perhaps partly this voluntary impoverishment that caused Beckett to turn from English to French, where the vocabulary is more limited, and where there is a greater divergence than in English between the literary language to which Beckett was habituated and the colloquial discourse his narrators employ.

As early as 1929, Beckett observed in his essay on Joyce, "No language is so sophisticated as English. It is abstracted to death." He compared English to Medieval Latin in order to establish an analogy between Dante's use of the vulgar tongue and Joyce's creation of one. Perhaps the all-powerful language of Joyce inhibited Beckett's development in English. Beckett himself contrasted the two: "The more Joyce knew the more he could. He's tending toward omniscience and omnipotence as an artist. I'm working with impotence, ignorance."[2]

---

[2] Israel Shenker, "Moody Man of Letters," New York *Times*, May 6, 1956, sec. 2, p. 1.

The emphasis should be placed on "working." It is a simple fact that Beckett's erudition compares with that of Joyce. Although they work differently, they both strive for maximum inclusiveness in their fiction. Joyce's reach is encyclopedic; he finds a syllable or symbol to suggest everything, from the most trivially accidental to the most mythically universal. Omniscient and omnipotent, detached and smiling, he creates a universe of unparalleled linguistic wealth. Beckett, in contrast (and perhaps in direct reaction), seeks ignorance, impotence, nakedness. He comes as close to them as literature can, but he cannot achieve them. He may change his language so that he speaks an alien tongue literally as well as metaphorically, but he cannot do away with language and still manage to think. And that is his curse, as it is ours—that man is, as Descartes defined him, "a thing that thinks."

Thus sentenced, thus cursed. Beckett's protagonists insist upon the ridiculous details of their physical situations—Murphy in his rocker, Molloy on his compulsive voyage, Malone in bed, the Unnamable in limbo, an uprooted Gogo and Didi by their rooted tree, a defenseless Hamm and Clov in their shelter, the partner of Pim and/or Bom in the mud, Winnie and Willie on a scorched earth beneath a hellish blazing sun. Mobile or immobile, in frantic activity or absurd tableau, they evoke laughter at their physical situations and pity for their metaphysical situation. Seeking sense and sensibility in an indifferent cosmos, reflecting the Absurdity of the Macrocosm in the absurd details of his microcosm, the Beckett hero cries out in the frustration of his humanity, which is our own.

A poet and not a philosopher, Beckett had to work through his own creations to attain his bleak, comic vision of the human condition. Thus, the early English fiction is inhabited by caricatures, and only from the heroes does Beckett modify his attitude between *More Pricks* and *Murphy*. In the short stories, Belacqua is seen through detached and mocking eyes, but Beckett tacitly admits his sympathy for Murphy: "All the puppets in this book whinge sooner or later, except Murphy, who is not a puppet." In the Magdalen Mental Mercyseat, Murphy's mind is even vouchsafed a vision of what the French heroes will seek in vain to glimpse: "that rare postnatal treat . . . the Nothing, than which in the guffaw of the Abderite naught is more real." Appropriately enough, Murphy's response—like Belacqua's in the hospital, like that of Democritus the laughing Abderite—is laughter.

Watt, who cannot laugh, is a grotesque throwback to Cooper, a servant in *Murphy*, and a grotesque foreshadowing of the French heroes, who finally cast off servitude. The grotesque has been identified by its assimilation of animal and human worlds, of real and dream worlds.[3] Although Watt's concerns are not with reality, it is nevertheless a kind of reality that he seeks at Mr. Knott's establishment, where events are as illogical and inexplicable as in dreams.

Ungainly and plodding, Watt consecrates his life to trying to understand Mr. Knott's establishment. Sam the narrator pokes fun at Watt's senses and reason, which fail their owner in his time of need, but Sam Beckett's sympathy for Watt (an ironic, ambivalent sympathy, to be sure) peeps through the account of Sam, surname unknown. Not so completely detached from Watt as he would have us believe, Sam-narrator dwells on the same physically disgusting and mentally agonizing details that preoccupy Sam Beckett in his French works, and,

[3] Wolfgang Kayser, *Das Groteske* (Oldenburg, 1957).

through Sam Beckett, his French heroes. Far from Bergson's analysis of the comic as mechanical aberration imposed on the *élan vital*, Beckett's comic heroes are limp rags of life lost in a stone-cold universe.

Beckett neither discovered nor invented the coldness of the cosmos, nor is he alone in finding indifference in the so-called moral as well as the natural order. The hypocrisy of faith, the stupidity of hope, and the brutality of charity are familiar attitudes in the contemporary scene, and contemporary art is riddled with the breakdown of belief, motivation, and communication. As the painter Burri expresses the poignancy of the human situation with his ludicrous sacks and scarlet gashes, Beckett's comic, violent bums become a metaphor for modern man, fallen too low for the contingencies of history or religion.

Unlike the biblical patriarchs who are ironically reflected in Watt, faithful servant of Mr. Knott, Beckett's French heroes have no job. Vagrants, paralytics, beggars, they move compulsively or do not move at all. Molloy is semiparalyzed, Malone is completely paralyzed, and the Unnamable is virtually bodiless except for a possible head and rump. Hilariously incongruous collections of impulse and habit, they are sentenced to recount their experience in all its unreconstructed absurdity. In those accounts, events blend into one another, along with places and times: characters change names, pop up and vanish, are invented and expunged: paragraphs disappear, sentences expand and contract, and phrases reflect forwards and backwards, suddenly denied or repeated. But the haphazard, irrational surface is actually a mosaic of extraordinary conceptual and linguistic control.

Trapped between birth and death, Beckett's French heroes fill the interim with stories, "And all funny: not one not funny." In the long interval between birth and death, while yearning for an exit through womb or tomb, these compulsive narrators spawn words as incoherent as the cries of the newborn, as incoherent as the death rattle, but the incoherence is calculated by Beckett.

To arrive at these approximations of the noises of the nascent and moribund, Beckett underwent intensive linguistic discipline. His early characters share with him a penchant for comic verbal elegance that depends upon breadth of vocabulary and reference. The titles of the early works, like the works themselves, contain puns: *Whoroscope, More Pricks Than Kicks*, "Enueg," *Murphy* (where Beckett declares, "In the begginning was the pun"). In these works, an intellectual laugh springs from linguistic techniques that are indifferent or irrelevant to truth: polished paradox, sneering irony, twisted quotation, erudite jargon. Even the heavier humor of misplaced literalism is lightly and elegantly applied. Beckett's wit glitters mainly in parody, where the tone is sometimes riotously, sometimes grotesquely, out of key with its subject. *Watt*, the bulk of whose prose is a heavy-handed parody of the workings of the rational understanding, opens and closes in light social satire, and it is enlivened midway by a caricature of an academic committee. But *Watt* also abounds in verbal repetition, flat contradiction, and ambivalent irony, all later transferred intact into Beckett's French work.

From the first burst into French prose, an incisive and vulgarly colloquial tongue replaces the elegant language of *Murphy* and the laborious logic of *Watt*. The cultivated English smile explodes into a Rabelaisian guffaw when pedantic jawbreakers give way to Basic-French-and-dirty-words, when a Latinate syntax gives way to pygmy phrases and giant sentences. The twisted quotations turn no longer about literature but about biblical or commonplace sayings, and, unlike the polished gems of the English fiction, they are deeply imbedded in the philosophic context. Only incidental in the English work, ingenuous literalism, flat self-contradiction, and hammered repetition become tools for comic creation and epistemological exploration. They are blunt, clumsy instruments, extensions of the hands that hold them, of the heads that conceive them. They do not, finally, discover or construct a universe: we laugh, finally, at the outlandish idea that they ever could, and yet the tension of their effort supports all of Beckett's work, inspiring bitter, hollow, mirthless laughter at their failure, which reflects ours.

In Beckett's latest work, Arsene's three laughs are merged; the ethical laugh is aroused by cruelty, the intellectual laugh by ignorance, but cruelty and ignorance dissolve in suffering. Bitter and hollow laughter are drowned in mirthless, dianoetic laughter—the only possible reaction to the impossible human situation, in which we live.

Cursed with a mind, man cannot be content with his animal body. Cursed with a body, he cannot retire into the life of the spirit. Forever alone, he is immersed in words, married to phenomena, and he spawns reasons before he knows what is happening to him; he spends the rest of his life foisting names on things, and things on names. If he is lucid beyond logic, he attempts to understand raw experience, but the pattern of ready-made things, names, and values intrudes upon his efforts at an intimate and idiosyncratic interpretation. He comes to doubt everything, and even to doubt the interpreting subject; his "I" is a working hypothesis that no longer works, and yet there is no one else he can be. Unable to penetrate into his microcosm, unable to break out into a macrocosm, he agonizes, poised awkwardly between them, and he is aware of his precarious position: "on the one hand the mind, on the other the world, I don't belong to either."

Beckett's extraordinary achievement has been to give dimension to this tightrope-walker, so that we care profoundly about his equilibrium. Beckett's is an intellectual accomplishment, for all the vaunted ignorance of his heroes. Using comic cliché phrases, he farcically deprives us of ready-made concepts. Using ludicrously simple events, he ironically invests them with metaphysical meaning. But he does not deal in philosophical problems; he plunges us into an emotional situation so that we alternate between panic and hilarity, as we anxiously watch the tottering of subject and object, of world and self, of *our* world and *our* self.

In Beckett's work, coherence is jarred at every level—the cosmos, the plot, the person, the sentence. In the "wordy-gurdy" of his protagonists' monologues, we are persuaded by our dizziness of his heroes' authenticity. They know no respect for time or place; they disdain sequence and proportion. But they must not be too readily confused with their creator. Unlike Sartre and Camus, who paint an absurd world in logical language and syntax, Beckett strives for a more mimetic art. Cosmic absurdity is reflected by non-concatenation of incidents, as in the fiction of Kafka; personal disintegration is reflected by syntactical fragmentation, as in the drama of Ionesco. Beckett uses the word and moods of our time, but he weaves them into a fabric of impressive design; the surface gibberish is packed with significance, the surface chaos with symbolism. Beckett's precise workmanship is readily apparent if we examine his revisions. Successive versions of his stories contain no modification in the abrupt *non sequiturs*, but there are many phrasal changes in order to achieve ludicrous incongruity, syntactical ambiguity, symbolic ambivalence, and more intense rhythms.

By use of a first-person, alogical narration, Beckett links his presentation of cosmic irony with his heroes' consciousness of that irony. Introspectionists who descend from Descartes, his protagonists show how miserably the line has deteriorated. Grotesque, ancient, crippled, hysterically caressing what they scarcely dare call possessions, thinking tenderly of their hats, clinging frantically to pencil, stick, or sack, Beckett's French "I's" mock themselves as they suffer. Gradually stripped of possessions and clothes, they grow larger in meaning as their silhouettes shrink. In *Comment c'est* the narrator is naked even of hat, bereft even of pencil, and literally dumb, reduced to voiceless, sentenceless, significant phrases. In *Happy Days* Winnie is reduced to a hatted head, thinking staccato thoughts in fewer and older phrases. As the very number of words is reduced, the tension is tautened between knowledge and ignorance, between sense and non-sense. With consummate verbal skill, Beckett involves us more deeply in his heroes, as they become more obsessively involved with themselves. And at the same time, we are more involved with *ourselves*. Beckett's fellow playwright Ionesco speaks for Beckett's heroes too when he writes: "By expressing my deepest obsessions, I express my deepest humanity."[4]

Instead of laughing in a civilized and detached way at comic figures whom we do not resemble, instead of reforming after laughing at our own weakness as seen in another, we come, in Beckett's work, to doubt ourselves through our laughter. But through the obsessions of Beckett's heroes, we understand our own deepest humanity. Since names are interchangeable, perhaps we too are nameless and unnamable. We laugh at the leg ailments, verbal difficulties, ignorance, and passion of Beckett's heroes, but our laughter is nervous and anxious. Are *our* feet solidly grounded, *our* words expressive of *our* meaning, *our* tears of grief or mirth? What shall we take as fact? We laugh in fear as we realize that there is no fact, only fiction. "Know thyself." What, that fiction? "Connaître, c'est mésurer." What, a fiction?

Beckett has achieved an ambiguously ironic confusion and communion of identity: Beckett, his creation the "I" who creates, his creation the "I" who sees. At this late stage of human history, when man cannot decipher his identity from the comic complexity of fictions and words, he nevertheless is compelled to seek that identity. Life and letters alike become a dianoetic joke of creations feeding upon their creators, with whom they are assimilable and irreconcilable. The artistic condition is no longer a pinnacle of privilege from which one may nod in neighborly fashion at God the Creator. Instead, creator and creature wallow together in dust or mud, whence they came. Or perhaps they never left it.

The modern man of letters who turns against letters was not fathered by Beckett, but no other modern writer—not Proust or Gide or Joyce or Mann—has integrated the act of creation so consistently and ironically into his own creation. Joyce held that the greatest love of a man was for his own lies, and yet the artist-liar is only one of his mythic prototypes. For Beckett, all literature and all life reduce to his portrait of the artist-liar as old bum: "You either lie or hold your peace," says Molloy, and Beckett's heroes do not hold their peace. Do we?

Beckett's art-lies, his fictions, know each other, if they know anything at all. Murphy's mind contains Belacqua, and the voiceless narrator of *Comment c'est*, recounting his life as the penitential task that all Beckett's heroes perform, likens

---

[4] Eugène Ionesco, "The Avant-Garde Theatre," *World Theatre VIII.* No. 3 (Autumn, 1959), quoted in Martin Esslin, "The Theatre of the Absurd," *Tulane Drama Review* (May, 1960), 7.

himself to Belacqua, comically turned on his side in the slime. In Beckett's un-published novel, Mercier speaks to Watt of Murphy, for the one reminds him of the other. Moran refers to Murphy, Watt, Yerk, Mercier. Malone groups himself with other Beckett fictions: "Then it will be all over with the Murphys, Merciers, Molloys, Morans and Malones, unless it goes on beyond the grave." Perhaps it does, since the Unnamable carries on a discourse with Molloy and Malone, Ma-hood and Worm, and others "from Murphy on"; he insists in vain that he is not they "who told me I was they, who I must have tried to be, under duress, or through fear, or to avoid acknowledging me." The crawling, voiceless creature of *Comment c'est* intermittently encounters and is Pim and Bom, voiced and voiceless aspects of Beckett's earlier fictions; reason and calculation, emotion and imagination—all are taught to man through his fiction, even if the fiction is him-self, and the dialogue reduced to a monologue of ready-made phrases, stubborn-ly, clumsily, ironically, searching for an individual and independent self. But the search itself is paradigmatic of all human endeavor.

Like his fiction, Beckett's drama focuses on man as artist-liar, often in the guise of artist-actor. It is this accent that distinguishes his drama from the com-parably comic anti-plays of Ionesco. Although Beckett and Ionesco both have learned from Artaud and Jarry to express serious theatrical concerns in spectacu-lar farcical terms, it is Beckett for whom theater is the more immediate meta-phor of the world. The worn-out acts of vaudeville and the threadbare devices of drama emphasize our presence at a spectacle, and symbolize our lives. In *Godot* each of the characters performs for an audience, and conflicting testimonies thread through the play. In *Endgame*, the artist is the hero whose chronicle seems to relate to his life in the penitential fashion that Belacqua's dream relates to his. In *Embers*, Henry's fictions, Bolton and Holloway, are possible doctors to cure him. In *Krapp's Last Tape*, Krapp attempts to fix the flux of himself through a tape recorder, for love has not accomplished this task. In *Happy Days*, Winnie needs the spectacle of Willie, as she needs to feel herself a spectacle in other eyes.

Beckett's heroes are aware of playing a role, as though they had read Epic-tetus the Stoic: "Remember that you are an actor in a drama, of such a kind as the author pleases to make it. . . . For this is your business, to act well the charac-ter assigned to you; to choose it is another's."[5] We are all actors, playing stock parts in the repertoire of the *commedia dell'arte*. Although ad lib dialogue is en-couraged, it must be couched in familiar phrases and re-enforced by violent slapstick. If there ever was a script, we cannot know it; much less can we know an author or audience.

Dramatic or fictional, Beckett's work paints an ironic portrait of man, Ev-eryman, as artist-liar. He paints in words—in the words that his heroes revile and unravel, in the words he weaves into one of the masterly prose styles of our time. Superbly controlling his medium, Beckett probes both source and product of language. The succinct redundancy of his dramatic dialogue is in ironic con-trast to the logorrhea of his fictional narrators.

Within each literary genre, Beckett undermines that very genre—fictional formulae in the fiction and dramatic conventions in the drama. By mocking the literary form within that form, Beckett questions the boundary between art and

[5] Quoted by Jean-Jacques Mayoux, "The Theatre of Samuel Beckett," *Perspective* (Autumn, 1959), 142.

life, between fiction and fact. Such interrogation is part of the traditional stock in trade of the fool, and Beckett plays it for all its farcical, metaphysical worth. He pommels existence with the questions of his characters, or with their frenzied affirmations immediately followed by more frenzied negations. These questions slap at life as well as art; for any interpretation of life is a construction, a game, a work of art; bordering on a reality that is necessarily unknown, unknowable, and frustratingly seductive.

"I'm working with impotence, ignorance," Beckett has explicitly admitted. "My little exploration is that whole zone of being that has always been set aside by artists as something unusable—as something by definition incompatible with art. I think anyone nowadays, who pays the slightest attention to his own experience finds it the experience of a non-knower, a non-can-er."[6]

"A non-knower, a non-can-er" is, however, still another role, that of the old comic Eiron or self-deprecator, the fool of his fictions. Aristotle, "qui savait tout," wrote that comedy paints men as worse than they are, and the Eiron paints himself as worse than he is. Beckett's comic ironist is ugly, small, poor, cruel, ignorant, miserable, and infinitely vulnerable. It is above all in that vulnerability that we recognize ourselves. As long as man remains ugly, small, poor, cruel, ignorant, miserable, and vulnerable, Beckett's ironic works will have lively and deadly relevance for us.

Through the years Beckett has hacked at his plots and characters; he has decimated his sentences and the number of his words, until he is left with a single protagonist in the generalized human situation, an "I" in quest of his "I" through fiction, who is in quest of his "I" through fiction, who, etc. Perhaps the old wedding jingle should be applied with a shotgun, for each "I" conceives another who conceives another who conceives another until we arrive full circle laughing—hysterical perhaps at our plight.

VIII
FROM THE
CLASSICS OF
COMIC THEORY

Preface to Tartuffe*

Molière

Here is a comedy that has excited a good deal of discussion and that has been under attack for a long time; and the persons who are mocked by it have made it plain that they are more powerful in France than all whom my plays have satirized up to this time. Noblemen, ladies of fashion, cuckolds, and doctors all kindly consented to their presentation, which they themselves seemed to enjoy along with everyone else; but hypocrites do not understand banter: they became angry at once, and found it strange that I was bold enough to represent their actions and to care to describe a profession shared by so many good men. This is a crime for which they cannot forgive me, and they have taken up arms against my comedy in a terrible rage. They were careful not to attack it at the point that had wounded them: they are too crafty for that and too clever to reveal their true character. In keeping with their lofty custom, they have used the cause of God to mask their private interests; and *Tartuffe*, they say, is a play that offends piety: it is filled with abominations from beginning to end, and nowhere is there a line that does not deserve to be burned. Every syllable is wicked, the very gestures are criminal, and the slightest glance, turn of the head, or step from right to left conceals mysteries that they are able to explain to my disadvantage. In vain did I submit the play to the criticism of my friends and the scrutiny of the public: all the corrections I could make, the judgment of the king and queen who saw the play, the approval of great princes and ministers of state who honored it with their presence, the opinion of good men who found it worthwhile, all this did not help. They will not let go of their prey, and every day of the week they have pious zealots abusing me in public and damning me out of charity.

I would care very little about all they might say except that their devices make enemies of men whom I respect and gain the support of genuinely good men, whose faith they know and who, because of the warmth of their piety, readily accept the impressions that others present to them. And it is this which forces me to defend myself. Especially to the truly devout do I wish to vindicate my play, and I beg of them with all my heart not to condemn it before seeing it, to rid themselves of preconceptions, and not aid the cause of men dishonored by their actions.

If one takes the trouble to examine my comedy in good faith, he will surely see that my intentions are innocent throughout, and tend in no way to make fun of what men revere; that I have presented the subject with all the precautions that its delicacy imposes; and that I have used all the art and skill that I could to

* Molière, Preface to *Tartuffe* [1669], Haskell M. Block, tr. and ed. (A.H.M. Publishing Corporation, 1958), pp. 1–7. Reprinted by permission of the A.H.M. Publishing Corporation, Arlington Heights, Illinois.

distinguish clearly the character of the hypocrite from that of the truly devout man. For that purpose I used two whole acts to prepare the appearance of my scoundrel. Never is there a moment's doubt about his character; he is known at once from the qualities I have given him; and from one end of the play to the other, he does not say a word, he does not perform an action which does not depict to the audience the character of a wicked man, and which does not bring out in sharp relief the character of the truly good man which I oppose to it.

I know full well that by way of reply, these gentlemen try to insinuate that it is not the role of the theater to speak of these matters; but with their permission, I ask them on what do they base this fine doctrine. It is a proposition they advance as no more than a supposition, for which they offer not a shred of proof; and surely it would not be difficult to show them that comedy, for the ancients, had its origin in religion and constituted a part of its ceremonies; that our neighbors, the Spaniards, have hardly a single holiday celebration in which a comedy is not a part; and that even here in France, it owes its birth to the efforts of a religious brotherhood who still own the Hotel de Bourgogne, where the most important mystery plays of our faith were presented; that you can still find comedies printed in gothic letters under the name of a learned doctor of the Sorbonne; and without going so far, in our own day the religious dramas of Pierre Corneille have been performed to the admiration of all France.

If the function of comedy is to correct men's vices, I do not see why any should be exempt. Such a condition in our society would be much more dangerous than the thing itself; and we have seen that the theater is admirably suited to provide correction. The most forceful lines of a serious moral statement are usually less powerful than those of satire; and nothing will reform most men better than the depiction of their faults. It is a vigorous blow to vices to expose them to public laughter. Criticism is taken lightly, but men will not tolerate satire. They are quite willing to be mean, but they never like to be ridiculed.

I have been attacked for having placed words of piety in the mouth of my impostor. Could I avoid doing so in order to represent properly the character of a hypocrite? It seemed to me sufficient to reveal the criminal motives which make him speak as he does, and I have eliminated all ceremonial phrases, which nonetheless he would not have been found using incorrectly. Yet some say that in the fourth act he sets forth a vicious morality; but is not this a morality which everyone has heard again and again? Does my comedy say anything new here? And is there any fear that ideas so thoroughly detested by everyone can make an impression on men's minds; that I make them dangerous by presenting them in the theater; that they acquire authority from the lips of a scoundrel? There is not the slightest suggestion of any of this; and one must either approve the comedy of *Tartuffe* or condemn all comedies in general.

This has indeed been done in a furious way for some time now, and never was the theater so much abused. I cannot deny that there were Church Fathers who condemned comedy; but neither will it be denied me that there were some who looked on it somewhat more favorably. Thus authority, on which censure is supposed to depend, is destroyed by this disagreement; and the only conclusion that can be drawn from this difference of opinion among men enlightened by the same wisdom is that they viewed comedy in different ways, and that some considered it in its purity, while others regarded it in its corruption and confused it with all those wretched performances which have been rightly called performances of filth.

And in fact, since we should talk about things rather than words, and since most misunderstanding comes from including contrary notions in the same word, we need only to remove the veil of ambiguity and look at comedy in itself to see if it warrants condemnation. It will surely be recognized that as it is nothing more than a clever poem which corrects men's faults by means of agreeable lessons, it cannot be condemned without injustice. And if we listened to the voice of ancient times on this matter, it would tell us that its most famous philosophers have praised comedy—they who professed so austere a wisdom and who ceaselessly denounced the vices of their times. It would tell us that Aristotle spent his evenings at the theater and took the trouble to reduce the art of making comedies to rules. It would tell us that some of its greatest and most honored men took pride in writing comedies themselves; and that others did not disdain to recite them in public; that Greece expressed its admiration for this art by means of handsome prizes and magnificent theaters to honor it; and finally, that in Rome this same art received extraordinary honors; I do not speak of Rome run riot under the license of the emperors, but of disciplined Rome, governed by the wisdom of the consuls, and in the age of the full vigor of Roman dignity.

I admit that there have been times when comedy became corrupt. And what do men not corrupt every day? There is nothing so innocent that men cannot turn it to crime; nothing so beneficial that its values cannot be reversed; nothing so good in itself that it cannot be put to bad uses. Medical knowledge benefits mankind and is revered as one of our most wonderful possessions; and yet there was a time when it fell into discredit, and was often used to poison men. Philosophy is a gift of Heaven; it has been given to us to bring us to the knowledge of a God by contemplating the wonders of nature; and yet we know that often it has been turned away from its function and has been used openly in support of impiety. Even the holiest of things are not immune from human corruption, and every day we see scoundrels who use and abuse piety, and wickedly make it serve the greatest of crimes. But this does not prevent one from making the necessary distinctions. We do not confuse in the same false inference the goodness of things that are corrupted with the wickedness of the corrupt. The function of an art is always distinguished from its misuse; and as medicine is not forbidden because it was banned in Rome, nor philosophy because it was publicly condemned in Athens, we should not suppress comedy simply because it has been condemned at certain times. This censure was justified then for reasons which no longer apply today; it was limited to what was then seen; and we should not seize on these limits, apply them more rigidly than is necessary, and include in our condemnation the innocent along with the guilty. The comedy that this censure attacked is in no way the comedy that we want to defend. We must be careful not to confuse the one with the other. There may be two persons whose morals may be completely different. They may have no resemblance to one another except in their names, and it would be a terrible injustice to want to condemn Olympia, who is a good woman, because there is also an Olympia who is lewd. Such procedures would make for great confusion everywhere. Everything under the sun would be condemned; now since this vigor is not applied to the countless instances of abuse we see every day, the same should hold for comedy, and those plays should be approved in which instruction and virtue reign supreme.

I know there are some so delicate that they cannot tolerate a comedy, who say that the most decent are the most dangerous, that the passions they present are all the more moving because they are virtuous, and that men's feelings are stirred by these presentations. I do not see what great crime it is to be affected by the sight of a generous passion; and this utter insensitivity to which they would lead us is indeed a high degree of virtue! I wonder if so great a perfection resides within the strength of human nature, and I wonder if it is not better to try to correct and moderate men's passions than to try to suppress them altogether. I grant that there are places better to visit than the theater; and if we want to condemn every single thing that does not bear directly on God and our salvation, it is right that comedy be included, and I should willingly grant that it be condemned along with everything else. But if we admit, as is in fact true, that the exercise of piety will permit interruptions, and that men need amusement, I maintain that there is none more innocent than comedy. I have dwelled too long on this matter. Let me finish with the words of a great prince of the comedy, *Tartuffe*.

Eight days after it had been banned, a play called *Scaramouche the Hermit* was performed before the court; and the king, on his way out, said to this great prince: "I should really like to know why the persons who make so much noise about Molière's comedy do not say a word about *Scaramouche*." To which the prince replied, "It is because the comedy of *Scaramouche* makes fun of Heaven and religion, which these gentlemen do not care about at all, but that of Molière makes fun of *them*, and that is what they cannot bear."

On the Essence of Laughter, and, in General, on the Comic in the Plastic Arts*[1]

Charles Baudelaire

I

I have no intention of writing a treatise on caricature: I simply want to acquaint the reader with certain reflections which have often occurred to me on the subject of this singular genre. These reflections had become a kind of obsession for me, and I wanted to get them off my chest. Nevertheless I have made every effort to impose some order, and thus to make their digestion more easy. This, then, is purely an artist's and a philosopher's article. No doubt a general history of caricature in its references to all the facts by which humanity has been stirred—facts political and religious, weighty or frivolous; facts relative to the disposition of the nation or to fashion—would be a glorious and important work. The task still remains to be done, for the essays which have been published up to the present are hardly more than raw materials. But I thought that this task should be divided. It is clear that a work on caricature, understood in this way, would be a history of facts, an immense gallery of anecdote. In caricature, far more than in the other branches of art, there are two sorts of works which are to be prized and commended for different and almost contrary reasons. One kind have value only by reason of the *fact* which they represent. No doubt they have a right to the attention of the historian, the archaeologist, and even the philosopher; they deserve to take their place in the national archives, in the biographical registers of human thought. Like the flysheets of journalism, they are swept out of sight by the same tireless breeze which supplies us with fresh ones. But the others—and it is with these that I want to concern myself especially—contain a mysterious, lasting, eternal element, which recommends them to the attention of artists. What a curious thing, and one truly worthy of attention, is the introduction of this indefinable element of beauty, even in works which are intended to represent his proper ugliness—both moral and physical—to man! And what is no less mysterious is that this lamentable spectacle excites in him an undying and incorrigible mirth. Here, then, is the true subject of my article.

A doubt assails me. Should I reply with a formal demonstration to the kind of preliminary question which no doubt will be raised by certain spiteful pundits of solemnity—charlatans of gravity, pedantic corpses which have emerged from

° Charles Baudelaire, "On the Essence of Laughter" [1855], in *The Mirror of Art*, Jonathan Mayne, tr. and ed. (Phaidon Press Ltd., 1955), pp. 131–153. [Footnotes in this selection have been renumbered.]

[1] Earliest traced publication in *Le Portefeuille*, 8th July 1855; reprinted, with minor variations, in *Le Présent*, 1st Sept. 1857, with the addition of the succeeding articles on French (1st Oct.) and Foreign (15th Oct.) Caricaturists.

the icy vaults of the *Institut* and have come again to the land of the living, like a band of miserly ghosts, to snatch a few coppers from the obliging administration? First of all, they would ask, is Caricature a genre? No, their cronies would reply, Caricature is not a genre. I have heard similar heresies ringing in my ears at academicians' dinners. It was these fine fellows who let the comedy of *Robert Macaire*[2] slip past them without noticing any of its great moral and literary symptoms. If they had been contemporaries of Rabelais, they would have treated him as a base and uncouth buffoon. In truth, then, have we got to show that nothing at all that issues from man is frivolous in the eyes of a philosopher? Surely, at the very least, there will be that obscure and mysterious element which no philosophy has so far analysed to its depths?

We are going to concern ourselves, then, with the essence of laughter and with the component elements of caricature. Later, perhaps, we shall examine some of the most remarkable works produced in this genre.

II

The Sage laughs not save in fear and trembling. From what authority-laden lips, from what completely orthodox pen, did this strange and striking maxim fall?[3] Does it come to us from the Philosopher-King of Judea? Or should we attribute it to Joseph de Maistre,[4] that soldier quickened with the Holy Spirit? I have a vague memory of having read it in one of his books, but given as a quotation, no doubt. Such severity of thought and style suits well with the majestic saintliness of Bossuet; but the elliptical turn of the thought and its quintessential refinement would lead me rather to attribute the honour to Bourdaloue, the relentless Christian psychologist. This singular maxim has kept recurring to my mind ever since I first conceived the idea of my article, and I wanted to get rid of it at the very start.

But come, let us analyse this curious proposition—

The Sage, that is to say he who is quickened with the spirit of Our Lord, he who has the divine formulary at his finger tips, does not abandon himself to laughter save in fear and trembling. The Sage trembles at the thought of having laughed; the Sage fears laughter, just as he fears the lustful shows of this world. He stops short on the brink of laughter, as on the brink of temptation. There is, then, according to the Sage, a certain secret contradiction between his special nature as Sage and the primordial nature of laughter. In fact, to do no more than touch in passing upon memories which are more than solemn, I would point out—and this perfectly corroborates the officially Christian character of the maxim—that the Sage *par excellence*, the Word Incarnate, never laughed.[5] In the eyes of One who has all knowledge and all power, the comic does not exist. And yet the Word Incarnate knew anger; He even knew tears.

Let us make a note of this, then. In the first place, here is an author—a

---

[2] The character of Robert Macaire (in the play *L'Auberge des Adrets*) had been created by the actor Frédérick Lemaître, in the 1820s. Later Daumier developed the character in a famous series of caricatures.

[3] Lavater's remark 'Le Sage sourit souvent et rit rarement' (*Souvenirs pour des voyageurs chéris*) has been suggested by G. T. Clapton; see Gilman p. 237, *n*. 32.

[4] On Baudelaire's debt to Joseph de Maistre, see Gilman pp. 63–66.

[5] This suggests a line in a poem by Baudelaire's friend Gustave le Vavasseur, published in 1843. *Dieux joyeux, je vous hais. Jésus n'a jamais ri.* See also Gilman p. 237, *n*. 32.

Christian, without doubt—who considers it as a certain fact that the Sage takes a very good look before allowing himself to laugh, as though some residue of uneasiness and anxiety must still be left him. And secondly, the comic vanishes altogether from the point of view of absolute knowledge and power. Now, if we inverted the two propositions, it would result that laughter is generally the apanage of madmen, and that it always implies more or less of ignorance and weakness. I have no wish, however, to embark recklessly upon a theological ocean, for which I should without doubt be insufficiently equipped with compass or sails; I am content just to indicate these singular horizons to the reader—to point them out to him with my finger.

If you are prepared, then, to take the point of view of the orthodox mind, it is certain that human laughter is intimately linked with the accident of an ancient Fall, of a debasement both physical and moral. Laughter and grief are expressed by the organs in which the command and the knowledge of good and evil reside—I mean the eyes and the mouth. In the earthly paradise—whether one supposes it as past or to come, a memory or a prophecy, in the sense of the theologians or of the socialists—in the earthly paradise, that is to say in the surroundings in which it seemed to man that all created things were good, joy did not find its dwelling in laughter. As no trouble afflicted him, man's countenance was simple and smooth, and the laughter which now shakes the nations never distorted the features of his face. Laughter and tears cannot make their appearance in the paradise of delights. They are both equally the children of woe, and they came because the body of enfeebled man lacked the strength to restrain them.° From the point of view of my Christian philosopher, the laugh on his lips is a sign of just as great a misery as the tears in his eyes. The Being who sought to multiply his own image has in no wise put the teeth of the lion into the mouth of man—yet man rends with his laughter; nor all the seductive cunning of the serpent into his eyes—yet he beguiles with his tears. Observe also that it is with his tears that man washes the afflictions of man, and that it is with his laughter that sometimes he soothes and charms his heart; for the phenomena engendered by the Fall will become the means of redemption.

May I be permitted a poetic hypothesis in order to help me prove the accuracy of these assertions, which otherwise many people may find tainted with the *a priori* of mysticism? Since the comic is a damnable element, and one of diabolic origin, let us try to imagine before us a soul absolutely pristine and fresh, so to speak, from the hands of Nature. For our example let us take the great and typical figure of Virginie,[6] who perfectly symbolizes absolute purity and naïveté. Virginie arrives in Paris still bathed in sea-mists and gilded by the tropic sun, her eyes full of great primitive images of waves, mountains and forests. Here she falls into the midst of a turbulent, overflowing and mephitic civilization, all imbued as she is with the pure and rich scents of the East. She is linked to humanity both by her birth and her love, by her mother and her lover, her Paul, who is as angelic as she and whose sex knows no distinction from hers, so to speak, in the unquenched ardours of a love which is unaware of itself. God she has known in the church of *Les Pamplemousses*—a modest and mean little church, and in the

---

° Philippe de Chennevières (c.b.), an early friend of Baudelaire's. He wrote a number of books, and had a distinguished career in the official world of art. The exact source of this idea has not been traced among his works.

[6] From Bernardin de Saint-Pierre's *Paul et Virginie*.

vastness of the indescribable tropic sky and the immortal music of the forests and the torrents. Certainly Virginie is a noble intelligence; but a few images and a few memories suffice her, just as a few books suffice the Sage. Now one day by chance, in all innocence, at the Palais-Royal, at a glazier's window, on a table, in a public place, Virginie's eye falls upon—a caricature! a caricature all very tempting for us, full-blown with gall and spite, just such as a shrewd and bored civilization knows how to make them. Let us suppose some broad buffoonery of the prizering, some British enormity, full of clotted blood and spiced with a monstrous 'Goddam!' or two: or, if this is more to the taste of your curious imagination, let us suppose before the eye of our virginal Virginie some charming and enticing morsel of lubricity, a Gavarni of her times, and one of the best—some insulting satire against the follies of the court, some plastic diatribe against the Parc-aux-Cerfs,[7] the vile activities of a great favourite, or the nocturnal escapades of the proverbial *Autrichienne*.[8] Caricature is a double thing; it is both drawing and idea—the drawing violent, the idea caustic and veiled. And a network of such elements gives trouble to a simple mind which is accustomed to understand by intuition things as simple as itself. Virginie has glimpsed; now she gazes. Why? She is gazing at the unknown. Nevertheless she hardly understands either what it means or what it is for. And yet, do you observe that sudden folding of the wings, that shudder of a soul that veils herself and wants to draw back? The angel has sensed that there is offence in it. And in truth, I tell you, whether she has understood it or not, she will be left with some strange element of uneasiness—something which resembles fear. No doubt, if Virginie remains in Paris and knowledge comes to her, laughter will come too: we shall see why. But for the moment, in our capacity as analysts and critics who would certainly not dare to assert that our intelligence is superior to that of Virginie, let us simply record the fear and the suffering of the immaculate angel brought face to face with caricature.

III

If you wish to demonstrate that the comic is one of the clearest tokens of the Satanic in man, one of the numerous pips contained in the symbolic apple, it would be enough to draw attention to the unanimous agreement of physiologists of laughter on the primary ground of this monstrous phenomenon. Nevertheless their discovery is not very profound and hardly goes very far. Laughter, they say, comes from superiority. I should not be surprised if, on making this discovery, the physiologist had burst out laughing himself at the thought of his own superiority. Therefore he should have said: Laughter comes from the idea of one's *own* superiority. A Satanic idea, if there ever was one! And what pride and delusion! For it is a notorious fact that all the madmen in the asylums have an excessively overdeveloped idea of their own superiority: I hardly know of any who suffer from the madness of humility. Note, too, that laughter is one of the most frequent and numerous expressions of madness. And now, see how everything falls into place. When Virginie, once fallen, has declined by one degree in purity, the idea of her own superiority will begin to dawn upon her; she will be more learned from the point of view of the world; and she will laugh.

[7] Louis XV's private brothel at Versailles.
[8] Marie Antoinette.

I said that laughter contained a symptom of failing; and, in fact, what more striking token of debility could you demand than a nervous convulsion, an involuntary spasm comparable to a sneeze and prompted by the sight of someone else's misfortune? This misfortune is almost always a *mental* failing. And can you imagine a phenomenon more deplorable than one failing taking delight in another? But there is worse to follow. The misfortune is sometimes of a very much lower kind—a failure in the physical order. To take one of the most commonplace examples in life, what is there so delightful in the sight of a man falling on the ice or in the street, or stumbling at the end of a pavement, that the countenance of his brother in Christ should contract in such an intemperate manner, and the muscles of his face should suddenly leap into life like a timepiece at midday or a clockwork toy? The poor devil has disfigured himself, at the very least; he may even have broken an essential member. Nevertheless the laugh has gone forth, sudden and irrepressible. It is certain that if you care to explore this situation, you will find a certain unconscious pride at the core of the laughter's thought. That is the point of departure. 'Look at me! *I* am not falling,' he seems to say. 'Look at me! *I* am walking upright. *I* would never be so silly as to fail to see a gap in the pavement or a cobblestone blocking the way.'

The Romantic school, or, to put it better, the Satanic school, which is one of its subdivisions, had a proper understanding of this primordial law of laughter; or at least, if they did not all understand it, all, even in their grossest extravagances and exaggerations, sensed it and applied it exactly. All the miscreants of melodrama, accursed, damned and fatally marked with a grin which runs from ear to ear, are in the pure orthodoxy of laughter. Furthermore they are almost all the grandchildren, legitimate or illegitimate, of the renowned wanderer Melmoth,[9] that great satanic creation of the Reverend Maturin. What could be greater, what more mighty, relative to poor humanity, than the pale, bored figure of Melmoth? And yet he has a weak and contemptible side to him, which faces against God and against the light. See, therefore, how he laughs; see how he laughs, as he ceaselessly compares himself to the caterpillars of humanity, he so strong, he so intelligent, he for whom a part of the conditional laws of mankind, both physical and intellectual, no longer exist! And this laughter is the perpetual explosion of his rage and his suffering. It is—you must understand—the necessary resultant of his contradictory double nature, which is infinitely great in relation to man, and infinitely vile and base in relation to absolute Truth and Justice. Melmoth is a living contradiction. He has parted company with the fundamental conditions of life; his bodily organs can no longer sustain his thought. And that is why his laughter freezes and wrings his entrails. It is a laugh which never sleeps, like a malady which continues on its way and completes a destined course. And thus the laughter of Melmoth, which is the highest expression of pride, is for ever performing its function as it lacerates and scorches the lips of the laugher for whose sins there can be no remission.[10]

[9] *Melmoth the Wanderer* (1820) was the masterpiece of its author, the Rev. C. R. Maturin (1782–1824). It was one of the most influential of all the novels of horror, and Baudelaire's great admiration for it was revealed in his desire to make a new French translation, on the grounds that the existing translation was inadequate. See G. T. Capton, 'Balzac, Baudelaire and Maturin,' *French Quarterly*, June and Sept. 1930; see also Mario Praz, *The Romantic Agony* (O.U.P., 2nd ed., 1951) pp. 116–118.

[10] 'A mirth which is not riot gaiety is often the mask which hides the convulsed and distorted features of agony—and laughter, which never yet was the expression of rapture, has often been the only intelligible language of madness and misery. Ecstasy only of smiles—despair laughs...' *Melmoth* (2nd ed., 1824), vol. III, p. 302.

IV

And now let us recapitulate a little and establish more clearly our principal propositions, which amount to a sort of theory of laughter. Laughter is satanic: it is thus profoundly human. It is the consequence in man of the idea of his own superiority. And since laughter is essentially human, it is, in fact, essentially contradictory; that is to say that it is at once a token of an infinite grandeur and an infinite misery—the latter in relation to the absolute Being of whom man has an inkling, the former in relation to the beasts. It is from the perpetual collision of these two infinites that laughter is struck. The comic and the capacity for laughter are situated in the laugher and by no means in the object of his laughter. The man who trips would be the last to laugh at his own fall, unless he happened to be a philosopher, one who had acquired by habit a power of rapid self-division and thus of assisting as a disinterested spectator at the phenomena of his own ego. But such cases are rare. The most comic animals are the most serious—monkeys, for example, and parrots. For that matter, if man were to be banished from creation, there would be no such thing as the comic, for the animals do not hold themselves superior to the vegetables, nor the vegetables to the minerals. While it is a sign of superiority in relation to brute creation (and under this heading I include the numerous pariahs of the *mind*), laughter is a sign of inferiority in relation to the wise, who, through the contemplative innocence of their minds, approach a childlike state. Comparing mankind with man, as we have a right to do, we see that primitive nations, in the same way as Virginie, have no conception of caricature and have no comedy (Holy Books never laugh, to whatever nations they may belong), but that as they advance little by little in the direction of the cloudy peaks of the intellect, or as they pore over the gloomy braziers of metaphysics, the nations of the world begin to laugh diabolically with the laughter of Melmoth; and finally we see that if, in these selfsame ultra-civilized nations, some mind is driven by superior ambition to pass beyond the limits of worldly pride and to make a bold leap towards pure poetry, then the resulting poetry, as limpid and profound as Nature herself, will be as void of laughter as is the soul of the Sage.

As the comic is a sign of superiority, or of a belief in one's own superiority, it is natural to hold that, before they can acheive the absolute purification promised by certain mystical prophets, the nations of the world will see a multiplication of comic themes in proportion as their superiority increases. But the comic changes its nature, too. In this way the angelic and the diabolic elements function in parallel. As humanity uplifts itself, it wins for evil, and for the understanding of evil, a power proportionate to that which it has won for good. And this is why I find nothing surprising in the fact that we, who are the children of a better law than the religious laws of antiquity—we, the favoured disciples of Jesus—should possess a greater number of comic elements than pagan anitquity. For this very thing is a condition of our general intellectual power. I am quite prepared for sworn dissenters to cite the classic tale of the philosopher who died of laughing when he saw a donkey eating figs, or even the comedies of Aristophanes and those of Plautus. I would reply that, quite apart from the fact that these periods were essentially civilized, and there had already been a considerable shrinkage of belief, their type of the comic is still not quite the same as ours. It even has a touch of barbarity about it, and we can really only adopt it by backward effort of mind, the result of which is called *pastiche*. As for the grotesque figures which antiquity has bequeathed us—the masks, the bronze figurines, the Hercules (all muscles), the little Priapi, with tongue curled in air and pointed ears (all cranium and phallus); and as for those prodigious phalluses on which the white daughters of Romulus innocently ride astride, those monstrous engines of generation, equipped with wings and bells—I believe that these things are all full of deep seriousness.[11] Venus, Pan and Hercules were in no sense figures of fun. It was not until after the coming of Christ, and with the aid of Plato and Seneca, that men began to laugh at them. I believe that the ancients were full of respect for drum-majors and for doers of mighty deeds of all kinds, and that none of those extravagant fetishes which I instanced a moment ago were anything other than tokens of adoration, or, at all events, symbols of power; in no sense were they intentionally comic emanations of the fancy. Indian and Chinese idols are unaware that they are ridiculous; it is in us, Christians, that their comicality resides.

V

It would be a mistake to suppose that we have got rid of every difficulty. The mind that is least accustomed to these aesthetic subtleties would very quickly be able to counter me with the insidious objection that there are *different varieties of laughter*. It is not always a disaster, a failing or an inferiority in which we take our delight. Many sights which provoke our laughter are perfectly innocent; not only the amusements of childhood, but even many of the things that tickle the palate of artists, have nothing to do with the spirit of Satan.

There is certainly some semblance of truth in that. But first of all we ought to make a proper distinction between laughter and joy. Joy exists in itself, but it has various manifestations. Sometimes it is almost invisible; at others, it expresses itself in tears. Laughter is only an expression, a symptom, a diagnostic. Symptom of what? That is the question. Joy is a unity. Laughter is the expression of a double, or contradictory, feeling; and that is the reason why a convulsion occurs. And so, the laughter of children, which I hold for a vain objection, is altogether different, even as a physical expression, even as a form, from the laughter of a man who attends a play, or who looks at a caricature, or from the terrible laughter of Melmoth—of Melmoth, the outcast of society, wandering somewhere between the last boundaries of the territory of mankind and the frontiers of the higher life; of Melmoth, who always believes himself to be on the point of freedom from his infernal pact, and longs without ceasing to barter that superhuman power, which is his disaster, for the pure conscience of a simpleton, which is his envy. For the laughter of children is like the blossoming of a flower. It is the joy of receiving, the joy of breathing, the joy of contemplating, of living, of growing. It is a vegetable joy. And so, in general, it is more like a smile—something analogous to the wagging of a dog's tail, or the purring of a cat. And if there still remains some distinction between the laughter of children and such expressions of animal contentment, I think that we should hold that this is because their laughter is not entirely exempt from ambition, as is only proper to little scraps of men—that is, to budding Satans.

But there is one case where the question is more complicated. It is the

---

[11]Curious readers will find examples reproduced in Fuchs, *Geschichte der erotischen Kunst*, 1908, vol. I, book 2, 'Das Altertum.'

laughter of man—but a true and violent laughter—at the sight of an object which is neither a sign of weakness nor of disaster among his fellows. It is easy to guess that I am referring to the laughter caused by the grotesque. Fabulous creations, beings whose authority and *raison d'être* cannot be drawn from the code of common sense, often provoke in us an insane and excessive mirth, which expresses itself in interminable paroxysms and swoons. It is clear that a distinction must be made, and that here we have a higher degree of the phenomenon. From the artistic point of view, the comic is an imitation: the grotesque a creation. The comic is an imitation mixed with a certain creative faculty, that is to say with an artistic *ideality*. Now human pride, which always takes the upper hand and is the natural cause of laughter in the case of the comic, turns out to be the natural cause of laughter in the case of the grotesque too, for this is a creation mixed with a certain imitative faculty—imitative, that is, of elements pre-existing in nature. I mean that in this case laughter is still the expression of an idea of superiority—no longer now of man over man, but of man over nature. Do not retort that this idea is too subtle; that would be no sufficient reason for rejecting it. The difficulty is to find another plausible explanation. If this one seems far-fetched and just a little hard to accept, that is because the laughter caused by the grotesque has about it something profound, primitive and axiomatic, which is much closer to the innocent life and to absolute joy than is the laughter caused by the comic in man's behaviour. Setting aside the question of utility, there is the same difference between these two sorts of laughter as there is between the *implicated* school of writing and the school of art for art's sake. Thus the grotesque dominates the comic from a proportionate height.

From now onwards I shall call the grotesque 'the absolute comic,' in antithesis to the ordinary comic, which I shall call 'the significative comic.' The latter is a clearer language, and one easier for the man in the street to understand, and above all easier to analyse, its element being visibly *double*—art and the moral idea. But the absolute comic, which comes much closer to nature, emerges as a *unity* which calls for the intuition to grasp it. There is but one criterion of the grotesque, and that is laughter—immediate laughter. Whereas with the significative comic it is quite permissible to laugh a moment late—that is no argument against its validity; it all depends upon one's quickness of analysis.

I have called it 'the absolute comic.' Nevertheless we should be on our guard. From the point of view of the definitive absolute, all that remains is *joy*. The comic can only be absolute in relation to fallen humanity, and it is in this way that I am understanding it.

VI

In its triple-distilled essence the absolute comic turns out to be the prerogative of those superior artists whose minds are sufficiently open to receive any absolute ideas at all. Thus, the man who until now has been the most sensitive to these ideas, and who set a good part of them in action in his purely aesthetic, as well as his creative work, is Theodore Hoffmann.[12] He always made a proper distinction between the ordinary comic and the type which he called 'the innocent comic.' The learned theories which he had put forth didactically, or thrown out in the

[12] On Hoffmann, and on the particular stories which Baudelaire cites in this section, see H. W. Hewett-Thayer's *Hoffmann, Author of the Tales* (Princeton and O.U.P., 1948).

form of inspired conversations or critical dialogues, he often sought to boil down into creative works; and it is from these very works that I shall shortly draw my most striking examples when I come to give a series of applications of the above-stated principles, and to pin a sample under each categorical heading.

Furthermore, within the absolute and significative types of the comic we find species, sub-species and families. The division can take place on different grounds. First of all it can be established according to a pure philosophic law, as I was making a start to do: and then according to the law of artistic creation. The first is brought about by the primary separation of the absolute from the significative comic: the second is based upon the kind of special capacities possessed by each artist. And finally it is also possible to establish a classification of varieties of the comic with regard to climates and various national aptitudes. It should be observed that each term of each classification can be completed and given a *nuance* by the adjunction of a term from one of the others, just as the law of grammar teaches us to modify a noun by an adjective. Thus, any German or English artist is more or less naturally equipped for the absolute comic, and at the same time he is more or less of an idealizer. I wish now to try and give selected examples of the absolute and significative comic, and briefly to characterize the comic spirit proper to one or two eminently artistic nations, before coming on to the section in which I want to discuss and analyse at greater length the talent of those men who have made it their study and their whole existence.

If you exaggerate and push the consequences of the significative comic to their furthest limits, you reach the *savage* variety, just as the synonymous expression of the innocent variety, pushed one degree further, is the *absolute* comic.

In France, the land of lucid thought and demonstration, where the natural and direct aim of art is utility, we generally find the significative type. In this genre Molière is our best expression. But since at the root of our character there is an aversion for all extremes, and since one of the symptoms of every emotion, every science and every art in France is an avoidance of the excessive, the absolute and the profound, there is consequently but little of the savage variety to be found in this country; in the same way our grotesque seldom rises to the absolute.

Rabelais, who is the great French master of the grotesque, preserves an element of utility and reason in the very midst of his most prodigious fantasies. He is directly symbolic. His comedy nearly always possesses the transparence of an allegory. In French caricature, in the *plastic* expression of the comic, we shall find this dominant spirit. It must be admitted that the enormous poetic good humour which is required for the true grotesque is found but rarely among us in level and continuous doses. At long intervals we see the vein reappear; but it is not an essentially national one. In this context I shall mention certain interludes of Molière, which are unfortunately too little read or acted—those of the *Malade Imaginaire* and the *Bourgeois Gentilhomme*, for example: and the carnival-esque figures of Callot. As for the essentially French comedy in the *Contes* of Voltaire, its *raison d'être* is always based upon the idea of superiority; it is entirely significative.

Germany, sunk in her dreams, will afford us excellent specimens of the absolute comic. There all is weighty, profound and excessive. To find true comic savagery, however, you have to cross the Channel and visit the foggy realms of spleen. Happy, noisy, carefree Italy abounds in the innocent variety. It was at the very heart of Italy, at the hub of the southern carnival, in the midst of the turbulent Corso, that Theodore Hoffmann discerningly placed his eccentric drama, *The Princess Brambilla*. The Spaniards are very well endowed in this matter. They are quick to arrive at the cruel stage, and their most grotesque fantasies often contain a dark element.

It will be a long time before I forget the first English pantomime that I saw played. It was some years ago, at the *Théâtre des Variétés*.[13] Doubtless only a few people will remember it, for very few seem to have taken to this kind of theatrical diversion, and those poor English mimes had a sad reception from us. The French public does not much like to be taken out of its element. Its taste is not very cosmopolitan, and changes of horizon upset its vision. Speaking for myself, however, I was excessively struck by their way of understanding the comic. It was said—chiefly by the indulgent, in order to explain their lack of success—that these were vulgar, mediocre artists—understudies. But that was not the point. They were English; that was the important thing.

It seemed to me that the distinctive mark of this type of the comic was *violence*. I propose to prove it with a few samples from my memories.

First of all, Pierrot was not the figure to which the late-lamented Deburau had accustomed us—that figure pale as the moon, mysterious as silence, supple and mute as the serpent, long and straight as a gibbet—that artificial man activated by eccentric springs. The English Pierrot swept upon us like a hurricane, fell down like a sack of coals, and when he laughed his laughter made the auditorium quake; his laugh was like a joyful clap of thunder. He was a short, fat man, and to increase his imposingness he wore a beribboned costume which encompassed his jubilant person as birds are encompassed with their down and feathers, or angoras with their fur. Upon his floured face he had stuck, crudely and without transition or gradation, two enormous patches of pure red. A feigned prolongation of the lips, by means of two bands of carmine, brought it about that when he laughed his mouth seemed to run from ear to ear.

As for his moral nature, it was basically the same as that of the Pierrot whom we all know—heedlessness and indifference, and consequently the gratification of every kind of greedy and rapacious whim, now at the expense of Harlequin, now of Cassandre or Léandre. The only difference was that where Deburau would just have moistened the tip of his finger with his tongue, he stuck both fists and both feet into his mouth.

And everything else in this singular piece was expressed in the same way, with passionate gusto; it was the dizzy height of hyperbole.

Pierrot walks past a woman who is scrubbling her doorstep; after rifling her pockets, he makes to stuff into his own her sponge, her mop, her bucket, water

---

[13] It has not proved possible to identify this pantomime beyond doubt, but, according to information kindly supplied by the Bibliothèque de l'Arsénal, it seems more than likely that it was a production entitled 'Arlequin, pantomime anglaise en 3 actes et 11 tableaux,' performed at the Théâtre des Variétés from the 4th until the 13th August, 1842. The newspaper *Le Corsair* (4th August) gives the following cast:—Arlequin: Howell.—Clown: Matthews (presumably the well-known clown, Tom Matthews).—Pantalon: Garders.—Colombine: Miss Maria Frood.—Une fée: Anne Plowman—Reine des fées: Emilie Fitzj (?). A review of this pantomime by Gautier, in *La Presse*, 14th Aug. 1842, has several points of agreement with Baudelaire's description. First, Gautier describes the apathy of the audience; secondly, he gives special praise to the clown's costume; finally, he refers to the incident of the clown's stealing his own head and stuffing it into his pocket (though the guillotine is not mentioned). Champfleury quotes the whole passage in his *Souvenirs des Funambules*, 1859, pp. 256–257, and provides evidence for dating the pantomime to the early 1840s when he ironically assigns the fragment to an article by Baudelaire 'sous presse depuis quinze ans seulement'.

and all! As for the way in which he endeavoured to express his love to her, any-one who remembers observing the phanerogamous habits of the monkeys in their famous cage at the Jardin des Plantes can imagine it for himself. Perhaps I ought to add that the woman's role was taken by a very long, very thin man, whose outraged modesty emitted shrill screams. It was truly an intoxication of laughter—something both terrible and irresistible.

For some misdeed or other, Pierrot had in the end to be guillotined. Why the guillotine rather than the gallows, in the land of Albion? . . . I do not know; presumably to lead up to what we were to see next. Anyway, there it was, the engine of death, there, set up on the French boards which were markedly sur-prised at this romantic novelty. After struggling and bellowing like an ox that scents the slaughter-house, at last Pierrot bowed to his fate. His head was severed from his neck—a great red and white head, which rolled noisily to rest in front of the prompter's box, showing the bleeding disk of the neck, the split vertebrae and all the details of a piece of butcher's meat just dressed for the counter. And then, all of a sudden, the decapitated trunk, moved by its irresistible obsession with theft, jumped to its feet, triumphantly 'lifted' its own head as though it was a ham or a bottle of wine, and with far more circumspection than the great St. Denis, proceeded to stuff it into its pocket!

Set down in pen and ink, all this is pale and chilly. But how could the pen rival the pantomime? The pantomime is the refinement, the quintessence of comedy; it is the pure comic element, purged and concentrated. Therefore, with the English actors' special talent for hyperbole, all these monstrous buffooneries took on a strangely thrilling reality.

Certainly one of the most remarkable things, in the sense of absolute com-edy—or if I may call it so, the metaphysics of absolute comedy—was the begin-ning of this beautiful piece, a prologue filled with a high aesthetic. The principal characters, Pierrot, Cassandre, Harlequin, Colombine and Léandre are facing the public, gentle and good as gold. They are all but rational beings and do not differ much from the fine fellows in the audience. The miraculous breath which is about to inspire them to such extraordinary antics has not yet touched their brains. A few quips from Pierrot can give no more than a pale idea of what he will be doing shortly. The rivalry between Harlequin and Léandre has just de-clared itself. A fairy takes Harlequin's side; she is the eternal protectress of mor-tals who are poor and in love. She promises him her protection, and, to give him immediate proof of it, she waves her wand in the air with a mysterious and au-thoritative gesture.

At once a dizzy intoxication is abroad; intoxication swims in the air; we breathe intoxication; it is intoxication that fills the lungs and renews the blood in the arteries.

What is this intoxication? It is the absolute comic, and it has taken charge of each one of them. The extraordinary gestures executed by Léandre, Pierrot and Cassandre make it quite clear that they feel themselves forcibly projected into a new existence. They do not seem at all put out. They set about preparing for the great disasters and the tumultuous destiny which awaits them, like a man who spits on his hands and rubs them together before doing some heroic deed. They flourish their arms, like windmills lashed by the tempest. It must be to loosen their joints—and they will certainly need it. All this is carried out to great gusts of laughter, full of a huge contentment. Then they turn to a game of leap-frog, and once their aptitude and their agility have been duly registered, there follows a dazzling volley of kicks, punches and slaps which blaze and crash like a battery of artillery. But all of this is done in the best of spirits. Every gesture, every cry, every look seems to be saying: 'The fairy has willed it, and our fate hurls us on—it doesn't worry *me!* Come, let's get started! Let's get down to business!' And then they *do* get down to business, through the whole fantastic work, which, properly speaking, only starts at this point—that is to say, on the frontier of the marvelous.

Under cover of this hysteria, Harlequin and Colombine have danced away in flight, and with an airy foot they proceed to run the gauntlet of their adventures.

And now another example. This one is taken from a singular author—a man of ranging mind, whatever may be said, who unites to the significative mockery of France the mad, sparkling lighthearted gaiety of the lands of the sun as well as the profound comic spirit of Germany. I am returning once again to Hoffmann.

In the story entitled *Daucus Carota, the King of the Carrots*, or by some translators *The King's Betrothed*, no sight could be more beautiful than the arrival of the great company of the Carrots in the farm-yard of the betrothed maiden's home. Look at all those little scarlet figures, like a regiment of English soldiers, with enormous green plumes on their heads, like carriage-footmen, going through a series of marvellous tricks and capers on their little horses! The whole thing is carried out with astonishing agility. The adroitness and ease with which they fall on their heads is assisted by their heads being bigger and heavier than the rest of their bodies, like those toy soldiers made of elderpith, which have lead weights in their caps.

The unfortunate young girl, obsessed with dreams of grandeur, is fascinated by this display of military might. But an army on parade is one thing; how different an army in barracks, furbishing its arms, polishing its equipment, or, worse still, ignobly snoring on its dirty, stinking campbeds! That is the reverse of the medal; the rest was but a magic trick, an apparatus of seduction. But her father, who is a wise man and well versed in sorcery, wants to show her the other side of all this magnificence. Thus, at an hour when the vegetables are sleeping their brutish sleep, never suspecting that any spy could catch them unawares, he lifts the flaps of one of the tents of this splendid army. Then it is that the poor dreaming girl sees all this mass of red and green soldiery in its appalling undress, wallowing and snoring in the filthy midden from which it first emerged. In its night-cap all that military magnificence is nothing more than a putrid swamp.

There are many other examples of the absolute comic that I might take from the admirable Hoffmann. Anyone who really wants to understand what I have in mind should read with care *Daucus Carota, Peregrinus Tyss, The Golden Pot*, and over and above all, *The Princess Brambilla*, which is like a catechism of high aesthetics. What pre-eminently distinguishes Hoffmann is his unintentional—and sometimes very intentional—blending of a certain measure of the significative comic with the most absolute variety. His most supernatural and fugitive comic conceptions, which are often like the visions of a drunken man, have a very conspicuous moral meaning; you might imagine that you had to do with the profoundest type of physiologist or alienist who was amusing himself by clothing his deep wisdom in poetic forms, like a learned man who might speak in parables and allegories.

Take for example, if you will, the character of Giglio Fava, the actor who suffered from a chronic dualism, in *The Princess Brambilla*. This *single* character changes personality from time to time. Under the name of Giglio Fava he swears enmity for the Assyrian prince, Cornelio Chiapperi; but when he is himself the Assyrian prince, he pours forth his deepest and the most regal scorn upon his rival for the hand of the Princess—upon a wretched mummer whose name, they say, is Giglio Fava.

I should perhaps add that one of the most distinctive marks of the absolute comic is that it remains unaware of itself. This is evident not only in certain animals, like monkeys, in whose comicality gravity plays an essential part, nor only in certain antique sculptural caricatures of which I have already spoken, but even in those Chinese monstrosities which delight us so much and whose intentions are far less comic than people generally think. A Chinese idol, although it be an object of veneration, looks very little different from a tumbletoy or a potbellied chimney-ornament.

And so, to be finished with all these subtleties and all these definitions, let me point out, once more and for the last time, that the dominant idea of superiority is found in the absolute, no less than in the significative comic, as I have already explained (at too great a length, perhaps): further, that in order to enable a comic emanation, explosion, or, as it were, a chemical separation of the comic to come about, there must be two beings face to face with one another; again, that the special abode of the comic is in the laugher, the spectator: and finally, that an exception must nevertheless be made in connection with the 'law of ignorance' for those men who have made a business of developing in themselves their feeling for the comic, and of dispensing it for the amusement of their fellows. This last phenomenon comes into the class of all artistic phenomena which indicate the existence of a permanent dualism in the human being—that is, the power of being oneself and someone else at one and the same time.

And so, to return to my primary definitions and to express myself more clearly, I would say that when Hoffmann gives birth to the absolute comic it is perfectly true that he knows what he is doing; but he also knows that the essence of this type of the comic is that it should appear to be unaware of itself and that it should produce in the spectator, or rather the reader, a joy in his own superiority and in the superiority of man over nature. Artists create the comic; after collecting and studying its elements, they know that such-and-such a being is comic, and that it is so only on condition of its being unaware of its nature, in the same way that, following an inverse law, an artist is only an artist on condition that he is a double man and that there is not one single phenomenon of his double nature of which he is ignorant.

From **An Essay on Comedy**[*]

George Meredith

There are plain reasons why the comic poet is not a frequent apparition, and why the great comic poet remains without a fellow. A society of cultivated men and women is required, wherein ideas are current, and the perceptions quick, that he may be supplied with matter and an audience. The semi-barbarism of merely giddy communities, and feverish emotional periods, repel him: and also a state of marked social inequality of the sexes; nor can he whose business is to address the mind be understood where there is not a moderate degree of intellectual activity.

Moreover, to touch and kindle the mind through laughter demands, more than sprightliness, a most subtle delicacy. That must be a natal gift in the comic poet. The substance he deals with will show him a startling exhibition of the dyer's hand, if he is without it. People are ready to surrender themselves to witty thumps on the back, breast, and sides; all except the head—and it is there that he aims. He must be subtle to penetrate. A corresponding acuteness must exist to welcome him. The necessity for the two conditions will explain how it is that we count him during centuries in the singular number. . . . Life, we know too well, is not a comedy, but something strangely mixed; nor is comedy a vile mask. The corrupted importation from France was noxious, a noble entertainment spoilt to suit the wretched taste of a villainous age; and the later imitations of it, partly drained of its poison and made decorous, became tiresome, notwithstanding their fun, in the perpetual recurring of the same situations, owing to the absence of original study and vigor of conception. Scene 5, Act 2, of the *Misanthrope*, owing, no doubt, to the fact of our not producing matter for original study, is repeated in succession by Wycherley, Congreve, and Sheridan, and, as it is at second hand, we have it done cynically—or such is the tone—in the manner of "below stairs." Comedy thus treated may be accepted as a version of the ordinary worldly understanding of our social life; at least, in accord with the current dicta concerning it. The epigrams can be made; but it is uninstructive, rather tending to do disservice. Comedy justly treated, as you find it in Molière, whom we so clownishly mishandled—the comedy of Molière throws no infamous reflection upon life. It is deeply conceived, in the first place, and therefore it cannot be impure. Meditate on that statement. Never did man wield so shrieking a scourge upon vice; but his consummate self-mastery is not shaken while administering it. Tartuffe and Harpagon, in fact, are made each to whip himself and his class—

---

[*] George Meredith, "An Essay on Comedy" [1877], collected works first published by Chapman & Hall, 1885–1895.

the false pietists, and the insanely covetous. Molière has only set them in motion. He strips Folly to the skin, displays the imposture of the creature, and is content to offer her better clothing, with the lesson Chrysale reads to Philaminte and Bélise. He conceives purely, and he writes purely, in the simplest language, the simplest of French verse. The source of his wit is clear reason; it is a fountain of that soil, and it springs to vindicate reason, common sense, rightness, and justice—for no vain purpose ever. The wit is of such pervading spirit that it inspires a pun with meaning and interest. His moral does not hang like a tail, or preach from one character incessantly cocking an eye at the audience, as in recent realistic French plays, but is in the heart of his work, throbbing with every pulsation of an organic structure. If life is likened to the comedy of Molière, there is no scandal in the comparison.

Congreve's *Way of the World* is an exception to our other comedies, his own among them, by virtue of the remarkable brilliancy of the writing, and the figure of Millamant. The comedy has no idea in it, beyond the stale one that so the world goes; and it concludes with the jaded discovery of a document at a convenient season for the descent of the curtain. A plot was an afterthought with Congreve. By the help of a wooden villain (Maskwell), marked gallows to the flattest eye, he gets a sort of plot in *The Double-Dealer*. His *Way of the World* might be called "The Conquest of a Town Coquette"; and Millamant is a perfect portrait of a coquette, both in her resistance to Mirabell and the manner of her surrender, and also in her tongue. The wit here is not so salient as in certain passages of *Love for Love*, where Valentine feigns madness, or retorts on his father, or Mrs. Frail rejoices in the harmlessness of wounds to a woman's virtue, if she keeps them "from air." In *The Way of the World*, it appears less prepared in the smartness, and is more diffused in the more characteristic style of the speakers. Here, however, as elsewhere, his famous wit is like a bullyfencer, not ashamed to lay traps for its exhibition, transparently petulant for the train between certain ordinary words and the powder-magazine of the improprieties to be fired. Contrast the wit of Congreve with Molière's. That of the first is a Toledo blade, sharp, and wonderfully supple for steel; cast for dueling, restless in the scabbard, being so pretty when out of it. To shine, it must have an adversary. Molière's wit is like a running brook, with innumerable fresh lights on it at every turn of the wood through which its business is to find a way. It does not run in search of obstructions, to be noisy over them; but when dead leaves and viler substances are heaped along the course, its natural song is heightened. Without effort, and with no dazzling flashes of achievement, it is full of healing, the wit of good breeding, the wit of wisdom.

"Genuine humor and true wit," says Landor, "require a sound and capacious mind, which is always a grave one. . . ." The life of the comedy is in the idea. As with the singing of the skylark out of sight, you must love the bird to be attentive to the song, so in this highest flight of the comic Muse, you must love pure comedy warmly to understand the *Misanthrope;* you must be receptive of the idea of comedy. And to love comedy you must know the real world, and know men and women well enough not to expect too much of them, though you may still hope for good. . . .

Now, to look about us in the present time, I think it will be acknowledged that, in neglecting the cultivation of the comic idea, we are losing the aid of a powerful auxiliary. You see Folly perpetually sliding into new shapes in a society possessed of wealth and leisure, with many whims, many strange ailments and strange doctors. Plenty of common sense is in the world to thrust her back when she pretends to empire. But the first-born of common sense, the vigilant Comic, which is the genius of thoughtful laughter, which would readily extinguish her at the outset, is not serving as a public advocate.

You will have noticed the disposition of common sense, under pressure of some pertinacious piece of light-headedness, to grow impatient and angry. That is a sign of the absence, or at least of the dormancy, of the comic idea. For Folly is the natural prey of the Comic, known to it in all her transformations, in every disguise; and it is with the springing delight of hawk over heron, hound after fox, that it gives her chase, never fretting, never tiring, sure of having her, allowing her no rest.

Contempt is a sentiment that cannot be entertained by comic intelligence. What is it but an excuse to be idly-minded, or personally lofty, or comfortably narrow, not perfectly humane? If we do not feign when we say that we despise Folly, we shut the brain. There is a disdainful attitude in the presence of Folly, partaking of the foolishness to comic perception; and anger is not much less foolish than disdain. The struggle we have to conduct is essence against essence. Let no one doubt of the sequel when this emanation of what is firmest in us is launched to strike down the daughter of Unreason and Sentimentalism—such being Folly's parentage, when it is respectable.

Our modern system of combating her is too long defensive, and carried on too ploddingly with concrete engines of war in the attack. She has time to get behind entrenchments. She is ready to stand a siege, before the heavily-armed man of science and the writer of the leading article or elaborate essay have primed their big guns. It should be remembered that she has charms for the multitude; and an English multitude, seeing her make a gallant fight of it, will be half in love with her, certainly willing to lend her a cheer. Benevolent subscriptions assist her to hire her own man of science, her own organ in the press. If ultimately she is cast out and overthrown, she can stretch a finger at gaps in our ranks. She can say that she commanded an army, and seduced men, whom we thought sober men and safe, to act as her lieutenants. We learn rather gloomily, after she has flashed her lantern, that we have in our midst able men, and men with minds, for whom there is no pole-star in intellectual navigation. Comedy, or the comic element, is the specific for the poison of delusion while Folly is passing from the state of vapor to substantial form. . . .

The comic poet is in the narrow field, or enclosed square, of the society he depicts; and he addresses the still narrower enclosure of men's intellects, with reference to the operation of the social world upon their characters. He is not concerned with beginnings or endings or surroundings, but with what you are now weaving. To understand his work and value it, you must have a sober liking of your kind, and a sober estimate of our civilized qualities. The aim and business of the comic poet are misunderstood, his meaning is not seized nor his point of view taken, when he is accused of dishonoring our nature and being hostile to sentiment, tending to spitefulness and making an unfair use of laughter. Those who detect irony in comedy do so because they choose to see it in life. Poverty, says the satirist, 'has nothing harder in itself than that it makes men ridiculous.' But poverty is never ridiculous to comic perception until it attempts to make its rags conceal its bareness in a forlorn attempt at decency, or foolishly to rival ostentation. Caleb Balderstone, in his endeavor to keep up the honor of a noble household in a state of beggary, is an exquisitely comic character. In the case of "poor relatives," on the other hand, it is the rich, whom they perplex, that are really comic; and to laugh at the former, not seeing the comedy of the latter, is to betray dullness of vision. Humorist and satirist frequently hunt together as ironists in pursuit of the grotesque, to the exclusion of the comic. That was an affecting moment in the history of the Prince Regent, when the First Gentleman of Europe burst into tears at a sarcastic remark of Beau Brummell's on the cut of his coat. Humor, satire, irony, pounce on it altogether as their common prey. The Comic Spirit eyes, but does not touch, it. Put into action, it would be farcical. It is too gross for comedy.

Incidents of a kind casting ridicule on our unfortunate nature, instead of our conventional life, provoke derisive laughter, which thwarts the comic idea. But derision is foiled by the play of the intellect. Most of doubtful causes in contest are open to comic interpretation, and any intellectual pleading of a doubtful cause contains germs of an idea of comedy.

The laughter of satire is a blow in the back or the face. The laughter of comedy is impersonal and of unrivaled politeness, nearer a smile—often no more than a smile. It laughs through the mind, for the mind directs it; and it might be called the humor of the mind.

One excellent test of the civilization of a country, as I have said, I take to be the flourishing of the comic idea and comedy; and the test of true comedy is that it shall awaken thoughtful laughter.

From **Laughter**[*]

Henri Bergson

The Comic in General—The Comic Element in Forms and Movements—Expansive Force of the Comic

What does laughter mean? What is the basal element in the laughable? What common ground can we find between the grimace of a merry-andrew, a play upon words, an equivocal situation in a burlesque and a scene of high comedy? What method of distillation will yield us invariably the same essence from which so many different products borrow either their obtrusive odour or their delicate perfume? The greatest of thinkers, from Aristotle downwards, have tackled this little problem, which has a knack of baffling every effort, of slipping away and escaping only to bob up again, a pert challenge flung at philosophic speculation.

Our excuse for attacking the problem in our turn must lie in the fact that we shall not aim at imprisoning the comic spirit within a definition. We regard it, above all, as a living thing. However trivial it may be, we shall treat it with the respect due to life. We shall confine ourselves to watching it grow and expand. Passing by imperceptible gradations from one form to another, it will be seen to achieve the strangest metamorphoses. We shall disdain nothing we have seen. Maybe we may gain from this prolonged contact, for the matter of that, something more flexible than an abstract definition,—a practical, intimate acquaintance, such as springs from a long companionship. And maybe we may also find that, unintentionally, we have made an acquaintance that is useful. For the comic spirit has a logic of its own, even in its wildest eccentricities. It has a method in its madness. It dreams, I admit, but it conjures up in its dreams visions that are at once accepted and understood by the whole of a social group. Can it then fail to throw light for us on the way that human imagination works, and more particularly social, collective, and popular imagination? Begotten of real life and akin to art, should it not also have something of its own to tell us about art and life?

At the outset we shall put forward three observations which we look upon as fundamental. They have less bearing on the actually comic than on the field within which it must be sought.

The first point to which attention should be called is that the comic does not exist outside the pale of what is strictly *human*. A landscape may be beautiful, charming and sublime, or insignificant and ugly; it will never be laughable. You may laugh at an animal, but only because you have detected in it some human attitude or expression. You may laugh at a hat, but what you are making fun of in this case, is not the piece of felt or straw, but the shape that men have given it,—the human caprice whose mould it has assumed. It is strange that so important a fact, and such a simple one too, has not attracted to a greater degree the attention of philosophers. Several have defined man as "an animal which laughs." They might equally well have defined him as an animal which is laughed at; for if any other animal, or some lifeless object, produces the same effect, it is always because of some resemblance to man, of the stamp he gives it or the use he puts it to.

Here I would point out, as a symptom equally worthy of notice, the *absence of feeling* which usually accompanies laughter. It seems at though the comic could not produce its disturbing effect unless it fell, so to say, on the surface of a soul that is thoroughly calm and unruffled. Indifference is its natural environment, for laughter has no greater foe than emotion. I do not mean that we could not laugh at a person who inspires us with pity, for instance, or even with affection, but in such a case we must, for the moment, put our affection out of court and impose silence upon our pity. In a society composed of pure intelligences there would probably be no more tears, though perhaps there would still be laughter; whereas highly emotional souls, in tune and unison with life, in whom every event would be sentimentally prolonged and re-echoed, would neither know nor understand laughter. Try, for a moment, to become interested in everything that is being said and done; act, in imagination, with those who act, and feel with those who feel; in a word, give your sympathy its widest expansion: as though at the touch of a fairy wand you will see the flimsiest of objects assume importance, and a gloomy hue spread over everything. Now step aside, look upon life as a disinterested spectator: many a drama will turn into a comedy. It is enough for us to stop our ears to the sound of music in a room, where dancing is going on, for the dancers at once to appear ridiculous. How many human actions would stand a similar test? Should we not see many of them suddenly pass from grave to gay, on isolating them from the accompanying music of sentiment? To produce the whole of its effect, then the comic demands something like a momentary anesthesia of the heart. Its appeal is to intelligence, pure and simple.

This intelligence, however, must always remain in touch with other intelligences. And here is the third fact to which attention should be drawn. You would hardly appreciate the comic if you felt yourself isolated from others. Laughter appears to stand in need of an echo. Listen to it carefully: it is not an articulate, clear, well-defined sound; it is something which would fain be prolonged by reverberating from one to another, something beginning with a crash, to continue in successive rumblings, like thunder in a mountain. Still, this reverberation cannot go on for ever. It can travel within as wide a circle as you please: the circle remains, none the less, a closed one. Our laughter is always the laughter of a group. It may, perchance, have happened to you, when seated in a railway carriage or at *table d'hôte*, to hear travellers relating to one another stories which must have been comic to them, for they laughed heartily. Had you been one of their company, you would have laughed like them, but, as you were not, you had no desire whatever to do so. A man who was once asked why he did not weep at a sermon when everybody else was shedding tears replied: "I don't belong to the parish!" What that man thought of tears would be still more true of laughter. However spontaneous it seems, laughter always implies a kind of secret freemasonry, or even complicity, with other laughers, real or imaginary. How often has it been said that the fuller the theatre, the more uncontrolled the laughter of the audience! On the other hand, how often has the remark been made that many comic effects are incapable of translation from one language to another, because they refer to the customs and ideas of a particular social group! It is through not understanding the importance of this double fact that the comic has been looked upon as a mere curiosity in which the mind finds amusement, and laughter itself as a strange, isolated phenomenon, without any bearing on the rest of human activity. Hence those definitions which tend to make the comic into an abstract relation between ideas: "an intellectual contrast," "a patent absurdity," etc., definitions which, even were they really suitable to every form of the comic, would not in the least explain why the comic makes us laugh. How, indeed, should it come about that this particular logical relation, as soon as it is perceived, contracts, expands and shakes our limbs, whilst all other relations leave the body unaffected? It is not from this point of view that we shall approach the problem. To understand laughter, we must put it back into its natural environment, which is society, and above all must we determine the utility of its function, which is a social one. Such, let us say at once, will be the leading idea of all our investigations. Laughter must answer to certain requirements of life in common. It must have a *social* signification.

Let us clearly mark the point towards which our three preliminary observations are converging. The comic will come into being, it appears, whenever a group of men concentrate their attention on one of their number, imposing silence on their emotions and calling into play nothing but their intelligence. . . .

Before going further, let us halt a moment and glance around. As we hinted at the outset of this study, it would be idle to attempt to derive every comic effect from one simple formula. The formula exists well enough in a certain sense, but its development does not follow a straightforward course. What I mean is that the process of deduction ought from time to time to stop and study certain culminating effects, and that these effects each appear as models around which new effects resembling them take their places in a circle. These latter are not deductions from the formula, but are comic through their relationship with those that are. To quote Pascal again, I see no objection, at this stage, to defining the process by the curve which that geometrician studied under the name of *roulette* or cycloid—the curve traced by a point in the circumference of a wheel when the carriage is advancing in a straight line: this point turns like the wheel, though it advances like the carriage. Or else we might think of an immense avenue such as are to be seen in the forest of Fontainebleau, with *crosses* at intervals to indicate the crossways: at each of these we shall walk round the cross, explore for a while the paths that open out before us, and then return to our original course. Now, we have just reached one of these mental crossways. *Something mechanical encrusted on the living* will represent a cross at which we must halt, a central image from which the imagination branches off in different directions. What are these directions? There appear to be three main ones. We will follow them one after the other, and then continue our onward course.

1. In the first place, this view of the mechanical and the living dovetailed into each other makes us incline towards the vaguer image of *some rigidity or other* applied to the mobility of life, in an awkward attempt to follow its lines

and counterfeit its suppleness. Here we perceive how easy it is for a garment to become ridiculous. It might almost be said that every fashion is laughable in some respect. Only, when we are dealing with the fashion of the day, we are so accustomed to it that the garment seems, in our mind, to form one with the individual wearing it. We do not separate them in imagination. The idea no longer occurs to us to contrast the inert rigidity of the covering with the living suppleness of the object covered: consequently, the comic here remains in a latent condition. It will only succeed in emerging when the natural incompatibility is so deep-seated between the covering and the covered that even an immemorial association fails to cement this union: a case in point is our head and top hat. Suppose, however, some eccentric individual dresses himself in the fashion of former times our attention is immediately drawn to the clothes themselves; we absolutely distinguish them from the individual, we say that the latter *is disguising himself*,—as though every article of clothing were not a disguise!—and the laughable aspect of fashion comes out of the shadow into the light.

Here we are beginning to catch a faint glimpse of the highly intricate difficulties raised by this problem of the comic. One of the reasons that must have given rise to many erroneous or unsatisfactory theories of laughter is that many things are comic *de jure* without being comic *de facto*, the continuity of custom having deadened within them the comic quality. A sudden dissolution of continuity is needed, a break with fashion, for this quality to revive. Hence the impression that this dissolution of continuity is the parent of the comic, whereas all it does is to bring it to our notice. Hence, again, the explanation of laughter by *surprise, contrast*, etc., definitions which would equally apply to a host of cases in which we have no inclination whatever to laugh. The truth of the matter is far from being so simple. . . .

2. Our starting-point is again "something mechanical encrusted upon the living." Where did the comic come from in this case? It came from the fact that the living body became rigid, like a machine. Accordingly, it seemed to us that the living body ought to be the perfection of suppleness, the ever-alert activity of a principle always at work. But this activity would really belong to the soul rather than to the body. It would be the very flame of life, kindled within us by a higher principle and perceived through the body, as though through a glass. When we see only gracefulness and suppleness in the living body, it is because we disregard in it the elements of weight, of resistance, and, in a word, of matter; we forget its materiality and think only of its vitality, a vitality which we regard as derived from the very principle of intellectual and moral life. Let us suppose, however, that our attention is drawn to this material side of the body; that, so far from sharing in the lightness and subtlety of the principle with which it is animated, the body is no more in our eyes than a heavy and cumbersome vesture, a kind of irksome ballast which holds down to earth a soul eager to rise aloft. Then the body will become to the soul what, as we have just seen, the garment was to the body itself—inert matter dumped down upon living energy. The impression of the comic will be produced as soon as we have a clear apprehension of this putting the one on the other. And we shall experience it most strongly when we are shown the soul *tantalised* by the needs of the body: on the one hand, the moral personality with its intelligently varied energy, and, on the other, the stupidly monotonous body, perpetually obstructing everything with its machine-like obstinacy. The more paltry and uniformly repeated these claims of the body, the more striking will be the result. But that is only a matter of degree,

and the general law of these phenomena may be formulated as follows: *Any incident is comic that calls our attention to the physical in a person, when it is the moral side that is concerned....*

3. Let us then return, for the last time, to our central image—something mechanical encrusted on something living. Here, the living being under discussion was a human being, a person. A mechanical arrangement, on the other hand, is a thing. What, therefore, incited laughter, was the momentary transformation of a person into a thing, if one considers the image from this standpoint. Let us then pass from the exact idea of a machine to the vaguer one of a thing in general. We shall have a fresh series of laughable images which will be obtained by taking a blurred impression, so to speak, of the outlines of the former and will bring us to this new law: *We laugh every time a person gives us the impression of being a thing....* The comic is that side of a person which reveals his likeness to a thing, that aspect of human events which, through its peculiar inelasticity, conveys the impression of pure mechanism, of automatism, of movement without life. Consequently it expresses an individual or collective imperfection which calls for an immediate corrective. This corrective is laughter, a social gesture that singles out and represses a special kind of absentmindedness in men and in event....

Hence the equivocal nature of the comic. It belongs neither altogether to art nor altogether to life. On the one hand, characters in real life would never make us laugh were we not capable of watching their vagaries in the same way as we look down at a play from our seat in a box; they are only comic in our eyes because they perform a kind of comedy before us. But, on the other hand, the pleasure caused by laughter, even on the stage, is not an unadulterated enjoyment; it is not a pleasure that is exclusively esthetic or altogether disinterested. It always implies a secret or unconscious intent, if not of each one of us, at all events of society as a whole. In laughter we always find an unavowed intention to humiliate, and consequently to correct our neighbor, if not in his will, at least in his deed. This is the reason a comedy is far more like real life than a drama is. The more sublime the drama, the more profound the analysis to which the poet has had to subject the raw materials of daily life in order to obtain the tragic element in its unadulterated form. On the contrary, it is only in its lower aspects, in light comedy and farce, that comedy is in striking contrast to reality: the higher it rises, the more it approximates to life; in fact, there are scenes in real life so closely bordering on high-class comedy that the stage might adopt them without changing a single word.

Selected Bibliography

There has been no attempt to make this bibliography as inclusive as possible. To do so would require a volume in itself. The books and articles listed here, in addition to the sources used for the text (listed elsewhere), constitute a basic working bibliography for all students interested in the subject of comedy.

Auden, W. H. *The Dyer's Hand.* New York: Random House, 1962.

Behrman, S. N. "What Makes Comedy High?". *New York Times,* March 30, 1952.

Bergler, Edmund. *Laughter and the Sense of Humor.* New York: Grune & Stratton, 1956.

Berry, Ralph. *Shakespeare's Comedies: Explorations in Form.* Princeton, N.J.: Princeton University Press, 1972.

Blistein, Elmer. *Comedy in Action.* Durham, N.C.: Duke University Press, 1964.

Brody, Morris W. "The Meaning of Laughter." *Psychoanalytic Quarterly,* Vol. 19, 1950.

Brown, John Russell. *Shakespeare and His Comedies.* London: Methuen, 1957.

Capp, Al. "The Comedy of Charlie Chaplin." *The Atlantic Monthly,* Vol. 185, February 1950.

Charney, Maurice (ed.). "Comedy: New Perspectives." *New York Literary Forum,* No. 1, 1978.

Charney, Maurice. *Comedy High and Low.* New York: Oxford University Press, 1978.

Clemons, Walter. "Anthony Burgess: Pushing On." *New York Times Book Review,* November 29, 1970.

Cook, Albert. *The Dark Voyage and the Golden Mean.* Cambridge, Mass.: Harvard University Press, 1949.

Cooper, Lane. *An Aristotelian Theory of Comedy.* New York: Kraus 1969.

Cornford, Francis M. *The Origin of Attic Comedy.* Cambridge, England: Cambridge University Press, 1934.

Dobrée, Bonamy. *Restoration Comedy.* Oxford: Oxford University Press, 1924.

Drew, Elizabeth. *Discovering Drama.* New York: Norton, 1937.

Duckworth, George. *The Nature of Roman Comedy: A Study in Popular Entertainment.* Princeton, N.J.: Princeton University Press, 1952.

Eastman, Max. *Enjoyment of Laughter.* New York: Simon & Schuster, 1936.

Eberhart, Richard. "Tragedy as Limitation: Comedy as Control and Resolution," *Tulane Drama Review,* Vol. 6, June 1962.

Elliott, R. C. *The Power of Satire.* Princeton, N.J.: Princeton University Press, 1960.

Enck, John J., Elizabeth T. Forter, Alvin Whitley (eds.). *The Comic in Theory and Practice.* Englewood Cliffs, N.J.: Prentice-Hall, 1960.

Feibleman, James. *In Praise of Comedy.* New York: Macmillan, 1939.

Fernandez, Ramon. *Molière, The Man Seen Through His Plays*. New York: Hill and Wang, 1958.

Fujimura, Thomas H. *The Restoration Comedy of Wit*. Princeton, N.J.: Princeton University Press, 1952.

Goldstein, Jeffrey H. and McGheg, Paul E. (eds.). *The Psychology of Humor: Theoretical Perspectives and Empirical Issues*. New York: Academic Press, 1972.

Gregory, J. C. *The Nature of Laughter*. London, Kegan Paul, 1924.

Greig, J. Y. T. *The Psychology of Laughter and Comedy*. New York: Dodd Mead, 1923.

Gurewitch, Morton. *Comedy: The Irrational Vision*. Ithaca, N.Y.: Cornell University Press, 1975.

Harrison, Jane. *Themis*. Cambridge, England: Cambridge University Press, 1927.

Hoy, Cyrus. *The Hyacinth Room*. New York: Knopf, 1964.

Huizinga, Johan. *Homo Ludens: A Study of the Play-Element in Culture*. Boston: Beacon Press, 1955.

Ionesco, Eugene. *Notes and Counternotes*. Trans. by Donald Watson. New York: Grove Press, 1964.

Kernan, Alvin. *The Cankered Muse*. New Haven, Conn.: Yale University Press, 1959.

Knights, L. C. "Notes on Comedy," from *The Importance of Scrutiny*. New York University Press, 1964.

Kronenberger, Louis. *The Thread of Laughter*. New York: Knopf, 1952.

Lauter, Paul (ed.). *Theories of Comedy*. Garden City, N.Y.: Doubleday (Anchor Books), 1964.

Legman, Gershon. *Rationale of the Dirty Joke: An Analysis of Sexual Humor*. New York: Grove Press, 1971.

Levin, Harry (ed.). *Veins of Humor*. Cambridge, Mass.: Harvard University Press, 1972.

McCollom, William G. *The Divine Average: A View of Comedy*. Cleveland, Ohio: Press of Case Western Reserve University, 1971.

Merchant, W. Moelwyn. *Comedy*. London: Methuen, 1972.

Meyerhold, Vsevolod. "Farce," *Tulane Drama Review*, Vol. 4, September 1959.

Monro, D. H. *Argument of Laughter*. Notre Dame, Ind.: University of Notre Dame Press, 1963.

Moore, W. G. *Molière: A New Criticism*. Oxford, England: Clarendon Press, 1969.

Myers, Henry A. "An Analysis of Laughter," *Sewanee Review*, Vol. 46, 1938.

Olson, Elder. *The Theory of Comedy*. Bloomington, Ind.: Indiana University Press, 1968.

Palmer, John. *Comedy*. London: Secker, 1914.

Perry, H. T. E. *Masters of Dramatic Comedy*. Cambridge, Mass.: Harvard University Press, 1939.

Piddington, Ralph. *The Psychology of Laughter: A Study in Social Adaptation*. New York: Gamut Press, 1963.

Salingar, Leo. *Shakespeare and the Traditions of Comedy*. Cambridge, England: Cambridge University Press, 1976.

Scott, Nathan A., Jr. "The Bias of Comedy and the Narrow Escape Into Faith," *The Christian Scholar*, Vol. XLIV, Spring 1961.

Segal, Erich. *Roman Laughter: The Comedy of Plautus*. Cambridge, Mass.: Harvard University Press, 1968.

Stephenson, Robert C. "Farce as Method," *Tulane Drama Review*, Vol. 5, December 1961.

Styan, J. L. *The Dark Comedy: The Development of Modern Comic Tragedy*. Cambridge, England: Cambridge University Press, 1968.

Swabey, Marie Collins. *Comic Laughter: A Philosophical Essay.* New Haven, Conn.: Yale University Press, 1961.

Sypher, Wylie (ed.). *Comedy.* Garden City, N.Y.: Doubleday (Anchor Books), 1956.

Tynan, Kenneth. *Curtains.* New York: Atheneum, 1961.

Vexler, Julius. "The Essence of Comedy," *Sewanne Review,* Vol. 43, 1935.

Welsford, Enio. *The Fool.* Garden City, N.Y.: Doubleday (Anchor Books), 1961.

Willeford, William. *The Fool and His Scepter: A Study in Clowns and Jesters and Their Audience.* Evanston, Ill.: Northwestern University Press, 1969.

Wimsatt, W. K. (ed.). *The Idea of Comedy: Ben Jonson to George Meredith.* Englewood Cliffs, N.J.: Prentice-Hall, 1969.

White, E. B. "Some Remarks on Humor," *The Second Tree From the Corner.* New York: Harper & Row, 1954.

84   9   8   7   6   5   4   3   2